Table of Contents

I. Reading
  A. Directions
  B. Sequencing
  C. Main Idea
II. Writing
  A. Capitalization
  B. Proofreading

Name _____

Root and Base Words

Many words consist of one or more **Greek** or **Latin root**. For example, the Greek root **tele** means "far." When it is combined with **vis**, the Latin root for "see," we get **television**.

Directions: Fill in the blanks below to learn the meaning of more roots.

1. Telephones allow us to hear sounds from far away. **Tele** means _far_, and **phone** comes from the Greek word meaning _away_.

2. **Ped** is a root word meaning "foot." Therefore, a **pedestrian** is a person who travels by _Ped ("foot")_.

3. **Graph** comes from the Greek word meaning "to write," and **auto** is the root word for "self." Thus, an **autograph** is _To write self_.

4. **Geo** is the Greek root for "Earth." **Geography**, then, is writing or drawing about the _Earth to write_.

5. **Bio** is the root word meaning "life." When someone writes an **autobiography**, he or she writes about _Self life to write_.

6. A **biographer** writes about ~~themselves~~ _there life_.

7. The word **pedometer** combines the root *ped* with *meter*, a root meaning "measurement." A **pedometer** is an instrument for _measuring_ the distance someone travels by _meters_.

8. **Logy** is a Greek root for "study." When combined with the root *graph*, we get *graphology* or the study of _To write study_.

9. **Biology** is the study of _life study_.

10. **Geology** is the study of _Earth study_.

11. Writing that comes from far away is called a ~~pedometer~~ _pedometer_.

12. Combine the root word for "sound" and the root word for "write." The machine we use to play records is a _____.

More Root and Base Words

Add new words to your vocabulary by understanding these Greek or Latin roots.

1. **Magna** or **magni** is the Latin root for "great." **Magnificent** is an adjective that means "excellent" or "great."

2. **Aqua** is the Latin word meaning "water." An **aquarium** is a place for keeping water plants and aquatic animals.

3. **Flor** is the Latin root for "flower." A **florist** sells or grows flowers for a living.

4. **Dict** is the Latin root meaning "to speak." **Diction** means the manner in which words are spoken.

5. **Micro** comes from the Greek word *mikros,* meaning "tiny" or "small." A **microscope** is an instrument that allows us to see very small things.

Directions: Use a dictionary to find two words formed from each of the above roots. Write words and their definitions in the blanks below.

Root	Dictionary Word	Definition
1. **magna** or **magni**	(a) _____	(a) _____
	(b) _____	(b) _____
2. **aqua**	(a) _____	(a) _____
	(b) _____	(b) _____
3. **flor**	(a) _____	(a) _____
	(b) _____	(b) _____
4. **dict**	(a) _____	(a) _____
	(b) _____	(b) _____
5. **micro**	(a) _____	(a) _____
	(b) _____	(b) _____

Name _____

Words With aqua and aque

aqua, aque	water
aqualung	breathing equipment for underwater swimming or diving
aquamarine	a bluish sea-green color
aquaplane	a wide board that is towed by a motorboat, like a single water ski
aquarium	an artificial pond or tank of water where live water animals and water plants are kept; a building where such collections are exhibited
aquatic	growing or living in water
aqueduct	a channel that carries large amounts of water

Directions: Divide the following words into parts so that **aqua (or aque)** is separate.

Example: aqua rium

1. aquamarine   _agua_   _marine_
2. aqualung   _aq agua_   _lung_
3. aquaplane   _aqua_   _plane_
4. aqueduct   _aque_   _duct_

Directions: Complete each sentence using a word from the word box.

1. To go scuba diving, you need to wear an _aqualung_.

2. The children bought a variety of fish for the _aquarium_.

3. Seaweed is an _aquatic_ plant.

4. The Romans used an _aquaplane_ to transport water from one place to another.

5. Susan liked to waterski, but her brother John preferred to use an _____.

Name _____

Words With dict

dict	to say
dictate	to say something aloud that will be written or recorded by another; to command or order
dictator	a ruler with unlimited power
diction	a style of speaking; the degree of preciseness or clarity in speech
predict	to foretell or say ahead of time that something will happen
verdict	a judgment or decision, especially that of a jury in a court case

Directions: Circle the root that means "to say" in the following words.

1. diction

2. predict

3. dictator

4. verdict

Directions: Complete each sentence using a word from the word box.

1. The foreman of the jury announced the _____: not guilty.

2. The actor was very careful of his _____ during the audition.

3. The manager will _____ the new rules to the employees.

4. I _____ that my little brother will have a dent in his new bike before the end of the week.

I. Reading
  A. Directions
  B. Sequencing
  C. Main Idea
II. Writing
  A. Capitalization
  B. Proofreading

Name _____

Prefix Crossword

A **prefix** is a word part added to the **beginning of a word** that changes its meaning.

Directions: Match the words in the word box with their definitions below. Write them in the correct places in the puzzle.

Across
1. not usual
2. fill again
3. middle of the night
4. set again

Down
5. not making sense
6. not certain
7. count wrongly
8. take away frost

GRADE

6

I. Reading
   A. Directions
   B. Sequencing
   C. Main Idea
II. Writing
   A. Capitalization
   B. Proofreading

Name _____

Understanding Prefixes

Directions: Match each word with its meaning. Write the number of the word by its meaning.

1. exhale — breathe in
2. inhale — breathe out

_____ breathe in

_____ breathe out

3. misread — read wrongly
4. reread — read again

_____ read wrongly

_____ read again

5. bicycle — three-wheeled cycle
6. tricycle — two-wheeled cycle

_____ three-wheeled cycle

_____ two-wheeled cycle

Directions: Use the words above to complete the sentences.

1. Allen likes to ___inhale___ the fresh mountain air.

2. Carmen is in a ___bicycle___ race today.

3. The model airplane you put together may not work if you ___misread___ the directions.

4. The toddler's ___tricycle___ is in the garage.

5. Matt wants to ___reread___ this book.

6. Take in a deep breath, then ___exhale___ .

I. Reading
A. Directions
B. Sequencing
C. Main Idea
II. Writing
A. Capitalization
B. Proofreading

Name _____

Prefix Puzzle

Directions: Match the words in the word box with their definitions below. Write them in the correct places in the puzzle.

Across

1. pay before

2. treat wrongly

3. not correct

4. not clear

Down

5. not like

6. not perfect

7. make new again

8. on shore

GRADE 6

I. Reading
A. Directions
B. Sequencing
C. Main Idea
II. Writing
A. Capitalization
B. Proofreading

Name _____

Prefix Meanings

Directions: Match each word with its meaning. Write the number of the word by its meaning.

1. increase   _____ become larger

2. decrease   _____ become smaller

3. indirect   _____ direct again

4. redirect   _____ not direct

5. inflate   _____ to let out air

6. deflate   _____ to blow air into

Directions: Use the words above to complete the sentences.

1. When I ___deflate___ the tire, it will be flat.

2. To make more soup, ___redirect___ the amount of water.

3. Nick took an ___indirect___ route to school.

4. If you are lost, a police officer can _____ you.

5. Here are twenty balloons to ___inflate___ for the party.

6. The price of shirts will ___decrease___ during the big sale.

GRADE 6

I. Reading
  A. Directions
  B. Sequencing
  C. Main Idea
II. Writing
  A. Capitalization
  B. Proofreading

Name _____

Words With con

Directions: Complete each sentence with a **con** word from the word box.

converged	controversy	contorted	conclude	consult
convince	conduct	conscious	congested	confetti
contrition	contestant	conservation	conjured	

1. The mall was _____ with swarms of sale-crazed customers.

2. Did you _____ your teacher that they are a good group?

3. Please _____ your doctor if your fever continues.

4. Peter's face _____ in pain as his horse stomped on his foot.

5. The two highways _____ before we reached Toronto.

6. Our _____ group hopes to plant 50 trees this Saturday.

7. The tearful toddler, filled with _____, told her dead goldfish that she only meant to take it for a walk.

8. Are you _____, Henry? Speak to me if you can hear me!

9. The brawny guide will _____ us to the bottom of the gorge.

10. Our meeting will _____ in twenty minutes.

11. There was a horrid _____ about the music selection chosen for the skating party.

12. What evil the wicked warlock _____ against his unsuspecting apprentice!

13. When the first _____ could not answer the riddle, he was sentenced to nine years hard dishwashing.

14. After our team won, we tossed _____ high into the air to celebrate.

Name _____

Missing Prefixes

Directions: Read the story. Use the prefixes in the word box to write in the missing prefixes.

un	tele	dis	re	mis

Star Trip

As usual, the Little Prince of Mars sat in front of his big-screen

_____ vision. "This life is very _____ interesting," he thought.
1   2

Just then, he heard a knock at the door. When he opened the door, a

messenger handed him a _____ gram. "There must be some
3

_____ take," said the Little Prince. But when he opened the envelope,
4

he was surprised. The _____ happy frown on his face _____ appeared.
5   6

He was going on a trip to the stars! The Little Prince

was _____ certain what to pack. He dashed for his _____ scope and
7   8

magic crystal kit. He packed and _____ packed his star travel
9

bag until everything fit. Someday he would _____ turn to his own planet,
10

but until then, he was ready for an adventure in the stars!

Name _____

Suffixes

A **suffix** is a word part added to the **end of a word** that changes its meaning.

Directions: Use the suffix definitions in the box to write a definition of each word below.

> **ist** means "one who practices"
> **ous** means "full of"
> **ance** means "the state of"

1. artist _____

2. courageous _____

3. admittance _____

4. appearance _____

5. guitarist _____

6. humorous _____

7. inheritance _____

8. mountainous _____

9. poisonous _____

10. violinist _____

_____

Name _____

Suffixes ful and ly

Directions: Add the suffix **ful** or **ly** to the word from the box that makes sense in the sentence.

harm	easy
care	glad
use	brave
rest	sudden
hope	clear

1. Please be _____ when you use the iron.

2. _____ a flock of geese swept across the sky.

3. Our vacation at the beach was so _____.

4. Sandy got an "A" on her speech because she spoke so _____.

5. Our team is _____ that we will make the playoffs.

6. Some activities are _____ to your health.

7. Manuel _____ climbed the tree to get his sister's escaped parakeet.

8. I will _____ deliver your papers for you while you are gone.

9. Your notes will be _____ as you prepare for the test.

10. The class aced the test _____.

Name _____

Suffixes less and ness

Directions: Add the suffix **less** or **ness** to complete each sentence.

1. We adopted a home _____ dog from the pound.

2. My favorite thing about the dog is the soft _____ of its fur.

3. The thick _____ of its fur keeps the dog warm.

4. Dark _____ scared our dog at first, so it slept in my brother's room.

5. It was use _____ to try to break the dog of that habit!

6. Our house was never spot _____ before the dog arrived, but it is definitely messy now.

7. Feeling at home with our new pet was pain _____.

8. We were not care _____ when we named our dog.

GRADE 6

I. Reading
A. Directions
B. Sequencing
C. Main Idea
II. Writing
A. Capitalization
B. Proofreading

Name _____

Selecting Suffixes

Directions: Write the word with a suffix from the word box that fits the definition.

supportive	patience
absence	intelligence
truthful	forgetful
thoughtful	doubtful
cheerful	active

1. thinking carefully _____

2. has trouble remembering _____

3. having a sunny attitude _____

4. keeping busy _____

5. disbelieving or questioning _____

6. always telling the truth _____

7. the state of not being present _____

8. smartness _____

9. showing great care or concern _____

10. ability to wait calmly _____

GRADE
6

I. Reading
  A. Directions
  B. Sequencing
  C. Main Idea
II. Writing
  A. Capitalization
  B. Proofreading

Name _____

Suffix Definitions

Directions: Write the definition of each word using the suffix definitions in the word box.

> **ness** means "quality of being"
> **ble** means "capable of being"

1. bleak<u>ness</u> _____

2. permiss<u>ible</u> _____

3. break<u>able</u> _____

4. blind<u>ness</u> _____

5. steadi<u>ness</u> _____

6. admiss<u>ible</u> _____

7. furri<u>ness</u> _____

8. believ<u>able</u> _____

Selecting More Suffixes

Directions: Complete each sentence using a word with a suffix from the word box.

collection	invitation
capable	improvements
peaceful	addition
wonderful	marvelous

1. My birthday was_____.

2. This is my _____ of stamps.

3. It is so _____ up in the mountains.

4. In _____ to dance lessons, I take piano and clarinet.

5. The _____ for the wedding came yesterday.

6. The movie was _____!

7. Dad is working on a few home _____.

8. He is not _____ of lifting all those heavy boxes himself.

Name _____

Analyzing Words and Their Parts

A **syllable** is a word or part of a word with only one vowel sound.

Directions: Fill in the missing syllables. Use words from the box. Write the number of syllables after each word. The first one has been done for you.

expense	exist	aquarium	acquire	request
exact	expand	exit	quality	excellent
quiz	quantity	expression	exhibit	squirm

1. ex**cel** lent (3)

2. _____ squirm ( )

3. _____ act ( )

4. _____ quiz ( )

5. aquar ___ um ( )

6. ac _____ ( )

7. quali _____ ( )

8. _____ it ( )

9. ex _____ sion ( )

10. _____ ist ( )

11. _____ quest ( )

12. ex _____ it ( )

13. _____ pense ( )

14. _____ pand ( )

15. quan _____ ty ( )

Directions: Write words that rhyme. Use the words in the box.

1. fizz _____

2. resist _____

3. fact _____

4. fence _____

5. sand _____

6. it's been sent _____

7. this is it _____

8. made for me _____

9. fit _____

10. worm _____

11. fire _____

12. best _____

A **root word** is a common stem which gives related words their basic meaning.

Directions: Write the root word for the bold word in each sentence.

1. I know **exactly** what I want. _____

2. Those shoes look **expensive**. _____

3. She didn't like my **expression** when I frowned. _____

4. We went to the train **exhibition** at the park. _____

Name _____

Dividing Words Into Syllables

Directions: Divide these words into syllables by putting a hyphen (-) between each syllable. The first one has done for you.

1. multiplication

   mul–ti–pli–ca–tion

2. discover

   _____

3. ultimate

   _____

4. transfer

   _____

5. continent

   _____

6. follow

   _____

7. British

   _____

8. American

   _____

9. president

   _____

10. discrimination

   _____

11. spectacular

   _____

12. commercial

   _____

13. probability

   _____

14. country

   _____

15. casual

   _____

16. political

   _____

17. wrestle

   _____

18. basketball

   _____

19. particular

   _____

20. cereal

   _____

21. picture

   _____

22. plumber

   _____

23. personal

   _____

24. sentence

   _____

Name _____

Tony's Tuxedo

banjo
buffalo
echo
halo
mosquito
patio
portfolio
ratio
rodeo
silo
soprano
stereo
studio
tobacco
tomato
tornado
tuxedo
zero

Directions: Write the words from the word box according to their number of syllables. The first one is done for you.

Two-Syllable Words

b a n • j o

___ ___ • ___

___ ___ • ___

___ ___ • ___

___ ___ • ___

Three-Syllable Words

___ • ___ ___ ___ • ___

___ • ___ ___ • ___

___ • ___ ___ • ___

___ ___ • ___ ___ • ___

___ • ___ ___ ___ • ___

___ ___ ___ • ___ ___ • ___

___ ___ • ___ ___ • ___

___ ___ • ___ ___ • ___

___ ___ • ___ ___ • ___

___ • ___ ___ • ___

___ ___ • ___ • ___

Four-Syllable Word

___ ___ ___ • ___ ___ • ___ ___ • ___

GRADE
6
I. Reading
  A. Directions
  B. Sequencing
  C. Main Idea
II. Writing
  A. Capitalization
  B. Proofreading

Name _____

This Is So Fine

Directions: Rewrite each sentence below, replacing the word **fine** with one of the synonyms given. Since the synonyms have slight differences in meaning, be careful to choose the correct one.

Fine: clear, delicate, elegant,
            small, sharp, subtle

1. The queen wore a **fine** gown encrusted with jewels.

   _____

   _____

2. I wash this blouse by hand because of its **fine** lace collar.

   _____

   _____

3. The sand in an hourglass must be very **fine** to trickle as it does.

   _____

   _____

4. We need **fine** weather for sailing.

   _____

   _____

5. Dad used a whetstone to put a **fine** edge on the knife.

   _____

   _____

6. Sometimes there is a **fine** line between innocence and guilt.

   _____

   _____

Name _____

Synonyms

Synonyms are words that mean nearly the **same**.

Directions: Write a word from the word box below its synonym.

refuse	occur	shake	choose
purchase	fright	rough	reply
copy	vacant	worth	pledge
genuine	depart	simple	tardy

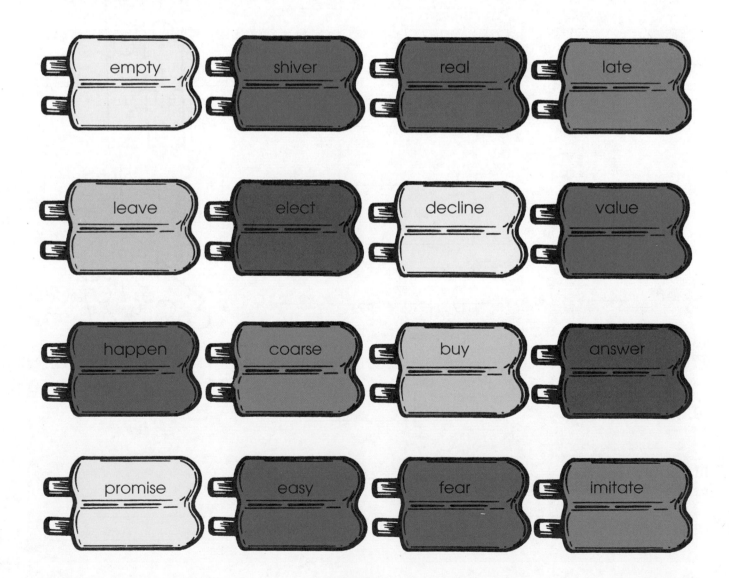

empty

shiver

real

late

leave

elect

decline

value

happen

coarse

buy

answer

promise

easy

fear

imitate

GRADE
6

I. Reading
   A. Directions
   B. Sequencing
   C. Main Idea
II. Writing
   A. Capitalization
   B. Proofreading

Name _____

Antonyms

Antonyms are words that mean the **opposite**.

Directions: Write the antonym for each word below.

1. near   _____

2. easy   _____

3. first   _____

4. high   _____

5. stand   _____

6. best   _____

7. boy   _____

8. left   _____

9. question   _____

10. north   _____

11. huge   _____

12. organized   _____

GRADE
6

I. Reading
A. Directions
B. Sequencing
C. Main Idea
II. Writing
A. Capitalization
B. Proofreading

Name _____

Antonyms

Snake Charmer

Directions: Circle an antonym for the <u>underlined</u> word in each sentence.

1.	The bike is <u>broken</u>.	fixed	old	lost
2.	Kim is the <u>tallest</u> girl.	oldest	shortest	cutest
3.	That <u>boy</u> is nice.	kid	girl	person
4.	Steve is very <u>happy</u>.	angry	funny	sad
5.	Can Mark <u>work</u> today?	run	play	eat
6.	Jump <u>over</u> the net.	under	beside	on
7.	I <u>found</u> the door key.	forgot	lost	hid
8.	It <u>started</u> on time.	played	showed	stopped
9.	I have a <u>hard</u> bed.	big	soft	tiny
10.	The movie is <u>short</u>.	long	funny	sad
11.	I was <u>early</u> today.	home	lost	late
12.	He drives too <u>fast</u>.	slow	hurry	far

GRADE 6

I. Reading
  A. Directions
  B. Sequencing
  C. Main Idea
II. Writing
  A. Capitalization
  B. Proofreading

Name _____

Mussel With Muscle

Homophones are words that are pronounced alike but have different meanings.

Directions: Write the correct homophone from the word box under each picture. Write the matching homophone below it.

cymbal	symbol	hangar	hanger	muscle
mussel	pare	pear	pause	paws
plain	plane	principal	principle	tacks
tax	waist	waste		

I. Reading
A. Directions
B. Sequencing
C. Main Idea
II. Writing
A. Capitalization
B. Proofreading

Name _____

What Do You Know?

Directions: Write the homophone for each word listed. Then, write the homophone pair that best completes each sentence. Use a dictionary if you need help.

allowed _____ loot _____

patients _____ passed _____

close _____ rung _____

board _____ rote _____

seller _____ threw _____

council _____ tied _____

weak _____ jam _____

1. The librarian _____ the children

   to read _____ to one another.

2. This _____ year

   _____ by so quickly.

3. The child _____ the entire

   passage by _____ .

4. According to the agreement, the _____

   must repair the _____ windows before the sale is final.

5. A priceless _____ was among the _____ stolen
   from the museum last night.

6. We _____ our boat to the dock and waited for low
   _____ .

7. Caring for so many _____ requires great _____ .

8. Please _____ the door of my _____ closet.

9. The attorney will _____ his clients before the next
   _____ meeting.

10. We were so _____ that we decided to leave the
    _____ meeting.

Name _____

A Crown of Wild Olive Leaves

Directions: Read the selections and fill in each blank with the correct homophones.

Imagine yourself as a spectator at the ancient Greek games! Use the word bank of homophones to fill in each blank within the sentence. Then, use the other homophone in the pair to write your own sentence on the line provided. Try to write sentences about the Olympics.

Word Bank

all—awl	scent—sent	waits—weights	site—sight
throne—thrown	way—weigh	him—hymn	toes—tows
mail—male	scene—seen	war—wore	one—won

---

1. In the ancient games all athletes were _____. Unmarried women were allowed to attend the spectacle, but married women were not.

   _____

2. The _____ for the games was chosen carefully so that it was in full view of an important landmark.

   _____

3. The temple of Zeus could be _____ from the Games. The games were dedicated in honor of this god.

   _____

4. One _____ that athletes relaxed was to swim in the pool at Olympia. But there were no swimming races in this one-and-only pool of ancient Greece.

   _____

5. Every four years, three heralds would be _____ from the town of nearby Elis to proclaim the games and announce the *Olympic Truce*.

   _____

6. These heralds carried staffs and _____ wreaths of olive leaves.

   _____

7. The long-jump participants carried heavy lead _____. Yet distances of over 16 meters were recorded!

   _____

   _____

GRADE
6

I. Reading
A. Directions
B. Sequencing
C. Main Idea
II. Writing
A. Capitalization
B. Proofreading

Name _____

8. The greatest honor was given to the winner of the stade. This was a run equal to about 192 meters. The winning sprinter had that year's Games named after _____.

_____

9. Runners began from a standing start, feet together, _____ gripping the grooves in the stone slabs which served as the starting line.

_____

10. Wrestlers _____ their events if their opponent had three falls. A fall was declared any time a wrestler's back or shoulder touched the ground.

_____

11. The Olympic Games were one of four all-Greek sports competitions. These games were open to _____ Greek men. At the all-Athens games, one event familiar to us today was a torch race.

_____

12. One chariot competitor, Emperor Nero, won his event even though he was _____ from his vehicle and failed to finish. Bribing the judges, Nero was named the champion with the excuse that he would have won if he had finished! After he died, the judges returned the bribe money.

_____

GRADE 6

I. Reading
A. Directions
B. Sequencing
C. Main Idea
II. Writing
A. Capitalization
B. Proofreading

Name _____

Present a Present

Homographs are spelled alike but are different in meaning or pronunciation.

Directions: Fill in the blank with the correct homograph. Place an accent mark on the appropriate syllable of each homograph.

compact
conduct
conflict
content
contest
convict
impact
insult
object
permit
present
protest
rebel
record
refund
refuse
subject
suspect

1. They had to _____ the _____ for committing another terrible crime.

2. A young _____ will often _____ against parents or teachers.

3. I am _____ with the _____ of my research paper.

4. The nasty _____ used to _____ him made him feel bad.

5. I will _____ myself to this _____ .

6. Someday, my parents will _____ me to get my driver's _____ .

7. The singer hopes to _____ a hit _____.

8. My mom will _____ if I throw this _____.

9. We are expected to _____ ourselves with self-control and overall good _____ .

10. I will _____ her with a lovely _____.

11. I _____ to touch that stinky _____.

12. I _____ he is the guilty _____ .

Directions: Write the six homographs that were not used in the correct category. For each homograph, place an accent mark on the appropriate syllable.

Verbs: _____   Nouns: _____

_____   _____

_____   _____

_____   _____

_____   _____

GRADE
6

I. Reading
  A. Directions
  B. Sequencing
  C. Main Idea
II. Writing
  A. Capitalization
  B. Proofreading

Name _____

The Right Choice

Directions: Unscramble the scrambled word in each sentence. Write it on the line. Then, underline the correct meaning of the word.

1. The (anem) _____ number between 2 and 8 is 5.

   intend   average   unkind

2. We heard the distant (yab) _____ of a wolf last night.

   body of water   howl   reddish-brown

3. Help (alib) _____ water from our boat before it sinks!

   throw water out with a container   pail handle   money for release

4. The race car driver has only one more (apl) _____ to complete.

   distance around a track   drink up   body part formed when you sit

5. The man reads the (emtre) _____ every month to see how much electricity we use.

   device that measures flow   rhythm of a poem   unit of length

6. Our pillows are filled with (nowd) _____ .

   grassy land   soft feathers   from higher to lower ground

7. The knight drew his (olif) _____ and charged at his enemy.

   keep from carrying out a plan   metal sheet   long narrow sword

8. We ate at the (unterco) _____ because all the booths were occupied.

   long table in a restaurant   one who counts   opposite

9. You'd better (cudk) _____ , or you'll bump your head on that branch.

   bird   lower suddenly   type of cloth

10. The (citk) _____ is known to cause certain diseases in animals and people.

    pillow covering   sound of a clock   a small insect

11. We have to learn the steps of the (elre) _____ for the school show.

    sway after being hit   spool for winding   dance

12. We left our waitress a twenty-percent (ipt) _____ .

    slant   end point   money for services

Name _____

Picture This!

A **compound word** is formed by two or more words.
Some compound words are written as one word. **Examples:** blueberry   motorcycle

Other compound words are joined by a hyphen. **Examples:** twenty-one editor-in-chief

Directions: Write the compound word for each of the following cartoons.

= _____   = _____

= _____   = _____

= _____   = _____

= _____   = _____

= _____   = _____

= _____   = _____

GRADE
6
I. Reading
  A. Directions
  B. Sequencing
  C. Main Idea
II. Writing
  A. Capitalization
  B. Proofreading

Name _____

Compound Puzzles

Directions: Solve the word puzzles. Read the first part of the compound word vertically. Then, write the other part of the compound word horizontally. How many words can you make?

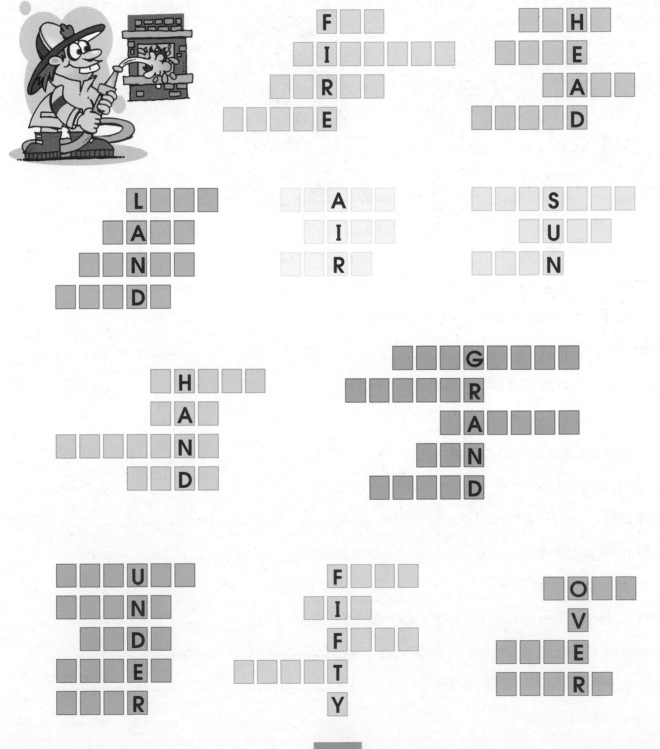

Name _____

Put-Them-Together Words

Directions: Choose a word from each box to make a compound word that correctly matches each definition.

folk	ginger	length
three-	trouble	land
court	live	vice-
seventy-	heart	head
chop	near-	sage

wise	broken	sighted
two	fourths	stock
brush	sticks	house
mark	president	quarters
tale	some	bread

Choose a word from each box.

1. not able to see far _____

2. annoying _____

3. story handed down among people _____

4. farm animals _____

5. grayish-green bushy plant of the dry plains _____

6. a fraction of a whole _____

7. in the direction of the length _____

8. main office of operations _____

9. building used for county government _____

10. a two-digit number _____

11. kind of spicy cake _____

12. thin wooden sticks used in pairs for eating _____

13. something easily seen and used as a guide _____

14. officer next in rank to president _____

15. crushed by sorrow _____

GRADE
6

I. Reading
  A. Directions
  B. Sequencing
  C. Main Idea
II. Writing
  A. Capitalization
  B. Proofreading

Name _____

Words in Context

Directions: Unscramble the scrambled compound word in each sentence by using context clues. Write the word correctly on the line provided.

_____ 1. Max has an emergency appointment with the dentist because he has a **chathoote**.

_____ 2. A torrential **ponrudwo** caused flooding along the rivers and streams.

_____ 3. Jennifer earned **newtty-evif** dollars babysitting last month.

_____ 4. We found an **rahowdear** while exploring what was once the site of a Native American village.

_____ 5. The President's weekly radio address was **starcabdo** live from the Oval Office of the White House.

_____ 6. The view from the Grand Canyon was absolutely **kingthebarta**.

_____ 7. We had **drah-delobi** eggs, toast, and juice for breakfast today.

_____ 8. My grandmother made a beautiful **chowkarpt** quilt with scraps from old clothing.

_____ 9. I bought a **pakprecab** book to read on the trip.

_____ 10. The Empire State Building was once the tallest **crassperky** in New York City.

_____ 11. My brother drove in the wrong direction down a **neo-awy** street.

_____ 12. The **teabsawsket** is full and needs to be emptied.

_____ 13. Our family is leaving on Monday for a **wot-ekwe** vacation at the beach.

_____ 14. My brother is the only **flet-headnd** pitcher and batter on our team.

_____ 15. After the concert, we went **gasteckba** to interview the performers.

Name _____

Messy Groups

Directions: Look at the groups in the chart below. Write a name for each one that tells how all its members are alike. Then, add two more members to each group.

Group Name	Animals With Fur
Members	bear
	dog
	cat
	lion
	wolf

Group Name	
Members	United States
	Mexico
	China

Group Name	
Members	Caribbean
	Atlantic
	Mediterranean

Group Name	
Members	lawyers
	scientists
	writers

Group Name	
Members	chirping
	growling
	shouting

Group Name	
Members	asteroids
	stars
	comets

GRADE
6

I. Reading
  A. Directions
  B. Sequencing
  C. Main Idea
II. Writing
  A. Capitalization
  B. Proofreading

Name _____

What's in an Ad?

Directions: Read the advertisements. Classify information in each one as a fact or opinion. Statements of fact can be proven true. Statements of opinion cannot be proven because they present beliefs, judgments, or feelings.

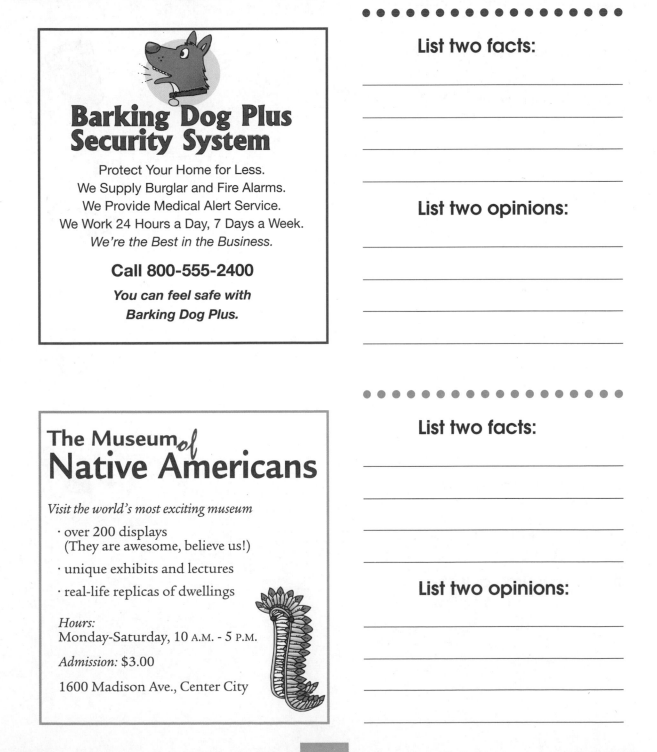

Barking Dog Plus Security System

Protect Your Home for Less.
We Supply Burglar and Fire Alarms.
We Provide Medical Alert Service.
We Work 24 Hours a Day, 7 Days a Week.
We're the Best in the Business.

Call 800-555-2400

You can feel safe with
Barking Dog Plus.

List two facts:

_____

_____

_____

List two opinions:

_____

_____

_____

The Museum *of* Native Americans

Visit the world's most exciting museum

· over 200 displays
  (They are awesome, believe us!)

· unique exhibits and lectures

· real-life replicas of dwellings

Hours:
Monday-Saturday, 10 A.M. - 5 P.M.

Admission: $3.00

1600 Madison Ave., Center City

List two facts:

_____

_____

_____

List two opinions:

_____

_____

_____

GRADE 6

I. Reading
   A. Directions
   B. Sequencing
   C. Main Idea
II. Writing
    A. Capitalization
    B. Proofreading

Name _____

Word Analogies

Classification means to put words together in groups. A **word analogy** expresses the relationship between words.

Directions: Complete each analogy with an appropriate word.

1. Cup is to adult as bottle is to _____

2. Four is to dog as two is to _____

3. Skin is to human as feathers are to _____

4. Paw is to dog as hoof is to _____

5. Hot is to oven as cold is to _____

6. Watch is to wrist as ring is to _____

7. Round is to ball as square is to _____

8. Calf is to cow as foal is to _____

9. Antlers are to deer as horns are to _____

10. Ink is to pen as paint is to _____

11. Rain is to spring as snow is to _____

12. Tadpole is to frog as caterpillar is to _____

I. Reading
   A. Directions
   B. Sequencing
   C. Main Idea
II. Writing
   A. Capitalization
   B. Proofreading

Name _____

More Analogies

Two of the most common analogies involve synonyms and antonyms.

Model 1: *Word* is to *word* as *word* is to _____.
                    (synonym)   (synonym)

Example: *Small* is to *little* as *big* is to *large*.

Model 2: *Word* is to *word* as *word* is to _____.
                    (antonym)   (antonym)

Example: *Beautiful* is to *ugly* as *happy* is to *sad*.

Directions: Read the definitions of the words in the word box. Complete the analogies below using words from the word box.

---

timid—*adj.* without courage

sullen—*adj.* gloomy, bad humored

foe—*n.* enemy

bold—*adj.* showing great courage

jovial—*adj.* full of laughter, jolly

climate—*n.* weather conditions

loathe—*v.* to dislike, to detest

comprehend—*v.* to understand

---

1. *Bad* is to *terrible* as *shy* is to _____.

2. *Bad* is to *good* as _____ is to *friend*.

3. *Car* is to *automobile* as *weather* is to _____.

4. *Teach* is to *instruct* as *understand* is to _____.

5. *Shout* is to *whisper* as *love* is to _____.

6. *Mean* is to *kind* as *shy* is to _____.

7. *Gentle* is to *rough* as *happy* is to _____.

8. *Pretty* is to *cute* as _____ is to *jolly*.

9. *Love* is to *like* as _____ is to *detest*.

10. *Bush* is to *shrub* as *enemy* is to _____.

GRADE
6

I. Reading
A. Directions
B. Sequencing
C. Main Idea
II. Writing
A. Capitalization
B. Proofreading

Name _____

Word Work

Directions: Look up each of the following words in a dictionary and write the definitions on the line. Then, use these words to complete each analogy below.

1. punctual _____

2. fragile _____

3. discard _____

4. fraudulent _____

5. peril _____

6. prohibit _____

7. monotonous _____

8. decade _____

9. augment _____

10. soothe _____

11. *Food* is to *eat* as *trash* is to _____.

12. *Late* is to *early* as *tardy* is to _____.

13. *Metal* is to *sturdy* as *glass* is to _____.

14. *Accept* is to *reject* as *allow* is to _____.

15. *Loud* is to *quiet* as *varied* is to _____.

16. *Real* is to *genuine* as *fake* is to _____.

17. *One hundred* is to *century* as *ten* is to _____.

18. *Hard* is to *soft* as *disturb* is to _____.

19. *Take* is to *give* as *subtract* is to _____.

20. *Walk* is to *stroll* as *danger* is to _____.

I. Reading
A. Directions
B. Sequencing
C. Main Idea
II. Writing
A. Capitalization
B. Proofreading

Name _____

Analogy Models

Directions: Read the analogy models. Then, circle the correct word to complete each analogy below. Use a dictionary if you need help.

Model 1:   *Tool* is to its *function* as *tool* is to its _____.
                                                                      (function)
Example: *Pen* is to *writing* as *shovel* is to *digging*.

Model 2:   *Title* is to *specialty* as *title* is to _____.
                                                          (specialty)
Example: *Dentist* is to *teeth* as *veterinarian* is to *animals*.

Model 3:   *Cause* is to *effect* as *cause* is to _____.
                                                        (effect)
Example: *Sadness* is to *tears* as *joy* is to *laughter*.

Model 4:   *Worker* is to *product* as *worker* is to _____.
                                                          (product)
Example: *Author* is to *book* as *artist* is to *painting*.

1. *Policeman* is to *crime* as *doctor* is to _____.
   a. illness   b. nurse   c. stethoscope   d. patient
2. *Carpenter* is to *hammer* as *doctor* is to _____.
   a. illness   b. nurse   c. stethoscope   d. patient
3. *Druggist* is to *pharmacy* as *teacher* is to _____.
   a. student   b. school   c. books   d. teach
4. *Baker* is to *bread* as *seamstress* is to _____.
   a. thread   b. needle   c. dress   d. sewing
5. *Scissors* are to *cut* as *ax* is to _____.
   a. chop   b. burn   c. tree   d. sharpen
6. *Sun* is to *sunburn* as *snow* is to _____.
   a. overcast   b. frostbite   c. umbrella d. climate
7. *Fire* is to *burn* as *cold* is to _____.
   a. ice   b. freeze   c. snow   d. wind
8. *Hunger* is to *eat* as *thirst* is to _____.
   a. food   b. cup   c. milk   d. drink

I. Reading
  A. Directions
  B. Sequencing
  C. Main Idea
II. Writing
  A. Capitalization
  B. Proofreading

Name _____

Fill Out the Form

Directions: Four people are going camping. Fill in the order form for their camping supplies. Remember to order enough supplies for four people. You can use your home address and phone number.

Item	Price	Order #	Item	Price	Order #
Super Sturdy Tent (4 person tent)	$200 each	97SJ800	First Aid Kit	$22 each	57CN249
Toasty Warm Sleeping Bag	$36 each	86GV394	Waterproof Camera	$25 each	16DK989
Tough Travel Backpack	$20 each	34TP283	Flashlight	$15 each	78PL234
PlastLight Water Bottle	$8 each	22SX436	Portable Stove	$40 each	9STO509

Carl's Camping Supplies

Name _____

Address _____

City _____ State _____ Zip Code _____

Phone Number _____

Item	Order #	Quantity	Price	Total

*Shipping
0–$200 = $10
$201–$400 = $20
$401 and up = $30

Thank you for your order!

Subtotal _____

*Shipping _____

Total _____

GRADE
6

I. Reading
A. Directions
B. Sequencing
C. Main Idea
II. Writing
A. Capitalization
B. Proofreading

Name _____

Recipe Puzzle

Directions: Put the steps for this recipe in the correct order. Write them on the lines provided. Then, write a list of ingredients you will need.

Pour batter into pans.

Preheat oven to 350°F.

Remove cakes from pans. Cool completely before frosting.

Grease sides and bottom of each pan.

Put cake mix, eggs, oil, and water in a large bowl.

Bake for 35-38 minutes.

Stir ingredients together for about 30 seconds.

Use a toothpick to check if cake is cooked. The toothpick should come out clean.

Cool in pan for 10 minutes.

Beat cake batter at medium speed for 2 minutes.

Carefully put pans in oven.

Yummy Cake Recipe

Ingredients _____

1. _____

2. _____

3. _____

4. _____

5. _____

6. _____

7. _____

8. _____

9. _____

10. _____

11. _____

I. Reading
  A. Directions
  B. Sequencing
  C. Main Idea
II. Writing
  A. Capitalization
  B. Proofreading

Name _____

Tie Your Shoe

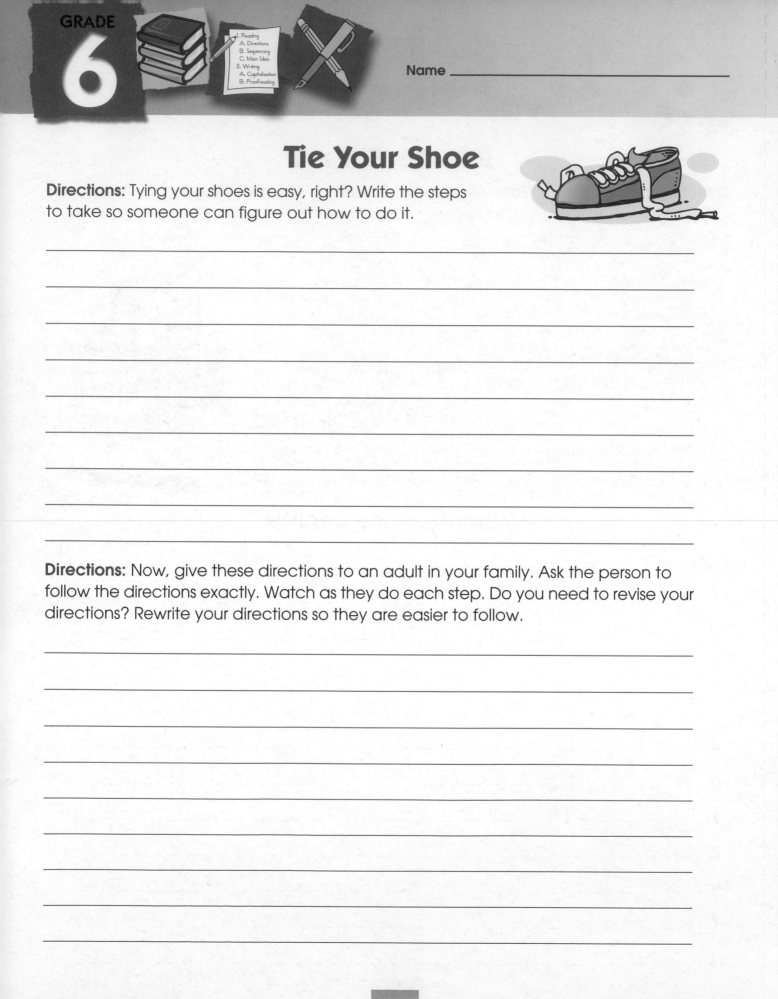

Directions: Tying your shoes is easy, right? Write the steps to take so someone can figure out how to do it.

_____

_____

_____

_____

_____

_____

_____

_____

Directions: Now, give these directions to an adult in your family. Ask the person to follow the directions exactly. Watch as they do each step. Do you need to revise your directions? Rewrite your directions so they are easier to follow.

_____

_____

_____

_____

_____

_____

_____

_____

Name _____

All in a Day

Directions: Read the activities. Then, write each next to a time that makes sense. Some lines will be blank.

Activities

Go to bed	Eat breakfast
Go to tennis practice	Play catch with a friend
Wake up	Eat dinner
Get out of school	Go to school
Do homework	Eat lunch

Hours in the Day

7 A.M. _____

8 A.M. _____

9 A.M. _____

10 A.M. _____

11 A.M. _____

12 P.M. _____

1 P.M. _____

2 P.M. _____

3 P.M. _____

4 P.M. _____

5 P.M. _____

6 P.M. _____

7 P.M. _____

8 P.M. _____

9 P.M. _____

GRADE 6

I. Reading
A. Directions
B. Sequencing
C. Main Idea
II. Writing
A. Capitalization
B. Proofreading

Name _____

Making a Mosaic

When you follow directions, be sure to read through them first, slowly. Look for special terms and time-order words, gather all materials, and follow the directions in the order they are written.

Directions: The pictures below show step-by-step directions for making a mosaic. Beside each picture, write the directions to explain each step. Be sure to use time-order words.

Step 1: _____

_____

_____

Step 2: _____

_____

_____

Step 3: _____

_____

_____

Step 4: _____

_____

_____

Step 5: _____

_____

_____

Step 6: _____

_____

_____

Name _____

Topic and Main Idea

Directions: Read each paragraph. Then, answer the questions.

You need a balanced diet to stay healthy. A balanced diet provides the amount of nutrients your body needs every day. By eating lots of different foods, you will get the nutrients you require to stay healthy.

1. What is the topic of this paragraph? Circle one.
   A. eating foods
   B. the importance of a balanced diet
   C. planning your diet

2. Which sentence states the main idea about the topic?
   A. When you eat lots of different foods you get the nutrients you require.
   B. A balanced diet provides the amount of nutrients your body needs every day.
   C. You need a balanced diet to stay healthy.

The food guide pyramid shows the five basic food groups. When choosing what to eat, you should think about these food groups. The food groups are Bread, Cereal, Rice, and Pasta; Vegetable; Fruit; Milk, Yogurt, and Cheese; and Meat, Poultry, Fish, Dry Beans, Eggs, and Nuts. The best way to plan a balanced diet is to choose a variety of foods from each of the five food groups.

3. What is the topic of this paragraph? Circle one.
   A. planning a balanced diet
   B. vegetables
   C. the food guide pyramid

4. Which sentence states the main idea about the topic? Circle one.
   A. The food guide pyramid shows the five basic food groups.

B. When choosing what to eat, you should think about these food groups.
C. The best way to plan a balanced diet is to choose a variety of foods from each of the five food groups.

You should avoid eating cookies, candy, and sweetened soft drinks. These foods have a lot of sugar and very little nutritional value. They may also cause you to gain weight and your teeth to decay.

5. What is the topic of this paragraph? Circle one.
   A. foods to avoid eating
   B. sugar
   C. how to avoid gaining weight

6. What is the unstated main idea? Circle one.
   A. Some foods have a lot of sugar and not much nutritional value.
   B. Cookies, candy, and sweetened soft drinks are not healthful foods.
   C. Foods with a lot of sugar can cause you to gain weight.

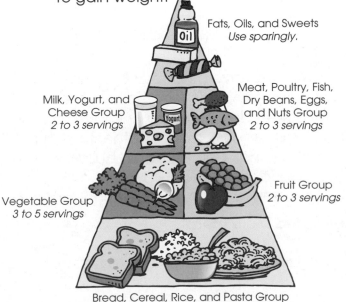

Fats, Oils, and Sweets
Use sparingly.

Milk, Yogurt, and Cheese Group
2 to 3 servings

Meat, Poultry, Fish, Dry Beans, Eggs, and Nuts Group
2 to 3 servings

Fruit Group
2 to 3 servings

Vegetable Group
3 to 5 servings

Bread, Cereal, Rice, and Pasta Group
6 to 11 servings

I. Reading
  A. Directions
  B. Sequencing
  C. Main Idea
II. Writing
  A. Capitalization
  B. Proofreading

Name _____

What's the Main Idea?

Often the main idea of a passage is **stated** in a sentence. Sometimes, however, you have to figure out the **unstated** main idea by looking at important details.

Directions: Read each paragraph. Then, write a sentence that states the main idea for each paragraph.

One of the most popular forms of entertainment today is playing computer games. Children are fascinated by these games. They are popular because they have exciting graphics, fun activities, and a wide variety of games.

Stated Main Idea: _____

_____

_____

Some radio stations play jazz. Others play rock. Still others play country. Some stations just report the news and weather. What a lot of variety we get from radio!

Unstated Main Idea: _____

_____

_____

Do you have a hobby? One kind of hobby involves collecting things. Some people collect stamps. Others may collect dolls or stuffed animals. Many people collect and trade sports cards. Another kind of hobby involves building things. Some people build models of ships and airplanes from kits or build large structures from Legos. Other hobbies involve music, art, dance, and sports.

Unstated Main Idea: _____

_____

_____

GRADE
6

I. Reading
  A. Directions
  B. Sequencing
  C. Main Idea
II. Writing
  A. Capitalization
  B. Proofreading

Name _____

What's the Idea?

Directions: Circle the sentence that best expresses the main idea of each paragraph.

1. Edmund began to question whether or not the lion in the Queen's courtyard was alive. The large creature looked as if it were about to pounce on a dwarf. But it did not move. Then Edmund noticed the snow on the lion's head and back. Only a statue would be covered like that!

   • The statue is snow-covered.

   • Edmund wonders if the lion is alive.

   • The lion is ready to jump.

2. The resting party of children and beavers heard the sound of jingling bells. Mr. Beaver dashed out of his hiding place and soon called the others to join him. He could hardly contain himself with excitement. Father Christmas is here!

   • Mr. Beaver is a brave animal.

   • Father Christmas has come to Narnia.

   • The group hears a jingling sound.

3. Poor Edmund! Because he came to the Queen, he expected her to reward him gratefully with Turkish delight. After all, he had traveled so far and had suffered miserably in the cold. When the Queen finally commanded that he receive food and drink, the cruel dwarf brought Edmund a bowl of water and a hunk of dry bread.

   • Edmund is not rewarded as he expects.

   • The young boy suffered from the cold.

   • Edmund receives bread and water.

4. Peter knew he must rescue Susan from the wolf. When the wolf charged, Susan climbed up a nearby tree. The wolf's snapping and snarling mouth was inches away. When Peter looked more closely, he realized that his sister was about to faint. Rushing in with his sword, Peter slashed at the beast.

   • Peter kills the wolf.

   • Peter realizes he must save his sister.

   • The wolf snarls at Susan.

I. Reading
   A. Directions
   B. Sequencing
   C. Main Idea
II. Writing
   A. Capitalization
   B. Proofreading

Name _____

Beth Is Sick

Poor Beth is sick, and she doesn't know why. She felt great yesterday, but this morning she woke up with a headache, a fever, and a horrible sore throat. Beth is disappointed because today is the day her class is going to the new science museum. Why did she have to be sick on a field trip day? How did she get ill so quickly?

Beth and Kim talk on the phone about Beth's situation for twenty minutes. Because they planned to be field trip partners, Kim is really sad Beth isn't going to school today. Kim tells Beth she probably got sick because she didn't wear a jacket to school yesterday, and it was a cold day. She tells Beth that if your body gets cold, you catch germs more easily. Beth tells Kim that is silly. She believes Kim has a virus.

Beth remembers learning about viruses in science class. Mr. Fridley told them that viruses are noncellular structures that can only be seen through an electron microscope, which magnifies them thousands of times. On its own, a virus is a lifeless particle that can't reproduce, but when a virus enters a living cell, it starts reproducing and can sometimes harm the host cell. Viruses that harm host cells cause disease like chicken pox, the flu, and colds. Mr. Fridley told them that shaking hands with or being sneezed or coughed on by an infected person may infect you with the virus. Beth believes that she became infected from someone since lots of people are sick at this time of year. Kim promises Beth a full report on the science museum.

Directions: Underline the main idea of the story.

Beth has a headache, fever, and a sore throat.

Beth and Kim try to discover why Beth is sick.

Viruses cause diseases.

Mr. Fridley taught them about viruses.

Directions: Check the correct answers.

Viruses...   ☐ can't be seen through an ordinary light microscope.
☐ pass easily from one person to another.
☐ are thousands of times bigger than regular cells.
☐ enter living cells and start reproducing.

What are some ways to avoid viruses? _____

_____

_____

GRADE
6

I. Reading
   A. Directions
   B. Sequencing
   C. Main Idea
II. Writing
   A. Capitalization
   B. Proofreading

Name _____

Support for the Main Idea

Sometimes the main idea is not stated directly. When this happens, you can use **supporting details** to infer the main idea.

Directions: Read each paragraph. Then, answer the questions.

Spiders and insects are small creatures. They both have thin, jointed legs and segmented bodies. Both spiders and insects can be found in a rainbow of colors and a variety of sizes.

1. What is the unstated main idea of this paragraph? _____

_____

2. List two details that support the main idea.

_____

_____

_____

Have you ever seen a spider's web? One web, called a *ladder web*, is long and narrow. Another web is called an *orb web*. This kind of web resembles a wheel.

1. What is the unstated main idea of this paragraph? _____

_____

2. List two details that support the main idea.

_____

_____

_____

GRADE 6

I. Reading
  A. Directions
  B. Sequencing
  C. Main Idea
II. Writing
  A. Capitalization
  B. Proofreading

Name _____

Some Do—Some Don't

Writers include **details** to help readers understand the selection. Some details **support the main idea**. Other details may provide additional information or enhance the story, but **do not support the main idea**.

Directions: Read the paragraphs below. Then, answer the questions.

Snakes come in all shapes and sizes. Some snakes, such as tree snakes, have long and thin bodies. This helps them blend into their environment. Other snakes, such as sea snakes, are thinner from side to side than from front to back. This shape helps them move through the water. Some snakes are even short and stubby.

1. What is the main idea of the paragraph? _____

_____

2. List two details that support the main idea. _____

_____

_____

3. Which details tell more about snakes but are not supporting details? _____

_____

_____

All mammals have fur or hair. These body coverings help keep mammals warm. Because mammals are warm-blooded, their body temperature stays about the same all the time, no matter what the temperature around them is. The fur of mammals keeps body warmth in and cold out.

1. What is the main idea of the paragraph? _____

_____

2. List two details that support the main idea. _____

_____

_____

3. Which details tell more about mammals but are not supporting details? _____

_____

_____

GRADE
6

I. Reading
A. Directions
B. Sequencing
C. Main Idea
II. Writing
A. Capitalization
B. Proofreading

Name _____

Picture the Details

Directions: Look at each illustration and main idea. Then, circle all supporting details that go with them.

Main Idea: The runners were lined up to begin the big race.

I. Which could be supporting details?

A. There were many fast runners.

B. The runners were waiting at the starting line.

C. The official had a stop watch.

D. The runners were wearing racing clothes.

Main Idea: Tina and Patty were looking for something unusual in the attic.

2. Which could be supporting details?

A. They have fun in the attic.

B. The attic is cold and dark.

C. They find old clothes in a trunk.

D. They think it is scary in the attic.

Main Idea: Roberto and several of his friends went to the beach yesterday.

3. Which could be supporting details?

A. Some people are afraid of swimming in the ocean.

B. Some children played games on the beach.

C. The water was rough.

D. Some children went swimming.

It's All in the Details

Directions: Read each main idea below. Write two supporting details that could be included with it in a paragraph. You can use a reference source, if necessary.

1. Christopher Columbus was a famous explorer.

_____

_____

_____

_____

2. Watching the Olympics is exciting!

_____

_____

_____

Directions: Choose one of the following topics. Write a paragraph about it that includes a main idea sentence and at least two sentences with supporting details.

| Celebrating Your Favorite Holiday | A Memorable Present |
| Your Special Talent | A New Family Member |

_____

_____

_____

_____

_____

_____

GRADE
6
I. Reading
A. Directions
B. Sequencing
C. Main Idea
II. Writing
A. Capitalization
B. Proofreading

Name _____

Context Clues Scramble

Directions: Unscramble the following words. (Hint: All of the words begin with **con**.) Then, write an unscrambled word to complete each sentence below. Use context clues to help you choose the best word.

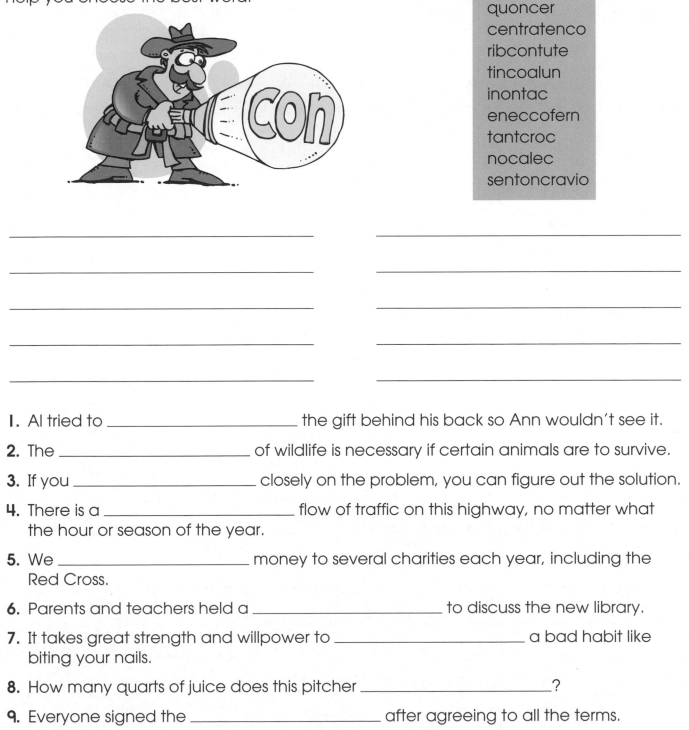

quoncer
centratenco
ribcontute
tincoalun
inontac
eneccofern
tantcroc
nocalec
sentoncravio

_____   _____

_____   _____

_____   _____

_____   _____

1. Al tried to _____ the gift behind his back so Ann wouldn't see it.

2. The _____ of wildlife is necessary if certain animals are to survive.

3. If you _____ closely on the problem, you can figure out the solution.

4. There is a _____ flow of traffic on this highway, no matter what the hour or season of the year.

5. We _____ money to several charities each year, including the Red Cross.

6. Parents and teachers held a _____ to discuss the new library.

7. It takes great strength and willpower to _____ a bad habit like biting your nails.

8. How many quarts of juice does this pitcher _____?

9. Everyone signed the _____ after agreeing to all the terms.

To Be More Precise

Directions: Complete the sentence for each dictionary entry to show how each word is used. Be sure to include explanations, antonyms, and synonyms as context clues in your sentences.

as sist ance (ə sis´ təns) help; aid:

Without your assistance, _____

_____

chron i cle (kron´ ə kəl) record of events in the order in which they happened; history; story:

The explorer kept a chronicle _____

_____

cou ra geous (kə rā´ jəs) brave; fearless; full of courage:

The courageous knight _____

_____

de mol ish (di mol´ ish) destroy; pull or tear down:

The old building was demolished _____

_____

drab (drab) dull; unattractive:

The woman dramatically altered the drab room by _____

_____

gen e ros i ty (jen´ ə ros´ ə tē) being generous; unselfishness; willingness to share:

As the result of their neighbor's generosity, _____

_____

gro tesque (grō tesk´) unnatural in shape, appearance, or manner; fantastic; odd:

The book is filled with pictures of grotesque creatures and other _____

_____

stead i ly (sted´ l ē) in a steady manner; firmly; uniformly:

The carpenter worked steadily _____

GRADE 6

I. Reading
A. Directions
B. Sequencing
C. Main Idea
II. Writing
A. Capitalization
B. Proofreading

Name _____

Context Clues

A **context clue** is a clue or **hint from the sentence** that helps you to figure out words that you don't know.

Directions: Read each sentence carefully. Guess the definition of each <u>underlined</u> word based on the context clues in the sentence. Then, use a dictionary to see how good your guess was.

1. He didn't want to miss that game because the coach had said it was a <u>crucial</u> one in deciding the championship.

   _____   _____
              your guess   dictionary definition

2. Although he tried to be <u>punctual</u>, he was always late.

   _____   _____
              your guess   dictionary definition

3. The confusing instructions that come with some home computers <u>perplex</u> many people.

   _____   _____
              your guess   dictionary definition

4. Light has a <u>velocity</u> of about 186,000 miles per second.

   _____   _____
              your guess   dictionary definition

5. Our pet bird <u>warbles</u> happily in his cage all day long.

   _____   _____
              your guess   dictionary definition

More Context Clues

Directions: Read each sentence. Guess the definition of the <u>underlined</u> word. Use a dictionary to check your guesses.

1. I get sunburned easily, so I <u>shun</u> long days at the beach.

_____   _____
         your guess   dictionary definition

2. He skied so well that no one could believe he was a <u>novice</u>.

_____   _____
         your guess   dictionary definition

3. We grew too many tomatoes, so we gave the <u>surplus</u> to the neighbors.

_____   _____
         your guess   dictionary definition

4. Our teacher <u>berated</u> us for being rude to the guest.

_____   _____
         your guess   dictionary definition

5. A promise of something for nothing is usually a <u>fraud</u>.

_____   _____
         your guess   dictionary definition

6. His <u>anguish</u> over his dog's death did not stop for many weeks.

_____   _____
         your guess   dictionary definition

7. If we want to stay on the team, we must <u>adhere</u> to the rules.

_____   _____
         your guess   dictionary definition

8. If our best hitter is ill, our chance of winning will <u>diminish</u>.

_____   _____
         your guess   dictionary definition

GRADE 6

I. Reading
   A. Directions
   B. Sequencing
   C. Main Idea
II. Writing
   A. Capitalization
   B. Proofreading

Name _____

Using Context Clues

Directions: Read each sentence. Guess the definition of the underlined word. Use a dictionary to check your guesses.

1. You will get a ticket from the policeman if you <u>exceed</u> the speed limit.

   _____   _____
   your guess   dictionary definition

2. The park ranger asked us to <u>discard</u> our litter in the basket.

   _____   _____
   your guess   dictionary definition

3. Although he was in great <u>peril</u>, he risked his life to save the child.

   _____   _____
   your guess   dictionary definition

4. That is a <u>fragile</u> vase, so please handle it with care.

   _____   _____
   your guess   dictionary definition

5. He didn't go to the dentist because he feared <u>excruciating</u> pain.

   _____   _____
   your guess   dictionary definition

6. The rain made your note <u>illegible</u>, so we did not know where you had gone.

   _____   _____
   your guess   dictionary definition

7. She has purchased many new stamps to <u>augment</u> her collection.

   _____   _____
   your guess   dictionary definition

8. The <u>obstinate</u> mule refused to budge from the street.

   _____   _____
   your guess   dictionary definition

GRADE
6

I. Reading
A. Directions
B. Sequencing
C. Main Idea
II. Writing
A. Capitalization
B. Proofreading

Name _____

Using More Context Clues

Directions: Read each sentence. Guess the definition of the <u>underlined</u> word. Use a dictionary to check your guesses.

1. His <u>monotonous</u> speech made half the audience fall asleep.

_____   _____
        your guess   dictionary definition

2. The fire department <u>prohibits</u> the use of candles in this theatre because of the fire danger.

_____   _____
        your guess   dictionary definition

3. Her <u>cordial</u> welcome made all her guests feel at home.

_____   _____
        your guess   dictionary definition

4. After the long hike, we all suffered from <u>fatigue</u>.

_____   _____
        your guess   dictionary definition

5. The elephant looked <u>enormous</u> to the small boy.

_____   _____
        your guess   dictionary definition

6. The snow <u>glistened</u> like jewels in the moonlight.

_____   _____
        your guess   dictionary definition

7. Yesterday was a very <u>hectic</u> day because our relatives arrived from Alaska and our dog had puppies.

_____   _____
        your guess   dictionary definition

8. When the man lost all his money, he became a <u>pauper</u>.

_____   _____
        your guess   dictionary definition

GRADE 6

I. Reading
  A. Directions
  B. Sequencing
  C. Main Idea
II. Writing
  A. Capitalization
  B. Proofreading

Name _____

Understanding Context Clues

Directions: For each sentence, circle the pair of words that completes the meaning of the sentence.

1. Their profits have been _____, and they wish to _____ their situation.
   a. decreasing—excuse
   b. declining—remedy
   c. comfortable—redress

2. Rats provide a _____ in reducing garbage, but this is outweighed by their _____ activities.
   a. help—useful
   b. trouble—dynamic
   c. service—harmful

3. Fact and Fancy were so _____ that no one could _____ them.
   a. connected—separate
   b. necessary—use
   c. respected—want

4. If one is to understand the _____, one must study the _____.
   a. facts—unnecessary
   b. unusual—sentences
   c. whole—parts

5. His father _____ him, for he realized the interest was more than a _____ fancy.
   a. encouraged—childish
   b. berated—sincere
   c. helped—mature

6. Safe driving prevents _____ and the awful _____ of knowing you have caused an accident.
   a. disease—remainder
   b. accidents—safe
   c. tragedy—remorse

Reviewing Context Clues

Directions: Circle the word which best fits each sentence.

Saving your (1) _____ to eat at a later date is not always (2) _____. It may not wait as long as you do!

1.	land	greed	luck	dessert
2.	golden	wise	fair	sure

Many (3) _____ may indeed make for light work, but only if they work (4) _____.

3.	shovels	seas	hands	kitchens
4.	together	alone	nearby	silently

"Put your money where your mouth is" may be a (5) _____-inflicting proverb; but it sure (6) _____ people quiet!

5.	plant	gold	wise	germ
6.	invests	keeps	shuts	tempts

Go ahead and rollerblade along life's (7) _____, but keep those knee pads (8) _____ for the bumps along the way.

7.	problems	highways	lamps	deeds
8.	ready	quick	dangerous	softly

Music may indeed (9) _____ a savage beast, but only if the (10) _____ has an instrument nearby.

9.	shoot	ride	calm	scale
10.	lion	trumpet	radio	musician

The saying "A fool and his money are soon (11) _____" should not be discussed when (12) _____ allowance from our parents.

11.	parted	happy	peaceful	shown
12.	sewing	waving	giving	asking

As Uncle Gene (13) _____ on his inflatable raft on the (14) _____, we knew that some men are islands!

13.	flew	fetched	floated	fared
14.	dock	lake	sink	house

Hurtling downward into a deep, dark (15) _____, Bernard exclaimed, "Why sure! Gotta (16) _____ before ya' leap!"

15.	mansion	Chevy	chasm	rim
16.	look	shave	care	buy

GRADE 6

I. Reading
  A. Directions
  B. Sequencing
  C. Main Idea
II. Writing
  A. Capitalization
  B. Proofreading

Name _____

Just the Facts, Please

Directions: Read Ricky's paragraph. Underline each sentence that states an opinion rather than a fact. Then, list one valid and faulty opinion. Opinions are considered valid if they are supported by facts and faulty if they are not.

There are some really goofy laws still on the books in cities and towns throughout the United States. Many of these laws were passed a long time ago. Why they were passed in the first place is beyond me! People back then sure had some strange ideas about right and wrong.

In New Jersey, for example, it is against the law to slurp your soup in a public restaurant, and in the city of Newark, you must have a written note from your doctor if you want to buy ice cream after 6:00 P.M.!

If you happen to live within the city limits of Flowery Branch, Georgia, you had better not yell, "Snake!" Kids who live in Minneapolis, Minnesota, will like this next law, especially if they don't have a dishwasher. You see, it's against the law to wipe dishes dry. The lawmakers believed that dishes should drip dry. If you are a boy in Pulaski, Illinois, watch out where you throw snowballs! It's against the law for you to throw them at trees. I suppose it's okay for girls to throw snowballs, though, because they aren't mentioned in the law. That's really unfair.

Now here's another, you'll enjoy. I'm sure you'd agree that most little kids like lollipops. Well, guess what! If you live in Spokane, Washington, you are not allowed to buy a lollipop if you are a child. It's the law! If your family car drips oil or anything else for that matter, Green Bay, Wisconsin, is not the place to be. There is a one-dollar fine for every drip your car makes on the pavement. Speaking of cars, if you like comics, don't get caught reading them if you are riding in a car in Norman, Oklahoma. It's against the law.

Now here's the best one. In Winnetka, Illinois, it's against the law to take your shoes off in a theater if your feet smell.

Valid Opinion _____

_____

_____

_____

Faulty Opinion _____

_____

_____

_____

GRADE
6

I. Reading
   A. Directions
   B. Sequencing
   C. Main Idea
II. Writing
   A. Capitalization
   B. Proofreading

Name _____

Is That a Fact?

Directions: Read each statement and write **O** if it states an opinion or **F** if it states a fact. Then, give a reason for each answer.

I. _____ The most impressive view of China's Great Wall is from a space shuttle as it orbits Earth.

_____

_____

2. _____ Built between 400s B.C. and A.D. 1600s, the Great Wall was the greatest engineering feat of its time.

_____

_____

3. _____ The Great Wall is the longest human-made structure in existence, with the main part stretching over 2,100 miles.

_____

_____

4. _____ If you include the Great Wall's side sections and spurs, you can add another 1,800 miles or so to its total length, making it as long as the Nile River.

_____

_____

5. _____ The Chinese should rebuild all the sections of the Great Wall that have crumbled over the centuries.

_____

_____

6. _____ Everyone says that the Great Wall is China's greatest national treasure.

_____

_____

GRADE
6
I. Reading
   A. Directions
   B. Sequencing
   C. Main Idea
II. Writing
   A. Capitalization
   B. Proofreading

Name _____

Reading Skills: Fact or Opinion?

A **fact** is information that can be proved. An **opinion** is information that tells how someone feels or what he or she thinks about something.

Directions: For each sentence, write **F** for fact or **O** for opinion. The first one has been done for you.

_____F_____ 1. Each of the countries in South America has its own capital.

_____ 2. All South Americans are good swimmers.

_____ 3. People like the climate in Peru better than in Brazil.

_____ 4. The continent of South America is almost completely surrounded by water.

_____ 5. The only connection with another continent is a narrow strip of land, called the Isthmus of Panama, which links it to North America.

_____ 6. The Andes Mountains run all the way down the western edge of the continent.

_____ 7. The Andes are the longest continuous mountain barrier in the world.

_____ 8. The Andes are the most beautiful mountain range.

_____ 9. The Amazon River is the second longest river in the world—about 4,000 miles long.

_____ 10. Half of the people in South America are Brazilians.

_____ 11. Life in Brazil is better than life in other South American countries.

_____ 12. Brazil is the best place for South Americans to live.

_____ 13. Cape Horn is at the southern tip of South America.

_____ 14. The largest land animal in South America is the tapir, which reaches a length of 6 to 8 feet.

I. Reading
A. Directions
B. Sequencing
C. Main Idea
II. Writing
A. Capitalization
B. Proofreading

Name _____

You Be the Judge

The lawyer is asking the witnesses many questions. Some of the answers are facts, and some are opinions. The judge will only accept facts.

Directions: Read each question and answer. Check **fact** or **opinion** next to each answer. If you checked fact, write a second answer that is an opinion. If you checked opinion, write a second answer that is a fact.

☐ fact
☐ opinion

1. question: Mr. Wallace, what was the stranger wearing?
    answer: He was wearing a blue coat, red scarf, black slacks, and black shoes.

☐ fact
☐ opinion

2. question: Mr. Henry, what did you hear from your window?
    answer: I heard a sound that must have been the intruder breaking in.

☐ fact
☐ opinion

3. question: Ms. Harris, what time did you notice the broken lock?
    answer: It was 10:15 P.M., just as I arrived home.

☐ fact
☐ opinion

4. question: Mrs. Patterson, do you know the owner of the stolen painting?
    answer: He is the nicest boss I have ever worked for.

☐ fact
☐ opinion

5. question: Mr. Samuels, was the painting insured?
    answer: Yes, the painting was insured for ten thousand dollars.

☐ fact
☐ opinion

6. question: Miss Ryan, did you see the defendant take the painting?
    answer: Of course he took it! It had to be him.

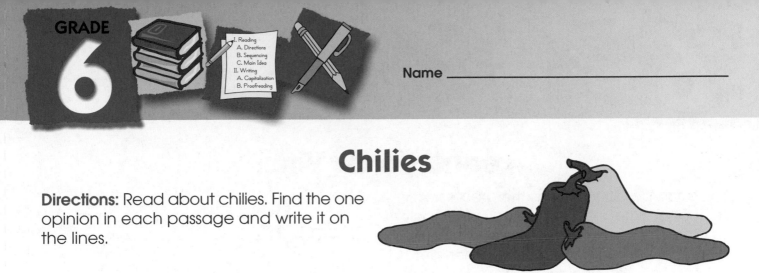

Name _____

Chilies

Directions: Read about chilies. Find the one opinion in each passage and write it on the lines.

Chilies are hot or sweet peppers. They are part of the "nightshade" family of plants that also includes potatoes and tomatoes. Potatoes and tomatoes taste better than chilies, though.

Opinion: _____

_____

Chilies were originally grown in Central and South America. By the 15th century, Europeans were cooking with them and drying them to use as a spice. European dishes taste better now than they did before chilies were used in them.

Opinion: _____

_____

Although it is really a Mexican recipe, every intelligent American loves *chili con carne*. It is made with spicy meat, beans, and chilies. Today, most Americans call that dish "chili."

Opinion: _____

_____

Some people think that all chilies are hot. Therefore, they never eat any of them. What a silly belief! There are many different kinds of red, yellow, and green chilies. Even red chilies can be sweet.

Opinion: _____

_____

I. Reading
  A. Directions
  B. Sequencing
  C. Main Idea
II. Writing
  A. Capitalization
  B. Proofreading

Name _____

Leonardo da Vinci

Leonardo da Vinci was the greatest artist of all time. He is remembered not only as a painter, but also as a sculptor, a musician, an inventor, an astronomer, a scientist, and an engineer.

Leonardo was born in 1452 in Vinci, Italy. As a young boy, he showed a talent for mathematics and painting. His father took him to Florence, Italy, to study painting and engineering. Florence was the best place to learn because so many gifted people lived there. Leonardo became well known in Florence as a young painter. Soon he was painting better than his teachers. In 1472, at the age of twenty, Leonardo was asked to join the painter's guild in Florence. The painter's guild was the best place for Leonardo. He could finally be recognized among other great artists.

When Leonardo was thirty years old, he decided to move to Milan, Italy. He began working for the Duke of Milan. The Duke wanted to make Milan a beautiful and

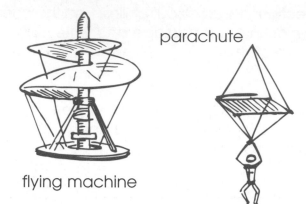

parachute

flying machine

famous city, like Florence. While in Milan, Leonardo painted the most famous painting in history—*The Last Supper*. People came from many countries to see the painting. Today, the painting is still found on the wall of the little church in Italy.

In 1499, Leonardo returned to Florence. There he painted his other famous painting, the *Mona Lisa*. The *Mona Lisa* was a painting of a twenty-four-year-old wife of a wealthy merchant. Her name was Lisa del Gioconda. Her mysterious smile is the most fascinating part of the painting.

Leonardo is remembered for other contributions. He sketched designs for flying machines and parachutes long before anyone believed people could fly. Leonardo also drew detailed sketches of the human body and how it worked. He wrote thousands of pages of notes on mathematics and science.

Leonardo da Vinci is the most important artist of all time not only because of his paintings, but also because of his scientific and mathematical inventions. Many of his sketches and notes have been used over the years to help scientists and inventors make new discoveries.

LEONARDO DAVINCI

70 Fact or Opinion

GRADE 6

I. Reading
A. Directions
B. Sequencing
C. Main Idea
II. Writing
A. Capitalization
B. Proofreading

Name _____

Leonardo da Vinci

Directions: Are the following statements facts or opinions? Write **F** if the statement is a fact and **O** if the statement is an opinion.

1. _____ Leonardo da Vinci is the most important artist of all time.

2. _____ Leonardo painted *The Last Supper* in a small church in Milan.

3. _____ As a child, Leonardo was talented at mathematics and painting.

4. _____ Many of Leonardo's sketches were used to help scientists and inventors make new discoveries.

5. _____ Leonardo was not happy until he joined the painter's guild in Florence.

6. _____ *The Last Supper* is the world's most famous painting.

7. _____ The Mona Lisa's mysterious smile is the most interesting part of that painting.

8. _____ To understand *The Last Supper*, you have to travel to the small church in Italy where it was painted.

9. _____ Leonardo returned to Florence in 1499.

10. _____ Florence was the best place for Leonardo to study as a young boy.

GRADE 6

I. Reading
   A. Directions
   B. Sequencing
   C. Main Idea
II. Writing
   A. Capitalization
   B. Proofreading

Name _____

What Do You Think?

Directions: Read each sentence. Write two sentences explaining what could have caused each event to happen.

1. The bird ceased its singing in the forest.

   a. _____

   b. _____

2. Tim came home crying. His backpack was open.

   a. _____

   b. _____

3. Five hundred people laughed at Lana as she stood in the bright light.

   a. _____

   b. _____

4. The saddled horse galloped onto the track without a jockey.

   a. _____

   b. _____

5. Pam sat soaking wet on the bench with her friends.

   a. _____

   b. _____

6. Martin stared with mouth agape at his teacher, Mr. Lancaster.

   a. _____

   b. _____

GRADE 6

I. Reading
A. Directions
B. Sequencing
C. Main Idea
II. Writing
A. Capitalization
B. Proofreading

Name _____

Reading Skills: Cause and Effect

A **cause** is the reason something happens. The **effect** is what happens as the result of the cause.

Directions: Read the paragraphs below. For each numbered sentence, circle the cause or causes and underline the effect or effects. The first one has been done for you.

(1) <u>All living things in the ocean are endangered</u> by (humans polluting the water.) Pollution occurs in several ways. One way is the dumping of certain waste materials, such as garbage and sewage, into the ocean. (2) The decaying bacteria that feed on the garbage use up much of the oxygen in the surrounding water, so other creatures in the area often don't get enough.

Other substances, such as radioactive waste material, can also cause pollution. These materials are often placed in the water in securely sealed containers. (3) But after years of being exposed to the ocean water, the containers may begin to leak.

Oil is another major source of concern. (4) Oil is spilled into the ocean when tankers run aground and sink or when oil wells in the ocean cannot be capped. (5) The oil covers the gills of fish and causes them to smother. (6) Diving birds get the oil on their wings and are unable to fly. (7) When they clean themselves, they are often poisoned by the oil.

Rivers also can contribute to the pollution of oceans. Many rivers receive the runoff water from farmlands. (8) Fertilizers used on the farms may be carried to the ocean, where they cause a great increase in the amount of certain plants. Too much of some plants can actually be poisonous to fish.

Worse yet are the pesticides carried to the ocean. These chemicals slowly build up in shellfish and other small animals. These animals then pass the pesticides on to the larger animals that feed on them. (9) The buildup of these chemicals in the animals can make them ill or cause their babies to be born dead or deformed.

GRADE 6

I. Reading
   A. Directions
   B. Sequencing
   C. Main Idea
II. Writing
   A. Capitalization
   B. Proofreading

Name _____

Television

The invention of the television changed the world in many important ways. Television has given people the opportunity to see and hear people, places, and events from around the world. More than 98 percent of all U.S. homes have a television. Television is now an important form of communication, allowing people instant access to current events.

Television does not have just one inventor. In the 1800s, an Italian inventor named Marconi discovered how to send signals through the air as electromagnetic waves. His invention was the radio. This set the stage for the invention of television. In the early 1900s, a young American named Philo Farnsworth began experimenting. He had an idea to send pictures as well as sound through the air. This idea resulted in the invention of the electronic television camera.

About the same time, an American scientist named Vladimir Zworykin invented the iconoscope and the kinescope. The iconoscope was a television camera. The kinescope was a picture tube to receive and show the picture. In 1929, Zworykin made the first television system.

But how does a television work? The picture that you see is the result of three steps. First, light and sound waves are changed into electronic signals. The light and sound waves come from the scene that is being televised. Next, these electronic signals are passed through the air to be received by individual television sets. Last, the television set unscrambles the signals. In this way, a picture is "moved" from the original scene to your television set.

These three steps happen because light and sound waves can be made into electronic signals. Light waves are picked up and changed into electronic signals by a camera. Sound waves are picked up and changed into electronic signals by a microphone. The camera signals are called video, and the microphone signals are called *audio*.

To produce electric signals in color, certain color signals are added to the video. Three primary colors of light—red, blue, and green—are used to produce pictures in color.

With the advent of digital technology, televisions have wider screens and pictures that are even clearer.

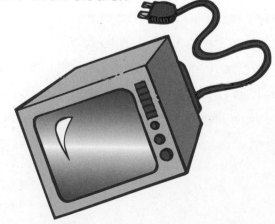

Television

Directions: Fill in the chart below with information from the passage.

Cause	Effect
1.	Television pictures appear in color.
A camera picks up light waves.	2.
Vladimir Zworykin invents the iconoscope and the kinescope.	3.
4.	The electronic television camera is invented.
5.	People can see and hear people, places, and events from around the world.
More than 98 percent of all U.S. homes have a television.	6.
7.	Electronic signals are received by television sets.
Marconi invents the radio.	8.
9.	A picture is "moved" from the original scene to a television set.
Digital technology is becoming readily available.	10.

I. Reading
  A. Directions
  B. Sequencing
  C. Main Idea
II. Writing
  A. Capitalization
  B. Proofreading

Name _____

Put Them Together

Directions: Find the causes and effects that make sense together. Write the complete cause/effect sentences on the lines provided.

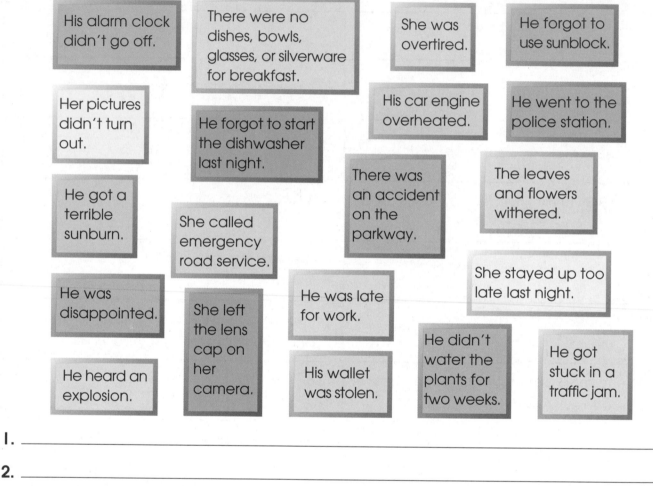

His alarm clock didn't go off.

There were no dishes, bowls, glasses, or silverware for breakfast.

She was overtired.

He forgot to use sunblock.

Her pictures didn't turn out.

He forgot to start the dishwasher last night.

His car engine overheated.

He went to the police station.

He got a terrible sunburn.

She called emergency road service.

There was an accident on the parkway.

The leaves and flowers withered.

He was disappointed.

He was late for work.

She stayed up too late last night.

She left the lens cap on her camera.

He didn't water the plants for two weeks.

He got stuck in a traffic jam.

He heard an explosion.

His wallet was stolen.

1. _____

2. _____

3. _____

4. _____

5. _____

6. _____

7. _____

8. _____

9. _____

10. _____

GRADE 6

I. Reading
  A. Directions
  B. Sequencing
  C. Main Idea
II. Writing
  A. Capitalization
  B. Proofreading

Name _____

Shiloh

A **simile** is a comparison using the words *like* or *as*.

Example: The pile of laundry was *as high as a mountain* by the time our washer was fixed.

Directions: Underline the similes in these sentences. Write another simile with the same or nearly the same meaning.

1. My dream leaks out like water in a paper bag.

   _____

2. I hold Shiloh as carefully as I carry Becky when she's asleep.

   _____

3. I'm as happy as a flea on a dog.

   _____

4. Keeping Shiloh a secret is like having a bomb waiting to go off.

   _____

5. I'm as tense as a cricket at night.

   _____

6. Ma hums to Shiloh like he's a baby in a cradle.

   _____

Directions: Complete these sentences with a simile of your own.

1. Shiloh looked at Dara Lynn like _____ .

2. Doc Murphy was as gentle as _____ with Shiloh.

3. Judd trying to be nice was like _____ .

4. The Prestons were happy as _____
   to have Shiloh.

GRADE 6

I. Reading
   A. Directions
   B. Sequencing
   C. Main Idea
II. Writing
   A. Capitalization
   B. Proofreading

Name _____

It's Like . . .

Directions: Underline the simile in each sentence. The first one has been done for you.

1. After staying up all night to study for her big test, Sarah looked <u>like a lifeless plant</u>.

2. When it came time to sing at choir practice, she sounded like a cat screeching at the top of its lungs.

3. But she still looked as pretty as a flower.

4. Fortunately, she felt as good as new after a short nap in the afternoon.

5. That's why she was able to run like the wind at track practice that evening.

6. Of course she was as hungry as a horse come dinnertime, after such a long day.

7. Sarah slept like a rock that night.

8. She was as happy as a clam to find out the next day that she got a "B" on her test!

9. No one would have ever guessed that she had studied like a maniac for it.

10. Sarah resolved that she would never again wait until the last minute to study; like clockwork, she would study a little bit each night for the entire semester.

Directions: Now, write five similes of your own. Don't forget to include *like* or *as* in each one.

_____

_____

_____

_____

_____

_____

_____

GRADE 6

I. Reading
  A. Directions
  B. Sequencing
  C. Main Idea
II. Writing
  A. Capitalization
  B. Proofreading

Name _____

Compared to What?

A **simile** compares two different things and states the comparison directly by using the word *as* or *like*. A **metaphor** makes a comparison without stating it directly.

Example: The basketball player was *a tower* next to his other teammates.

Directions: Underline the metaphors in the following sentences. The first one has been done for you.

1. The airplane was <u>a bullet in the sky</u>.

2. From the plane, the river was a silver ribbon winding through the landscape.

3. The clouds were ghostly battleships sailing across the sky.

4. The snow-capped peaks were ice cream cones jutting into the sky.

5. The sunset was a bonfire in the sky.

6. The plane's shadow was a giant bird skimming effortlessly across the farm fields below.

7. Chicago was on fire with lights as we approached the airport at dusk.

8. The exciting city was a breath of fresh air to us folks from the country.

Directions: Now, write five metaphors of your own.

_____

_____

_____

_____

_____

_____

_____

I. Reading
  A. Directions
  B. Sequencing
  C. Main Idea
II. Writing
  A. Capitalization
  B. Proofreading

Name _____

Which Is Which?

Directions: Label each sentence **simile** or **metaphor**.

1. _____ There was no use trying to help Rachel with her problem; all she did was bark at me.

2. _____ The neighbors' music was so loud that we felt like we were at a rock concert.

3. _____ The breeze was like a cool drink on a hot day.

4. _____ After a few days, the house was a work of art.

5. _____ The chair looked ugly, but it was as comfortable as a worn shoe.

6. _____ The blueberries we picked were precious jewels of sweetness.

7. _____ Karen smelled like a bouquet of flowers in the springtime.

8. _____ Grandma's pie tasted like a slice of heaven.

9. _____ "Stop being such a couch potato and do something with your day!" her mom cried.

10. _____ The house was a train wreck on stilts.

11. _____ Mike has a hard exterior, but on the inside he's all cream cheese.

12. _____ The terrible smell, which was as foul as rotten eggs, hit us as soon as we walked through the door.

13. _____ My little brother is the family policeman; he opens his mouth whenever he notices someone doing something they're not supposed to.

14. _____ I was prepared to babysit for Belinda's two brothers, but when she showed up with a whole army of kids, I had to put my foot down.

15. _____ Don't let his innocent looks fool you; he's as sly as a fox.

GRADE

6

I. Reading
A. Directions
B. Sequencing
C. Main Idea
II. Writing
A. Capitalization
B. Proofreading

Name _____

Calling All Idioms

An **idiom** is a word or phrase that has taken on a different meaning than its actual one. Some idioms are so common that we don't even think about them. The expression "putting your foot in your mouth," for example, means saying something embarrassing or stupid.

Directions: Underline the idioms in the following sentences. The first one has been done for you.

1. You're lucky you keep winning, but <u>don't push your luck</u>.

2. My dad called me on the carpet after viewing my report card.

3. We're all in the same boat here!

4. Jared was putting me on.

5. By a vote of 8-3, the board turned down the proposal.

6. Since Mr. Smith was absent, they asked Ms. Nakano to fill in.

7. We ran into Nicki and Sammy at the fair.

8. The pizza at City Pies is out of this world.

Directions: Write a sentence using each of the idioms from the box:

break down	grow up	set up	run down
strike out	bottle up	shake down	check out

_____

_____

_____

_____

_____

_____

_____

GRADE 6

I. Reading
  A. Directions
  B. Sequencing
  C. Main Idea
II. Writing
  A. Capitalization
  B. Proofreading

Name _____

Extra! Extra!

Directions: The following are opening sentences for articles that appeared in the most recent edition of *Mercerville Monthly*. Read each one and predict the purpose of the article. Write **persuade**, **inform**, or **entertain** on the line.

There's no doubt in my mind that Michael Jordan is the best basketball player that has ever lived.

1. _____

On Friday night, the Town Council voted unanimously to create a scholarship fund to send Mercerville's brightest students to college.

2. _____

Everyone has been wondering about our town's newest, most famous resident, comedian Slick Anderson. Well, Slick took me on a tour of his multi-million-dollar estate today, and what he showed me made me laugh so hard my stomach hurt. Wait until you hear about Slick's collection of humorous cartoon memorabilia!

3. _____

Café de Cochon, located at 33 Main Street, serves light French food at reasonable prices.

4. _____

Some people say the solution to Mercerville's beetle problem is to spray a deadly insecticide. But why risk poisoning our pets, the environment, and even ourselves? I have a better plan for getting rid of the unwanted beetles, and not only is it safer for the environment but it won't cost the townspeople any money.

5. _____

Six houses have been burglarized since the town's Neighborhood Watch program was dismantled, according to Police Chief Carmen DeSoto.

6. _____

As mayor of this town, Bob Thorpe has done nothing but deceive people. Mike Fernandez is an honest and hardworking alternative to Mr. Thorpe, and everyone should vote for him on Election Day.

7. _____

How is it that this town can raise thousands of dollars for the Mercerville High boys' basketball team but the championship-winning girls' team can't even afford new uniforms? It's time for Mercerville to give female athletes the respect they deserve!

8. _____

GRADE

6

I. Reading
  A. Directions
  B. Sequencing
  C. Main Idea
II. Writing
  A. Capitalization
  B. Proofreading

Name _____

No Day at the Beach

Directions: Read each story fragment. Then, write a possible outcome. When you have finished, read your completed story!

    All week, my family had been looking forward to spending Saturday at Brewster Beach. Then, on Friday night, my little sister got an earache, and my mom said we'd probably have to take her to the doctor the next day. Fortunately,

_____

_____

    Saturday started out as a beautiful day. We all woke up early and my dad made waffles. We put on our swimsuits and packed the car. But, when my mom tried to start the car, it

_____

_____

    Eventually, we were able to get on the road, and we were all in good spirits again. But then, it began to rain! We were five minutes from the beach when sheets of water fell from the sky. We thought the rain would ruin our day for sure. So we pulled over, and

_____

_____

    When we finally got to the beach, all the other families were already packing their things to go. My sister begged to stay for an hour or so, so we spread out our blanket even though the air was getting cool. I decided to feel the water. But I had no sooner dipped in my big toe when I was attacked by a swarm of mosquitoes! They were everywhere!

_____

_____

    We were all grumpy that night. What a disaster! I have a feeling it'll be a while before we plan another trip to Brewster Beach.

_____

Name _____

What Will Happen?

Directions: Read each situation. Then, use what you know to make a prediction.

"Have a good day, and please don't forget to shut the windows before you leave for school!" said Mrs. Martin, rushing to catch her bus.

Max was eating breakfast and finishing the homework assignment he had forgotten to do last night. Twenty minutes later, he looked up at the clock. If he didn't hurry, he would miss his bus. Max shoved his homework and books into his backpack and ran out the door, making sure it was locked.

It was during math class that Max heard thunder and a howling wind and noticed the dark storm clouds.

"Oh, no," Max moaned to himself.

1. Predict what Max will find when he gets home. _____

_____

_____

Mary Beth had 10 more problems to finish before she could meet her friends. If she hadn't wasted so much time on the computer after dinner while she was supposed to be doing homework, she could have been outside having fun with them right now. Within a half-hour Mary Beth was out the door.

Only a few minutes later, she heard her mother calling her. "Mary Beth! It's time to come in!"

She barely had a chance to play. Reluctantly, Mary Beth left her friends and went inside. She was determined to do things differently tomorrow.

2. Predict what Mary Beth will do differently. _____

_____

_____

The Johnsons are away for the week. They have hired Dennis to get their mail and newspaper each afternoon while they are gone.

When Dennis gets home from school on Monday, he collects their mail and paper.

On Tuesday, he has soccer practice all afternoon and forgets. On Wednesday, he goes to a friend's house and stays overnight. Except for Monday, in fact, Dennis forgets to get the mail and paper every day that week.

3. Predict the outcome when the Johnsons return from their trip. _____

_____

_____

I. Reading
  A. Directions
  B. Sequencing
  C. Main Idea
II. Writing
  A. Capitalization
  B. Proofreading

Name _____

What Happens Next?

Directions: Do you like to read comic strips? Have you ever tried to predict the outcome before reading the last frame? Well, here's your chance to show what you know about cats, predict what will happen, and be an artist, too! Read the frames below. Then, draw the ending.

GRADE 6

I. Reading
   A. Directions
   B. Sequencing
   C. Main Idea
II. Writing
   A. Capitalization
   B. Proofreading

Name _____

Athlete Mix-Up

Directions: Read each description of an athlete. Draw a conclusion about what type of athlete is described. Write your answers on the lines.

1. My sport can be played outside or inside. I don't usually play on a team, but, sometimes, I have a partner. I have to hit a ball over a net, but not with my hands. Once I pulled a muscle while practicing my killer serve.

   I'm a _____ .

2. My sport is almost always played outside. I don't play on a team. I have to hit a ball over and over again, but not with my hands. My dream is to someday make a "hole in one." I can take a cart instead of walking to get from one part of the course to another.

   I'm a _____ .

3. My sport is always played inside. It involves trying to knock over things. I don't have to wear a uniform when I compete in my sport, but I do have to wear special shoes. I am happy when I make a "strike."

   I'm a _____ .

4. My sport is played outside by teams. There are lots of skills involved in my sport: kicking, throwing, catching, and running. Some of my teammates are pretty big, especially the linebacker. He looks even

bigger when he's wearing his uniform and all his padding.

   I'm a _____ .

5. When I was a little kid, I fantasized about swinging through the trees like a monkey. Now, I can swing, jump, dance, and do flips, too. My sport is usually played inside. I practice my routine and try to be graceful so I will impress the judges on competition day.

   I'm a _____ .

6. My sport can be played outside or inside. However, it can't be played outside when the weather is cold. I go fast by kicking my legs as I pull with my arms. Sometimes, I race against other people, and, sometimes, I race against the clock. In long races, I have teammates who take over when I have finished my laps.

   I'm a _____ .

7. Look, no hands needed in my sport! I am not allowed to touch the ball with my hands. Usually I kick it, but I can bounce it off my head, too. I run from one end of the field to the other, trying to get the ball past the goalie and into the net.

   I'm a _____ .

GRADE 6

I. Reading
   A. Directions
   B. Sequencing
   C. Main Idea
II. Writing
   A. Capitalization
   B. Proofreading

Name _____

The Missing Painting

Directions: Read the following mystery and answer the questions.

Detective Doolittle couldn't sleep. He was puzzled by the facts of his latest case. A priceless painting had been reported stolen from the home of Neptune Island's wealthiest resident, Eloise Rappaport. He didn't find any evidence and there were no witnesses, either. Who could have sneaked into the Rappaport home in broad daylight and stolen a painting the size of a refrigerator? It just didn't seem possible.

The next day, Detective Doolittle drove back to the crime scene. Miss Rappaport let him in and took him to the library where the robbery had taken place.

"So tell me again, in your own words, what happened," said Doolittle.

"Well," said Miss Rappaport, "It was Saturday afternoon and it was very hot—you know, usual July weather. I had just come back from lunch at my friend Marcia's house when I noticed that the library door was open. It was around 2:30. I didn't think much of it so I went upstairs to change for the cocktail party I was to go to that night. When I came back downstairs, I heard the phone ringing. I went to pick up the extension in the library—that's when I noticed that my painting was missing!"

"And you didn't see or hear anything strange that day?" the detective asked.

"No, but there is something that's been bothering me. At the time I didn't think anything of it but I saw my neighbor, Fred, on his way into the Post Office the very next day with a giant box, big enough to fit my painting in, marked 'Fragile.' I offered to give him a ride home but he acted really strange and ran away. I've always thought he was a weird fellow."

"Hmmm …" said Detective Doolittle. He was frustrated; he'd never had so much trouble cracking a case before. Something about Miss Rappaport's story was troubling him. "Thanks for your help. I'll be going now. Just one more question—who was on the phone when you took that call in the library that day?"

"Oh," she said, "it was the gardener, Theresa. She was calling to tell me she wouldn't be in that day because she had to drive her daughter to kindergarten. I'll tell you, she has been trouble since I hired her last summer. I wouldn't be surprised if she was the one who took the painting!"

"Maybe she did, Miss Rappaport," said Detective Doolittle angrily, "but you're the one who's lying!"

1. Why does Detective Doolittle say that Miss Rappaport is lying?_____

_____

_____

2. What do you think happened to the painting? What makes you think so?_____

_____

_____

3. On another sheet of paper, write a conclusion to the story.

GRADE
6

I. Reading
  A. Directions
  B. Sequencing
  C. Main Idea
II. Writing
  A. Capitalization
  B. Proofreading

Name _____

I Conclude . . .

Directions: When you read, you use information in the text as well as what you know to draw conclusions. Read the following facts and think about what you know. Make a check mark next to the correct conclusion. Then, write another conclusion for each of the facts.

1. Dolphins sleep just under the surface of the water but come up for air at three to four minute intervals.

   _____ Dolphins are not fish but mammals.

   _____ Dolphins are light sleepers.

   _____

2. Hydroponics, the cultivation of plants in water, was once used by the ancient Aztecs and Chinese, and is currently in use year-round in many greenhouses where the climate makes it impossible to grow plants outside.

   _____ Hydroponics is not a new method of growing plants.

   _____ Hydroponics is an efficient method of plant cultivation.

   _____

3. Between 1950 and 1996, the population of New York City went from 7,891,957 to 7,380,906, while the population of Dallas went from 434,462 to 1,053,292.

   _____ New York City is one of the largest cities in the world.

   _____ The population of a city can increase or decrease over time.

   _____

4. An elephant eats about 1/20 of its own body weight daily, while a mouse eats as much as its weight.

   _____ An elephant eats an enormous amount of food each day.

   _____ A smaller animal such as the mouse eats more in relation to its size.

   _____

5. In less than a decade, the landfills in over half of the 50 states will be filled to capacity.

   _____ We are running out of room for all the garbage we produce.

   _____ Landfills are not the best solution for disposing of garbage.

   _____

GRADE 6

I. Reading
  A. Directions
  B. Sequencing
  C. Main Idea
II. Writing
  A. Capitalization
  B. Proofreading

Name _____

Summarizing

A **summary** is a brief retelling of the main ideas of a reading selection. To summarize, write the author's most important points in your own words.

Directions: Write a two-sentence summary for each paragraph.

The boll weevil is a small beetle that is native to Mexico. It feeds inside the seed pods, or bolls, of cotton plants. The boll weevil crossed into Texas in the late 1800s. It has since spread into most of the cotton-growing areas of the United States. The boll weevil causes hundreds of millions of dollars worth of damage to cotton crops each year.

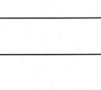

Summary: _____

_____

_____

Each spring, female boll weevils open the buds of young cotton plants with their snouts. They lay eggs inside the buds, and the eggs soon hatch into worm-like grubs. The grubs feed inside the buds, causing the buds to fall from the plant. They eat their way from one bud to another. Several generations of boll weevils may be produced in a single season.

Summary: _____

_____

_____

The coming of the boll weevil to the United States caused tremendous damage to cotton crops. Yet, there were some good results, too. Farmers were forced to plant other crops. In areas where a variety of crops were raised, the land is in better condition than it would have been if only cotton had been grown.

Summary: _____

_____

_____

GRADE

6

I. Reading
A. Directions
B. Sequencing
C. Main Idea
II. Writing
A. Capitalization
B. Proofreading

Name _____

At the Movies

Directions: What is your favorite movie of all time? Imagine that you are the arts and entertainment writer for a major newspaper. Write a summary of this movie including its topic, main idea, names of main characters, and the important events that took place. Then, write a paragraph at the end to tell why you think people should see it.

_____

_____

_____

_____

_____

_____

_____

_____

_____

_____

_____

_____

_____

_____

_____

_____

GRADE 6

I. Reading
   A. Directions
   B. Sequencing
   C. Main Idea
II. Writing
   A. Capitalization
   B. Proofreading

Name _____

Neon Lights

Directions: A summary should include only the important details from a selection. Read the paragraph. Summarize it on the lines below. Then, go back and circle the sentences from the article that contained details that were not important for your summary.

When we think of neon lights, we think of the signs we see in store windows. That light is different from the light produced by an ordinary light bulb in a lamp. The light in neon lamps is produced by neon, a gas found in the air all around us. Neon gas, which is what is in neon lights, is colorless. When the sign is turned on, an electric current flows through the tube. The electrons in the neon gas get a burst of energy from the electric current. As each electron settles down, it releases a photon of light. The photons travel to our eyes and we see red light. Even though this light appears to glow continuously, the electrons are really like little lights blinking on and off. When the sign is turned off again, the neon gas becomes colorless.

_____

_____

_____

_____

_____

_____

_____

_____

_____

_____

I. Reading
  A. Directions
  B. Sequencing
  C. Main Idea
II. Writing
  A. Capitalization
  B. Proofreading

Name _____

Summarizing a Personal Narrative

Directions: Read the following narrative. Then, follow the directions.

My Greatest Fear

I am scared of spiders. I realize this is not a logical fear, but I cannot help myself. I have been frightened by spiders since I was very young. For the following three reasons, spiders will never be pets of mine.

The first reason that I am scared of spiders is their appearance. I do not like their eight wispy, creepy legs. Spiders are never easily seen, but rather dark and unattractive. They are often hairy, and the mere thought of multiple eyeballs gives me shivers.

Spiders are not well-behaved. They are sly and always ready to sneak up on innocent victims. Spiders have habits of scurrying across floors, dropping from ceilings, and dangling from cobwebs. One never knows what to expect from a spider.

Finally, I am scared of spiders due to a "spider experience" as a child. Having just climbed into bed, I noticed a particularly nasty-looking spider on the ceiling over my bed. My father came in to dispose of it, and it fell into bed with me. The thought of it crawling over me drove me from the bed shrieking. After that, I checked the ceiling nightly before getting into bed.

Many people love spiders. They are good for the environment and are certainly needed on our planet. However, because of my fear, irrational though it may be, I'd rather just avoid contact with arachnids.

Directions: Write a four-sentence summary of the narrative.

_____

_____

_____

_____

_____

_____

GRADE 6

I. Reading
A. Directions
B. Sequencing
C. Main Idea
II. Writing
A. Capitalization
B. Proofreading

Name _____

Facts to Back It Up

The statements you read in a newspaper article should be **objective**, or based on facts and not the writer's opinion. The writer should provide these facts to back up the story.

Directions: Read the following article carefully. Then, follow the instructions at the bottom of the page.

New Movie Theater Planned
By Marilyn Moore

Everyone who lives in the Oakdale section of town is excited about the movie theater planned for construction. The site where they want to build it is an empty lot. There is nothing there but trees and a bike path. Having a big movie theater is better than having only trees. The architect's plans for the building are perfect. And they will build a new sidewalk to let people who live south of Lawrence Street walk there. People will spend lots of time at the movie theater because everyone loves movies. The biggest benefit of having the theater is that when it opens, all the kids my age will get part-time jobs there.

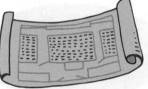

1. Circle all the facts that are given in the article.

2. Underline all the sentences from the article that reflect the author's opinion.

3. Tell why you do or do not think the article is objective. _____

_____

_____

4. On the lines below, rewrite this article so that it is objective.

_____

_____

_____

_____

_____

_____

GRADE 6

I. Reading
A. Directions
B. Sequencing
C. Main Idea
II. Writing
A. Capitalization
B. Proofreading

Name _____

To Get the Vote

Directions: Read the following passage. Then, answer the questions.

Imagine how different life would be if women had never been given the right to vote! Before 1920, no woman in the United States could vote in an election. There were also laws that limited their right to own property, and many colleges and employers would not accept female applicants.

In the mid-1800s, women and men all over the country began speaking out in favor of giving women more rights. In 1848, a conference was held in Seneca Falls, New York, to bring together people who believed in more rights for women. Many famous people attended the conference including Elizabeth Cady Stanton, Lucretia Mott, Frederick Douglass, and Sojourner Truth. They felt that, as long as women were unable to vote, other rights could be denied to them as well.

The struggle for women's right to vote continued for many years. Susan B. Anthony, another activist, actually cast a vote in the 1872 presidential election and was arrested as a result. During her trial, she told the judge that she had voted "to educate all women to do precisely as I have done, rebel against your man-made, unjust, unconstitutional forms of law."

Her plan may have worked, because the demand for the right to vote only increased in the late 19th and early 20th centuries. Finally, in 1920, Congress added the 19th Amendment to the Constitution: "The right of citizens of the United States to vote shall not be denied or abridged by the United States or by any State on account of sex."

1. What was the author's purpose for writing this passage— to inform, entertain, persuade, or express beliefs? _____
_____

2. What is the main idea of this passage? _____
_____
_____

3. Why do you think activists believed that women would be denied many rights as long as they could not vote? _____
_____
_____

4. How would your life be different if women had never been given the right to vote? On another sheet of paper, write a paragraph to explain your answer.

GRADE 6

I. Reading
  A. Directions
  B. Sequencing
  C. Main Idea
II. Writing
  A. Capitalization
  B. Proofreading

Name _____

Keep Behavin'

It was time for another of Mr. Fridley's science classes on behaviors. This time, the class was going to discuss learned behaviors. Mr. Fridley explained that learned behaviors are behaviors that change as a result of experience.

First, Mr. Fridley explained learning by association. This type of learning connects a stimulus with a particular response. He asked if anyone could give him an example. Lee suggested that when the bell rings at the end of class, the students put away their pens and pick up their books. Mr. Fridley congratulated Lee on his answer and said that the students learned to associate the stimulus of the bell with the response of leaving class.

There are several kinds of learning by association. One results In a conditioned response—a desired response to an unusual stimulus. Mr. Fridley reminded them of Ivan Pavlov's experiments with dogs. In the experiments, Pavlov found that dogs salivated when they smelled meat. Pavlov began ringing a bell every time he was about to give meat to a dog. In time, the dog salivated when the bell rang, whether or not there was any meat. Pavlov had trained the dogs to respond to the bell instead of the food.

Another kind of learning by association involves teaching animals to act in a certain way by rewarding them for their behavior. This is called positive reinforcement and may be as simple as a rat pressing a lever to get food. This type of learning, however, may also involve a complex series of tasks.

Match:

conditioned response   study hard—get a good grade

positive reinforcement   hear siren—panic

Underline:

Both types of learning by association involve . . .

a stimulus.   a learned association.

a response.   experiments.

Circle:

If a squirrel learns to climb into a bird feeder to obtain food, it has learned by . . .

conditioned response.   unconditioned response.

positive reinforcement.   negative reinforcement.

Write examples of something you have learned by conditioned response and something you have learned by positive reinforcement. _____

_____

Name _____

What's the Difference?

One day, David and Donald were discussing alligators. David insisted that alligators and crocodiles were the same animal but that people called them by different names. Donald insisted, however, that the two animals were entirely different reptiles. Kim walked up just in time to save the boys from further squabbling. Kim, who had lived in Florida for ten years, could settle this one.

She told David that alligators and crocodiles are separate reptiles. She told them that although they are similar-looking and are both called *crocodilians*, they are very different. Both have a long, low, cigar-shaped body, short legs, and a long, powerful tail to help them swim. But most crocodiles have a pointed snout instead of a round one like the alligator's. She also pointed out that while both have tough hides, long snouts, and sharp teeth to grasp their prey, the crocodile is only about two-thirds as heavy as an American alligator of the same length and can therefore move much more quickly. David and Donald were impressed with Kim's knowledge.

Kim also told the boys another way to tell the two reptiles apart. She said that both have an extra long lower fourth tooth. This tooth fits into a pit in the alligator's upper jaw, while in the crocodile, it fits into a groove in the side of the upper jaw and shows when the crocodile's mouth is closed. David and Donald thanked Kim for the information, looked at each other sheepishly, and walked away laughing.

Match:

crocodile   fourth tooth shows when mouth is shut
                   round snout
                   called *crocodilian*
alligator   fourth tooth is in a pocket in upper jaw
                   pointed snout

Directions: Write three ways alligators and crocodiles are alike and three ways they are different.

Alike	Different
_____	_____
_____	_____
_____	_____

Name two other animals that are sometimes thought to be the same.

_____   _____

I. Reading
A. Directions
B. Sequencing
C. Main Idea
II. Writing
A. Capitalization
B. Proofreading

Name _____

Cats and Dogs

Directions: Magda is comparing and contrasting her cat Spike and her dog Fritz. Here's her chart.

	SPIKE	FRITZ
Tricks	does nothing on command	fetches, sits, shakes, begs
Destructiveness	claws furniture and drapes	chews shoes, slippers, and anything left around
Food	eats only one kind of cat food and only when he feels like it	eats anything and everything edible including stuff I don't like
Grooming	loves to be brushed	loves to be brushed
Breath	not too bad if you like fish, which I don't	bad enough to knock you out
Friendliness	cuddly *only* when he wants to be cuddled	always happy, wagging tail, licking my face, wanting to play
Vet Visits	could not care less	has to be dragged through the door

I. Use Magda's chart to explain how Spike and Fritz are alike. _____

_____

_____

2. Use Magda's chart to explain how Spike and Fritz are different. _____

_____

_____

3. Do you think one makes a better pet than the other? Why or why not?_____

_____

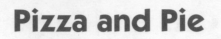

Name _____

Pizza and Pie

Directions: You can use a **Venn diagram** to compare and contrast things, ideas, facts, and people. As you study the delicious-looking pizza and blueberry-peach pie, list their similarities and their distinguishing characteristics on the diagram below.

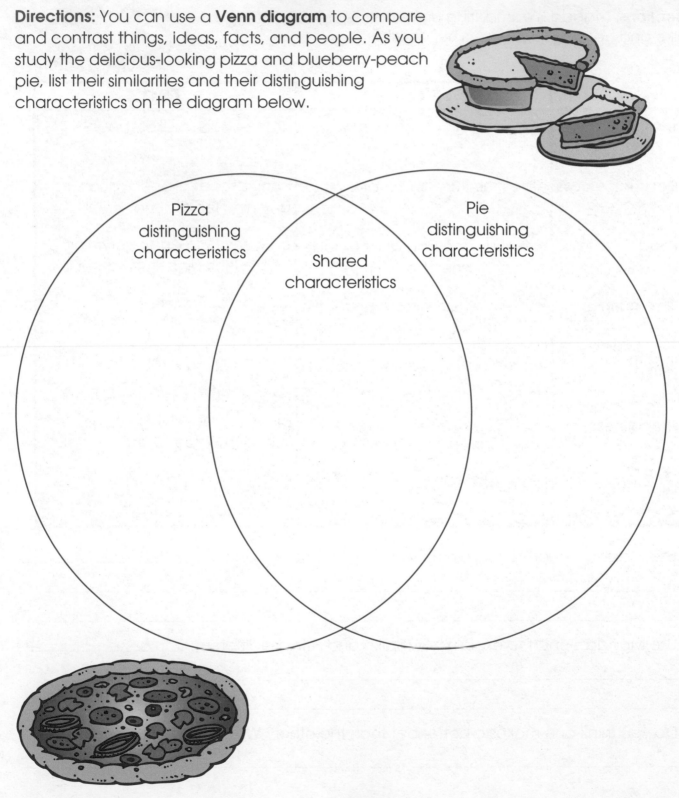

Pizza
distinguishing
characteristics

Shared
characteristics

Pie
distinguishing
characteristics

Comparing and Contrasting

GRADE 6

I. Reading
A. Directions
B. Sequencing
C. Main Idea
II. Writing
A. Capitalization
B. Proofreading

Name _____

Stranger Than Fiction

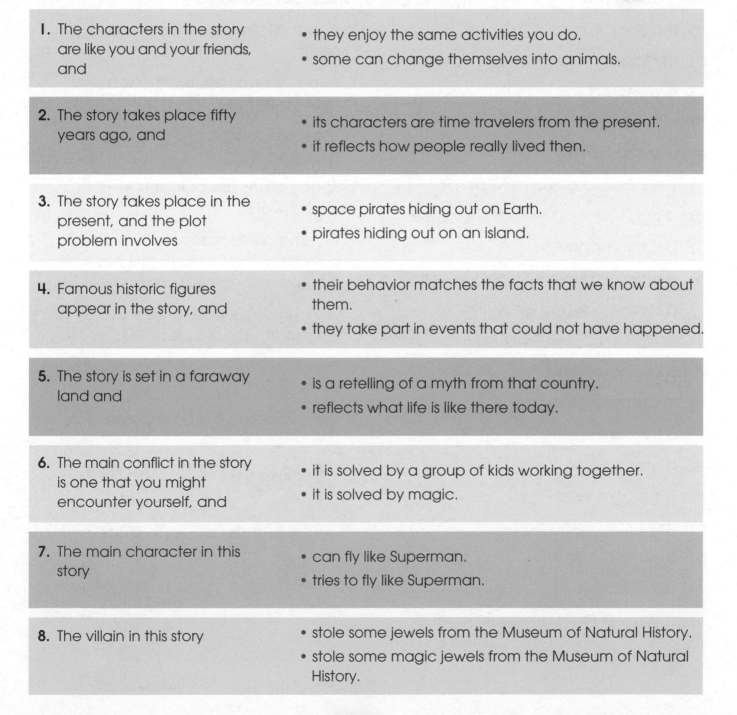

Realistic Fiction
Fantasy

Fiction is about make-believe events. **Realistic fiction** is based on events that *could* happen in real life, but **fantasy** is based on impossible events.

Directions: For each sentence beginning, choose the ending that would best occur in a fantasy story. Draw a line to that ending.

1. The characters in the story are like you and your friends, and
   - they enjoy the same activities you do.
   - some can change themselves into animals.

2. The story takes place fifty years ago, and
   - its characters are time travelers from the present.
   - it reflects how people really lived then.

3. The story takes place in the present, and the plot problem involves
   - space pirates hiding out on Earth.
   - pirates hiding out on an island.

4. Famous historic figures appear in the story, and
   - their behavior matches the facts that we know about them.
   - they take part in events that could not have happened.

5. The story is set in a faraway land and
   - is a retelling of a myth from that country.
   - reflects what life is like there today.

6. The main conflict in the story is one that you might encounter yourself, and
   - it is solved by a group of kids working together.
   - it is solved by magic.

7. The main character in this story
   - can fly like Superman.
   - tries to fly like Superman.

8. The villain in this story
   - stole some jewels from the Museum of Natural History.
   - stole some magic jewels from the Museum of Natural History.

GRADE 6

I. Reading
   A. Directions
   B. Sequencing
   C. Main Idea
II. Writing
   A. Capitalization
   B. Proofreading

Name _____

Make It Real

Directions: Liz wants to enter a story-writing contest. She wrote down all the ideas that came into her head. Then, she decided that she wants to make her story realistic. Circle the details that she might use in her story.

Possible settings:

a) the year 2525

b) the present

c) five years ago

d) a small town

e) a softball field

f) a spaceship going to Neptune

g) a castle where time is standing still

h) a surprise party

i) a mermaid's cave under the sea

j) a rocket going to the Moon

Possible characters:

k) the Boogie Monster

l) a talking frog

m) a pet pig

n) a sixth-grade girl

o) someone's grandfather

p) a girl who can fly

q) a mermaid

r) a boy who can do magic tricks

Possible plot problems:

s) A softball team has never won a game.

t) A magic pearl fell into the sea and must be found.

u) The main character wants to impress a new neighbor.

v) Space aliens are planning to steal Earth's water.

w) The character has to answer a riddle in order to free himself or herself from the prison of an evil princess.

x) The character gets upset when Grandfather moves in.

y) The character's two best friends have been quarreling.

z) The characters in a book come to life.

Get real!

GRADE
6

I. Reading
  A. Directions
  B. Sequencing
  C. Main Idea
II. Writing
  A. Capitalization
  B. Proofreading

Name _____

It's Impossible!

Directions: Eli is visiting his cousin Jacob. He'd like to read a fantasy story at bedtime. He selects some books and reads a passage from each. Make a check mark in front of each passage that could have come from a fantasy book. Then, underline the words or sentences that make you feel sure of this.

☐ Suddenly the banging, clattering, and crashing stopped. The furious roar of the wind died down. The eerie silence was almost as scary as the raging of the storm. Ben started toward the cellar stairs, but his uncle pulled him back. "It's not safe yet," he said. "We're just in the eye of the tornado."

☐ Miranda closed her eyes and counted to ten, just as the old woman had told her to do. When she opened her eyes again, she was still sitting on the grass with Snowball, her cat, beside her. The difference, however, was that she was now scarcely any taller than the cat. Snowball narrowed his eyes and growled softly at her.

☐ Carlos waded to the shore, holding tight to the silver coin that Adrian had given him. What had Adrian said? "If you need help, rub the coin and say my name and I will be there. But I will come only once." Beyond the shimmering white beach stretched the dense, gloomy forest that he must pass through to reach Evershade.

☐ It seemed impossible that a castle should have so many halls and all of them so much alike, Gabrielle thought to herself as she darted around yet another corner. She was desperate to find a staircase. She dreaded being caught where she shouldn't have

been, yet she also hoped that someone would find her soon and lead her back to her tour group.

☐ The road beyond the wooden bridge forked in two directions. One followed the stream burbling and twinkling under the bridge. The other path, nearly overgrown with weeds, led up the hillside and toward the rocky cliffs. Emma hesitated, her map now useless. "If I were you, I'd go to the left," remarked an ancient turtle that had been sunning itself on the bank. It then slid into the water with a soft plop.

☐ Jun watched his older brother with envy. This was going to be Ho's first year in the dragon, and he had taken what seemed like hours to dress. Now, he was carefully combing and recombing his hair in front of the mirror. "No one's going to see anything but your feet," Jun said crossly. "You'd think you were going to lead the whole parade."

GRADE
6

I. Reading
  A. Directions
  B. Sequencing
  C. Main Idea
II. Writing
  A. Capitalization
  B. Proofreading

Name _____

Choices, Choices

Directions: Read each summary and write two more sentences that could be added to it. The first sentence should suggest a realistic plot. The second should turn the story into a fantasy. The first one has been done for you.

1. Brooke and Brendan's family has inherited Aunt May's old house in the country. They decide to spend the summer fixing it up. As they are cleaning out the basement, Brooke and Brendan make a surprising discovery.

   They find a scrapbook with photos of a girl who looks like she could be Brooke's twin.

   They discover a tunnel that leads to a different world each time they follow it.

2. Juan's older brother and his friends say Juan isn't good enough to play basketball with them. Feeling sad, Juan goes to practice by himself in the empty schoolyard.

   _____

   _____

   _____

3. Mrs. Maychek is a quiet, shy old woman who lives in the apartment next door to Malik's family. One day, Malik rescues Mrs. Maychek's cat from a fierce bulldog and carries the injured cat to its owner. Mrs. Maychek invites Malik inside and gives him cake and cocoa. Then, Malik notices something interesting as he looks around the living room.

   _____

   _____

4. Tony's friends have all gone away for the summer, and he is sure he'll have a rotten summer. However, Uncle Matthew stops by with an "unbirthday" gift that he says will solve Tony's problem. The gift is a box full of envelopes, and he is to open one each day. Eagerly, he tears open the first envelope.

   _____

   _____

   _____

GRADE 6

I. Reading
   A. Directions
   B. Sequencing
   C. Main Idea
II. Writing
   A. Capitalization
   B. Proofreading

Name _____

The Author's Purpose

Authors write to entertain, inform, or persuade. To **entertain** means to hold the attention of or to amuse someone. A fiction book about outer space entertains its reader, as does a joke book.

To **inform** means to give factual information. A cookbook informs the reader of new recipes. A newspaper tells what is happening in the world.

To **persuade** people means to convince them. Newspaper editorial writers try to persuade readers to accept their opinions. Doctors write health columns to persuade readers to eat nutritious foods.

Directions: Read each of the passages below. Tell whether they entertain, inform, or persuade. (They may do more than one.) Give the reasons why.

George Washington was born in a brick house near the Potomac River in Virginia on Feb. 11, 1732. When he was 11 years old, George went to live with his half-brother, Lawrence, at Mount Vernon.

Author's Purpose: _____

Reason: _____

When George Washington was a child, he always measured and counted things. Maybe that is why he became a surveyor when he grew up. Surveyors like to measure and count things, too.

Author's Purpose: _____

Reason: _____

George Washington was the best president America has ever had. He led a new nation to independence. He made all the states feel as if they were part of the United States. All presidents should be as involved with the country as George Washington was.

Author's Purpose: _____

Reason: _____

_____

I. Reading
A. Directions
B. Sequencing
C. Main Idea
II. Writing
A. Capitalization
B. Proofreading

Name _____

Llamas

Directions: Read each paragraph. Tell whether it informs, entertains, or persuades. One paragraph does more than one. Then, write your reasons on the lines below.

A llama (LAH'MAH) is a South American animal that is related to the camel. It is raised for its wool. Also, it can carry heavy loads. Some people who live near mountains in the United States train llamas to go on mountain trips. Llamas are sure-footed because they have two long toes and toenails.

Author's Purpose: _____

Reason: _____

Llamas are the best animals to have if you're planning to backpack in the mountains. They can climb easily and carry your supplies. No one should ever go for a long hiking trip in the mountains without a llama.

Author's Purpose: _____

Reason: _____

Llamas can be stubborn animals. Sometimes, they suddenly stop walking for no reason. People have to push them to get them moving again. Stubborn llamas can be frustrating when hiking up a steep mountain.

Author's Purpose: _____

Reason: _____

Greg is an 11-year-old boy who raises llamas to climb mountains. One of his llamas is named Dallas. Although there are special saddles for llamas, Greg likes to ride bareback.

Author's Purpose: _____

Reason: _____

_____

Now, use a separate sheet of paper to inform readers about llamas.

GRADE

6

I. Reading
  A. Directions
  B. Sequencing
  C. Main Idea
II. Writing
  A. Capitalization
  B. Proofreading

Name _____

Roller Coasters

Directions: Read each paragraph and determine the author's purpose. Then, write down your reason on the line below.

Roller coaster rides are thrilling. The cars chug up the hills and then fly down them. People scream and laugh. They clutch their seats and sometimes raise their arms above their heads.

Author's Purpose: _____

Reason: _____

The first roller coasters were giant slides made of ice in Russia. That was more than 300 years ago! The slides were about 70 feet high, and people had to climb steep ladders to reach their tops. Riders got into carts and slid down very fast. Then, they climbed the ladders again. Early roller coasters were more work than fun.

Author's Purpose: _____

Reason: _____

The first roller coaster in America was built in 1884. It cost only a nickel to ride the "Switchback Gravity Pleasure Railway" at Coney Island in New York. Roller coasters did not become very popular until the late 1920s.

Author's Purpose: _____

Reason: _____

Have you ever ridden a giant roller coaster? Some of the most famous ones in the world include the "Mamba" at Worlds of Fun in Kansas City, Missouri; the "Ultra Twister" at Six Flags Astroworld in Houston, Texas; and the "Magnum" at Cedar Point in Sandusky, Ohio. Roller coasters are fun because they have thrilling twists and turns. Some go very high and some turn upside down. Everyone should go on a roller coaster at least once in his or her life.

Author's Purpose: _____

Reason: _____

_____

Now, use a separate sheet of paper to persuade people to ride roller coasters.

Name _____

Review

Directions: Follow the instructions for each section.

1. Write a paragraph about a sport in which you are informing your audience.

_____

_____

_____

_____

_____

2. Write a paragraph about the circus in which you are entertaining your audience.

_____

_____

_____

_____

_____

3. Write a paragraph about the desire for a later bedtime in which you are persuading your audience.

_____

_____

_____

_____

_____

_____

I. Reading
  A. Directions
  B. Sequencing
  C. Main Idea
II. Writing
  A. Capitalization
  B. Proofreading

Name _____

A Reason for Everything!

Directions: Below are the beginnings of some letters that David wrote. Tell why he wrote each one. Make sure to include the author's purpose for writing: to inform, to entertain, to persuade, or to express feelings, opinions, or beliefs.

Dear Aunt Grace,

Thanks so much for the kaleidoscope kit you sent for my birthday. I never would have guessed that making a kaleidoscope was so much fun. I have finished one, and I am about to try making some of the others shown in the book.

Dear Miguel,

We arrived in Monterey yesterday. Monterey was California's capital city under the Mexican government, so it has many historic buildings. Today, we visited the old state custom house, a whaling station, and an old adobe house that is a museum. The adobe house had an old-fashioned garden and live farm animals you could pet.

Dear Jeff,

It's too bad you are away at camp. I have to tell you what you missed. While the Yees were away, they had a student house-sit and care for their hamster. He didn't know much about hamsters. Well, the hamster got out, and the house-sitter looked all over for it. He finally found it but had a terrible time catching it. When the Yees got back, they found a mouse in the hamster hut!

Dear Editor,

Rocky Point Beach has become so littered that it is starting to look like a junkyard. You can see newspapers, cans, bottles, and food wrappers everywhere. I even saw parts of an old wet suit, a broken baby carrier, and a supermarket cart. The Recreation Department does not have the funds to clean it up, so it is up to the public. Two classes from my school will be there for a clean-up day on April 13. We'd like everyone who cares about the beach to come out and join us at 9:00 A.M.

GRADE
6

I. Reading
    A. Directions
    B. Sequencing
    C. Main Idea
II. Writing
    A. Capitalization
    B. Proofreading

Name _____

Paws With a Cause

Paws With a Cause (PAWS) is a nonprofit organization that provides specially trained "hearing" and "service" dogs to people with disabilities. It began in 1979 in Byron Center, Michigan, and was originally called Ears for the Deaf.

At first, the organization trained dogs to assist the hearing impaired. Over time, they expanded their service to training "service" dogs. A service dog allows a physically challenged person to have more independence. In addition, PAWS trains dogs to help individuals with multiple handicaps.

PAWS trainers select dogs from animal shelters and humane societies across the United States. Over 95 percent of the hearing dogs have been saved from possible death at these shelters. These dogs are then taken to the training center, where they spend several months in specific skill training.

The dogs' training consists of three parts. All the dogs are given basic obedience training. They learn to respond to commands such as "sit," "come," and "down." Dogs being trained for the hearing impaired are also given specific sound-alert training. These dogs learn to respond to six sounds: door knock, doorbell ring, two types of telephone rings, alarm clock, smoke alarm, and an intruder. Service dogs receive advanced training geared to the individual person's needs. They may learn how to turn off lights, pick up dropped objects, close doors, or serve as a support for walking. The third phase of training takes place at the recipient's home. A field trainer helps

the dog bond with a new owner, learn commands, and get familiar with the needs and routines of the owner.

A trained dog is expensive. A hearing dog costs approximately $5,000. A service dog costs around $8,500. Individuals with disabilities may purchase the dogs with their own money. PAWS has an active donation fund to assist individuals with the expenses incurred, but the waiting period is lengthy. Some organizations sponsor walk-a-thons or other fund drives to raise money for a member of their community. Also, generous students have earned money through creative methods such as the "Read-a-Million-Minutes" program.

In addition to rescuing many dogs from animal shelters and then training them for specific service, PAWS spends a great deal of time educating the public. Through community awareness presentations, PAWS is helping the public understand the legal rights of dogs for the hearing impaired and service dogs and the need for these dogs. With the help of these dogs, having a disability does not mean living with an inability.

GRADE 6

Name _____

Paws With a Cause

Directions: One way the author demonstrates a purpose for writing is in the information he or she chooses to include. Complete the story map with details from the passage.

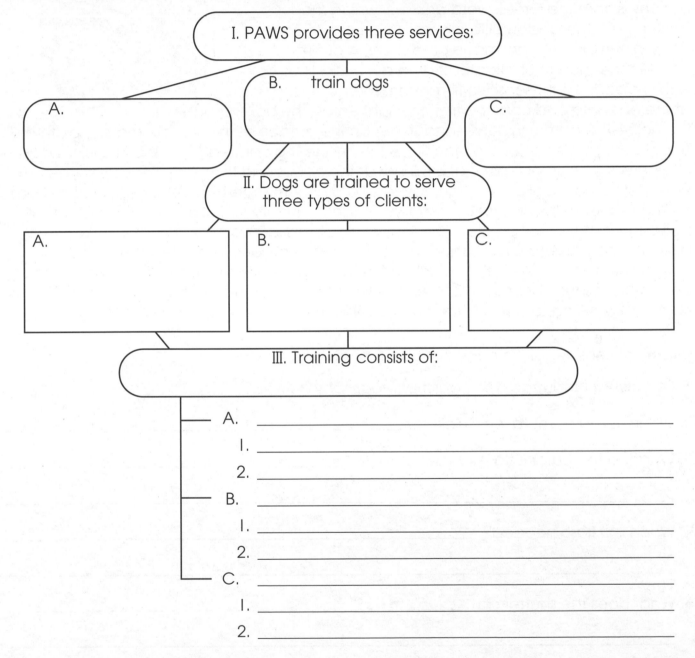

I. PAWS provides three services:

A.

B.   train dogs

C.

II. Dogs are trained to serve three types of clients:

A.

B.

C.

III. Training consists of:

A. _____

   1. _____

   2. _____

B. _____

   1. _____

   2. _____

C. _____

   1. _____

   2. _____

IV. Write a sentence summarizing the author's purpose in giving these details in "Paws With a Cause."

_____

_____

Name _____

Comprehension: Fun With Photography

The word *photography* means "writing with light."
Photo is from the Greek word *photos*, which means "light."
Graphy is from the Greek word *graphic*, which means
"writing." Cameras don't literally write pictures, of course.
Instead, they imprint an image onto a piece of film.

Even the most sophisticated camera is basically a box
with a piece of light-sensitive film inside. The box has a hole
at the opposite end from the film. The light enters the box through
the hole—the camera's lens—and shines on the surface of the film to create a picture.
The picture that's created on the film is the image the camera's lens is pointed toward.

A lens is a circle of glass that is thinner at the edges and thicker in the center. The outer
edges of the lens collect the light rays and draw them together at the center of the lens.

The shutter helps control the amount of light that enters the lens. Too much light will
make the picture too light. Too little light will result in a dark picture. Electronic flash—either
built into the camera or attached to the top of it—provides light when needed.

Cameras with automatic electronic flashes provide the additional light automatically.
Electronic flashes—or simply "flashes," as they are often called—require batteries. If your
flash quits working, a dead battery is probably the cause.

Directions: Answer these questions about photography.

1. From what language is the word *photography* derived? _____

2. Where is the camera lens thickest? _____

3. What do the outer edges of the lens do? _____

_____

4. When is a flash needed? _____

_____

5. What does the shutter do? _____

_____

_____

_____

GRADE 6

I. Reading
   A. Directions
   B. Sequencing
   C. Main Idea
II. Writing
   A. Capitalization
   B. Proofreading

Name _____

Comprehension: Photography Terms

Like other good professionals, photographers make their craft look easy. Their skill—like that of the graceful ice skater—comes from years of practice. Where skaters develop a sense of balance, photographers develop an "eye" for pictures. They can make important technical decisions about photographing, or "shooting," a particular scene in the twinkling of an eye.

It's interesting to know some of the technical language that professional photographers use. "Angle of view" refers to the angle from which a photograph is taken. "Depth of field" is the distance between the nearest point and the farthest point that is in focus in a photo.

"Filling the frame" refers to the amount of space the object being photographed takes up in the picture. A close-up picture of a dog, flower, or person would fill the frame. A far-away picture would not.

"ASA" refers to the speed of different types of films. "Speed" means the film's sensitivity to light. The letters *ASA* stand for the American Standards Association. Film manufacturers give their films ratings of 200ASA, 400ASA, and so on to indicate film speed. The higher the number on the film, the higher its sensitivity to light, and the faster its speed. The faster its speed, the better it will be at clearly capturing sports images and other action shots.

Directions: Answer these question about photography terms.

1. Name another term for photographing. _____

2. This is the distance between the nearest point and the farthest point that is in focus in a photo.

   _____

3. This refers to the speed of different types of film. _____

4. A close-up picture of someone's face would

   ☐ provide depth of field.   ☐ create an ASA.   ☐ fill the frame.

5. To photograph a swimming child, which film speed is better?

   ☐ 200ASA   ☐ 400ASA

Name _____

Comprehension: Photographing Animals

Animals are a favorite subject of many young photographers. Cats, dogs, hamsters, and other pets top the list, followed by zoo animals and the occasional lizard.

Because it's hard to get them to sit still and "perform on command," some professional photographers refuse to photograph pets. There are ways around the problem of short attention spans, however.

One way to get an appealing portrait of a cat or dog is to hold a biscuit or treat above the camera. The animal's longing look toward the food will be captured by the camera as a soulful gaze. Because it's above the camera—out of the camera's range—the treat won't appear in the picture. When you show the picture to your friends afterwards, they will be impressed by your pet's loving expression.

If you are using fast film, you can take some good, quick shots of a pet by simply snapping a picture right after calling its name. You'll get a different expression from your pet using this technique. Depending on your pet's disposition, the picture will capture an inquisitive expression or possibly a look of annoyance, especially if you've awakened Rover from a nap!

Taking pictures of zoo animals requires a little more patience. After all, you can't wake up a lion! You may have to wait for a while until the animal does something interesting or moves into a position for you to get a good shot. When photographing zoo animals, don't get too close to the cages, and never tap on the glass or throw things between the bars of a cage! Concentrate on shooting some good pictures, and always respect the animals you are photographing.

Directions: Answer these questions about photographing animals.

1. Why do some professionals dislike photographing animals?_____

_____

2. What speed of film should you use to photograph quick-moving pets? _____

3. To capture a pet's loving expression, hold this out of camera range._____

4. Compared to taking pictures of pets, what does photographing zoo animals require?

_____

_____

GRADE 6

I. Reading
A. Directions
B. Sequencing
C. Main Idea
II. Writing
A. Capitalization
B. Proofreading

Name _____

Main Idea/Recalling Details: Kites

Kites are a familiar sight on breezy fall days. They come in a great variety of sizes, colors, and designs. It is not known who invented kites, but kites have been flown since the beginning of recorded history. While today children and adults use them for recreation, throughout history kites have had other uses.

In the United States, kites have been used in weather and other scientific research experiments. Before airplanes and weather balloons, the National Weather Service had kites carry weather instruments as high as 4 miles above the earth. In addition, the United States military used kites for observing the enemy and sending messages between troops.

In other countries, kites had cultural and religious importance. The ancient Chinese flew kites over their homes to drive out evil spirits. The Chinese still enjoy kites so much that one day each year they celebrate Kites' Day.

On some Pacific islands, kites were thought to have spiritual qualities. They were believed to symbolize both sides of nature—life and death. On some Polynesian islands, kites were used as protection against evil. These kites were often shaped like birds and used as soaring messengers to the heavens. In Hawaii, kites were also used to establish land ownership. A kite was released in the air, and a claim was given for the area where it came down.

Directions: Answer these questions about kites.

1. The main idea is:

   ☐ Kites come in a great variety of sizes, color, and designs.

   ☐ While today kites are used for recreation, throughout history they have had other uses.

2. Besides recreation, name two ways kites have been used in the United States.

   _____

   _____

3. What country celebrates a holiday called Kites' Day? _____

4. How did Hawaiians use kites to decide land ownership? _____

   _____

GRADE 6

I. Reading
A. Directions
B. Sequencing
C. Main Idea
II. Writing
A. Capitalization
B. Proofreading

Name _____

Comprehension: Aerodynamics

Kites are able to fly because of the principle of aerodynamics. This big word simply means the study of forces that are put into action by moving air. Three main forces work to keep a heavier-than-air kite flying—lift, gravity, and drag.

This is how it works: The flying lines, or strings, are attached to the kite to hold it at a slant. The wind pushes against the underside of the kite. At the same time, the wind rushes around the edges of the kite and "drags" some of the air from the upper side. This creates a partial vacuum there. The push of the air underneath is greater than the push of the air from the top, so the kite is held in the air. An airplane is held in the air in much the same way, except that it must keep moving rapidly to make the pressure above and below its wings different. The wind does this for the kite. In a steady airstream, a kite doesn't move backward or forward. It seems to be unaffected by gravity. This is possible because the lifting force of the wind overcomes the downward force of gravity.

If you have ever ridden a bicycle into a strong wind, you may have felt some of the forces of aerodynamics. If you held your hand out to your side, you could feel the air stream flowing around your hand. With your fingers pointed into the wind and your hand held level, there is little lift or drag. But if you raised your fingers slightly, the wind lifted your hand upwards. Raising your hand higher increases the drag and decreases the lift. Your hand is pushed downward. A kite flying in the sky is subject to these same forces.

Directions: Answer these questions about aerodynamics.

1. What is aerodynamics? _____

_____

2. What three forces are at work to hold a kite in the air?

_____   _____   _____

3. An airplane is held in the air in much the same way, except that it must keep moving rapidly to keep the air above and below its wings different.

    True   False

GRADE 6

I. Reading
  A. Directions
  B. Sequencing
  C. Main Idea
II. Writing
  A. Capitalization
  B. Proofreading

Name _____

Comprehension: Getting Your Kite to Fly

There are some basic things to know about kite flying that can help you enjoy the sport more. Here are a few of the most important ones.

First, if you have ever seen someone flying a kite in a movie, you probably saw him or her get the kite off the ground by running into the wind. However, this is not the way to launch a kite. Most beginners will find a "high-start" launch to be the easiest. For a high-start launch, have a friend stand about 100 feet away, facing into the wind. Your friend should face you and hold the kite gently. Place some tension on the flying line by pulling gently on it. With a steady breeze behind you, tug gently on the line, and the kite will rise. If your kite begins to dive, don't panic or pull on the line. Dropping the reel will cause it to spin out of control and could cause someone to be hurt. Simply let the line go slack. This usually will right the kite in midair.

For a kite that is pulling hard away from you, have a friend stand behind you and take up the slack line as you bring it in. Hand over hand, pull down the kite. It is very important to have gloves on to do this, or you may burn or cut your hands. It is recommended that you always wear gloves while kite flying.

When two kite lines get crossed, pulling may cause enough friction to cut one or both of the lines. Instead of pulling, both fliers should walk toward one another until their lines uncross as they pass.

Directions: Circle **True** or **False** for these statements about kite flying.

1. To launch a kite, run into the wind holding the kite behind you.   True   False

2. In a high-start launch, a friend stands about 100 feet away from you, holding the kite.   True   False

3. If your kite begins to dive from the sky, immediately drop the reel.   True   False

4. It is recommended that you always wear gloves when kite flying.   True   False

Name _____

Comprehension: Colonists Come to America

After Christopher Columbus discovered America in 1492, many people wanted to come live in the new land. During the 17th and 18th centuries, a great many Europeans, especially the English, left their countries and settled along the Atlantic Coast of North America between Florida and Canada. Some came to make a better life for themselves. Others, particularly the Pilgrims, the Puritans, and the Quakers, came for religious freedom.

A group of men who wanted gold and other riches from the new land formed the London Company. They asked the king of England for land in America and for permission to found a colony. They founded Jamestown, the first permanent English settlement in America, in 1607. They purchased ships and supplies, and located people who wanted to settle in America.

The voyage to America took about eight weeks and was very dangerous. Often, fierce winds blew the wooden ships off course. Many were wrecked. The ships were crowded and dirty. Frequently, passengers became ill, and some died. Once in America, the early settlers faced even more hardships.

Directions: Answer these questions about the colonists coming to America.

1. How long did it take colonists to travel from England to America? _____

2. Name three groups that came to America to find religious freedom.

   _____   _____   _____

3. Why was the London Company formed? _____
   _____

4. What was Jamestown? _____
   _____

5. Why was the voyage to America dangerous? _____
   _____

GRADE
6

I. Reading
  A. Directions
  B. Sequencing
  C. Main Idea
II. Writing
  A. Capitalization
  B. Proofreading

Name _____

Recalling Details: Early Colonial Homes

When the first colonists landed in America, they had to find shelter quickly. Their first homes were crude bark and mud huts, log cabins, or dugouts, which were simply caves dug into the hillsides. As soon as posssible, the settlers sought to replace these temporary shelters with comfortable houses.

Until the late 17th century, most of the colonial homes were simple in style. Almost all of the New England colonists—those settling in the northern areas of Massachusetts, Connecticut, Rhode Island, and New Hampshire—used wood in building their permanent homes. Some of the buildings had thatched roofs. However, they cought fire easily, and so were replaced by wooden shingles. The outside walls also were covered with wooden shingles to make the homes warmer and less drafty.

In the middle colonies—New York, Pennsylvania, New Jersey, and Delaware—the Dutch and German colonists often made brick or stone homes that were two-and-a-half or three-and-a-half stories high. Many southern colonists—those living in Virginia, Maryland, North Carolina, South Carolina, and Georgia—lived on large farms called *plantations*. Their homes were usually made of brick.

In the 18th century, some colonists became wealthy enough to replace their simple homes with mansions, often like those being built by the wealthy class in England. They were called *Georgian houses* because they were popular during the years that Kings George I, George II, and George III ruled England. Most were made of brick. They usually featured columns, ornately carved doors, and elaborate gardens.

Directions: Answer these questions about early colonial homes.

1. What were the earliest homes of the colonists?

_____

2. What were the advantages of using wooden shingles?

_____

3. What did Dutch and German colonists use to build their homes?

_____

4. What were Georgian homes?

_____

GRADE 6

I. Reading
   A. Directions
   B. Sequencing
   C. Main Idea
II. Writing
   A. Capitalization
   B. Proofreading

Name _____

Recalling Details: The Colonial Kitchen

The most important room in the home of a colonial family was the kitchen. Sometimes it was the only room in the home. The most important element of the kitchen was the fireplace. Fire was essential to the colonists, and they were careful to keep one burning at all times. Before the man of the house went to bed, he would make sure that the fire was carefully banked so it would burn all night. In the morning, he would blow the glowing embers into flame again with a bellows. If the fire went out, one of the children would be sent to a neighbor's for hot coals. Because there were no matches, it would sometimes take a half hour to light a new fire, using flint, steel, and tinder.

The colonial kitchen, quite naturally, was centered around the fireplace. One or two large iron broilers hung over the hot coals for cooking the family meals. Above the fireplace, a large musket and powder horn were kept for protection in the event of an attack and to hunt deer and other game. Also likely to be found near the fireplace was a butter churn, where cream from the family's cow was beaten until yellow flakes of butter appeared.

The furniture in the kitchen—usually benches, a table, and chairs—were made by the man or men in the family. It was very heavy and not very comfortable. The colonial family owned few eating utensils—no forks and only a few spoons, also made by members of the family. The dishes included pewter plates, "trenchers"—wooden bowls with handles—and wooden mugs.

Directions: Answer these questions about the colonial kitchen.

1. What was the most important element of the colonial kitchen? _____

2. In colonial days, why was it important to keep a fire burning in the fireplace?

   _____

3. Name two uses of the musket.

   _____   _____

4. Who made most of the furniture in the early colonial home?

   _____

GRADE 6

I. Reading
  A. Directions
  B. Sequencing
  C. Main Idea
II. Writing
  A. Capitalization
  B. Proofreading

Name _____

Main Idea: The *Gettysburg Address*

On November 19, 1863, President Abraham Lincoln gave a short speech to dedicate a cemetery for Civil War soldiers in Gettysburg, Pennsylvania, where a famous battle was fought. He wrote five drafts of the *Gettysburg Address*, one of the most stirring speeches of all time. The war ended in 1865.

> Four score and seven years ago, our fathers brought forth on this continent a new nation, conceived in liberty, and dedicated to the proposition that all men are created equal.
>
> Now we are engaged in a great civil war, testing whether that nation, or any nation so conceived and so dedicated, can long endure. We are met on a great battlefield of that war. We have come to dedicate a portion of that field as a final resting place for those who here gave their lives that this nation might live. It is altogether fitting and proper that we should do this.
>
> But, in a larger sense, we cannot dedicate—we cannot consecrate—we cannot hallow—this ground. The brave men, living and dead, who struggled here have consecrated it far above our poor power to add or detract. The world will little note nor long remember what we say here, but it can never forget what they did here. It is for us the living, rather, to be dedicated to the unfinished work which they who fought here have thus far so nobly advanced. It is rather for us to be here dedicated to the great task remaining before us—that from these honored dead we take increased devotion to that cause for which they gave their last full measure of devotion—that we here highly resolve that these dead shall not have died in vain— that this nation, under God, shall have a new birth of freedom—and that government of the people, by the people, for the people shall not perish from this earth.

Directions: Answer the questions about the *Gettysburg Address*.

1. Circle the main idea:

This speech will be long remembered as a tribute to the dead who died fighting in the Civil War.

This speech is to honor the dead soldiers who gave their lives so that the nation could have freedom for all citizens.

2. What happened on the ground where the cemetery stood? _____

_____

_____

GRADE 6

I. Reading
  A. Directions
  B. Sequencing
  C. Main Idea
II. Writing
  A. Capitalization
  B. Proofreading

Name _____

Comprehension:
The *Emancipation Proclamation*

On September 22, 1862, a year before delivering the *Gettysburg Address*, President Lincoln delivered the *Emancipation Proclamation*, which stated that all slaves in Confederate states should be set free. Since the Confederate states had already seceded (withdrawn) from the Union, they ignored the proclamation. However, the proclamation did strengthen the North's war effort. About 200,000 black men—mostly former slaves—enlisted in the Union Army. Two years later, the 13th Amendment to the Constitution ended slavery in all parts of the United States.

I, Abraham Lincoln, do order and declare that all persons held as slaves within said designated States and parts of States are, and henceforward shall be, free; and that the Executive Government of the United States, including military and naval authorities thereof, shall recognize and maintain the freedom of said persons.

And I hereby enjoin upon the people so declared to be free to abstain from all violence, unless in necessary self-defense; and I recommend to them that, in all cases where allowed, they labor faithfully for reasonable wages.

And I further declare and make known that such persons of suitable condition will be received into the armed forces of the United States to garrison forts, positions, stations, and other places, and to man vessels of all sorts in said service.

(This is not the full text of the *Emancipation Proclamation*.)

Directions: Answer the questions about the *Emancipation Proclamation*.

1. How did the *Emancipation Proclamation* strengthen the North's war effort?

_____

2. Which came first, the *Emancipation Proclamation* or the *Gettysburg Address*?

_____

3. Which amendment to the Constitution grew out of the *Emancipation Proclamation*?

_____

4. *Secede* means to ☐ quit.　　☐ fight.　　☐ withdraw.

I. Reading
  A. Directions
  B. Sequencing
  C. Main Idea
II. Writing
  A. Capitalization
  B. Proofreading

Name _____

Comprehension: Lincoln and the South

Many people think that Abraham Lincoln publicly came out against slavery from the beginning of his term as president. This is not the case. Whatever his private feelings, he did not criticize slavery publicly. Fearful that the southern states would secede, or leave, the Union, he pledged to respect the southern states' rights to own slaves. He also pledged that the government would respect the southern states' runaway slave laws. These laws required all citizens to return runaway slaves to their masters.

Clearly, Lincoln did not want the country torn apart by a civil war. In the following statement, written in 1861 shortly after he became president, he made it clear that the federal government would do its best to avoid conflict with the southern states.

> I hold that, in contemplation of the universal law and the Constitution, the Union of these states is perpetual. . . . No state, upon its own mere motion, can lawfully get out of the Union. . . . I shall take care, as the Constitution itself expressly enjoins upon me, that the laws of the Union be faithfully executed in all the states. . . . The power confided to me will be used to hold, occupy, and possess the property and places belonging to the government, and to collect the duties and imposts. . . .
>
> In your hands, my dissatisfied fellow-countrymen, and not in mine, is the momentous issue of civil war. The government will not assail you. You can have no conflict without yourselves being the aggressors. You have no oath registered in heaven to destroy the government, while I shall have the most solemn one to "preserve, protect, and defend" it.

Directions: Use context clues for these definitions.

1. What is the correct definition of *assail*? _____

2. What is the correct definition of *enjoin*? _____

3. What is the correct definition of *contemplation*?_____

_____

Directions: Answer these questions about Lincoln and the southern states.

1. Lincoln is telling the southern states that the government

  ☐ does want a war.   ☐ doesn't want a war.   ☐ will stop a war.

2. As president, Lincoln pledged to "preserve, protect, and defend"

  ☐ slavery.   ☐ the northern states.   ☐ the Union.

I. Reading
A. Directions
B. Sequencing
C. Main Idea
II. Writing
A. Capitalization
B. Proofreading

Name _____

Comprehension: Away Down South in Dixie

Although many southerners disapproved of slavery, the pressure to go along with the majority who supported slavery was very strong. Many of those who thought slavery was wrong did not talk about their opinions. It was dangerous to do so!

The main reason the southern states seceded from the Union in 1861 was because they wanted to protect their right to own slaves. They also wanted to increase the number of slaves so they could increase production of cotton and other crops that slaves tended. Many Civil War monuments in the South are dedicated to a war that was described as "just and holy."

"Dixie," a song written in 1859 that is still popular in the South, sums up the attitude of many southerners. As the song lyrics show, southerners' loyalties lay not with the Union representing all the states, but with the South and the southern way of life.

Dixie
I wish I was in Dixie, Hoo-ray! Hoo-ray!
In Dixie land I'll take my stand
To live and die in Dixie.
Away, away, away down south in Dixie!
Away, away, away down south in Dixie!
(This is not the full text of the song.)

Directions: Answer these questions about southerners and "Dixie."

1. Why did southerners who disapproved of slavery keep their opinions to themselves?

_____

_____

2. Why did southerners want more slaves? _____

_____

3. What are the words on some southern Civil War monuments? _____

_____

4. What "stand" is referred to in "Dixie"?

☐ stand for slavery   ☐ stand against slavery   ☐ stand for cotton

GRADE 6

I. Reading
  A. Directions
  B. Sequencing
  C. Main Idea
II. Writing
  A. Capitalization
  B. Proofreading

Name _____

Comprehension: Our National Anthem

Written in 1814 by Francis Scott Key, our American national anthem is stirring, beautiful, and difficult to sing. Key wrote the song while aboard a ship off the coast of Maryland, where one long night he watched the gunfire from a British attack on America's Fort McHenry. The following morning, he wrote "The Star-Spangled Banner" when, to his great joy, he saw the American flag still flying over the fort—a sign that the Americans had not lost the battle.

The Star-Spangled Banner

Oh say, can you see, by the dawn's early light,
What so proudly we hail'd at the twilight's last gleaming?
Whose broad stripes and bright stars, thro' the perilous fight,
O'er the ramparts we watch'd were so gallantly streaming?
And the rockets' red glare, the bombs bursting in air,
Gave proof thro' the night that our flag was still there.
Oh say, does that star-spangled banner yet wave
O'er the land of the free and the home of the brave?

Oh, the shore dimly seen thro' the mists of the deep,
Where the foe's haughty host in dread silence reposes,
What is that which the breeze, o'er the towering steep,
As it fitfully blows, half conceals, half discloses?
Now it catches the gleam of the morning's first beam,
In full glory reflected, now shines on the stream:
'Tis the star-spangled banner: O, long may it wave
O'er the land of the free and the home of the brave!

Directions: Answer these questions about the first two verses of "The Star-Spangled Banner."

1. Who wrote "The Star-Spangled Banner"? _____

2. What is "The Star-Spangled Banner"? _____

3. In what year was the song written? _____

4. At what time of day was the song written? _____

5. Tell what is meant by the lines " . . . the rockets' red glare, the bombs bursting in air/Gave proof through the night that our flag was still there."

_____

_____

Name _____

Comprehension: "America the Beautiful"

   Written in 1895 by Katherine Lee Bates, "America the Beautiful" is another very popular patriotic song. It is so popular, in fact, that some people would like to see it replace "The Star-Spangled Banner" as the United States' national anthem. Ms. Bates was inspired to write the song while visiting Colorado, where she was struck by the splendor of the mountains. Today, "America the Beautiful" remains a tribute to our country's natural beauty.

America the Beautiful
Oh beautiful for spacious skies,
For amber waves of grain,
For purple mountains majesties
Above the fruited plain!
America! America!
God shed His grace on thee,
And crown thy good
With brotherhood
From sea to shining sea!

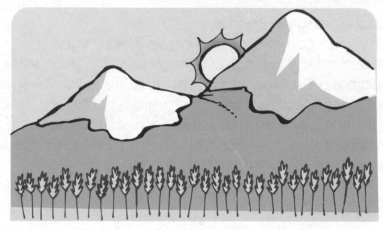

Directions: Use context clues or a dictionary to answer these questions about "America the Beautiful."

1. What is the correct definition of *tribute*? _____

2. What is the correct definition of *amber*? _____

   What other word might you use for *amber* in the song? _____

3. What is the singular form of *majesties*? What does it mean in the song? _____

_____

4. "From sea to shining sea" means the oceans to the east and west of the United States. What are their names?

_____   _____

5. Do you think "America the Beautiful" should be our national anthem? Why or why not?

_____

_____

I. Reading
A. Directions
B. Sequencing
C. Main Idea
II. Writing
A. Capitalization
B. Proofreading

Name _____

Comprehension: Civil War Marching Song

When soldiers march, they sometimes sing a song to help them keep in step. One of the most famous marching songs of the Civil War was the "Battle Hymn of the Republic," written in 1861 by Julia Ward Howe. Mrs. Howe wrote the song after visiting a Union army camp in the North. The words are about how God is on the side of the soldiers.

Battle Hymn of the Republic
Mine eyes have seen the glory of the coming of the Lord,
He is trampling out the vintage where the grapes of wrath are stored,
He has loosed the fateful lightning of his terrible swift sword,
His truth is marching on.

Glory, glory hallelujah! Glory, glory hallelujah!
Glory, glory hallelujah! His truth is marching on.

I have seen him in the watchfires of a hundred circling camps,
I have builded him an altar in the evening dews and damps,
I can read his righteous sentence by the dim and flaring lamps,
His day is marching on.

Glory, glory hallelujah! Glory, glory hallelujah!
Glory, glory hallelujah! His truth is marching on.

Directions: Answer these questions about the "Battle Hymn of the Republic."

1. Who wrote the "Battle Hymn of the Republic"? _____

2. When was the song written? _____

3. What war was in progress at the time? _____

4. Why did soldiers sing while they marched? _____

_____

5. What marches on along with the soldiers? _____

6. What did the soldiers sing about building in the evening?

_____

GRADE
6

I. Reading
  A. Directions
  B. Sequencing
  C. Main Idea
II. Writing
  A. Capitalization
  B. Proofreading

Name _____

Recalling Details: The Island Continent, Australia

Australia is the only country that fills an entire continent. It is the smallest continent in the world but the sixth largest country. Australia, called the island continent, is totally surrounded by water—the Indian Ocean on the west and south, the Pacific Ocean on the east, and the Arafura Sea, which is formed by these two oceans coming together, to the north.

The island continent is, in large part, a very dry, flat land. Yet it supports a magnificent and unusual collection of wildlife. Because of its remoteness, Australia is home to plants and animals that are not found anywhere else in the world. Besides the well-known kangaroo and koala, the strange animals of the continent include the wombat, dingo, kookaburra, emu, and, perhaps the strangest of all, the duckbill platypus.

There are many physical features of Australia that also are unique, including the central part of the country known as the "Outback," which consists of three main deserts—the Great Sandy, the Gibson, and the Great Victoria. Because much of the country is desert, more than half of all Australians live in large, modern cities along the coast. There are also many people living in the small towns on the edge of the Outback, where there is plenty of grass for raising sheep and cattle. Australia rates first in the world for sheep raising. In fact, there are more than 10 times as many sheep in Australia as there are people!

Directions: Answer these questions about Australia.

1. What are the three large bodies of water that surround Australia?

   _____ _____ _____

2. Besides the kangaroo and the koala, name three other unusual animals found only in Australia.

   _____ _____ _____

3. What three deserts make up the "Outback"?

   _____ _____ _____

GRADE 6

I. Reading
   A. Directions
   B. Sequencing
   C. Main Idea
II. Writing
   A. Capitalization
   B. Proofreading

Name _____

Comprehension: The Aborigines

The native, or earliest known, people of Australia are the Aborigines (ab-ur-IJ-uh-neez). They arrived on the continent from Asia more than 20,000 years ago. Before the Europeans began settling in Australia during the early 1800s, there were about 300,000 Aborigines. But the new settlers brought diseases that killed many of these native people. Today, there are only about 125,000 Aborigines living in Australia, many of whom now live in the cities.

The way of life of the Aborigines, who still live like their ancestors, is closely related to nature. They live as hunters and gatherers and do not produce crops or raise livestock. The Aborigines have no permanent settlements, only small camps near watering places. Because they live off the land, they must frequently move about in search of food. They have few belongings and little or no clothing.

Some tribes of Aborigines, especially those that live in the desert, may move 100 times in a year. They might move more than 1,000 miles on foot during that time. These tribes set up temporary homes, such as tents made of bark and igloo-like structures made of grass.

The Aborigines have no written language, but they have developed a system of hand signals. These are used during hunting when silence is necessary and during their elaborate religious ceremonies when talking is forbidden.

Directions: Circle **True** or **False** for these statements about Aborigines.

1. The Aborigines came from Europe to settle in Australia.   True   False

2. The Aborigines live as hunters and gatherers rather than as farmers.   True   False

3. The tribes move about often to find jobs.   True   False

4. The people move often to help them raise their livestock.   True   False

5. Aborigine tribes always move 200 times a year.   True   False

GRADE 6

I. Reading
   A. Directions
   B. Sequencing
   C. Main Idea
II. Writing
   A. Capitalization
   B. Proofreading

Name _____

Main Idea/Comprehension: The Boomerang

The Aborigines have developed a few tools and weapons, including spears, flint knives, and the boomerang. The boomerang comes in different shapes and has many uses. This curved throwing stick is used for hunting, playing, digging, cutting, and even making music.

You may have seen a boomerang that, when thrown, returns to the thrower. This type of boomerang is sometimes used in duck hunting, but it is most often used as a toy and for sporting contests. It is lightweight—about three-fourths of a pound—and has a big curve in it. However, the boomerang used by the Aborigines for hunting is much heavier and is nearly straight. It does not return to its thrower.

Because of its sharp edges, the boomerang makes a good knife for skinning animals. The Aborigines also use boomerangs as digging sticks, to sharpen stone blades, to start fires, and as swords and clubs in fighting. Boomerangs sometimes are used to make music—two clapped together provide rhythmic background for dances. Some make musical sounds when they are pulled across one another.

To throw a boomerang, the thrower grasps it at one end and holds it behind his head. He throws it overhanded, adding a sharp flick of the wrist at the last moment. It is thrown into the wind to make it come back. A skillful thrower can do many tricks with his boomerang. He can make it spin in several circles or make a figure eight in the air. He can even make it bounce on the ground several times before it soars into the air and returns.

Directions: Answer these questions about boomerangs.

1. The main idea is:

   ☐ The Aborigines have developed a few tools and weapons, including spears, flint knives, and the boomerang.

   ☐ The boomerang comes in different shapes and has many uses.

2. To make it return, the thrower tosses the boomerang

   ☐ into the wind.   ☐ against the wind.

3. List three uses for the boomerang.

   _____

   _____

   _____

GRADE 6

I. Reading
A. Directions
B. Sequencing
C. Main Idea
II. Writing
A. Capitalization
B. Proofreading

Name _____

Comprehension: The Kangaroo

Many animals found in Australia are not found anywhere else in the world. Because the island continent was separated from the rest of the world for many years, these animals developed in different ways. Many of the animals in Australia are called *marsupials*. Marsupials are animals whose babies are born underdeveloped and are then carried in a pouch on the mother's body until they are able to care for themselves. The kangaroo is perhaps the best known of the marsupials.

There are 45 kinds of kangaroos, and they come in a variety of sizes. The smallest is the musky rat kangaroo, which is about a foot long, including its hairless tail. It weighs only a pound. The largest is the gray kangaroo, which is more than 9 feet long, including its tail, and can weigh 200 pounds. When moving quickly, a kangaroo can leap 25 feet and move at 30 miles an hour!

A baby kangaroo, called a *joey*, is totally helpless at birth. It is only three-quarters of an inch long and weighs but a fraction of an ounce. The newly born joey immediately crawls into its mother's pouch and remains there until it is old enough to be independent—which can be as long as eight months.

Kangaroos eat grasses and plants. They can cause problems for farmers and ranchers in Australia because they compete with cattle for pastures. During a drought, kangaroos may invade ranches and even airports looking for food.

Directions: Answer these questions about kangaroos.

1. What are marsupials? _____

   _____

2. What is the smallest kangaroo? _____

3. What is a baby kangaroo called? _____

4. Why did Australian animals develop differently from other animals? _____

   _____

GRADE 6

I. Reading
   A. Directions
   B. Sequencing
   C. Main Idea
II. Writing
   A. Capitalization
   B. Proofreading

Name _____

Comprehension: The Koala

The koala lives in eastern Australia in the eucalyptus (you-ca-LIP-tes) forests. These slow, gentle animals hide by day, usually sleeping in the trees. They come out at night to eat. Koalas eat only certain types of eucalyptus leaves. Their entire way of life centers on this unique diet. The koala's digestive system is specially adapted for eating eucalyptus leaves. In fact, to other animals, these leaves are poisonous!

The wooly, round-eared koala looks like a cuddly teddy bear, but it is not related to any bear. It is a marsupial like the kangaroo. And, like the joey, a baby koala requires a lot of care. It will remain constantly in its mother's pouch until it is six months old. After that, a baby koala will ride piggyback on its mother for another month or two, even though it is nearly as big as she is. Koalas have few babies—only one every other year. While in her pouch, the baby koala lives on its mother's milk. After it is big enough to be on its own, the koala will almost never drink anything again.

Oddly, the mother koala's pouch is backwards—the opening is at the bottom. This leads scientists to believe that the koala once lived on the ground and walked on all fours. But at some point, the koala became a tree dweller. This makes an upside-down pouch very awkward! The babies keep from falling to the ground by holding on tightly with their mouths. The mother koala has developed strong muscles around the rim of her pouch that also help to hold the baby in.

Directions: Answer these questions about koalas.

1. What is the correct definition for *eucalyptus*?

☐ enormous   ☐ a type of tree   ☐ rain

2. What is the correct definition for *digestive*?

☐ the process in which food is absorbed in the body
☐ the process of finding food
☐ the process of tasting

3. What is the correct definition for *dweller*?

☐ one who climbs   ☐ one who eats   ☐ one who lives in

GRADE 6

I. Reading
A. Directions
B. Sequencing
C. Main Idea
II. Writing
A. Capitalization
B. Proofreading

Name _____

Comprehension: The Wombat

Another animal unique to Australia is the wombat. The wombat has characteristics in common with other animals. Like the koala, the wombat is also a marsupial with a backwards pouch. The pouch is more practical for the wombat, which lives on the ground rather than in trees. The wombat walks on all fours so the baby is in less danger of falling out.

The wombat resembles a beaver without a tail. With its strong claws, it is an expert digger. It makes long tunnels beneath cliffs and boulders in which it sleeps all day. At night, it comes out to look for food. It has strong, beaver-like teeth to chew through the various plant roots it eats. A wombat's teeth have no roots, like a rodent's. Its teeth keep growing from the inside as they are worn down from the outside.

The wombat, which can be up to 4 feet long and weighs 60 pounds when full grown, eats only grass, plants, and roots. It is a shy, quiet, and gentle animal that would never attack. But when angered, it has a strong bite and very sharp teeth! And, while wombats don't eat or attack other animals, the many deep burrows they dig to sleep in are often dangerous to the other animals living nearby.

Directions: Answer these questions about the wombat.

1. How is the wombat similar to the koala? _____

_____

_____

2. How is the wombat similar to the beaver? _____

_____

_____

3. How is the wombat similar to a rodent? _____

_____

_____

GRADE
6

I. Reading
   A. Directions
   B. Sequencing
   C. Main Idea
II. Writing
   A. Capitalization
   B. Proofreading

Name _____

Comprehension: The Duckbill Platypus

Australia's duckbill platypus is a most unusual animal. It is very strange-looking and has caused a lot of confusion for people studying it. For many years, even scientists did not know how to classify it. The platypus has webbed feet and a bill like a duck. It doesn't have wings, but has fur instead of feathers. It has four legs instead of two. The baby platypus gets milk from its mother, like a mammal, but it is hatched from a tough-skinned egg, like a reptile. A platypus also has a poisonous spur on each of its back legs that is like the tip of a viper's fangs. Scientists have put the platypus—along with another strange animal from Australia called the spiny anteater—in a special class of mammal called *monotremes*.

The platypus has an amazing appetite! It has been estimated that a full-grown platypus eats about 1,200 earthworms, 50 crayfish, and numerous tadpoles and insects every day. The platypus is an excellent swimmer and diver. It dives under the water of a stream and searches the muddy bottom for food.

A mother platypus lays one or two eggs, which are very small—only about an inch long—and leathery in appearance. During the 7 to 14 days it takes for the eggs to hatch, the mother never leaves them, not even to eat. The tiny platypus, which is only a half-inch long, cuts its way out of the shell with a sharp point on its bill. This point is known as an "egg tooth," and it will fall off soon after birth. (Many reptiles and birds have egg teeth, but they are unknown in other mammals.) By the time it is 4 months old, the baby platypus is about a foot long—half its adult size—and is learning how to swim and hunt.

Directions: Answer these questions about the duckbill platypus.

1. In what way is a duckbill platypus like other mammals? _____

   _____

2. In what way is it like a reptile?_____

3. What other animal is in the class of mammal called *monotremes*?

   _____

4. What makes up the diet of a platypus? _____

5. On what other animals would you see an "egg tooth"? _____

Main Idea: Small Dinosaurs

When most people think of dinosaurs, they visualize enormous creatures. Actually, there were many species of small dinosaurs—some were only the size of chickens.

Like the larger dinosaurs, the Latin names of the smaller ones usually describe the creature. A small but fast species of dinosaur was Saltopus, which means "leaping foot." An adult Saltopus weighed only about 2 pounds and grew to be approximately 2 feet long. Fossils of this dinosaur, which lived about 200 million years ago, have been found only in Scotland.

Another small dinosaur with an interesting name was Compsognathus, which means "pretty jaw." About the same length as the Saltopus, the Compsognathus weighed about three times more. It's unlikely that these two species knew one another, since Compsognathus remains have been found only in France and Germany.

A small dinosaur whose remains have been found in southern Africa is Lesothosaurus, which means "Lesotho lizard." This lizard-like dinosaur was named only partly for its appearance. The first half of its name is based on the place its remains were found—Lesotho, in southern Africa.

Directions: Answer these questions about small dinosaurs.

1. Circle the main idea:

   People who think dinosaurs were big are completely wrong.

   There are several species of small dinosaurs, some weighing only 2 pounds.

2. How much did Saltopus weigh? _____

3. Which dinosaur's name means "pretty jaw"?_____

Name _____

Comprehension: Dinosaur History

Dinosaurs are so popular today that it's hard to imagine this not always being the case. The fact is, no one had any idea that dinosaurs ever existed until about 150 years ago.

In 1841, a British scientist named Richard Owen coined the term *Dinosauria* to describe several sets of recently discovered large fossil bones. *Dinosauria* is Latin for "terrible lizards," and even though some dinosaurs were similar to lizards, modern science now also links dinosaurs to birds. Today's birds are thought to be the closest relatives to the dinosaurs.

Like birds, most dinosaurs had fairly long legs that extended straight down from beneath their bodies. Because of their long legs, many dinosaurs were able to move fast. They were also able to balance themselves well. Long-legged dinosaurs, such as the Iguanodon, needed balance to walk upright.

The Iguanodon walked on its long hind legs and used its stubby front legs as arms. On the end of its arms were five hoof-like fingers, one of which functioned as a thumb. Because it had no front teeth for tearing meat, scientists believe the Iguanodon was a plant eater. Its large, flat back teeth were useful for grinding tender plants before swallowing them.

Directions: Answer these questions about the history of dinosaurs.

1. How were dinosaurs like today's birds? _____

_____

_____

2. This man coined the term *Dinosauria*.

☐ Owen Richards   ☐ Richard Owens   ☐ Richard Owen

3. Which of these did the Iguanodon not have?

☐ short front legs   ☐ front teeth   ☐ back teeth

4. List other ways you can think of that dinosaurs and birds are alike. _____

_____

_____

_____

_____

GRADE 6

I. Reading
A. Directions
D. Sequencing
C. Main Idea
II. Writing
A. Capitalization
B. Proofreading

Name _____

Comprehension: Tyrannosaurus Rex

The largest meat-eating animal ever to roam Earth was Tyrannosaurus Rex. *Rex* is Latin for "king," and because of its size, Tyrannosaurus certainly was at the top of the dinosaur heap. With a length of 46 feet and a weight of 7 tons, there's no doubt this dinosaur commanded respect!

Unlike smaller dinosaurs, Tyrannosaurus wasn't tremendously fast on its huge feet. It could stroll along at a walking speed of 2 to 3 miles an hour. Not bad, considering Tyrannosaurus was pulling along a body that weighed 14,000 pounds! Like other dinosaurs, Tyrannosaurus walked upright, probably balancing its 16-foot-long head by lifting its massive tail.

Compared to the rest of its body, Tyrannosaurus' front claws were tiny. Scientists aren't really sure what the claws were for, although it seems likely that they may have been used for holding food. In that case, Tyrannosaurus would have had to lower its massive head down to its short claws to take anything in its mouth. Maybe it just used the claws to scratch nearby itches!

Because of their low metabolism, dinosaurs did not require a lot of food for survival. Scientists speculate that Tyrannosaurus ate off the same huge piece of meat—usually the carcass of another dinosaur—for several weeks. What do you suppose Tyrannosaurus did the rest of the time?

Directions: Answer these questions about Tyrannosaurus Rex.

1. Why was this dinosaur called "Rex"? _____

_____

2. For what might Tyrannosaurus Rex have used its claws? _____

_____

3. How long was Tyrannosaurus Rex? _____

4. Tyrannosaurus weighed

☐ 10,000 lbs.   ☐ 12,000 lbs.   ☐ 14,000 lbs.

5. Tyrannosaurus ate

☐ plants.   ☐ other dinosaurs.   ☐ birds.

GRADE
6

I. Reading
A. Directions
B. Sequencing
C. Main Idea
II. Writing
A. Capitalization
B. Proofreading

Name _____

Comprehension: Dinosaur Fossils

Imagine putting together the world's largest jigsaw puzzle. That is what scientists who reassemble the fossil bones of dinosaurs must do to find out what the creatures looked like. Fossilized bones are imbedded, or stuck, in solid rock, so scientists must first get the bones out of the rocks without breaking or otherwise damaging them. This task requires enormous patience.

In addition to hammers, drills, and chisels, sound waves are used to break up the rock. The drills, which are similar to high-speed dentist drills, cut through the rock very quickly. As the bones are removed, scientists begin trying to figure out how they attach to one another. Sometimes the dinosaur's skeleton is preserved just as it was when it died. This, of course, shows scientists exactly how to reassemble it. Other times, parts of bone are missing. It then becomes a guessing game to decide what goes where.

When scientists discover dinosaur fossils, it is called a "find." A particularly exciting find in 1978 occurred in Montana when, for the first time, fossilized dinosaur eggs, babies, and several nests were found. The species of dinosaur in this exciting find was Maiasaura, which means "good mother lizard." From the size of the nest, which was 23 feet, scientists speculated that the adult female Maiasaura was about the same size.

Unlike birds' nests, dinosaur nests were not made of sticks and straw. Instead, since they were land animals, nests were made of dirt hollowed out into a bowl shape. The Maiasaura's nest was 3 feet deep and held about 20 eggs.

Directions: Answer these questions about dinosaur fossils.

1. Name four tools used to remove dinosaur bones from rock. _____

_____

_____

2. What do scientists do with the bones they remove? _____

_____

3. The type of dinosaur fossils found in Montana in 1978 were

☐ Mayiasaura.   ☐ Masaura.   ☐ Maiasaura.

4. When scientists discover dinosaur fossils, it is called a

☐ found.   ☐ find.   ☐ nest.

GRADE 6

I. Reading
A. Directions
B. Sequencing
C. Main Idea
II. Writing
A. Capitalization
B. Proofreading

Name _____

Comprehension: Dinosaur Tracks

Some scientists refer to dinosaurs' fossilized tracks as "footprints in time." The tracks that survived in Texas for 120 million years had been made in sand or mud. These large footprints were of the Apatosaurus. The footprints were more than 3 feet across!

Although Apatosaurus had a long, heavy tail, there is no sign that the tail hit the ground along with the feet. Scientists speculate that the place where the tracks were found was once a riverbed, and that Apatosaurus' tail floated in the water and thus left no tracks. Another theory is that the dinosaur always carried its tail out behind it. This second theory is not as popular, because scientists say it's unlikely the dinosaur would consistently carry its long, heavy tail off the ground. When Apatosaurus rested, for example, the tail would have left its mark.

Besides Texas, fossilized tracks have been found in England, Canada, Australia, and Brazil. Some tracks have also been found in New England. The tracks discovered in Canada were quite a find! They showed a pattern made by 10 species of dinosaurs. In all, about 1,700 fossilized footprints were discovered. Maybe the scientists uncovered what millions of years ago was a dinosaur playground!

Directions: Answer these questions about dinosaur tracks.

1. Circle the main idea:

   Fossilized dinosaur tracks provide scientists with information from which to draw conclusions about dinosaur size and behavior.

   Fossilized dinosaur tracks are not very useful because so few have been found in the United States.

2. Explain how a dinosaur might have crossed a river without its tail leaving a track.

   _____

3. Name five countries where dinosaur tracks have been found. _____

   _____

4. Circle the valid generalization about dinosaur tracks.

   The fact that 10 species of tracks were found together proves dinosaurs were friends with others outside their groups.

   The fact that 10 species of tracks were found together means the dinosaurs probably gathered in that spot for water or food.

GRADE
6

I. Reading
A. Directions
B. Sequencing
C. Main Idea
II. Writing
A. Capitalization
B. Proofreading

Name _____

Recalling Details: The Earth's Atmosphere

The most important reason that life can exist on Earth is its atmosphere—the air around us. Without it, plant and animal life could not have developed. There would be no clouds, weather, or even sounds, only a death-like stillness and an endlessly black sky. Without the protection of the atmosphere, the sun's rays would roast the Earth by day. At night, with no blanketing atmosphere, the stored heat would escape into space, dropping the temperature of the planet hundreds of degrees.

Held captive by Earth's gravity, the atmosphere surrounds the planet to a depth of hundreds of miles. However, all but 1 percent of the atmosphere is in a layer about 20 miles deep just above the surface of the Earth. It is made up of a mixture of gases and dusts. About 78 percent of it is a gas called *nitrogen*, which is very important as food for plants. Most of the remaining gas, 21 percent, is called *oxygen*, which all people and animals depend on for life. The remaining 1 percent is made up of a blend of other gases—including carbon dioxide, argon, ozone, and helium—and tiny dust particles. These particles come from ocean salt crystals, bits of rocks and sand, plant pollen, volcanic ash, and even meteor dust.

You may not think of air as matter, as something that can be weighed. In fact, the Earth's air weighs billions and billions of tons. Near the surface of the planet, this "air pressure" is greatest. Right now, about 10 tons of air is pressing in on you. Yet, like the fish living near the floor of the ocean, you don't notice this tremendous weight because your body is built to withstand it.

Directions: Answer these questions about the Earth's atmosphere.

1. What is the atmosphere? _____

2. Of what is the atmosphere made? _____

3. What is the most abundant gas in the atmosphere? _____

4. Which of the atmosphere's gases is most important to humans and animals?

   _____

5. What is air pressure? _____

GRADE 6

I. Reading
   A. Directions
   B. Sequencing
   C. Main Idea
II. Writing
   A. Capitalization
   B. Proofreading

Name _____

Comprehension: Causes and Effects of Weather

The behavior of the atmosphere, which we experience as weather and climate, affects our lives in many important ways. It is the reason no one lives on the South Pole. It controls when a farmer plants the food we will eat, which crops will be planted, and whether those crops will grow. The weather tells you what clothes to wear and how you will play after school. Weather is the sum of all the conditions of the air that may affect the Earth's surface and its living things. These conditions include the temperature, air pressure, wind, and moisture. Climate refers to these conditions but generally applies to larger areas and longer periods of time, such as the annual climate of South America rather than today's weather in Oklahoma City.

Climate is influenced by many factors. It depends first and foremost on latitude. Areas nearest the equator are warm and wet, while the poles are cold and relatively dry. The poles also have extreme seasonal changes, while the areas at the middle latitudes have more moderate climates, neither as cold as the poles nor as hot as the equator. Other circumstances may alter this pattern, however. Land near the oceans, for instance, is generally warmer than inland areas.

Elevation also plays a role in climate. For example, despite the fact that Africa's highest mountain, Kilimanjaro, is just south of the equator, its summit is perpetually covered by snow. In general, high land is cooler and wetter than nearby low land.

Directions: Check the answers to these questions about the causes and effects of weather.

1. What is the correct definition for *atmosphere*?

   ☐ the clouds   ☐ the sky   ☐ where weather occurs

2. What is the correct definition for *foremost*?

   ☐ most important   ☐ highest number   ☐ in the front

3. What is the correct definition for *circumstances*?

   ☐ temperatures   ☐ seasons   ☐ conditions

4. What is the correct definition for *elevation*?

   ☐ height above Earth   ☐ nearness to equator   ☐ snow covering

5. What is the correct definition for *perpetually*?

   ☐ occasionally   ☐ rarely   ☐ always

GRADE 6

I. Reading
  A. Directions
  B. Sequencing
  C. Main Idea
II. Writing
  A. Capitalization
  B. Proofreading

Name _____

Comprehension: Hurricanes

The characteristics of a hurricane are powerful winds, driving rain, and raging seas. Although a storm must have winds blowing at least 74 miles an hour to be classified as a hurricane, it is not unusual to have winds above 150 miles per hour. The entire storm system can be 500 miles in diameter, with lines of clouds that spiral toward a center called the "eye." Within the eye itself, which is about 15 miles across, the air is actually calm and cloudless. But this eye is enclosed by a towering wall of thick clouds where the storm's heaviest rains and highest winds are found.

All hurricanes begin in the warm seas and moist winds of the tropics. They form in either of two narrow bands to the north and south of the equator. For weeks, the blistering sun beats down on the ocean water. Slowly, the air above the sea becomes heated and begins to swirl. More hot, moist air is pulled skyward. Gradually, this circle grows larger and spins faster. As the hot, moist air at the top is cooled, great rain clouds are formed. The storm's fury builds until it moves over land or a cold area of the ocean where its supply of heat and moisture is finally cut off.

Hurricanes that strike North America usually form over the Atlantic Ocean. West coast storms are less dangerous because they tend to head out over the Pacific Ocean rather than toward land. The greatest damage usually comes from the hurricanes that begin in the western Pacific, because they often batter heavily populated regions.

Directions: Answer these questions about hurricanes.

1. What is necessary for a storm to be classified as a hurricane? _____

_____

2. What is the "eye" of the hurricane? _____

3. Where do hurricanes come from? _____

4. How does a hurricane finally die down? _____

_____

5. Why do hurricanes formed in the western Pacific cause the most damage?

_____

GRADE 6

I. Reading
   A. Directions
   B. Sequencing
   C. Main Idea
II. Writing
   A. Capitalization
   B. Proofreading

Name _____

Comprehension: Thunderstorms

With warm weather comes the threat of thunderstorms. The rapid growth of the majestic thunderhead cloud and the damp, cool winds that warn of an approaching storm are familiar in most regions of the world. In fact, it has been estimated that at any given time 1,800 such storms are in progress around the globe.

As with hurricanes and tornadoes, thunderstorms are formed when a warm, moist air mass meets with a cold air mass. Before long, bolts of lightning streak across the sky, and thunder booms. It is not entirely understood how lightning is formed. It is known that a positive electrical charge builds near the top of the cloud, and a negative charge forms at the bottom. When enough force builds up, a powerful current of electricity zigzags down an electrically charged pathway between the two, causing the flash of lightning.

The clap of thunder you hear after a lightning flash is created by rapidly heated air that expands as the lightning passes through it. The distant rumbling is caused by the thunder's sound waves bouncing back and forth within clouds or between mountains. When thunderstorms rumble through an area, many people begin to worry about tornadoes. But they need to be just as fearful of thunderstorms. In fact, lightning kills more people than any other severe weather condition. In 1988, lightning killed 68 people in the United States, while tornadoes killed 32.

Directions: Answer these questions about thunderstorms.

1. How many thunderstorms are estimated to be occurring at any given time around the world?

   _____

2. When are thunderstorms formed?

   _____

3. What causes thunder?

   _____

4. On average, which causes more deaths, lightning or tornadoes?

   _____

Name _____

Nouns

A **noun** names a person, place, thing, or idea.
There are several types of nouns.

Examples:

> **proper nouns:** Joe, Jefferson Memorial
> **common nouns:** dog, town
> **concrete nouns:** book, stove
> **abstract nouns:** fear, devotion
> **collective nouns:** audience, flock

A word can be more than one type of noun.

Example: Dog is both a common and a concrete noun.

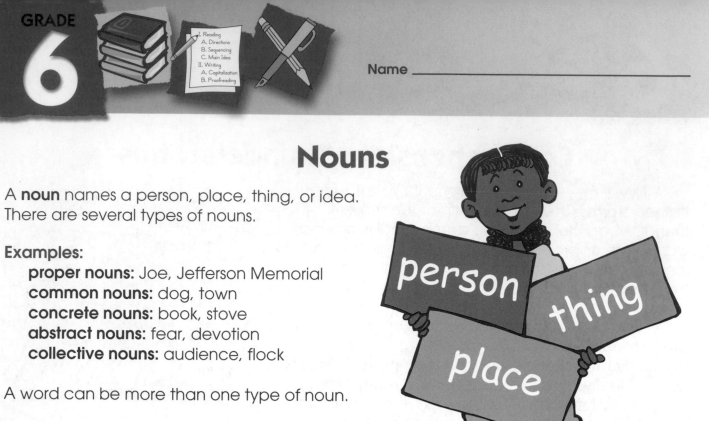

Directions: Write the type or types of each noun on the lines.

1. desk _____

2. ocean _____

3. love _____

4. cat _____

5. herd _____

6. compassion _____

7. reputation _____

8. eyes _____

9. staff _____

10. day _____

11. Roosevelt Building _____

12. Mr. Timken _____

13. life _____

14. porch _____

15. United States _____

I. Reading
A. Directions
B. Sequencing
C. Main Idea
II. Writing
A. Capitalization
B. Proofreading

Name _____

Possessive Nouns

A **possessive** noun owns something. To make a singular noun possessive, add an apostrophe and **s**. **Example:** mayor**'s** campaign.

To make a plural noun possessive when it already ends with **s**, add only an apostrophe. **Example:** dogs**'** tails

To make a plural noun possessive when it doesn't end with **s**, add an apostrophe and **s**. **Example:** men**'s** shirts

Directions: Write the correct form of the word for each sentence in the group. Words may be singular, plural, singular possessive, or plural possessive. The first one has been done for you.

teacher

1. How many <u>teachers</u> does your school have?

2. Where is the <u>teacher's</u> coat?

3. All the <u>teachers'</u> mailboxes are in the school office.

reporter

4. Two _____ were assigned to the story.

5. One _____ car broke down on the way to the scene.

6. The other _____ was riding as a passenger.

7. Both _____ notes ended up missing.

child

8. The _____ are hungry.

9. How much spaghetti can one _____ eat?

10. Put this much on each _____ plate.

11. The _____ spaghetti is ready for them.

mouse

12. Some _____ made a nest under those boards.

13. I can see the _____ hole from here.

14. A baby _____ has wandered away from the nest.

15. The _____ mother is coming to get it.

Name _____

Concrete or Abstract?

A **concrete noun** is something you can see, touch, taste, hear, or smell. An **abstract noun** is something you may not be able to see—an idea, a feeling, an emotion, or a quality.

Directions: Underline all the nouns and pronouns in the story. Then, write the concrete nouns on the left side of the chart and the abstract nouns on the right. If a noun is repeated, you don't have to rewrite it.

Michael told Stephie she was going to ride her bicycle today. She put her hands on the handlebars. He could see the fear on her face as she began to cry.

He held the bike as she pushed on the pedals. Her balance was good and the bike started to move. Her ability to ride was better today than ever before. Her anger at him was going away.

Then, Michael let go without telling her. She rode the bicycle all by herself. She didn't pick up much speed, but she did ride around the whole block by herself.

When Stephie was finished, she realized that she had ridden the bike on her own. Michael saw the pride on her face, and they went inside to tell their dad about her accomplishment.

Concrete Nouns		Abstract Nouns
_____	_____	_____
_____	_____	_____
_____	_____	_____
_____	_____	_____
_____	_____	_____
_____	_____	_____
_____	_____	_____

Name _____

Collective Crossword

A **collective noun** names a group of things.

Examples: a class of students   a troupe of mimes   a committee of citizens

Directions: Use the clues below to complete the crossword puzzle. If necessary, use a dictionary or encyclopedia to help you.

Across:

2. a group of sailors on a ship
4. a group of spectators
5. a group of athletes who play on the same side
6. a group of sheep
7. a group of people related to each other
9. a group of newborn kittens

Down:

1. a group of lions
3. a group of fish
4. a group of ants
7. a group of ships
8. three of the same kind (of anything)

GRADE
6

I. Reading
   A. Directions
   B. Sequencing
   C. Main Idea
II. Writing
   A. Capitalization
   B. Proofreading

Name _____

Possessive Pronouns

Possessive pronouns show ownership. **My, mine, your, yours, his, her, hers, their, theirs, our, ours**, and **its** are possessive pronouns.

Directions: Circle the possessive pronouns in each sentence.

1. My dogs chase cats continually.

2. Jodi put her sunglasses on the dashboard.

3. His mother and mine are the same age.

4. The cat licked its paw.

5. Their anniversary is February 1.

6. This necklace is yours.

7. We will carry our luggage into the airport.

8. Our parents took us to dinner.

9. My brother broke his leg.

10. Her report card was excellent.

11. Raspberry jam is my favorite.

12. Watch your step!

13. The house on the left is mine.

14. My phone number is unlisted.

15. Our garden is growing out of control.

16. Our pumpkins are ten times larger than theirs.

Mine!

Name _____

Interrogative Pronouns

An **interrogative pronoun** asks a question. There are three interrogative pronouns: **who**, **what**, and **which**.

Use **who** when speaking of persons.
Use **what** when speaking of things.
Use **which** when speaking of persons or things.

Examples:
   Who will go? **What** will you do? **Which** of these is yours?

Who becomes **whom** when it is a direct object or an object of a preposition. The possessive form of **whom** is **whose**.

Examples:
   To **whom** will you write?
   Whose computer is that?

Directions: Write the correct interrogative pronoun.

1. _____ wet raincoat is this?

2. _____ is the president of the United States?

3. _____ is your name?

4. _____ dog made this muddy mess?

5. _____ cat ran away?

6. _____ of you is the culprit?

7. _____ was your grade on the last test?

8. To _____ did you report?

9. _____ do you believe now?

10. _____ is the leader of this English study group?

GRADE 6

I. Reading
   A. Directions
   B. Sequencing
   C. Main Idea
II. Writing
   A. Capitalization
   B. Proofreading

Name _____

Reflexive Pronouns

Reflexive pronouns reflect the action of the verb back to the subject.

Myself, **yourself**, **herself**, **himself**, **itself**, **ourselves**, **yourselves**, and **themselves** are reflexive pronouns.

Examples: Roger made **himself** a model of the space shuttle.
The shuttle landed **itself**, using only gravity to pull it down.

Directions: Complete each sentence with the appropriate reflexive pronoun.

1. The Davenport children congratulated _____ on the good spot they found.

2. We sure found _____ a good viewpoint from which to watch the shuttle landing.

3. David imagined _____ trying to maneuver in a space shuttle that was hurtling toward Earth.

4. "I told _____ that I will become a commander someday," Earl said.

5. Deborah enjoyed _____ at the shuttle launch.

6. "You could train _____ for space travel if you built a model simulator," David's parents suggested.

Directions: Write the reflexive pronoun from the box that matches each subject listed below.

1. Peter _____

2. The dog _____

3. Gwen _____

4. Monica and I _____

5. Heather and Kimberly _____

6. You and Carolyn _____

7. I _____

8. You _____

myself
yourself
himself
yourselves
themselves
itself
herself
ourselves

GRADE 6

I. Reading
   A. Directions
   B. Sequencing
   C. Main Idea
II. Writing
   A. Capitalization
   B. Proofreading

Name _____

Pursuing Pronouns

A **personal pronoun** takes the place of one or more nouns. An **interrogative pronoun** introduces a question. A **relative pronoun** introduces a group of words that acts as an adjective.

Examples: **I** am excited about the track meet today.

(personal pronoun)

What event does Bill plan to enter?
(interrogative pronoun)

The track meet, **which** we went to last week, was an exciting event. (relative pronoun)

Directions: Write **personal**, **interrogative**, or **relative** in the blank to identify each boldfaced pronoun.

1. **Which** sprinting race is your favorite? _____

2. **We** both like the same type of running shoes. _____

3. The high jump is a challenge **that** I would like to take on. _____

4. **Who** would like to warm up with me? _____

5. A boy **whom** I knew won the track meet. _____

6. **You** are a natural when it comes to long-distance running. _____

7. Is it true that **she** would like to join our running club? _____

8. **Whose** house should the team go to for the end-of-the-year party? _____

Directions: Complete each sentence with a pronoun.

1. I tried to find my shoes _____ were lost. (relative)

2. _____ told us it won't be a problem for them to run today. (personal)

3. The boy _____ won the race is a great runner. (relative)

4. _____ would like to be our fourth runner in the relay race? (interrogative)

Name _____

How Possessive!

Possessive pronouns take the place of possessive nouns. For example, instead of saying "That is Samantha's sandwich," you can say, "That is **her** sandwich."

Notice that the noun follows the pronoun and there is no apostrophe. A possessive pronoun can also be used without a noun following it. You can say, "That is **hers**."

Directions: Use context clues to figure out the missing possessive pronouns. Write them on the lines.

"Hi! I'm Sam. What's _____ name?" said Sam.

"Hi. _____ name is Sidney," replied the boy.

"Nice to meet you, Sidney. Meet _____ friend Simon and

_____ sister, Samantha. We're about to eat _____ lunches.

Did you bring _____?"

"No," answered Sidney. "I left _____ at home." Then, he placed

_____ backpack on the table.

"No problem," said Sam. "You can have some of _____. We have plenty.

I have two tuna sandwiches. Simon and Samantha have subs. _____ mom

makes the best sandwiches."

"Thanks," said Sidney, showing them _____ big, toothy smile.

Challenge: Now, rewrite each of these sentences so it contains a possessive pronoun with no noun following it.

1. My favorite kind of sandwich is grilled cheese; what is your favorite kind of sandwich?

_____

2. I left my lunch at home, but Sara promised that I could have some of her lunch.

_____

3. My sister is in the fifth grade, but your sister is older.

_____

4. I offered Tommy some of my potato chips, but he said he wanted to eat his first.

_____

I. Reading
  A. Directions
  B. Sequencing
  C. Main Idea
II. Writing
  A. Capitalization
  B. Proofreading

Name _____

Pronoun Play-Off

A **subject pronoun** is used as the subject of a sentence or after a linking verb. An **object pronoun** is used as a direct object, an indirect object, or an object of a preposition.

Directions: Here's a game for you to play. Patricia Proud is a pronoun pro. She has written five sentences with subject and object pronouns. Can you beat her score? Here's what to do:

1. Read Patricia Proud's sentences.
2. Write the correct label in the circle underneath each underlined word: label subject pronouns **S**, direct object pronouns **DO**, indirect object pronouns **IO**, and objects of a preposition **OP**.
3. Calculate Patricia's score as follows:
   subject pronoun = 1 point   object of a preposition = 3 points
   direct object = 2 points   indirect object = 4 points.
4. Then, write five sentences of your own. Underline and label all the subject and object pronouns.
5. Figure out your score. Who won?

Patricia's Sentences   **Patricia's Score:** _____

1. My friends said that <u>they</u> really amused <u>them</u> with their antics.
   ◯   ◯

2. <u>You</u> and your friends pulled quite a joke on <u>us</u>.
   ◯   ◯

3. My parents and <u>I</u> gave <u>her</u> a gift for her eleventh birthday.
   ◯   ◯

4. <u>They</u> listened as <u>we</u> told <u>them</u> what happened to <u>you</u>.
   ◯   ◯   ◯   ◯

5. Jack's brother told <u>me</u> that <u>you</u> need help, so <u>we</u> will take care of <u>it</u> for <u>you</u> and <u>him</u>.
   ◯   ◯   ◯   ◯   ◯   ◯

Your Sentences   **Your Score:** _____

_____

_____

_____

GRADE 6

I. Reading
A. Directions
B. Sequencing
C. Main Idea
II. Writing
A. Capitalization
B. Proofreading

Name _____

Spelling: Plurals

Is **heros** or **heroes** the correct spelling? Many people aren't sure. These rules have exceptions, but they will help you spell the plural forms of most words that end with **o**.

heros or heroes?

- If a word ends with a consonant and **o**, add **es**: hero**es**.
- If a word ends with a vowel and **o**, add **s**: radio**s**.

Here are some other spelling rules for plurals:

- If a word ends with **s**, **ss**, **x**, **ch**, or **sh**, add **es**: bus**es**, kiss**es**, tax**es**, peach**es**, wish**es**.
- If a word ends with **f** or **fe**, drop the **f** or **fe** and add **ves**: lea**f**, lea**ves**; wi**fe**, wi**ves**.
- Some plurals don't end with **s** or **es**: **geese**, **deer**, **children**.

Directions: Write the plural forms of the words.

1. Our area doesn't often have (tornado). _____

2. How many (radio) does this store sell every month? _____

3. (Radish) are the same color as apples. _____

4. Does this submarine carry (torpedo)? _____

5. Hawaii has a number of active (volcano). _____

6. Did you pack (knife) in the picnic basket? _____

7. We heard (echo) when we shouted in the canyon. _____

8. Where is the list of (address)? _____

9. What will you do when that plant (reach) the ceiling? _____

10. Sometimes my dad (fix) us milkshakes. _____

11. Every night, my sister (wish) on the first star she sees. _____

12. Who (furnish) the school with pencils and paper? _____

13. The author (research) every detail in her books. _____

I. Reading
A. Directions
B. Sequencing
C. Main Idea
II. Writing
A. Capitalization
B. Proofreading

Name _____

Generating Gerunds

Gerunds are verbs that end in **ing** and are used as nouns.

Examples: **Laughing** is my sister's favorite pastime.
Jimmy's responsibility will be **sweeping** the porch.

Directions: Use gerunds to fill in the blanks below. Be sure your answers make sense with the meaning of the paragraph!

The Obstacle Course

_____ isn't everything when you compete in an obstacle course. First, you have to complete the course once to register a starting time. Then, your challenge is to do the course in a faster time. The competitors at today's obstacle course really gave it their all.

_____ was the hardest part for Kurt. He couldn't keep his two feet together. _____ was easier because he could jump and run at the same time. In the end, he improved his time by one whole minute.

_____ was the hardest part for Trish. Her arms just didn't move as fast as she wanted them to. On the other hand, she thought that _____ over the pond was easy. She improved her time by more than a minute. Other

competitors said that _____ was the easiest part of the course. But everyone agreed that _____ down the water slide was the most fun. The _____ from the crowd was loudest at the human-made mud pond. Everyone screamed with laughter when Maxwell slid into it.

In the end, Donna had the most improved time. She was given a ribbon and a free pass to a nearby water park. But all the kids that participated enjoyed themselves. Sometimes, just_____ your hardest is the best reward!

Name _____

To Infinitives and Beyond!

An **infinitive** is a verb, usually preceded by **to**, that is used as a noun, adjective, or adverb.

Examples: Everyone wanted **to leave**.
To turn down Alice's offer would be rude.
My little brother tried **to solve** the problem.

Directions: Underline the infinitives in each sentence.

1. *When Aliens Attack Part 2* is the movie to watch this summer!

2. The tennis player was determined to win the game.

3. I invited Dr. Lewis to speak to my class on Career Day.

4. "Not to be a pain," she said, "but can you turn down the TV while I do my homework?"

5. Angie's mother insisted that we were to come to the park as soon as the movie was over.

6. Yvetta's ability to make friends turned her into one of the most well-liked kids in school.

7. I told my little sister not to answer the door to strangers while I was across the street.

8. Even though she found it to be difficult, Michelle learned to play the violin beautifully.

9. The girl longed to run, skip, and ride her bicycle for the whole month she had to use crutches.

Challenge: Now, use infinitives to write five sentences of your own.

_____

_____

_____

_____

_____

_____

GRADE 6

I. Reading
A. Directions
B. Sequencing
C. Main Idea
II. Writing
A. Capitalization
B. Proofreading

Name _____

Scrambled Verbs

Here's a game for two players that tests what you know about verb tenses.

You will need: a number cube, adhesive tape, a timer or stopwatch, two crayons or markers of different colors, scratch paper, a pencil

Directions:

1. First, cover a number cube with adhesive tape. Then, write present, past, and future on the faces of the cube. Write each verb tense on two faces.

2. Each player must select a crayon or marker.

3. The first player should set the timer for 1 minute.

4. Then, this player must choose a verb from the chart below and unscramble it. He or she should write it in the box.

5. Then, he or she rolls the cube to determine a verb tense.

6. This player must use the verb correctly in a sentence. If it is used correctly, the player can color in the square. If not, the other player gets a chance to use the verb in a sentence and color the square. Then, the second player can take a regular turn.

7. Continue taking turns in this fashion.

8. The first player to complete a row across, down, or diagonally wins the game. Remember, you have only 1 minute per turn!

mitda	shlaf	casee	dysut	remgee
parepa	chekts	actprice	velpode	veres
rowk	covedris	FREE	rashe	cande
riccel	ageman	tollecc	shinif	macres
dritec	sitnel	blimc	vidpore	oncusef

I. Reading
A. Directions
B. Sequencing
C. Main Idea
II. Writing
A. Capitalization
B. Proofreading

Name _____

Just Perfect

Here are three more verb tenses to remember:

present perfect action started in the past and just completed or still going on.
I **have started** my homework already.

past perfect action completed before another action.
I **had finished** my math homework long before her call.

future perfect action that will be started and completed in the future.
I **will have finished** all my homework long before I go to bed.

Now, this page is just perfect!

Directions: Arrange each group of words to make a complete sentence. Then, write the sentence, underline the verb, and write its tense. The first one has been done for you.

1. _present perfect_   to traveled My summer this has countries six family far so

My family <u>has traveled</u> to six countries so far this summer.

2. _____   of by will visited trip the end our We 12 countries have

_____

3. _____   until week had Egypt in never a camel a I ridden ago

_____

4. _____   on trip most some tasted the foods have of I unusual this

_____

5. _____   flown to this tomorrow will By have Greece time we

_____

6. _____   written to home I my postcards back have at least 50 to friends

_____

7. _____   film pyramids had I of the taken only shots realized few a
I when the camera out was of

_____

GRADE 6

I. Reading
A. Directions
B. Sequencing
C. Main Idea
II. Writing
A. Capitalization
B. Proofreading

Name _____

How Irregular!

Some verbs are **irregular**. That means you don't just add **d** or **ed** when you change the verb to the past participle.

Example: I **ate** pancakes yesterday.
I **have eaten** breakfast already.

Directions: Find and circle the past tense and past participle for each of the following irregular verbs. Words may appear up, down, across, diagonally, and backwards. Then, use the circled words to complete the sentences below.

tear	strive	arise
lie	break	fall
write	ride	

F	A	L	L	E	N	X	Y
Z	B	T	O	R	E	Z	F
N	S	T	R	O	V	E	E
E	L	A	Y	D	I	A	L
D	E	B	R	E	R	R	L
D	T	N	R	I	T	O	A
I	O	X	R	O	S	S	I
R	R	B	R	O	K	E	N
X	W	R	I	T	T	E	N

1. My sister and I _____ at 7:00 A.M. Our parents had _____ an hour earlier to start the campfire.

2. I _____ off my horse yesterday. I have never _____ off a horse before.

3. I had already _____ several miles along the rocky trail when the accident occurred, but I got back on and _____ back to camp.

4. Last night, a raccoon _____ into our cooler to look for food. That's better than the bear that had _____ into Mr. Alexander's cabin last summer.

5. After a long hike, I _____ down on a flat rock. I had only _____ there about two minutes when I saw a bald eagle fly overhead.

6. My sister _____ to reach the top of the mountain before everyone else, but then she has always _____ to be the first at everything.

7. I slipped and _____ a hole in my jeans. When I took off my jacket, I noticed that I had _____ that, too.

8. I was flipping through the pages of my journal when I found an unopened note my friend had _____ me. I immediately read it and _____ her back.

Name _____

More Irregularities

For some irregular verbs, the past tense and past participle are the same.

Example: The past tense and past participle of the verb **stand** is **stood**.
We **stand** to salute the flag.
The children **stood** in line for 15 minutes.
Our house has **stood** for 150 years.

Directions: To complete each sentence, write the past tense or past participle of the verb that is bold. Then, write the boxed letters in order at the bottom of the page to answer the riddle.

1. **shine**   It has been days since the sun has __ ☐ __ __ __ .

2. **deal**   The president's speech __ ☐ __ __ __ with education.

3. **slide**   The children ☐ __ __ __ down the hill.

4. **flee**   The frightened child __ ☐ __ __ to safety.

5. **hold**   The boy had __ ☐ __ __ on as long as he could.

6. **spin**   The car had __ ☐ __ __ out of control.

7. **leave**   Everyone __ __ __ ☐ about an hour ago.

8. **sit**   He __ ☐ __ at the bus stop for over an hour.

9. **keep**   You have never __ __ __ ☐ a single promise!

10. **hang**   The portrait had __ __ ☐ __ in the hall for generations.

11. **lay**   They had no sooner __ __ ☐ __ down when the children ran through the room in their muddy shoes.

12. **catch**   I had __ __ __ ☐ __ __ a glimpse of her just in time.

13. **shrink**   Ann cried when she saw that her new sweater had __ ☐ __ __ __ so much.

14. **sting**   The hornet __ ☐ __ __ __ me on the leg.

How could the man go without sleep for seven days and not be tired?

☐☐ ☐☐☐☐ ☐☐☐ ☐☐ ☐☐☐☐☐ .

GRADE 6

I. Reading
  A. Directions
  B. Sequencing
  C. Main Idea
II. Writing
  A. Capitalization
  B. Proofreading

Name _____

Choose, Chose, Chosen

Irregular verbs can be confusing because you don't just add **d** or **ed** to form the past tense or the past participle. You also don't need a helping verb such as **have**, **has**, or **had** to form the past tense, but you do need a helping verb with a past participle.

Examples: **present:** I **choose** to read.
           past: You **chose** wisely.
           past participle: He **has chosen** a blue shirt.

Directions: Underline the correct verb form from the choices in parentheses.

1. I (brung, brought) my wallet with me but I have (forgot, forgotten) my keys again!

2. I had (did, done) everything humanly possible to help so I (went, gone) home.

3. I accidentally (threw, thrown) away all the notes I had (took, taken) in science class last week.

4. My friends (saw, seen) me coming before I had (saw, seen) them.

5. Jack (began, begun) to realize that he had (chose, chosen) the wrong clothes to wear on such a cold day.

6. We had not (knew, known) until this morning that you (were, been) in town.

7. Mack's parents had (forbade, forbidden) him to swim in the river, but he (swam, swum) there anyway.

8. Have you always (got, gotten) up so early, or have you just (began, begun) to get up at daybreak?

9. My computer had just (froze, frozen) for the third time, so I (gave, given) up and (wrote, written) my report by hand.

10. No one (knew, known) that I had (wrote, written) the song myself until I (sang, sung) it for them.

11. Mindy and I have not (spoke, spoken) since the last time she (was, been) at her grandparents' house.

12. It had (grew, grown) too cold to stay outside any longer, so everyone (came, come) inside.

GRADE 6

I. Reading
   A. Directions
   B. Sequencing
   C. Main Idea
II. Writing
   A. Capitalization
   B. Proofreading

Name _____

Putting It All Together

Directions: Underline the incorrect forms of irregular verbs in each sentence. Then, write the correct ones on the line.

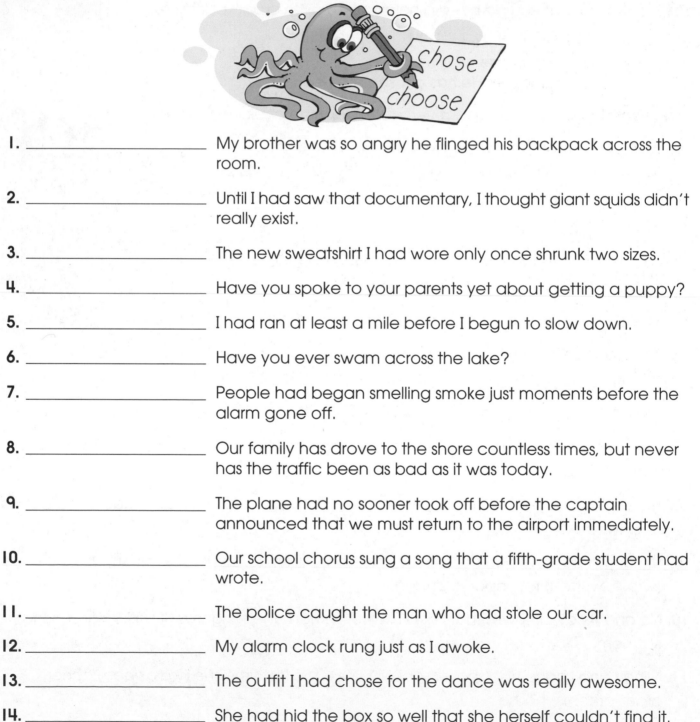

1. _____ My brother was so angry he flinged his backpack across the room.

2. _____ Until I had saw that documentary, I thought giant squids didn't really exist.

3. _____ The new sweatshirt I had wore only once shrunk two sizes.

4. _____ Have you spoke to your parents yet about getting a puppy?

5. _____ I had ran at least a mile before I begun to slow down.

6. _____ Have you ever swam across the lake?

7. _____ People had began smelling smoke just moments before the alarm gone off.

8. _____ Our family has drove to the shore countless times, but never has the traffic been as bad as it was today.

9. _____ The plane had no sooner took off before the captain announced that we must return to the airport immediately.

10. _____ Our school chorus sung a song that a fifth-grade student had wrote.

11. _____ The police caught the man who had stole our car.

12. _____ My alarm clock rung just as I awoke.

13. _____ The outfit I had chose for the dance was really awesome.

14. _____ She had hid the box so well that she herself couldn't find it.

15. _____ My brother sweared that he hadn't told anyone.

I. Reading
A. Directions
B. Sequencing
C. Main Idea
II. Writing
A. Capitalization
B. Proofreading

Name _____

Who's Who?

Adjectives can be used to compare. Add **er** to most adjectives of one or two syllables to compare two people, places, or things. Add **est** to most adjectives of one or two syllables to compare three or more people, places, or things.

Directions: Write **er** or **est** to complete each adjective in the story. Then, write the name of each sibling above his or her picture and circle the item that each one purchases.

Maggie is the old_____ but not the tall_____ of five siblings. Although Max is the young_____ of all, he is tall_____ than both Maggie and Missy. Morris is young_____ than Maggie but not short_____ than Maggie or Missy. Melvin, the quiet_____ of the five, is also the small_____ . Who's who?

Maggie, Morris, Max, Missy, and Melvin are shopping at the Coolkids' store at the mall. It has absolutely everything. As an avid stuffed animal collector, Maggie is buying the large_____ of two pandas. Max, who is always looking for a bargain, will get the cheap_____ video he can find. Missy loves to read. She has just enough money to buy a book with the funni_____ jokes and riddles ever written. It is also the thick_____ and heavi_____ kids' book she's ever bought. Melvin really likes jigsaw puzzles. Today, he found four puzzles he'd like to have. He has decided on the puzzle with the few_____ number of pieces. Morris is trying to decide between two skateboards. After trying out both of them, he picks the long_____ and narrow_____ one. Which item did each sibling buy?

Name _____

This, That, These, Those

The adjectives **this** and **that** are singular. The adjectives **these** and **those** are plural. **This** and **these** refer to things that are nearby. **That** and **those** refer to things that are farther away.

Examples: **This** elevator we are riding is called a "lift" in England.
Those apartments across the street are called "flats."

Directions: Use **this** and **that** correctly in the sentences below.

1. _____ cookie I have in my hand is called a "biscuit" in England.

2. _____ car trunk over there is called a "boot."

3. _____ parking lot is called a "car park."

4. _____ vacation we took last year would be called a "holiday."

5. _____ box of French fries Monica has is called "chips."

6. _____ can of fruit on the shelf is called a "bottle" of fruit.

Directions: Use **these** and **those** correctly in the sentences below.

1. _____ dollars she is handing you are the English form of currency called "pounds."

2. Isn't it interesting how _____ baby carriages across the street are called "prams"?

3. _____ bathrooms we just passed are called "loos."

4. _____ 7 gallons of gas you purchased at the last gas station would be called "petrol" in England.

5. All _____ soccer games you had fun playing in would be called "football games."

6. _____ differences show that even though people in both countries speak English, we are separate and unique in our own language.

GRADE 6

I. Reading
   A. Directions
   B. Sequencing
   C. Main Idea
II. Writing
   A. Capitalization
   B. Proofreading

Name _____

Did You Know?

A **proper adjective** is formed from a proper noun. It always begins with a capital letter.

Directions: Identify the proper adjectives in the animal facts below and use proofreaders' marks to capitalize them.

Here's how to use proofreaders' marks to capitalize letters:

german   irish

scottish

1. The komodo dragon is actually a lizard, not a dragon.

2. The south american Goliath spider is four inches long, has a $10\frac{1}{2}$ inch leg span, 1-inch fangs, and eats birds.

3. The animal we call the american buffalo is really a bison.

4. The california condor is a large bird that eats the remains of dead animals.

5. The african elephant is larger than the indian elephant.

6. The nile crocodile will remain underwater more than an hour in order to surprise its unsuspecting prey.

7. Unable to do anything but fight, amazon ants steal the larvae of other ants and keep them as slave ants to build their homes and feed them.

8. The alaskan brown bear is one of several mammals that is a scavenger, feeding on dead seals, walruses, and whales.

9. In european folklore, the hoot of an owl is a warning of death.

10. The male darwin frog has a pouch in his mouth in which he hatches eggs.

11. The adult siberian tiger, the largest big cat, reaches a length of 10 feet and a weight of 585 pounds.

12. The kiwi, a new zealand bird, is unable to fly.

13. Pandas eat chinese bamboo shoots; koalas eat australian eucalyptus leaves.

14. It is said that siamese cats, a breed that likely originated in Thailand, were trained to guard the king's palace and attack intruders by jumping on their backs.

15. The chihuahua is the smallest breed of dog and was named after the mexican state of the same name.

I. Reading
A. Directions
B. Sequencing
C. Main Idea
II. Writing
A. Capitalization
B. Proofreading

Name _____

Proper Nouns and Adjectives

Proper nouns and **adjectives** always begin with a capital letter.

Examples: Mount Rainier
the Sahara Desert (**the** is usually not capitalized)
the English language
Italians

Directions: Use proofreaders' marks to show each geographical name that should be capitalized.

australia is the smallest continent on Earth. The western half of this continent is dominated by the great sandy desert, the gibson desert, and the great victoria desert. Two mountain ranges, the macdonnell range and the musgrave range, are located in this area. The great dividing range is a long mountain chain that runs along australia's eastern coastline. Surrounding this small continent are the indian ocean, the timor sea, the arafura sea, the coral sea, and the pacific ocean. You may have read about the great barrier reef, which lies between its northeast shoreline and the coral sea.

australia is divided into six main areas: western australia, south australia, the northern territory, queensland, new south wales, and victoria. The capital of australia is canberra, which is located in new south wales. Its highest point is mt. kosciusko, which is southwest of canberra. Two large lakes, lake eyre and lake torrens, lie in south australia. The darling, warrego, and murray rivers flow through the southeast corner. Much of australia's land is used for grazing sheep and cattle.

Directions: Use proofreaders' marks to show each word that should be capitalized.

1. americans and the english speak the english language.

2. english is a germanic language, as are german and dutch.

3. swedish, norwegian, and danish are also germanic languages.

4. italian and spanish are two romance languages.

5. The romance languages come from latin, the language of all romans.

6. The languages of the russians, poles, czechs, and slavs have a common origin.

7. Many africans speak hebrew and arabic.

8. The language of indians and pakistanis is hindustani.

9. Many american students study french and german.

10. spanish and latin are also often studied.

GRADE 6

I. Reading
    A. Directions
    B. Sequencing
    C. Main Idea
II. Writing
    A. Capitalization
    B. Proofreading

Name _____

Comparing With Adjectives

The **comparative** form of an adjective is used to compare two nouns. It is formed in two ways: by adding the suffix **er** to the adjective or by using the words **more** or **less** with the adjective.

Examples:

David is a fast**er** runner than Thomas.
David is **more** diligent at track practice than Thomas.

The **superlative** form of an adjective is used to compare three or more nouns. It is also formed in two ways: by adding the suffix **est** to the adjective or by using the words **most** or **least** with the adjective.

Examples:

David is the fast**est** runner on the track team.
David is the **most** diligent worker on the track team.

Directions: Circle the adjective of comparison in each of the following sentences. On the line, write if the adjective is written using the comparative form or the superlative form.

1. Central High has the shortest basketball team in the league. _____

2. One of their most skillful plays is to pass the ball through their opponents' legs. _____

3. Central wins a lot of games because the team's players are more clever dribblers than the opposing players. _____

4. The opposing team is dizzier because Central dribbles circles around them. _____

5. The toughest game of the year was against South High. _____

6. Central's captain won the game with the fanciest shot of the game.

   _____

GRADE
6

I. Reading
A. Directions
B. Sequencing
C. Main Idea
II. Writing
A. Capitalization
B. Proofreading

Name _____

What Did You Say?

Adverbs can show comparison. To compare two actions, add the suffix **er** or use the words **more** or **less**. This is called using the **comparative degree**.

To compare more than two actions, add the suffix **est** or use the words **most** or **least**. This is called using the **superlative degree**.

The spellings of some adverbs change when you use comparative and superlative degrees. Here are some examples:

eagerly	more eagerly	most eagerly
carefully	less carefully	least carefully
well	better	best
low	lower	lowest

Directions: Benjamin Bing brags about everything, but he always uses adverbs incorrectly. Read what Benjamin has to say. Underline each mistake. Then, rewrite each sentence correctly.

1. Everyone knows I can do wheelies more better and more long than you can! _____

   _____

2. My older brother swims the most fast of all the kids at camp. _____

   _____

3. Our dog Spike growls ferociouslier than the dog next door. _____

   _____

4. I think the Rockets hockey team plays the most skillfulliest of all the teams. _____

   _____

5. I finished my homework even more quicklier today than yesterday. _____

   _____

6. I'm a great tennis player because I serve the ball more hard than the other players.

   _____

   _____

7. My mother jogs more farther in 15 minutes than your mother does. _____

   _____

8. My sister writes more rapidlier and neatlier than Jenny does. _____

   _____

GRADE
6

I. Reading
A. Directions
B. Sequencing
C. Main Idea
II. Writing
A. Capitalization
B. Proofreading

Name _____

Where and When

Some adverbs such as **here**, **there**, **outside**, and **nearby** tell where something is located. Other adverbs such as **always**, **never**, **today**, and **early** tell when something is taking place.

Directions: Write the adverb that correctly completes the sentence and fits in the puzzle. Each adverb must tell either **when** or **where**. The first one has been done for you.

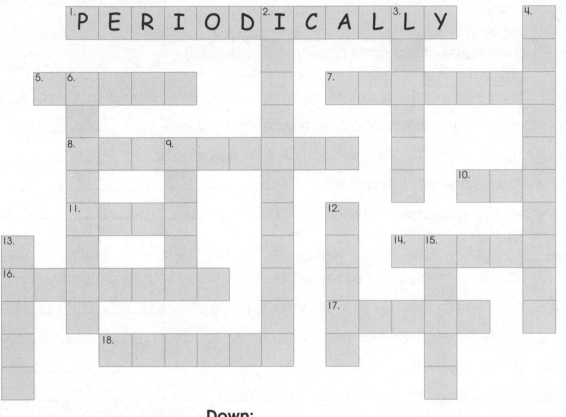

Across:

1. We _____ go to the movies.
5. I take a vitamin _____.
7. Please play _____.
8. We saw him _____.
10. Do it right _____!
11. Please come _____.
14. The sky is _____.
16. Nothing lasts _____.
17. Not late but _____.
18. He lives _____.

Down:

2. Come here _____!
3. I haven't seen you _____.
4. We've looked _____.
6. We can't find it _____.
9. Please sit _____.
12. Don't ever say _____.
13. Do you come here _____?
15. She hid the cookies _____ the breadbox.

Name _____

More About Adverbs

Adverbs that modify verbs function as adverbs of time, place, or manner. Adverbs that modify adjectives or other adverbs function as adverbs of degree, also called intensifiers.

Examples: We went to the big game **today**. (time)
People were selling programs **everywhere**. (place)
He was **really** tired after his workout. (degree)

Directions: Circle each adverb. Tell if it is an adverb of time, place, manner, or degree.

1. The roads were impassable because it snowed today. _____

2. We unwillingly resigned ourselves to staying at home. _____

3. Could we travel there in this storm? _____

4. We would be greatly cheered by a weather change. _____

Directions: Circle each intensifier or adverb of degree. Draw an arrow to the word it modifies. On the line, identify the modified word as an adverb or adjective.

1. She was quite easily upset by any change in plans. _____

2. We made rather extensive plans for our summer vacation. _____

3. We are planning an extremely exciting trip. _____

4. She very firmly refused to go at all. _____

Many adverbs have a **positive**, a **comparative**, and a **superlative** form.

| soon, softly | sooner, more softly | soonest, most softly |

Directions: Rewrite each sentence twice. Use the comparative form of the underlined adverb first, then use the superlative form.

1. He ran <u>fast</u> in the race. _____

   _____

2. She walked home from school <u>quickly</u>. _____

   _____

   _____

168

GRADE

6

I. Reading
  A. Directions
  B. Sequencing
  C. Main Idea
II. Writing
  A. Capitalization
  B. Proofreading

Name _____

Confusing Adjectives and Adverbs

Good, **bad**, **sure**, and **real** are adjectives. They modify nouns.
Examples: That was a **good** dinner. He made a **bad** choice.

Badly, **surely**, and **really** are adverbs.
They modify verbs, adjectives, and other adverbs.
Examples: He ran **badly**. He **really** wanted to go.

Better, **worse**, **best**, and **worst** are adjectives if they
modify nouns. They are adverbs if they modify verbs,
adverbs, or adjectives.
Examples: That's my **best** work. (adjective)
  He sang **best** last night. (adverb)

Well is an adjective if it refers to health.
Well is an adverb if it tells how something is done.
Examples: She feels **well** today. (adjective)
  He rode the horse **well**. (adverb)

Directions: Circle the correct word in parentheses. On the line, write whether it is an adverb
or adjective. Then, underline the word(s) in the sentence it modifies.

1. Tim was (sure, surely) he could go to the museum. _____

2. He wanted to go with his friends (bad, badly). _____

3. He (sure, surely) could finish his work before noon. _____

4. Susan had done a (good, well) job of convincing him to try. _____

5. Tim thought he could manage (good, better) with a schedule. _____

6. He could make (better, well) time if he was organized. _____

7. His list of chores was (worse, bad) than he thought. _____

8. Tim first cleaned up his room (real, really) well. _____

9. He just had to see the (real, really) dinosaur fossil. _____

10. Tim felt (well, good) and whistled as he worked. _____

11. He always worked (best, good) under pressure. _____

12. It turned out to be a (real, really) pleasure to help. _____

Simple Subjects

The **simple subject** of a sentence tells who or what the sentence is about. It is a noun or a pronoun.

Example: My **mom** is turning forty this year.
Mom is the simple subject.

Directions: Circle the simple subject in each sentence.

1. The cat ate all its food.

2. They watched the basketball game.

3. Loretta is going to lunch with her friend.

4. José likes strawberry jam on his toast.

5. The reporter interviewed the victim.

6. She turned down the volume.

7. The farm animals waited to be fed.

8. Can you lift weights?

9. The fan did little to cool the hot room.

10. Thomas Jefferson was one of the founding fathers of our country.

11. I have a lot to do tonight.

12. Will you go to the movie with us?

13. We enjoyed the day at the park.

14. Our pet is a dog.

15. She retrieved her homework from the garbage.

GRADE
6

I. Reading
   A. Directions
   B. Sequencing
   C. Main Idea
II. Writing
   A. Capitalization
   B. Proofreading

Name _____

Simple Predicates

The **simple predicate** of a sentence tells what the subject does, is doing, did, or will do. The simple predicate is always a verb.

Example:
My mom **is turning** forty this year.
"Is turning" is the simple predicate.

Directions: Underline the simple predicate in each sentence. Include all helping verbs.

1. I bought school supplies at the mall.

2. The tiger chased its prey.

3. Mark will be arriving shortly.

4. The hamburgers are cooking now.

5. We will attend my sister's wedding.

6. The dental hygienist cleaned my teeth.

7. My socks are hanging on the clothesline.

8. Where are you going?

9. The dog is running toward its owner.

10. Ramos watched the tornado in fear.

11. Please wash the dishes after dinner.

12. My dad cleaned the garage yesterday.

13. We are going hiking at Yellowstone today.

14. The picture shows our entire family at the family picnic.

15. Our coach will give us a pep talk before the game.

Name _____

A Lemonade Lesson

When two or more sentences contain the same predicate but different subjects, you can combine them to form a single sentence with a **compound subject**. To do this you can use **and** or **or** to combine the subjects.

When two sentences have the same subject but different predicates, you can combine them to form a single sentence with a **compound predicate**. To do this you can use **or**, **and**, or **but** to combine the verbs.

Directions: Revise this story so that all the sentences have compound subjects or compound predicates. The first one has been done for you.

1. We were hot after working in the garden. We were really thirsty, too. <u>We were hot and really thirsty after working in the garden.</u>

2. My sisters wanted some lemonade. I wanted some lemonade, too. _____
   _____

3. I grabbed a bunch of lemons. I carefully cut them in half. _____
   _____

4. Annie looked all over for the pitcher. Annie finally found it. _____
   _____

5. Donna squeezed all the lemons by hand. She poured the juice into a pitcher.
   _____

6. Annie added an equal amount of ice water. She stirred with the long wooden spoon.
   _____

7. Donna said, "You can get three glasses. You can pour the lemonade now."
   _____

8. Annie said, "Hurry up! We're thirsty." Donna said, "Hurry up! We're thirsty."
   _____

9. Annie took a big gulp and swallowed. Donna took a big gulp and swallowed. I took a big gulp and swallowed.
   _____
   _____

GRADE
6

I. Reading
A. Directions
B. Sequencing
C. Main Idea
II. Writing
A. Capitalization
B. Proofreading

Name _____

Predicate Power

Predicate nouns and **predicate adjectives** are used with forms of the verb **to be** and other linking verbs. They refer back to the subject of the sentence.

	predicate noun	predicate adjective
Example:	John is a **friend**.	John is really **funny**.

Directions: 1. Write any noun or pronoun on the subject line.

2. Write a form of the verb **to be** on the predicate line. Here are some examples:

is	was	have, has been	will be
are	were	had been	could have been

Be sure the verb agrees with your subject.

3. Pick a scrambled word. The first letter is underlined. After unscrambling the word, write it on the last line. If it is a noun, add an article such as **a**, **an**, or **the**, or make the noun plural so that it makes sense.

uch<u>g</u>or _____	e<u>g</u>goruso _____	a<u>p</u>leruse _____
nin<u>w</u>er _____	c<u>y</u>kyu _____	halent<u>e</u>p _____
razeri<u>b</u> _____	c<u>r</u>usidiulo _____	nesto<u>r</u>m _____
<u>d</u>ibelercni _____	a<u>b</u>yetu _____	casti<u>f</u>nat _____

Subject	Form of verb "to be"	Predicate noun or adjective
1. _____	_____	_____
2. _____	_____	_____
3. _____	_____	_____
4. _____	_____	_____
5. _____	_____	_____
6. _____	_____	_____
7. _____	_____	_____
8. _____	_____	_____
9. _____	_____	_____

GRADE
6

I. Reading
  A. Directions
  B. Sequencing
  C. Main Idea
II. Writing
  A. Capitalization
  B. Proofreading

Name _____

Agreement of Subject and Verb

A **singular subject** takes a singular verb.
Example: Bill washes the dishes.

A **plural subject** takes a plural verb.
Example: They watch television.

A **compound subject** connected by **and** takes a plural verb.
Example: Mary and Bill read books.

For a **compound subject** connected by
either/or or **neither/nor**, the verb agrees with
the subject closer to it.
Examples: Either my aunt or my uncle
takes us to games. Neither my grandfather
nor my grandmothers are over 85 years old.

A **singular indefinite pronoun** as the subject takes
a singular verb (anybody, anyone, everybody,
everyone, no one, somebody, someone, something).
Example: Everyone enjoys games.

Directions: Write the correct present-tense form of each verb on the line.

1. Everyone _____ wearing interesting hats. (enjoy)

2. Many people _____ hats for various activities. (wear)

3. One factory _____ only felt hats. (make)

4. Either bamboo grass or the leaves of a pine tree _____ wonderful straw
   hats. (make)

5. Factories _____ straw hats, too. (produce)

6. Somebody _____ the straw material. (braid)

7. Either machines or a worker _____ the braided material. (bleach)

8. Chemicals and gelatins _____ straw hats. (stiffen)

9. Ironing _____ the hat-making process. (finish)

GRADE
6

I. Reading
A. Directions
B. Sequencing
C. Main Idea
II. Writing
A. Capitalization
B. Proofreading

Name _____

Dear Agent 001 . . .

The **object of a preposition** is a noun or pronoun that follows a preposition in a phrase.

Directions: A friend is sending you a note. Just in case someone intercepts it, she's written all the direct objects and objects of prepositions in disappearing ink. Try to figure out what the message says. Write a noun or a pronoun in each blank.

Dear Agent 001,

I'm writing _____ from _____, I should be doing _____, but I just don't feel like it. I hope you-know-who doesn't see _____, but even if she does, she won't be able to read _____ because I'm using _____.

Anyway, I wanted to tell _____ about _____ for _____ on _____, but we really and it's okay with _____. I've already asked do need to make _____. It's only two weeks from _____. Can you meet _____ at _____ after _____? I can be there by there. I'll stop at _____. It only takes about _____ to get and buy some _____, and _____, so we'll have something to snack on while we talk. By the way, I don't have to be home until _____, so we have plenty of _____ to work out everything. Please tell _____ to come along, too, but whatever you do, don't let _____ know about _____ because I really want to surprise _____. Oops. I have to go!

See _____ and _____ later.

GRADE
6

I. Reading
   A. Directions
   B. Sequencing
   C. Main Idea
II. Writing
   A. Capitalization
   B. Proofreading

Name _____

Missing Objects

Directions: Each of the following sentences tells about a well-known character from a nursery rhyme or fairy tale. Each sentence is also missing either a direct object or an indirect object. Use the ^ symbol to show where the missing object should be. Then, insert it. The first one has been done for you.

1. After they were summoned by Old King Cole, the three fiddlers played _^ a merry tune.
        him

2. Mrs. Muffet fixed her lovely young daughter.

3. Old Mother Hubbard threw a big bone after returning from the market.

4. The very practical third little pig built himself.

5. Each time Pinocchio tells another lie, his nose grows longer.

6. Jill handed Jack and ran up the hill with him to get some water.

7. The pie man didn't offer any of his wares for he had no money.

8. Red Riding Hood brought a basket of goodies.

9. Hansel broke off a chunk of gingerbread from the witch's cottage and gave his sister Gretel.

10. A trickster gave a handful of magical beans for the cow.

11. Jack fetched on the hill.

12. Baa, baa, black sheep gave to his master.

I. Reading
A. Directions
B. Sequencing
C. Main Idea
II. Writing
A. Capitalization
B. Proofreading

Name _____

Be Brief

An **abbreviation** is the shortened form of a word. Many abbreviations begin with a capital letter and end with a period. **Initials** are a type of abbreviation you can use for certain names and expressions. They replace a word or a whole name.

Directions: Lisa Lewis is always making lists. To save time, she uses abbreviations and initials. Read Lisa's list and underline the abbreviations and initials she used. Then, list the abbreviations and initials and write what each means. Don't forget to include capital letters and periods where they belong.

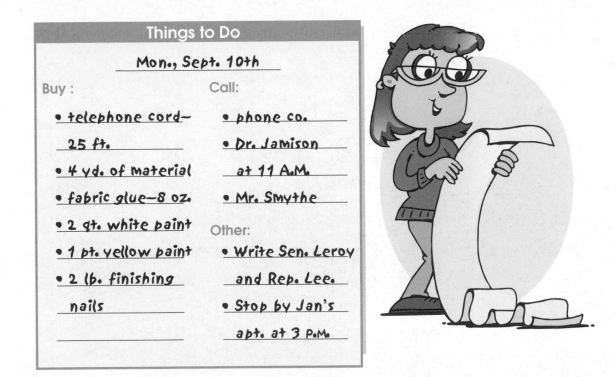

Things to Do

Mon., Sept. 10th

Buy :
- telephone cord— 25 ft.
- 4 yd. of material
- fabric glue—8 oz.
- 2 qt. white paint
- 1 pt. yellow paint
- 2 lb. finishing nails

Call:
- phone co.
- Dr. Jamison at 11 A.M.
- Mr. Smythe

Other:
- Write Sen. Leroy and Rep. Lee.
- Stop by Jan's apt. at 3 P.M.

1. _____ _____
2. _____ _____
3. _____ _____
4. _____ _____
5. _____ _____
6. _____ _____
7. _____ _____
8. _____ _____

9. _____ _____
10. _____ _____
11. _____ _____
12. _____ _____
13. _____ _____
14. _____ _____
15. _____ _____
16. _____ _____

Name _____

State It

The United States Postal Service has a standard abbreviation for every state. For example, Alabama is abbreviated as AL, Kansas as KS, and Tennessee as TN. When you write an address in letters and on envelopes, you should use these abbreviations. Can you identify all fifty states and the postal abbreviation for each? Test yourself and see.

Directions: Write the abbreviation for each state on the map.

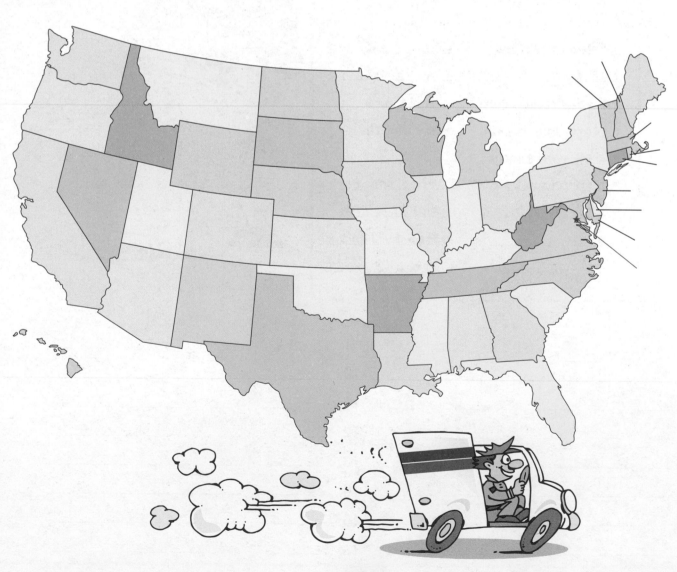

178

Name _____

Abbreviation Station

Directions: How well do you know your abbreviations? Play this game to find out. Each player needs a coin and small button to use as a marker.

1. Flip the coin to determine how many spaces to move your marker. Move 2 spaces if it's heads up, and 1 space if it's tails up.

2. You will land on an abbreviation. Tell what it means and how to use it. For example, *Dr.* is the abbreviation for the title "Doctor." It is written before a person's name.

3. The first player who goes from START to FINISH along any of the paths wins. Then, write all the words on the lines.

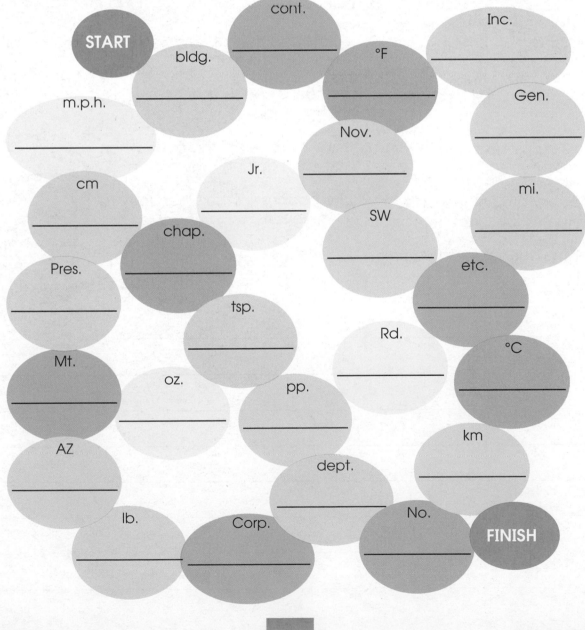

GRADE 6

I. Reading
  A. Directions
  B. Sequencing
  C. Main Idea
II. Writing
  A. Capitalization
  B. Proofreading

Name _____

A Recipe for a Sentence

And, but, yet, or, and **so** are **coordinating conjunctions**. Use them to join together words, phrases, and sentences. Be sure to add a comma before a conjunction when you use it to combine two sentences.

Directions: Read the sentences in the first column. Find related sentences in the second column. Look in the third column to find the best conjunction to combine the sentences. Write your new sentences on the lines below.

1. Stir together 1 cup butter and $1\frac{1}{2}$ cups brown sugar in a bowl.	Then, add two eggs.	or
	Stir.	so
2. Put 2 cups flour into another bowl and add 1 teaspoon baking soda.	Also add 1 cup of nuts with the chips if you like nuts.	but
		and
3. Combine the wet and dry ingredients.	Place the spoonfuls about $1\frac{1}{2}$ inches apart.	and
4. Add 2 cups chocolate chips to the mixture.	Take them out of the oven when they turn golden brown.	but
5. Drop spoonfuls of the batter onto a cookie sheet.	The cookies will rise when they're in the oven.	
6. Bake the cookies for 10 minutes.		

_____

_____

_____

_____

_____

_____

_____

_____

The Best of Three

A **subordinating conjunction** such as **although**, **after**, **when**, or **while** joins a dependent clause to an independent clause in a sentence. You can write most sentences with a subordinating conjunction in one of two different ways.

Example: **When** my friends arrived, I was still doing my homework.
        I was still doing my homework **when** my friends arrived.

When a sentence begins with a subordinating conjunction, use a comma to separate the two clauses.

Directions: Read each group of subordinating conjunctions and the pair of sentences that goes with it. Choose the best conjunction to join the sentences. Then, write the new sentences you can make on the lines underneath.

1. **while unless because**   She refuses to speak to me. I apologize to her.

   _____

   _____

2. **since when until**   You hear what I have to say. Don't say a word.

   _____

   _____

3. **while whether where**   I make dinner. You can set the table.

   _____

   _____

4. **as if   even though   as soon as**   I still couldn't go. I'd finished my homework.

   _____

   _____

5. **although as if after**   Our parents called us. We hurried home.

   _____

   _____

6. **wherever whenever whereas**   You want to leave. Just let us know.

   _____

   _____

I. Reading
  A. Directions
  B. Sequencing
  C. Main Idea
II. Writing
  A. Capitalization
  B. Proofreading

Name _____

Speechless!

Directions: Read the beginning part of each sentence. Then, choose one of these subordinating conjunctions to begin a clause that will complete the sentence. The first one is done for you.

as soon as	nor	so that
if	while	because
when	after	before
until	since	whenever
for	unless	even though

1. You'd better take off those shoes <u>if they are muddy!</u>

2. Please fix me a sandwich _____

_____

3. I am really nervous _____

_____

4. I'll be there _____

_____

5. Don't forget to walk the dog _____

_____

6. Take out the garbage _____

_____

7. I am grounded for two weeks _____

_____

8. I'm gluing it back together _____

_____

9. I'm not doing the dishes tonight _____

_____

GRADE 6

I. Reading
    A. Directions
    B. Sequencing
    C. Main Idea
II. Writing
    A. Capitalization
    B. Proofreading

Name _____

Riddle Time

Some prepositional phrases are like adjectives. They describe nouns or pronouns and tell **how many**, **what kind**, and **which one**.

Other prepositional phrases are like adverbs. They describe verbs, adjectives, and other adverbs and tell **how**, **when**, **where**, and **to what extent**.

Directions: Read the following riddles. Underline the prepositional phrase or phrases in each riddle and write **adjective** or **adverb** to tell how the phrase is functioning in the sentence. Then, try to answer the riddles.

1. A man drove a car with a flat tire across the country but didn't know it was flat. How was this possible?

   _____

2. What can you draw without a pencil and paper? _____

3. What's the first thing you do in the morning? _____

4. Why did the secretary place a clock under her desk? _____

   _____

5. What do you call the science of shopping? _____

6. What's worse than a millipede with sore feet? _____

   _____

7. Why can't you catch a cold going up in an elevator? _____

   _____

8. Which weighs more, a pound of feathers or a pound of potatoes? _____

   _____

9. Why did the baseball team sign a player with two heads? _____

   _____

10. How can you say rabbit without the letter r? _____

11. What goes around a yard but cannot move? _____

12. How could six people stand under a small umbrella and not get wet?

    _____

Name _____

One Long Sentence

Prepositions like **inside**, **near**, and **under** tell location. Other prepositions such as **toward**, **through**, and **past** tell direction. Still other prepositions like **during**, **until**, and **since** tell time.

Directions: Meet Marvin. About the only time you won't see Marvin on his bike is when he's at school. Unscramble the prepositions below. Then, write the longest sentence you can about Marvin's bike ride, using as many prepositional phrases as possible. The sentence has been started and ended for you.

yb _____	newtbee _____	vero _____
pu _____	soscar _____	tunli _____
stap _____	oveab _____	tenx ot _____
logan _____	wond _____	wradot _____
debyno _____	insec _____	undora _____
noit _____	druen _____	freboe _____
hebnid _____	rane _____	nupo _____
hateneb _____	morf _____	rughoth _____
noot _____	beedis _____	

Marvin rode his bike out of the garage, _____

_____

_____

_____

_____ and he still got home before noon!

GRADE
6

I. Reading
  A. Directions
  B. Sequencing
  C. Main Idea
II. Writing
  A. Capitalization
  B. Proofreading

Name _____

The Object Is . . .

A **prepositional phrase** begins with a preposition and ends with the object of the preposition. When you use a pronoun as the object of a preposition, be sure to use an object pronoun. The object pronouns are **me**, **you**, **him**, **her**, **it**, **us**, and **them**.

Directions: As you read the following story, you will notice that Greg did not complete the prepositional phrases. Help him out by adding the missing objects and any other words that describe the object.

Last night, my friend Steve and I decided to sleep outside in

_____. According to _____, the weather forecast

called for clear skies with _____. I found the sleeping bags underneath

_____ in _____. I also packed some snacks for

_____. We could hardly wait for it to get dark. We unrolled our sleeping

bags and put them _____, just beyond _____. It

finally got dark. Soon we'd hear the owls and some of the other critters that live in the

woods around _____. Steve and I played some games and talked

about _____ . Then, we had a snack and crawled into

_____. We were just about asleep when we were startled by a rustling sound.

     "It's probably just a raccoon," I said, as I nervously reached for

_____. Steve didn't say anything, but I could tell he was scared.

Well, it wasn't a critter. It was my little brother Tommy, dragging his blanket and pillow

behind _____.

     "What are you doing here?" I asked. "You know, Tommy, you almost scared the

wits out of _____ ,"

     "Sorry, Greg," he said. "I wanted to sleep outside with _____."

     "Well, okay." I sighed. "Just wrap the blanket around _____ and

come lie down next to _____.

     "Goodnight, Greg and Steve," said Tommy, "and thanks."

I. Reading
   A. Directions
   B. Sequencing
   C. Main Idea
II. Writing
   A. Capitalization
   B. Proofreading

Name _____

Prepositional Phrases

A **prepositional phrase** is a group of words that begins with a preposition and ends with a noun or pronoun. It can act as an adjective or adverb.

Examples: Pineapple is also grown **outside of Hawaii**. (adverb)
The sandwiches **with the peanut butter** were the best ones. (adjective)
We ate the peanut butter sandwiches **at night**. (adverb)

Directions: Underline the prepositional phrase in each sentence.

1. Peanuts are enjoyed around the world.

2. Peanuts are native to South America.

3. Peanut pods develop beneath the ground.

4. The pegs, which are the pod stems, push their way under the soil.

5. Peanuts are part of the legume family.

6. Most peanuts are grown in Africa and Asia.

Directions: Tell whether each prepositional phrase acts as an **adjective** or an **adverb**.

1. Wait until choir practice is over to eat peanut butter. _____

2. Peanut butter on a spoon is a delicious and quick snack. _____

3. Have you ever enjoyed celery with peanut butter and raisins? _____

4. Try your peanut butter sandwich with cold milk. _____

5. I love peanut butter on toast. _____

6. I enjoy eating peanuts at a ball game. _____

GRADE
6

I. Reading
  A. Directions
  B. Sequencing
  C. Main Idea
II. Writing
  A. Capitalization
  B. Proofreading

Name _____

Preposition, Adverb, or Verb?

Don't confuse prepositions with adverbs or with phrases made of **to** plus a verb.

Examples: All the students went **to** the zoo. (preposition)
We really wanted **to** go. (verb part)
We started getting excited **before** the trip. (preposition)
Have you gone to the zoo **before**? (adverb)

Directions: Identify each **bold** word as a preposition, adverb, or verb part.

1. It was incredible how they had trained the animals **to** move like that! _____

2. A monkey followed me **to** the concession stand. _____

3. A beautiful dove flew **around** the audience. _____

4. A seal tossed a ball **around** to show off. _____

5. We took pictures of the walrus **before** the show. _____

6. I had never seen a walrus up close **before**. _____

7. The walrus waddled beyond the stage over **to** the audience. _____

8. My friends were brave, and they decided **to** stay and pet him. _____

9. David asked us, "Who wants **to** see the Dolphin Show at 2:00?" _____

10. The whale catapulted **to** the top and grabbed the fish. _____

11. The monkeys would have liked **to** swing through the trees. _____

12. I looked **up** when I heard the parrot talk. _____

13. I noticed a pigeon flying **around**. _____

14. The elephants came **near**. _____

15. The pigeon carried the message **to** its destination. _____

16. The chimpanzees shouted **across** the water. _____

GRADE
6

I. Reading
  A. Directions
  B. Sequencing
  C. Main Idea
II. Writing
  A. Capitalization
  B. Proofreading

Name _____

Simple, Compound, and Complex Sentences

A simple sentence has a complete subject and predicate.
Example: The little brown rabbit hopped all around the yard.

A compound sentence has two or more simple sentences joined together.
Example: Patrick tried to pick the rabbit up, but it quickly hopped away.

A complex sentence contains one independent clause and one or more dependent clauses.
Example: After several tries, Patrick finally caught the frightened rabbit.

Directions: Label the sentences below as simple, compound, or complex.

1. Jack and Sam were planning their summer vacation. _____

2. Jack, who loved to hike and climb, wanted to go to the mountains. _____

3. Sam called the travel agency, but no one answered the phone. _____

4. They needed some advice about their travel plans. _____

5. Since they had been to the mountains last year, Sam thought going to a lake would be better this time. _____

6. They finally decided to fish the first week of their vacation and head for the mountains the second week. _____

Directions: Write the sentences below according to the directions.

1. Write a simple sentence with a compound subject.

_____

2. Write a simple sentence with a compound verb.

_____

3. Write a compound sentence using *and* as the conjunction.

_____

4. Write a complex sentence using the subordinating conjunction *after*.

_____

GRADE
6

I. Reading
   A. Directions
   B. Sequencing
   C. Main Idea
II. Writing
   A. Capitalization
   B. Proofreading

Name _____

Windy Weather

Remember: Follow punctuation rules whenever you write a sentence.

Periods are used at the end of a sentence.

Commas are used to separate items in a list or to separate parts of a sentence.

Question marks are placed at the end of a question.

Exclamation points end a command or sentence that expresses a strong emotion.

Directions: Read the following letter and insert the commas or end marks that are missing from each sentence.

Dear Scarecrow Tin Man and Lion

Hey guys how are you Thanks to everyone's help I arrived safely back in Kansas The balloon ride was so much fun Being so high up in the air was scary at first but I got used to it I was almost sad when the exciting journey was over You know what they say, though—there's no place like home

Auntie Em and Uncle Henry were happy to see me They said they missed me very much while I was in Oz It was great to see them too. Would you like to visit me here in Kansas Auntie Em says you can come for supper anytime Just look for the Wizard's balloon so you can hitch a ride I really miss you guys and I would love it if you'd come for a visit Hope to see you soon

Love
Dorothy

Directions: Now, write your own letter to a friend or family member you haven't seen in a long time. Make sure to write in complete sentences. When you are done, go back and circle all the periods, commas, question marks, and exclamation points you used.

Dear _____

_____

_____

_____

_____

_____

GRADE
6

I. Reading
A. Directions
B. Sequencing
C. Main Idea
II. Writing
A. Capitalization
B. Proofreading

Name _____

Did Not! Did Too!

Use **quotation marks** to show someone's exact words or thoughts.

Example: "I loved the present you gave me," she cried.

Directions: Insert quotation marks wherever they are needed in the story below.

I can't believe you barged into my room without knocking! Rita said.

I did knock, Robbie replied. You just didn't hear me because you were yapping on the phone.

Well, I heard your giant feet crashing down the hall. Bigfoot! Rita teased.

Robbie frowned. Don't call me Bigfoot! he warned. At least I don't have big ears like you. You're on the phone so much, your ears are enormous.

Mom, Robbie's picking on me! Rita yelled.

Robbie yelled, No, Mom, Rita's picking on me!

Since you two have nothing better to do, I have some chores for you, their mother called to them.

Robbie and Rita looked at each other. Quick! Robbie said. We'll go in my room and say we're studying for a math test. That always works!

Great idea, bro! You're the best! Rita said.

GRADE
6

I. Reading
   A. Directions
   B. Sequencing
   C. Main Idea
II. Writing
   A. Capitalization
   B. Proofreading

Name _____

Fix the Ads

Use capital letters at the beginning of a sentence and at the beginning of proper nouns and adjectives.

Directions: Rewrite the following newspaper ads using capital letters in the correct places.

is time running out for You? do you have Some time on your hands? whatever your problem, connie's clock store Can Help! stop by our store on main street to see our huge selection! just remember to hurry, Because "time waits for No One!"

_____

_____

_____

_____

_____

got a strong longing for Chocolate? a burning yearning for candy hearts? at david's candy Depot, you'll find chocolates in all shapes and sizes, caramels and Nougats to satisfy your sweet tooth, and Delicious jellybeans in 100 gourmet flavors. so stop by our store in the greenleaf mall. tell the clerk, "david sent me," and you'll get a free sample of our famous chocolate cherries!

_____

_____

_____

_____

_____

_____

GRADE 6

I. Reading
   A. Directions
   B. Sequencing
   C. Main Idea
II. Writing
   A. Capitalization
   B. Proofreading

Name _____

One Noisy Storm

There can be more than one way to say something correctly, so try using different types of sentences when you write.

Example: The old jalopy started making noise, then slowed down and puttered to a stop. The old jalopy started making noise. It slowed down and puttered to a stop.

The old jalopy first started making noise, then slowed down, then finally puttered to a stop. The old jalopy started making noise. Then, it slowed down and puttered to a stop.

Directions: Rewrite each of the following sentences in at least two different ways. You can rearrange the words if you want to, and even change them slightly, but be sure not to change the original meaning of the sentence.

1. Scooby had always been a silly cat, but that morning he was acting strangely.

   _____

   _____

2. He was jumping and howling more than usual. He even pounced on our other cat, Fluffernutter, while she was sleeping!

   _____

   _____

3. Fluffernutter woke up and started acting crazy, too.

   _____

   _____

4. The two of them made so much noise that our dog, Lucy, came to see what was going on.

   _____

   _____

5. Lucy started barking and ran into the bathroom. She wouldn't come out.

   _____

   _____

GRADE

6

I. Reading
  A. Directions
  B. Sequencing
  C. Main Idea
II. Writing
  A. Capitalization
  B. Proofreading

Name _____

Commas

Use **commas** . . .

   . . . after introductory phrases
   . . . to set off nouns of direct address
   . . . to set off appositives from the words that go with them
   . . . to set off words that interrupt the flow of the sentence
   . . . to separate words or groups of words in a series

Examples:

   Introductory phrase: Of course, I'd be happy to attend.
   Noun of direct address: Ms. Williams, please sit here.
   To set off appositives: Lee, **the club president**, sat beside me.
   Words interrupting flow: My cousin, **who's 13**, will also be there.
   Words in a series: I ate **popcorn**, **peanuts**, **oats**, and **barley**.

Directions: Identify how the commas are used in each sentence.
            Write: **I** for introductory phrase
                    N for noun of direct address
                    A for appositive
                    WF for words interrupting flow
                    WS for words in a series

_____ **1.** Yes, she is my sister.

_____ **2.** My teacher, Mr. Hopkins, is very fair.

_____ **3.** Her favorite fruits are oranges, plums, and grapes.

_____ **4.** The city mayor, Carla Ellison, is quite young.

_____ **5.** I will buy bread, milk, fruit, and ice cream.

_____ **6.** Her crying, which was quite loud, soon gave me a headache.

_____ **7.** Stephanie, please answer the question.

_____ **8.** So, do you know her?

_____ **9.** Unfortunately, the item is not returnable.

_____ **10.** My sister, my cousin, and my friend will accompany me on vacation.

_____ **11.** My grandparents, Rose and Bill, are both 57 years old.

I. Reading
A. Directions
B. Sequencing
C. Main Idea
II. Writing
A. Capitalization
B. Proofreading

Name _____

Quotation Marks

Quotation marks are used to enclose a speaker's exact words. Use commas to set off a direct quotation from other words in the sentence.

Examples:
Kira smiled and said, "Quotation marks come in handy."
"Yes," Josh said, "I'll take two."

Directions: If quotation marks and commas are used correctly, write **C** in the blank. If they are used incorrectly, write an **X** in the blank. The first one has been done for you.

__C__ 1. "I suppose," Elizabeth remarked, "that you'll be there on time."

_____ 2. "Please let me help! insisted Mark.

_____ 3. I'll be ready in 2 minutes!" her father said.

_____ 4. "Just breathe slowly," the nurse said, "and calm down."

_____ 5. "No one understands me" William whined.

_____ 6. "Would you like more milk?" Jasmine asked politely.

_____ 7. "No thanks, her grandpa replied, "I have plenty."

_____ 8. "What a beautiful morning!" Jessica yelled.

_____ 9. "Yes, it certainly is" her mother agreed.

_____ 10. "Whose purse is this?" asked Andrea.

_____ 11. It's mine" said Stephanie. "Thank you."

_____ 12. "Can you play the piano?" asked Heather.

_____ 13. "Music is my hobby." Jonathan replied.

_____ 14. Great!" yelled Harry. Let's play some tunes."

_____ 15. "I practice a lot," said Jayne proudly.

"This is exactly what I'm saying! You can tell by my quotation marks!"

Name _____

The Rule Is . . .

Directions: Do you know when to use colons and semicolons? Study the examples. Then, see if you can state the rules.

1. Dear Sir or Madam:

This is to inform you that you have been selected to. . .

What's the rule?

Use a colon _____ in a _____.

2. Here's what you'll need to bring along for the day trip to the beach: bathing suit, beach towel, sunscreen, sunglasses, sun hat, flip-flops, lunch, snacks, and pail.

What's the rule?

Use a colon _____.

3.

ARRIVALS				
AIRLINE	**FLIGHT**	**CITY**	**GATE**	**TIME**
National	3214	Denver	B12	12:45 P.M.
Southern	1242	Miami	B18	1:15 P.M.

What's the rule?

Use a colon _____.

4. Abraham Lincoln stood before the crowd and declared:

Four score and seven years ago our fathers brought forth, upon this continent, a new nation, conceived in Liberty, and dedicated to the proposition that all men are created equal. Now we are engaged in a great civil war, testing whether...

What's the rule?

Use a colon _____.

5. TURTLE: I bet you can't get from here to there as fast as I can.
RABBIT: I think you've lost your wits, Turtle!
TURTLE: I will not call it quits until we have raced, Sir.

What's the rule?

Use a colon _____.

6. Soccer practice is after school, and band practice is after lunch.
Soccer practice is after school; band practice is after lunch.

What's the rule?

Use a semicolon in place of _____ in a _____ sentence.

GRADE
6

I. Reading
   A. Directions
   B. Sequencing
   C. Main Idea
II. Writing
   A. Capitalization
   B. Proofreading

Name _____

The List

Underline titles of books, magazines, works of art, plays, movies, television shows, and names of ships and planes. Use quotation marks around titles of chapters, short stories, short poems, and songs.

Directions: Here's Miss Muffet's list of the Top Ten Things to Do While on Vacation. The little Miss's list has a few errors, though. Help her out by underlining and adding quotation marks to titles and names as necessary.

1. Practice my dramatic reading of The Spider and the Fly for my appearance on Star Search.

2. Prepare the manuscript for my book 101 Uses of Curds and Whey and send to Mother Goose Publishing Company.

3. Rent the movie of E.B. White's Charlotte's Web.

4. Record my rock version of Eentsy Weentsy Spider and send to the Backstreet Boys.

5. Attend the unveiling of Pablo Picasso's recently discovered painting Muffet and Spider at the National Museum of Art.

6. Finish my article, How to Live With Spiders and Like It, for Ranger Rick.

7. Go for a ride on the Out to Sea, my friend Bobby Shafto's private yacht.

8. Read the chapter Major Order of Arachnids in Kids' Guide to Insects & Spiders.

9. Get tickets for Tarantella, the new Broadway musical that everyone's talking about.

10. Arrange for a screen test for a possible role in the sequel to Arachnophobia.

GRADE
6

I. Reading
   A. Directions
   B. Sequencing
   C. Main Idea
II. Writing
   A. Capitalization
   B. Proofreading

Name _____

Semicolon

A **semicolon** is used to join two independent clauses that are closely related if a conjunction is not used. An **independent clause** is a group of words that could stand as a complete sentence by itself.

Examples:

The boys were in trouble; they were late for dinner.

(These sentences are closely related. The second explains the first.)

It was the third of September.
The boys were in trouble.

(These sentences aren't closely related. Write them as two separate sentences.)

Directions: Read each pair of sentences. Rewrite those that could be joined by a semicolon.

1. The tiny hummingbird builds a small nest. Its jelly bean-sized eggs fit nicely into it.

_____

2. Some birds build with unusual materials. You may find string or ribbon woven into a nest. _____

_____

3. A nest's location can tell you a bird's diet. Most birds live near their food supply.

_____

4. A gull's nest is on the shore. Gulls eat fish and other kinds of seafood.

_____

5. A woodpecker lives in a hole in a tree. It eats insects that live in trees.

_____

6. Some birds take over old nests. Purple martins live in birdhouses.

_____

7. A woodpecker makes a hole to live in and later moves out. An elf owl moves right into it. _____

8. A swan builds a nest among the reeds. The reeds help hide the nest from the swan's enemies. _____

_____

GRADE 6

I. Reading
  A. Directions
  B. Sequencing
  C. Main Idea
II. Writing
  A. Capitalization
  B. Proofreading

Name _____

Colons and Lists

Use a **colon** when writing a list of items if "follows" or "the following" is used in the introduction and the list of items immediately follows. Commas (and sometimes semicolons) are used to separate the items in the list.

Example: The clown was wearing **the following:** striped pants, a polka-dot shirt, floppy shoes, and baggy socks.

Do not use a colon if the list of items is introduced by such words as "namely," "for instance," "for example," or "that is." Instead, set off the phrase with commas.

Example: A clown could wear, **for example**, striped pants, a polka-dot shirt, floppy shoes, and baggy socks.

Directions: There are eight different outfits that could be made from the clothes listed. Fill in the blanks and correctly punctuate the eight different lists.

    Ties (striped, paisley)   **Shirts (white, blue)**   **Pants (khaki, gray)**

1. John could wear the following a striped tie white shirt and khaki pants.

2. He could also wear for instance a striped tie _____ shirt and khaki pants.

3. John could wear the outfit as follows a paisley tie white shirt and khaki pants.

4. He might try wearing for example a _____ tie blue shirt and khaki pants.

5. He could try namely a striped tie white shirt and gray pants.

6. Otherwise, he might try as follows a striped tie _____ shirt and gray pants.

7. He could outfit himself in the following a paisley tie white shirt and _____ pants.

8. John could choose a last choice as follows a paisley tie _____ shirt and gray pants.

Interjections

An **interjection** that shows strong feeling is followed by an exclamation point. The next word begins with a capital letter.
Example: Quiet! He's not finished yet.

An **interjection** that shows mild feeling is followed by a comma. The next word is not capitalized.
Example: Oh, is that correct?

Directions: Rewrite the sentences to show strong feeling. Punctuate and capitalize properly.

1. hurrah we won the game.

_____

2. whew that was a close one.

_____

Directions: Rewrite the sentences on the lines. Punctuate and capitalize properly.

1. yes you may go to the movies.

_____

2. well we're glad you're finally here.

_____

Directions: Rewrite the sentences below correctly.

1. hush you don't want to upset her.

_____

2. well we're glad you came to the meeting.

_____

3. quiet you'll wake up everyone.

_____

GRADE
6

I. Reading
  A. Directions
  B. Sequencing
  C. Main Idea
II. Writing
  A. Capitalization
  B. Proofreading

Name _____

Finding Spelling Errors

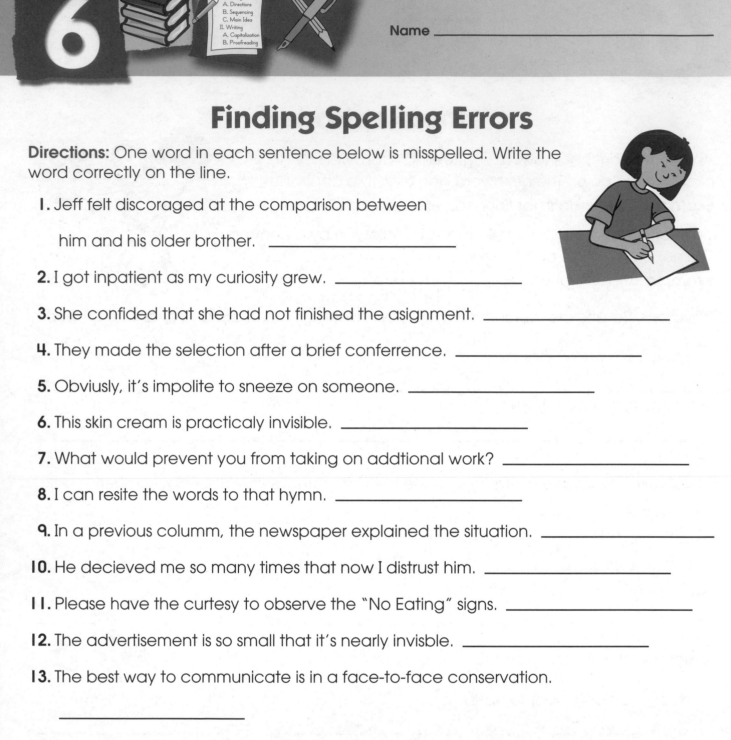

Directions: One word in each sentence below is misspelled. Write the word correctly on the line.

1. Jeff felt discoraged at the comparison between

   him and his older brother. _____

2. I got inpatient as my curiosity grew. _____

3. She confided that she had not finished the asignment. _____

4. They made the selection after a brief conferrence. _____

5. Obviusly, it's impolite to sneeze on someone. _____

6. This skin cream is practicaly invisible. _____

7. What would prevent you from taking on addtional work? _____

8. I can resite the words to that hymn. _____

9. In a previous columm, the newspaper explained the situation. _____

10. He decieved me so many times that now I distrust him. _____

11. Please have the curtesy to observe the "No Eating" signs. _____

12. The advertisement is so small that it's nearly invisble. _____

13. The best way to communicate is in a face-to-face conservation.

    _____

14. In a cost comparson, salmon is more expensive than tuna. _____

15. Poplarity among friends shouldn't depend on your accomplishments.

    _____

16. Her campaign was quite an acheivement. _____

17. He condemmed it as a poor imitation. _____

GRADE
6

I. Reading
  A. Directions
  B. Sequencing
  C. Main Idea
II. Writing
  A. Capitalization
  B. Proofreading

Name _____

Finding Spelling Errors

Directions: Circle all misspelled words. Write the words correctly on the lines at the end of each paragraph. If you need help, consult a dictionary.

Sabrina wanted to aquire a saltwater acquarum. She was worried about the expence, though, so first she did some reseach. She wanted to learn the exxact care saltwater fish need, not just to exsist but to florish. One sorce said she needed to put water in the aquarium and wait 6 weeks before she added the fish. "Good greif!" Sabrina thought. She got a kitten from her nieghbor instead.

_____

_____

_____

One stormy day, Marcel was babysitting his neice. He happened to obsurve that the sky looked darker than norml. At first he ignorred it, but then he noticed a black cloud exxpand and grow in hieght. Then a tail dropped down from the twisting cloud and siezed a tree! "It's a tornado!" Marcel shouted. "Maybe two tornados! This is an emergensy!" For a breef moment Marcel wished he hadn't shouted, because his niece looked at him with a very frightened expresion. Just then, the cieling began to sag as if it had a heavy wieght on it. "This is an excelent time to visit the basement," he told the little girl as calmy as possible.

_____

_____

_____

Just before Mother's Day, Bethany went to a flourist to buy some flowers for her mother. "Well, what is your reqest?" the clerk asked. "I don't have much money," Bethany told him. "So make up your mind," he said impatiently. "Do you want qualitiy or quanity?" Bethany wondered if he was giving her a quizz. She tried not to sqwirm as he stared down at her. Finally she said, "I want cortesy," as she headed for the exxit.

_____

_____

_____

I. Reading
A. Directions
B. Sequencing
C. Main Idea
II. Writing
A. Capitalization
B. Proofreading

Name _____

Correcting Errors

Directions: Find six errors in each paragraph. Write the words correctly on the lines after each paragraph. Use a dictionary if you need help.

My brother Jim took a math coarse at the high school that was too hard for hymn. My father didn't want him to take it, but Jim said, "Oh, you're just too critcal, Dad. Oviously, you don't think I can do it." Jim ingored Dad. That's norm at our house.

_____

_____

Well, the first day Jim went to the course, he came home with a solem expreion on his face, like a condemed man. "That teacher assined us five pages of homework!" he said. "And two addtional problems that we have to reserch!"

_____

_____

"He sounds like an excelent, profesional teacher," my dad said. "We need more teachers of that qwalitu in our schools." Jim squirmed in his seat. Then he gradualy started to smile. "Dad, I need some help with a personl problem," he said. "Five pages of problems, right?" Dad asked. Jim smiled and handed Dad his math book. That's tipical at our house, too.

_____

_____

One day, we had a meddical emergensy at home. My sisters' hand got stuck in a basket with a narrow opening, and she couldn't pull it out. I thought she would have to wear the basket on her hand permanentally! First, I tried to stretch and exxpand the baskets opening, but that didn't work.

_____

_____

Then I smeared a quanity of butter on my sisters hand, and she pulled it right out. I thought she would have the curtesy to thank me, but she just stomped away, still mad. How childsh! Sometimes she seems to think I exxist just to serve her. There are more importanter things in the world than her happiness!

_____

_____

Name _____

Complete Sentences

A **complete sentence** has both a simple subject and a simple predicate. It is a complete thought. Sentences which are not complete are called **fragments**.

Example:
    Complete sentence: The wolf howled at the moon.
    Sentence fragment: Howled at the moon.

Directions: Write **C** on the line if the sentence is complete. Write **F** if it is a fragment.

1. _____ The machine is running.

2. _____ What will we do today?

3. _____ Knowing what I do.

4. _____ That statement is true.

5. _____ My parents drove to town.

6. _____ Watching television all afternoon.

7. _____ The storm devastated the town.

8. _____ Our friends can go with us.

9. _____ The palm trees bent in the wind.

10. _____ Spraying the fire all night.

Directions: Rewrite the sentence fragments from above to make them complete sentences.

_____

_____

_____

_____

_____

GRADE
6

I. Reading
  A. Directions
  B. Sequencing
  C. Main Idea
II. Writing
  A. Capitalization
  B. Proofreading

Name _____

Run-On Sentences

A **run-on sentence** occurs when two or more sentences are joined together without punctuation or a joining word. Run-on sentences should be divided into two or more separate sentences.

Example:
  Run-on sentence: My parents, sister, brother, and I went to the park we saw many animals we had fun.
  Correct: My parents, sister, brother, and I went to the park. We saw many animals and had fun.

Directions: Rewrite the run-on sentences correctly.

1. The dog energetically chased the ball I kept throwing him the ball for a half hour.

_____

_____

_____

2. The restaurant served scrambled eggs and bacon for breakfast I had some and they were delicious.

_____

_____

_____

3. The lightning struck close to our house it scared my little brother and my grandmother called to see if we were safe.

_____

_____

_____

_____

_____

Run-On Wreck!

There is usually more than one way to fix a run-on sentence. You can rewrite it as two or more separate sentences. You can insert a comma or semicolon. You might also insert a conjunction such as **and**, **but**, or **with**.

Directions: Rewrite each of the following run-on sentences in two different ways. The first one is done for you.

1. Sunday's Street Fair was very crowded, there were more than ten thousand people there.

   <u>Sunday's Street Fair was very crowded. There were more than ten thousand people there./ Sunday's Street Fair was very crowded; there were more than ten thousand people there.</u>

2. There were lots of booths set up they were on First Avenue and Second Avenue, too.

   _____

   _____

   _____

3. You could buy lots of things at the fair, there were clothes, videos, pet supplies, food, and more.

   _____

   _____

   _____

4. My best friend found a cute T-shirt it had a funny saying on it.

   _____

   _____

   _____

5. We had so much fun at the fair and now I can't wait until next year's!

   _____

   _____

   _____

Variety Is the Spice of Life

Writing is more interesting when sentences are written in different ways. Sentences may be short or long, begin with phrases or clauses, or change their order.

Directions: Rewrite the paragraphs below. Divide some sentences and combine others. Vary their beginnings.

My sister broke her leg playing soccer. She was playing center. She was in a tournament. She tripped over the ball when she tried to trap the ball and fell to the ground immediately. An ambulance came and an ambulance had on its siren and she went away in the ambulance.

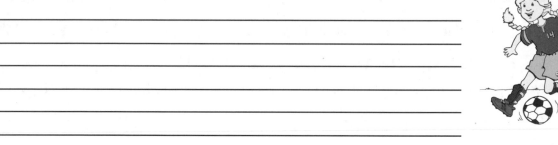

_____

_____

_____

_____

_____

The school year was about to begin. I had to get ready for it. Mother took me to the store. I had to get a notebook. I had to get paper. I had to get pens with blue ink and pencils with erasers. I saw my friends at the store. They were getting ready for school too.

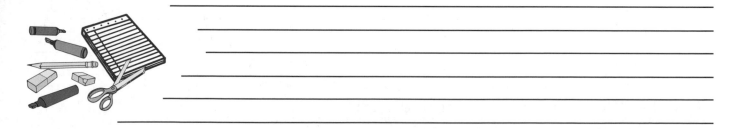

_____

_____

_____

_____

Jamie's mother got a new car. It was a good-looking one. The car was bright red and it had a sun roof and it had a stereo and it could go fast. It had four speeds. Jamie could not give anyone a lift there were only two seats. Jamie was not old enough to drive. He sat in the seat next to his mom.

_____

_____

_____

_____

GRADE
6

I. Reading
  A. Directions
  B. Sequencing
  C. Main Idea
II. Writing
  A. Capitalization
  B. Proofreading

Name _____

At the Car Wash

Directions: Rewrite each of the following sentences to include more adjectives and adverbs. The first one has been done for you.

1. My school held a car wash.

   My school held a huge car wash last weekend.

2. We were raising money for a new playground.

   _____

3. The playground we have now is too small.

   _____

4. The new playground will have two slides and a jungle gym.

   _____

5. It will also have separate swings for big kids and little kids.

   _____

6. I put soap on the cars at the car wash.

   _____

7. My best friend rinsed the cars off.

   _____

8. My older brother collected the money.

   _____

9. Many people came to the car wash.

   _____

10. It was a success.

   _____

GRADE
6

I. Reading
   A. Directions
   B. Sequencing
   C. Main Idea
II. Writing
   A. Capitalization
   B. Proofreading

Name _____

Stronger Sentences

Sometimes the noun form of a word is not the best way to express an idea. Compare these two sentences:

They made preparations for the party.
They prepared for the party.

The second sentence, using **prepared** as a verb, is shorter and stronger.

Directions: Write one word to replace a whole phrase. Cross out the words you don't need. The first one has been done for you.

1. She ~~made a suggestion~~ that we go on Monday.
   suggested

2. They arranged decorations around the room.

3. Let's make a combination of the two ideas.

4. I have great appreciation for what you did.

5. The buses are acting as transportation for the classes.

6. The group made an exploration of the Arctic Circle.

7. Please make a selection of one quickly.

8. The lake is making a reflection of the trees.

9. The family had a celebration of the holiday.

10. Would you please provide a solution for this problem?

11. Don made an imitation of his cat.

12. Please give a definition of that word.

13. I made an examination of the broken bike.

14. Dexter made an invitation for us to join him.

> Write one word to replace a whole phrase.

Name _____

Great Combinations

You can combine sentences by eliminating words that are repeated. When you eliminate words to put two or more subjects together into one sentence, you are making a **compound subject**. Make sure your subject agrees with your verb.

Example: **Lisa** went to soccer practice after school. **Tori** went to soccer practice.
Lisa and Tori went to soccer practice.

When you eliminate words to put two or more verbs together into one sentence, you are making a **compound predicate**.

Example: I **built** the birdhouse myself. I **painted** the birdhouse myself.
I **built and painted** the birdhouse myself.

Directions: Combine the following sets of sentences. Then, label each new sentence correctly with the words **compound subject** or **compound predicate** to tell which it contains.

1. My town just started a new recycling program. My town is asking everyone to participate.

   _____

   _____

2. We have to separate plastic, glass, aluminum, and paper. We have to put them all in different containers.

   _____

   _____

   _____

3. My sister has the job of taking the containers out to the curb so the truck can pick them up. I have the job of taking the containers out to the curb so the truck can pick them up.

   _____

   _____

   _____

4. The truck picks up the containers. Then, the truck takes the containers to a recycling plant in the next town.

I. Reading
  A. Directions
  B. Sequencing
  C. Main Idea
II. Writing
  A. Capitalization
  B. Proofreading

Name _____

All About Teddy

Conjunctions are words that join words or groups of words. Using conjunctions is a good way to combine sentences.

Example: My teacher will be there. My best friend will not be there.
My teacher will be there, **but** my best friend will not be.

Directions: Combine each pair of sentences below by using one of the conjunctions from the box. There may be more than one way to combine the sentences, and some conjunctions may be used more than once.

but	because	after	since	if
and	although	before	when	

1. Theodore Roosevelt was born on October 27, 1858. He died on January 16, 1919.

_____

_____

2. Roosevelt became vice president of the United States under William McKinley. McKinley was assassinated and Roosevelt became president.

_____

_____

3. As president, Roosevelt arranged for the Panama Canal to be built. He also resolved disagreements between big mining companies and their workers.

_____

_____

4. He set aside over 200 million acres of land for parks and nature reserves. He wanted to preserve America's natural resources for future generations.

_____

_____

5. Roosevelt ran for president again in 1912. He was defeated by Woodrow Wilson.

_____

_____

GRADE
6

I. Reading
   A. Directions
   B. Sequencing
   C. Main Idea
II. Writing
   A. Capitalization
   B. Proofreading

Name _____

Report-a-Sauras, Part 1

Directions: You are writing a report about dinosaurs. In each paragraph, you want to answer a certain research question. The following is a list of notes you took at the library. Write each piece of information under the paragraph it goes with.

- Dinosaurs roamed the earth for more than 180 million years, but they became extinct over 65 million years ago.

- By studying fossils, paleontologists can learn about the sizes of the different dinosaurs.

- Almost everything we know about dinosaurs comes from looking at fossils.

- Scientists who study dinosaur fossils are called *paleontologists*.

- Before paleontologists can study fossils, they must dig them from the ground and clean them very carefully.

- Then, the fossils can be taken to a university or museum and studied.

- By studying fossils, paleontologists can learn what the different types of dinosaurs ate.

- Fossils were formed from dinosaurs when their remains hardened into stone or were surrounded by mud or sand that hardened into stone.

- Fossils are formed over long periods of time from the bones, eggs, and other remains of dinosaurs.

- By studying fossils, paleontologists can learn how the different types of dinosaurs cared for their young.

First paragraph: When did the dinosaurs live?

_____

_____

Second paragraph: What are fossils, and why are they important?

_____

_____

_____

_____

_____

_____

GRADE 6

I. Reading
A. Directions
B. Sequencing
C. Main Idea
II. Writing
A. Capitalization
B. Proofreading

Name _____

Report-a-Sauras, Part 2

Directions: Continue to write each piece of information from page 211 under the paragraph it goes with.

Third paragraph: What are paleontologists, and what do they do?

_____

_____

_____

_____

_____

_____

_____

_____

_____

Fourth paragraph: What can paleontologists learn from looking at fossils?

_____

_____

_____

_____

_____

_____

_____

_____

_____

Name _____

Give Me One Reason

Directions: Place each line of information below in the correct spot on the outline. A few are already done for you. Check off the information as you use it.

I would be supervising other children	Program offers tutoring for younger kids
I would be working as a member of a team	Reading
To keep busy after school	Math
To help other children	Science
Program offers activities for younger kids	You wouldn't have to worry about me while you're at work
To gain responsibility	Arts and crafts
Program runs until 5:00	Playground games

Reasons I Should Join the After-School Program

I. To Help Other Children

    A. _____

        1. _____

        2. _____

        3. Math

    B. Program offers activities for younger kids

        1. Arts and crafts

        2. _____

II. To Gain Responsibility

    A. I would be supervising other children

    B. _____

III. _____

    A. Program runs until 5:00

    B. _____

I. Reading
A. Directions
B. Sequencing
C. Main Idea
II. Writing
A. Capitalization
B. Proofreading

Name _____

The Three-Alarm Outline

Directions: Read the following article. Then, fill in the outline below with points from the story. Remember: Each subsection you fill in must answer the main question posed for that section.

On June 11, a terrible fire ripped through the old hat factory on Martin Street. For a short period of time the fire threatened a store nearby, but it was contained thanks to the local fire department.

It is believed that the fire started in a pile of rags that was too close to an old electrical outlet.

The fire started at around 9:30 in the morning and by 10:00 the whole building was in flames. It took nearly three hours for firefighters to extinguish the blaze.

Ms. Liza Smith, of 32 Martin Street, reported the fire at 9:45 when she smelled smoke. "I thought for a while that the smell was coming from my house, and I was very scared," she said. "But when I went outside to wait for the fire department, I realized that the smell was coming from across the street." It took nearly 20 firefighters to put out the blaze.

By the time the fire was out, the entire building was destroyed. Fortunately, no one was injured.

I. What happened?

A._____

II. What was the cause?

A._____

III. When did it happen?

A._____

B. _____

IV. Who was involved?

A._____

B. _____

V. What was the result?

A._____

B. _____

I. Reading
  A. Directions
  B. Sequencing
  C. Main Idea
II. Writing
  A. Capitalization
  B. Proofreading

Name _____

Writing: Outlining

An **outline** is a skeletal description of the main ideas and important details of a reading selection. Making an outline is a good study aid. It is particularly useful when you must write a paper.

Directions: Read the paragraphs, and then complete the outline below.

Weather has a lot to do with where animals live. Cold-blooded animals have body temperatures that change with the temperature of the environment. Cold-blooded animals include snakes, frogs, and lizards. They cannot live anywhere the temperatures stay below freezing for long periods of time. The body temperatures of warm-blooded animals do not depend on the environment. Any animal with hair or fur—including dogs, elephants, and whales—is warm-blooded. Warm-blooded animals can live anywhere in the world where there is enough food to sustain them.

Some warm-blooded animals live where snow covers the ground all winter. These animals have different ways to survive the cold weather. Certain animals store up food to last throughout the snowy season. For example, the tree squirrel may gather nuts to hide in his home. Other animals hibernate in the winter. The ground squirrel, for example, stays in its burrow all winter long, living off the fat reserves in its body.

Title: _____

Main Topic: I. _____

  Subtopic: A. Cold-blooded animals' temperatures change with environment.

  Detail: I. _____

  Subtopic: B. _____

  Detail: I. They can live anywhere there is food.

Main Topic: II. _____

  Subtopic: A. Animals have different ways to survive the cold.

  Details: I. _____

         2. _____

Name _____

Organizing Paragraphs

A **topic sentence** states the main idea of a paragraph and is usually the first sentence. **Support sentences** follow, providing details about the topic. All sentences in a paragraph should relate to the topic sentence. A paragraph ends with a **conclusion sentence**.

Directions: Rearrange each group of sentences into a paragraph, beginning with the topic sentence. Cross out the sentence in each group that is not related to the topic sentence. Write the new paragraph.

Now, chalk drawings are considered art by themselves. The earliest chalk drawings were found on the walls of caves. Chalk is also used in cement, fertilizer, toothpaste, and makeup. Chalk once was used just to make quick sketches. Chalk has been used for drawing for thousands of years. Then, the artist would paint pictures from the sketches.

_____

_____

_____

_____

Dams also keep young salmon from swimming downriver to the ocean. Most salmon live in the ocean but return to fresh water to lay their eggs and breed. Dams prevent salmon from swimming upriver to their spawning grounds. Pacific salmon die after they spawn the first time. One kind of fish pass is a series of pools of water that lead the salmon over the dams. Dams are threatening salmon by interfering with their spawning. To help with this problem, some dams have special "fish passes" to allow salmon to swim over the dam.

_____

_____

_____

_____

_____

_____

I. Reading
  A. Directions
  B. Sequencing
  C. Main Idea
II. Writing
  A. Capitalization
  B. Proofreading

Name _____

It Doesn't Belong

Directions: In each paragraph, there is one sentence that doesn't belong. Circle the topic sentence, and underline the unnecessary sentence.

1. March is my favorite month of the year. I like March because you never know what to expect. Sometimes it snows. It usually rains a lot in April. Sometimes it can be very hot in March. March is the kind of month when anything can happen!

2. Yesterday, my mom and I planted flowers in our garden. My sister was at work yesterday afternoon. We planted daffodils, irises, and petunias. It was a lot of hard work, but I bet our garden will look great when all those flowers are in bloom!

3. We had an incredible thunderstorm last night! It rained so hard, it sounded like someone was playing drums on our roof. And the thunder was so loud, all the windows rattled. There was a lot of lightning too. During the storm, we heard a huge crash. I looked outside and saw a big branch had fallen next to the house. We were lucky it didn't hit anybody! It's not raining today.

4. Tomorrow, I will go to work with my dad for "Take Your Daughters to Work Day." My dad is the manager of a sporting goods store. My mom works in an office. I like going to work with Dad because it's never boring at the store. There is lots of sports equipment to play with and one of Dad's co-workers, Theresa, always plays catch with me on her break.

GRADE 6

I. Reading
  A. Directions
  B. Sequencing
  C. Main Idea
II. Writing
  A. Capitalization
  B. Proofreading

Name _____

Hollywood Hound

Start a new paragraph every time you begin writing about a new idea or a new person begins speaking.

Directions: Lola Labrador is covering a movie premiere for *Hollywood Hound*. Help Lola organize her article into paragraphs by marking a paragraph indent symbol ¶ wherever Lola should start a new paragraph.

The air was full of wagging tails and excited barks when I arrived at the Canine Cinema. Tonight was the premiere of Hollywood's most eagerly awaited film, "Mission Impawsible." The crowd surged forward with an excited woof as the first long black limousine arrived. Out stepped Thandie Newfoundland, the beautiful female star of the film. Thandie looked stunning in a sparkly diamond collar with matching diamond bracelets on her paws, and diamond earrings glistening in the fur of each ear. "How do you feel about being in this movie?" I asked the pretty pooch. "Lola, it's a dream come true," she responded. "My tail's been wagging ever since my big chase scene with the exploding Frisbee." Suddenly, excited howls filled the air. Who should step out of a limo but the star of "Mission Impawsible" himself, Tom Chow! What a handsome dog he was, with his black leather jacket and muscular paws. "Got to run," Tom called as he hurried inside with a wave to his fans. "I need to get a big bucket of doggie treats before the movie starts!"

GRADE

6

I. Reading
  A. Directions
  B. Sequencing
  C. Main Idea
II. Writing
  A. Capitalization
  B. Proofreading

Name _____

Lost in the Zoo

One good way to start a paragraph is with an attention-grabbing introduction. If you can, finish your paragraph with a conclusion that sums up the paragraph's main point.

Directions: Write an **I** next to each statement that could make a good introduction to a paragraph. Write a **C** next to each sentence that could make a good conclusion.

1. _____ What's big, scaly, and has a really bad temper? The Komodo dragon!

2. _____ As you can see, you don't have to be big to be dangerous!

3. _____ Would you know what to do if you came face to face with a wild animal? Read on for some helpful tips for your next wildlife adventure.

4. _____ So the next time you hear someone say dragons aren't real, tell them about the Komodo dragon—a living, breathing monster!

5. _____ Even though wild animals can be deadly, if you follow the steps I just mentioned, you can keep yourself safe in the wild.

6. _____ When you think of deadly animals, you probably think of sharks, lions, or grizzly bears; but the animal that has killed more people in history isn't one of these creatures! It's the lowly mosquito.

Directions: Now, write a paragraph about your favorite animal. Include an attention-grabbing introduction and a concluding sentence that sums up your main point.

_____

_____

_____

_____

_____

_____

GRADE
6

I. Reading
  A. Directions
  B. Sequencing
  C. Main Idea
II. Writing
  A. Capitalization
  B. Proofreading

Name _____

The School Newspaper

There are many different kinds of paragraphs. **Persuasive** paragraphs try to convince the reader; **expository** paragraphs give information about a topic and contains facts, opinions, or both; **descriptive** paragraphs describe things or events in detail.

Directions: Read each paragraph. On the lines below each one, tell what kind of paragraph it is (**persuasive**, **expository**, or **descriptive**) and its main message. The first one has been done for you.

1. Yesterday after school, the principal met with the new advisory board. This advisory board is made up of three teachers chosen by the principal, and three students chosen by the student body. The board hopes to address problems within the school and find ways for students and teachers to work together to solve them.

   Descriptive; the principal met with the advisory board to find ways for teachers and students to work together to solve problems.

2. Is it just me, or is the cafeteria food getting worse? Yesterday's special looked and tasted like cardboard. We used to have pizza all the time, but now we hardly ever have it. I think it would be great if we could have pizza more often instead of that gross cardboard stuff.

   _____

   _____

   _____

3. I plan to vote for Chris McGuinness for class president. Why? Because he's honest and hard-working. Remember how great the Fall Fiesta Dance was last week? Chris did all of the organizing. If he can do such a great job planning a dance, just think of how good he'll be as our president!

   _____

   _____

4. Chase Dribble scored the winning basket for our team with an amazing three-pointer from center court. This last-minute victory means our school will be going to the state championships next Saturday!

   _____

   _____

GRADE
6

I. Reading
    A. Directions
    B. Sequencing
    C. Main Idea
II. Writing
    A. Capitalization
    B. Proofreading

Name _____

The Art of Persuasion

A good **persuasive paragraph** contains several elements. It contains a **topic sentence** that tells the author's opinion. It contains **support sentences** that give the author's reasons for feeling this way; these sentences may include **examples** to support or prove the author's argument. Finally, it includes a strong **concluding sentence** that sums up the author's opinion.

Directions: Complete each sentence below to express your own opinion. Then, turn each one into the topic sentence for a persuasive paragraph.

1. The best thing to do when you're feeling down is _____

_____

_____

_____

_____

_____

2. The most fun day of the year is always _____

_____

_____

_____

_____

_____

GRADE
6

I. Reading
  A. Directions
  B. Sequencing
  C. Main Idea
II. Writing
  A. Capitalization
  B. Proofreading

Name _____

In a Blink

A **descriptive paragraph** contains a topic sentence telling who or what will be described. It also contains support sentences that introduce or give details about the topic, using specific examples.

Directions: Read this descriptive paragraph. Circle the topic sentence and underline the supporting sentences. If you see a sentence that does not relate to the main topic, cross it out.

Have you ever seen a firefly? The firefly is a type of beetle that is known for producing a yellowish or greenish light. All beetles have wings. The firefly produces light from a small organ on its abdomen called a *lantern*. The lantern contains special chemicals to make light. In most fireflies, the light blinks on and off; they actually use this to communicate with one another. When a male firefly blinks his light on and off, he is showing females that he is ready to mate.

Female fireflies may blink their lights to show interest in mating, but sometimes they do it to trick male fireflies. A female firefly will blink her light at a male as if she wants to mate, but the joke's on him—she eats him instead! Female black widow spiders are known for killing their male counterparts.

Directions: Now, write a descriptive paragraph of your own. Describe anything you want—your favorite food, a friend, a game you like to play. Remember to include a topic sentence and supporting sentences.

_____

_____

_____

_____

_____

_____

Name _____

Keeping It Casual

You don't need to have a topic sentence or supporting sentences in every paragraph you write. When you write a letter or a diary entry, for example, you don't need to make a point and back it up in every paragraph. However, it's a good idea to start a new paragraph whenever you start talking about something new. This warns your reader that you will be changing the subject.

Directions: Write a diary entry to tell what you did yesterday. Include any important activities you did, thoughts or feelings you had, or plans you made. Make sure to begin a new paragraph whenever you introduce something new.

Date: _____

Dear Diary, _____

_____

_____

_____

_____

_____

_____

_____

_____

_____

_____

_____

_____

_____

GRADE 6

I. Reading
  A. Directions
  B. Sequencing
  C. Main Idea
II. Writing
  A. Capitalization
  B. Proofreading

Name _____

Prompt Paragraphs

Writing prompts are comments or questions that get your imagination working. In school and on standardized tests, you will be asked to write paragraphs or short essays in response to writing prompts.

Directions: Respond to the writing prompts below by writing one paragraph to go with each. Make sure to include a topic sentence and supporting sentences in each paragraph.

1. What is your favorite genre of writing? Why?

_____
_____
_____
_____
_____
_____

2. If you could have dinner with any one of the American presidents, past or present, who would it be? Why? What would you say to him?

_____
_____
_____
_____
_____
_____

GRADE 6

I. Reading
A. Directions
B. Sequencing
C. Main Idea
II. Writing
A. Capitalization
B. Proofreading

Name _____

Building Paragraphs

Directions: Read each group of questions and the topic sentence. On another sheet of paper, write support sentences that answer each question. Number your support sentences in order. Make any necessary changes so the sentences fit together in one paragraph. Then, write your paragraph after the topic sentence.

Questions: Why did Jimmy feel sad?
What happened to change how he felt?
How does he feel when he comes to school now?

Jimmy used to look so solemn when he came to school. _____

_____

_____

_____

Questions: Why did Jennifer want to go to another country?
Why couldn't she go?
Does she have any plans to change that?

Jennifer always wanted to visit a foreign country. _____

_____

_____

_____

Questions: What was Paulo's "new way to fix spaghetti"?
Did anyone else like it?
Did Paulo like it himself?

Paulo thought of a new way to fix spaghetti. _____

_____

_____

_____

Prewriting Predicament

Prewriting is the process you go through before actually sitting down to write a story or report. There are several steps in the prewriting process.

Directions: Solve the crossword puzzle.

Across

3. First, _____ for ideas.

5. If necessary, _____ for more information.

6. Take _____ on the information you need or details you will include.

Down

1. Make an _____.

2. _____ your notes into groups that make sense.

4. Now, you're ready to write a _____ draft of your report or story!

I. Reading
A. Directions
B. Sequencing
C. Main Idea
II. Writing
A. Capitalization
B. Proofreading

Name _____

Proofreading Puzzler

Directions: Proofread the following article for capitalization, punctuation, grammar, and spelling mistakes. Use the proofreading symbols below to mark any mistakes you find.

℘ delete	# space	ℬ lowercase
∧ insert	ḇ capitalize	¶ new paragraph
(a e) transpose		

What do a Saint Bernard, a Chihuahua, and a german Shepherd have in common? That's easy—they are all dogs! But why don't all dogs look alike Most terriers are small and low to the ground. Long ago, terriers were used to hunt rats and badgers. The dogs would follow the rats and badgers into their underground homes. Terriers are good diggers there small size helps them get into tight places.

Greyhounds are racing dogs. They run very fast. a greyhound's long legs help it run? Another part of this dog's body that helps it run is its lungs. Just look at the greyhound's large chest! This dog's lungs is large and can hold a lot of air.

I. Reading
A. Directions
B. Sequencing
C. Main Idea
II. Writing
A. Capitalization
B. Proofreading

Name _____

It's in the Revision

Revising is the process of reviewing your work and making changes to improve your writing. Once you've finished the prewriting stage and written a rough draft, you should—

- reread your work and look for problems.
- correct spelling and grammar errors.
- watch out for wordy phrases.
- get rid of text that does not relate to your topic.
- make sure your writing is clear and interesting.
- ask someone else to read your first draft.
- write your final draft.

Directions: Revise the following story according to the steps shown above.

This year I had the best summer vacaton ever. My whole family went to Masachusets, where grandparents live. They live near the ocean on cape cod. While we were there we did a lot of fun stuff. My grand father taught me how to play chess, and I found out that I'm good at it. My little sister had day camp so I didn't have to watch her all day like I usually do in the summer. I took sailing lessons. My boat tipped over many times but I learned how to take the water out of the boat and get back on it. I hope I can go back to cape cod next summer!

_____

_____

_____

_____

_____

_____

_____

_____

_____

GRADE 6

I. Reading
A. Directions
B. Sequencing
C. Main Idea
II. Writing
A. Capitalization
B. Proofreading

Name _____

A Message to You

Directions: Imagine that you are entering a writing contest. You will be writing a report about the Civil Rights movement and telling why it was important. Write the steps you will take to write your report, from the very first step to writing your final draft.

1. _____

   _____

2. _____

   _____

3. _____

   _____

4. _____

   _____

5. _____

   _____

6. _____

   _____

7. _____

   _____

8. _____

   _____

9. _____

   _____

10. _____

   _____

GRADE
6

I. Reading
   A. Directions
   B. Sequencing
   C. Main Idea
II. Writing
   A. Capitalization
   B. Proofreading

Name _____

Show and Tell

There are two main kinds of descriptive writing: **narrative** writing uses imagery and figures of speech to describe someone or something. **Reports** describe someone or something with facts.

Directions: Read each item. Write **narrative** if you would be more likely to read it in a narrative. Write **report** in you would be more likely to read it in a report.

1. Jennifer stood 5'10" tall and weighed 125 pounds.   _____

2. Jennifer looks like a willowy tree blowing in the breeze.   _____

3. The kitten was a whirling little ball of fluff. With delicate white paws
   and a white chest against the rest of her black fur, she looked like
   she was wearing a tuxedo.   _____

4. The small, active kitten had fluffy fur. Her paws and chest were
   white, and the rest of her fur was black.   _____

5. The temperature was 16°F with 30 mile-per-hour winds. Snowfall
   was measured at 16 inches with drifts of four feet.   _____

6. It was the worst storm I had ever seen. The wind was howling, it
   was wicked cold, and the snow was piled high and coming down
   fast.   _____

Directions: Choose a topic that interests you. Write a paragraph about your topic in the style of a narrative or a report. Then, label your paragraph **narrative** or **report**.

_____

_____

_____

_____

_____

_____

_____

_____

_____

GRADE 6

I. Reading
  A. Directions
  B. Sequencing
  C. Main Idea
II. Writing
  A. Capitalization
  B. Proofreading

Name _____

Woof!

Directions: One way to describe something is to compare it to something else. Read the following description of two dogs named Bruiser and Happy. Then, fill in the chart below with details from the description.

Bruiser and Happy are best friends. They are very much alike in some ways and very different in other ways.

Both dogs are very friendly. They are smart, too. Training each of them was easy. Both can do all the standard dog tricks—roll over, fetch, sit, stay, and bark on command. They both love to go in the car, especially to the park. At the park, they love to chase each other around and run after sticks. Both dogs love it when we cook out. They sit and watch the grill hoping for a little sample of meat.

Bruiser and Happy do have their differences. Obviously Bruiser is huge, while Happy is tiny. When Bruiser barks, it sounds like an explosion. Happy's bark is more a *yip* than a real bark. When Bruiser runs, you can feel the earth shake. He even scares some people. Happy is too little to scare anyone. In fact, my cat even scares him. Bruiser sleeps on the floor. But Happy sleeps in my bed. Sorry, Bruiser!

How Happy and Bruiser Are Alike

_____

_____

_____

_____

_____

How Happy and Bruiser Are Different

_____

_____

_____

_____

_____

Directions: On the lines below, write your own description of two things. Be sure to explain how they are alike and how they are different.

_____

_____

_____

Creating Word Pictures

Painters create pictures with colors. Writers create pictures with words. Adding adjectives and adverbs, using specific nouns, verbs, similes, and metaphors in sentences help create word pictures.

Notice how much more interesting and informative these two rewritten sentences are.

Original sentence
The animal ate its food.

Rewritten sentences
Like a hungry lion, the starving cocker spaniel wolfed down the entire bowl of food in seconds.

The raccoon delicately washed the berries in the stream before nibbling them slowly, one by one.

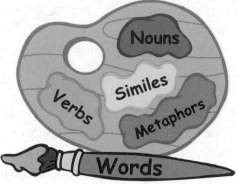

Directions: Rewrite each sentence twice, creating two different word pictures.

1. The person built something.

_____

_____

2. The weather was bad.

_____

_____

3. The boy went down the street.

_____

_____

4. The children helped.

_____

_____

GRADE

6

I. Reading
  A. Directions
  B. Sequencing
  C. Main Idea
II. Writing
  A. Capitalization
  B. Proofreading

Name _____

Describe It!

Directions: You have just been the first person on Earth to see a space alien— shown at the right. It's very important that you give the most accurate description you can to the government investigators and reporters waiting to hear every detail. Take a good look. Then, write the most accurate description you can.

_____

_____

_____

_____

_____

_____

_____

_____

_____

_____

_____

_____

_____

_____

_____

_____

_____

I. Reading
A. Directions
B. Sequencing
C. Main Idea
II. Writing
A. Capitalization
B. Proofreading

Name _____

Persuasive Writing

To **persuade** means to convince someone that your opinion is correct. "Because I said so," isn't a very convincing reason. Instead, you need to offer reasons, facts, and examples to support your opinion.

Directions: Write two reasons or facts and two examples to persuade someone.

1. Riding a bicycle "no-handed" on a busy street is a bad idea.

   Reasons/Facts: _____

   _____

   Examples: _____

   _____

   _____

2. Taking medicine prescribed by a doctor for someone else is dangerous.

   Reasons/Facts: _____

   _____

   Examples: _____

   _____

   _____

3. Learning to read well will help you in every other subject in school.

   Reasons/Facts: _____

   _____

   Examples: _____

   _____

   _____

GRADE 6

I. Reading
   A. Directions
   B. Sequencing
   C. Main Idea
II. Writing
   A. Capitalization
   B. Proofreading

Name _____

Hire Me!

Persuasive writing tries to convince the reader of something. When you write a persuasive essay, you must back up your opinions with facts.

Directions: A landscape company has advertised for a young helper to do yard work. Imagine that you are applying for the job. Read each pair of sentences, and circle the letter of the sentence that is more persuasive. Remember that in persuasive writing, you want to back up opinions with facts.

H. I am writing to apply for the job of yard work assistant because I am well qualified for it.
N. I want that job that you had in the paper.

O. I don't mind working if it's not too hot or raining.
I. I can provide references from two neighbors as to my skills and reliability.

W. I want to use those cool riding mowers.
R. I have used all kinds of lawn equipment and am eager to learn more.

E. I have been doing yard work since I was six years old.
A. I haven't done much yard work, but it doesn't look that hard.

Y. I can work mornings only, except for Tuesdays and Fridays and only if you let me know at least a week in advance.
D. I am ready to start and would be able to work any time you needed me.

Write the letters you circled to complete the following sentence.
If you wrote these sentences in a letter you would get _____.
Write the letters you didn't circle to complete the following sentence.
If you included these sentences in a letter, there is _____ you would get the job.

Directions: Look through the want ads in your local newspaper. Imagine you are an adult, and pick a job you would like to have. Jot down a few notes on the lines below. Then, on another sheet of paper, write a letter applying for the job. Include the education and experience that you might need to get the job.

_____

_____

_____

Name _____

Back It Up!

Directions: Find a fact from **Column B** to back up each opinion in **Column A**. Write the letter that goes with each choice on the line.

Column A

1. _____ Many kids think the cafeteria food stinks.

2. _____ The cafeteria is crowded.

3. _____ The cafeteria serves unhealthy food.

4. _____ Safety is not a problem.

5. _____ Sixth graders are responsible about litter.

Column B

A. The seating capacity of the cafeteria is 150 kids per lunch period, yet it is now used by 200 kids each lunch period.

B. In a poll, 82 percent of sixth graders said they hate the cafeteria food.

C. Since this school is located in the middle of town, kids can go to stores to get lunch items without having to cross busy streets.

D. In the last three months, sixth graders have participated in three large recycling and community clean-up projects.

E. In the last month, 80 percent of hot lunch items were fried and greasy.

Directions: On the lines below, write a persuasive essay about something you would like to change about your school. Be sure to back up each opinion with a fact.

_____

_____

_____

_____

_____

_____

GRADE 6

I. Reading
   A. Directions
   B. Sequencing
   C. Main Idea
II. Writing
   A. Capitalization
   B. Proofreading

Name _____

Let's Talk Business

Directions: Read the letter below. Then, write a reply as if you were Mr. Mechanic. Be sure to include all six parts of a business letter in your response: **heading**, **inside address**, **salutation**, **body**, **closing**, and **signature**.

999 Speedy Lane
Hot Dog, California 90102
February 29, 2000

Mike Mechanic, Chief Engineer
Superfast Bikes
1 Superfast Track
Boston, Massachusetts 01234

Dear Mr. Mechanic:

I am writing to tell you about what has happened to me since I ordered a Superfast Racing Bike from your company. The good news is that I have won three road races. None of my friends can keep up with me. The bad news is that I became the first kid in Massachusetts to get a speeding ticket for riding a bicycle. Imagine that! My dad had to pay $50! I'll be paying him off until Christmas.

I sure didn't like getting that ticket, but it gave me an idea. How would you like to use me and my ticket in an ad for the Superfast Line? Let me know. My agent will be happy to talk to your people about agreeable terms.

Sincerely,

Mickey Modest

_____

_____

_____

_____

_____

_____

GRADE
6

I. Reading
  A. Directions
  B. Sequencing
  C. Main Idea
II. Writing
  A. Capitalization
  B. Proofreading

Name _____

Turn the Radio On

Guglielmo Marconi made a big contribution to modern life. Here are notes about his life, placed in chronological order.

Directions: After you read the notes, answer the questions that follow.

• Guglielmo Marconi was born in 1874.

• He received private education until he entered the Livorno Technical Institute.

• Heinrich Hertz discovered and created radio waves in 1888.

• Marconi read an article written in 1894 that proposed that radio waves could replace the telegraph for sending messages.

• Marconi practiced with radio waves and could send and receive signals two miles.

• He took out a patent on his invention in 1896.

• The British navy began to use Marconi's instruments on some of its ships.

• Marconi sent a message 31 miles across the English Channel in 1899.

• In late 1901, the inventor transmitted a radio message across the Atlantic Ocean.

• In 1909, he was awarded the Nobel Prize in physics for his discoveries.

• Guglielmo Marconi died in 1937.

I. Number these pieces of information in order:

_____ private education   _____ British navy   _____ read article   _____ born

      _____ Atlantic Ocean   _____ two miles

2. Number these pieces of information in order.

_____ patent   _____ Nobel   _____ died   _____ Livorno

      _____ Heinrich   _____ English Channel

3. Write one sentence which captures the essence of this inventor's achievement.

_____

Name _____

Franklin Facts

Directions: Here are paragraphs about the life of patriot Benjamin Franklin. Underline the effect in each cause-and-effect paragraph below. Then, choose a title from the box below and write it in the blank to match the paragraph.

1. _____
Josiah Franklin was not a father blinded by his pride. When he saw that his son Ben was unhappy with the family candle-making trade, he sent him to work for an older son.

2. _____
Deborah Read was unable to marry Ben Franklin. This was due to the lack of proof that her long-missing first husband was really dead.

3. _____
Observing Boston's volunteer fire company and noting his own city's problem with fires, Franklin instituted a number of firefighting companies for Philadelphia.

4. _____
Franklin traveled far along the eastern coast of the American colonies to inspect and improve the post offices during his tenure as the colonial Postmaster General.

5. _____
Because Franky, Franklin's second son, died of smallpox at the age of four, Franklin regretted that he had not had the boy inoculated.

6. _____
While experimenting with electrical shock on a turkey, Franklin accidentally shocked himself, knocking himself unconscious for several minutes.

7. _____
Angered by the murder of twenty Indians in 1763, Franklin wrote an attack on the white frontiersman who had killed these helpless victims.

8. _____
Franklin knew that the American colonies, in their quarrels with England, were weak individually. As a result he wrote, "Gentlemen, we must now all hang together, or we shall most assuredly hang separately."

9. _____
Franklin sailed to France because the Americans desperately needed loans for their war with Great Britain.

10. _____
Franklin was puzzled that our young nation, which called for liberty and equality, practiced what he considered the abominable practice of slavery.

Titles

A Loving Father
Uncovering Murder
Improving the Mail
Fighting the Fires Together
A Lost Husband

A Parent Grieves
Finding Financial Aid
An Electric Shock
Banding Together
Liberty for All

Victorious

Directions: Read the time line to complete the story web below.

1940—Wilma Rudolph is born in Clarksville, Tennessee. She weighs four pounds. She has nineteen older brothers and sisters.

1945—At the age of five, Wilma contracts scarlet fever and polio. This leaves her with a left leg that is twisted inward. News spreads that she will never walk again.

Childhood: Although unable to walk, Wilma exercises. The nearest hospital willing to treat black people is 50 miles away. The local school will not accept her because of her disability.

Childhood: She is able to obtain a steel leg brace from the hospital. She can now go to school. Still she is unable to play with others. She exercises on her own.

Childhood: One Sunday as Wilma and her family come to church, Wilma removes her leg brace and walks without help.

1952—Wilma is able to take off her brace for the last time. Wilma and her mother mail the brace back to the hospital.

Teens: Wilma begins to play basketball. She had studied and memorized the moves of this game while watching classmates earlier.

Teens: In high school Wilma leads her team to the state championships. They lose in the finals. A college coach scouts the state final, and Wilma is given an athletic scholarship to attend the university and participate in track and field.

1960—Wilma represents the United States in the Olympic Games. She wins the gold medal in both the 100-meter and 200-meter events, despite a twisted ankle. Her 400-meter relay team also wins a gold medal.

1962—Wilma Rudolph becomes a second-grade teacher and a high school coach.

1994—Wilma Rudolph dies.

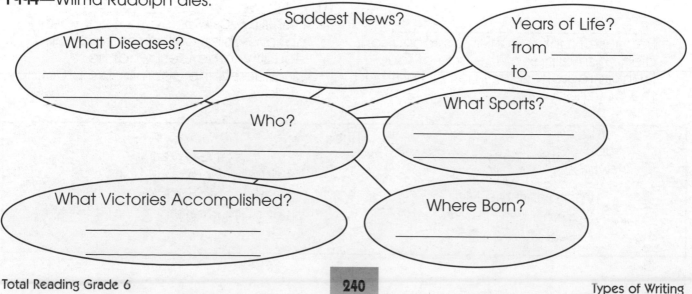

I. Reading
  A. Directions
  B. Sequencing
  C. Main Idea
II. Writing
  A. Capitalization
  B. Proofreading

Name _____

True Stories From the Sea

Directions: Here are six short descriptions of animals from under the ocean. Can you match each with a title that fits its description?

Titles: What Big Eyes You Have!   Breathe Deeply
                 Keep Out of the Light   Dill Pickle
                 The Cadillac of Fish

The anglerfish lures its prey with a part of its fin which serves as its fishing pole. This fin, located between the eyes of the anglerfish, emits a small light which glows from the very tip. When a curious shrimp checks out this light, he is promptly devoured.

_____

Few large sharks are found in deep sea water, but that is where the megamouth shark resides. It swims with its mouth wide open, feeding upon the tiny plankton that migrate through its territory. This huge fish is as long as a large automobile. Discovered in 1976, the megamouth's scientific name is translated as "giant yawner of the open sea."

_____

The kraken is a giant squid. While no healthy kraken has ever been seen or photographed, scientists believe it may grow to 57 feet in length. Squid have ten long tentacles covered with toothed suckers. These help the creature hold its prey. The kraken also possesses a hard, sharp beak for crushing its victims. This keen-sighted creature has the largest eyes of all earth's animals . . . almost 18 inches in diameter!

_____

The deep sea cucumber is not a plant! It's an animal. This creature, which can live 30,000 feet below the ocean surface, is about the size of a pickle. And it reminds some people of a bumpy-backed piglet. It gets its food by sucking or chewing mud from the ocean floor. _____

The elephant seal can hold its breath for a long time. With its huge lungs and specialized circulatory system, this mammal can remain underwater for one hour at a time. Typically it may spend 20 hours each day below the surface of the water. It dives deep to eat squid. Possibly it spends much of its time in the depths to avoid its rival, the great white shark. _____

I. Reading
A. Directions
B. Sequencing
C. Main Idea
II. Writing
A. Capitalization
B. Proofreading

Name _____

Where Do I Start?

To start a **research report**, you can use these steps.

James Madison

CONSTITUTION

1. Choose a topic area.
2. Brainstorm ideas.
3. Identify the specific topic you want to write about.
4. Identify possible reference sources.
5. Find the sources and take notes from each one.

Directions: Read about what one student did to start a research report.
Draw a line matching each sentence in **Column A** to the correct step from **Column B**.

Column A

1. I want to write a report about a famous American.

2. Let's see: presidents, entertainers, athletes, business people . . . I think I'll choose a famous president.

3. I don't know much about President James Madison. I think I'll choose him.

4. There is a good article about James Madison in my encyclopedia.

5. Madison had an important role in the writing of the U.S. Constitution before he became president.

Column B

A. Find the sources and take notes from each one.

B. Choose a topic area.

C. Identify possible reference sources.

D. Brainstorm ideas.

E. Identify the specific topic you want to write about.

Directions: Think of a topic that you would like to research and report on. Write what you would do to brainstorm and find information for your report.

_____

_____

_____

_____

_____

I. Reading
A. Directions
B. Sequencing
C. Main Idea
II. Writing
A. Capitalization
B. Proofreading

Name _____

What Do I Need To Know?

Directions: Asking the right questions is a big part of writing a successful research report. Read this paragraph about President James Madison. Which of the questions on the list can you find answers to in the paragraph? Underline those questions.

James Madison was born in Virginia in 1751 and died in 1836. As a young man he married Dolley Payne Todd. He eventually became the fourth president of the U.S., serving from 1809–1817. He was elected to serve after his good friend Thomas Jefferson, who was the third president. Madison was a congressman, secretary of state, and president, but he is most famous for his work in writing the U.S. Constitution and the Bill of Rights. He believed in political and religious freedom for all Americans.

1. When was Madison born?

2. When was Madison president?

3. What games did Madison like to play when he was a kid?

4. What school did Madison attend?

5. What did Madison do before he became president?

6. What were his greatest accomplishments?

7. Why is he considered an important American?

8. What were his favorite TV shows?

9. Who were some of his friends and political allies?

10. Why did Madison support the Bill of Rights?

Directions: Think about the research topic you picked on the previous page. On the lines below, write a list of good research questions to ask about it.

_____

_____

_____

_____

_____

_____

I. Reading
  A. Directions
  B. Sequencing
  C. Main Idea
II. Writing
  A. Capitalization
  B. Proofreading

Name _____

The Right Stuff

Directions: Circle the resource book you would use to find . . .

1. A recipe for baking homemade bread.

   encyclopedia   cookbook   *The Life of a Beaver*

2. A description of how beavers make dams.

   almanac   *The Life of a Beaver*   *The Guinness Book of World Records*

3. A map of the United Kingdom.

   thesaurus   world atlas   *The Guinness Book of World Records*

4. The ingredients for Turkish Delight.

   The Life of a Beaver   world atlas   cookbook

5. Information about the author, C. S. Lewis.

   almanac   encyclopedia   *Guidebook for Art Instructors*

6. The name of the world's most massive dam.

   The Guinness Book of World Records   dictionary   thesaurus

7. The oldest words in the English language.

   almanac   atlas   *The Guinness Book of World Records*

8. Another word for "trouble."

   thesaurus   atlas   cookbook

9. Why a beaver slaps its tail.

   dictionary   *The Life of a Beaver*   atlas

10. The pronunciation of "courtier."

   The Hobbit   dictionary   almanac

11. What camphor is used for.

   dictionary   *The Life of a Beaver*   thesaurus

GRADE 6

I. Reading
A. Directions
B. Sequencing
C. Main Idea
II. Writing
A. Capitalization
B. Proofreading

Name _____

Note This!

Directions: Mr. Dizzy is ready to teach a lesson on note-taking, but he has scrambled the index cards containing the main points of his lesson. Read the note cards. Circle the ones that belong in the lesson on note-taking.

Record supporting ideas and link them to main ideas.

Summarize main ideas.

Use abbreviations whenever possible.

Review your notes soon after taking them to fill in any missing ideas.

The idea is to take as many notes as possible.

Write down every word.

Listen for main ideas.

Make sure you can read what you are writing.

Write slowly and neatly in your very best handwriting.

Discard notes after taking them.

Directions: Find a reference book that has information on the topic you chose on page 242. Use the tips you underlined above to take notes. Write your notes on the lines below.

_____

_____

_____

_____

_____

_____

_____

GRADE
6

I. Reading
   A. Directions
   B. Sequencing
   C. Main Idea
II. Writing
   A. Capitalization
   B. Proofreading

Name _____

Vivid Visuals

Visuals such as maps, graphs, and charts can often explain something better than words can. The key is to know which visual to use to best explain your point.

Directions: Victor Visual has lots of visuals to choose from. He's just a little confused about which one to use for each topic. For each of the topics listed, write the name of the best visual to use.

1. _____ to explain how to get from school to Victor's house.

2. _____ to show Victor's height from first grade to sixth grade.

3. _____ to show which states border the Pacific Ocean.

4. _____ to show the favorite ice cream flavors of sixth graders.

5. _____ to point out the location of the Mississippi River.

6. _____ to tell the number of yucky lunches served in the cafeteria each month for 10 months.

7. _____ to tell the percentage of sixth graders that take each bus route.

8. _____ to show the route taken by Victor's school bus.

GRADE 6

I. Reading
A. Directions
B. Sequencing
C. Main Idea
II. Writing
A. Capitalization
B. Proofreading

Name _____

Internet Inquiry

The Internet is like an entire research library right inside your computer. You must know how to use the Internet properly to get the most out of what it has to offer.

Directions: Match each research subject with the Web site where you could find related information.

A. www. britannica.com (encyclopedia)
B. www. columbussymphony.org
C. www.nytimes.com
D. msn.foxsports.com
E. www.ed.gov/index.jhtml
F. www.ibm.com/us
G. www.stanford.edu
H. www.metmuseum.org
I. www.velveticecream.com
J. www.weather.com

1. _____ paintings in the Metropolitan Museum in New York City

2. _____ the box score of last night's Chicago Cubs game

3. _____ courses offered at Stanford University

4. _____ current information from the U.S. Department of Education

5. _____ latest information about IBM computers

6. _____ current flavors of Velvet Ice Cream

7. _____ information about the first Moon landing

8. _____ upcoming concerts by the Columbus Symphony Orchestra

9. _____ the weather today in Atlanta, Dallas, and Seattle

10. _____ information about yesterday's speech by the president

Directions: If you have access to the Internet, check out three of the Web sites above. On the lines below, write a sentence for each site to summarize the kind of information you found there.

_____

_____

_____

_____

Name _____

Look It Up!

A **dictionary** gives word definitions and pronunciations.
A **thesaurus** provides synonyms and antonyms for words.
An **encyclopedia** has information on most subject matter.
An **almanac** contains information about recent events.
An **atlas** has maps and population information.

Directions: To complete the crossword puzzle, figure out which reference source you would use to find the information described in each clue.

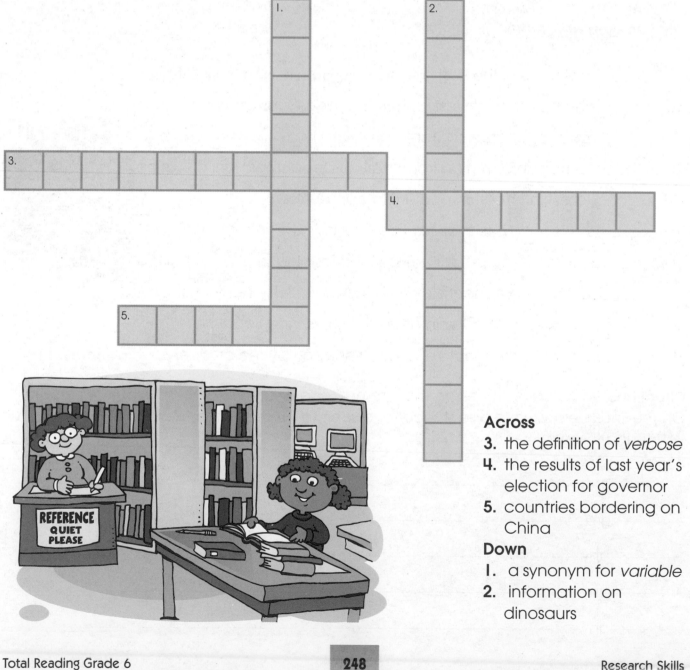

Across

3. the definition of *verbose*
4. the results of last year's election for governor
5. countries bordering on China

Down

1. a synonym for *variable*
2. information on dinosaurs

GRADE 6

I. Reading
A. Directions
B. Sequencing
C. Main Idea
II. Writing
A. Capitalization
B. Proofreading

Name _____

Chorus Program

Directions: Mr. Musichead is tired of his kids complaining about the chorus music. This year, he decided to let the kids vote on what kind of music they should perform. Look at the results of the election and enter the votes on the chart.

Of 100 fifth graders:
45 chose pop tunes
35 chose show tunes
18 chose classical pieces
2 chose hymns

Of 95 sixth graders:
40 chose pop tunes
40 chose show tunes
10 chose classical pieces
5 chose hymns

Of 105 seventh graders:
55 chose show tunes
30 chose pop tunes
20 chose classical pieces

	Pop	Show	Classical	Hymn
Fifth Grade	_____	_____	_____	_____
Sixth Grade	_____	_____	_____	_____
Seventh Grade	_____	_____	_____	_____
Total	_____	_____	_____	_____

Pie chart: Hymn (2%), Classical (16%), Pop (35%), Show (47%)

Directions: Use the chart to help you write each type of music in the correct place on the pie chart. Then, answer the questions.

1. Which grade liked pop tunes the most? _____

2. Which grade liked classical music best? _____

3. How many students voted altogether? _____

4. How many students altogether voted for show tunes? _____

5. How many more seventh graders preferred pop tunes to show tunes? _____

Name _____

Table of Contents

The **table of contents**, located in the front of books or magazines, tells a lot about what is inside.

A table of contents in a book lists the headings and page numbers for each chapter. **Chapters** are the parts into which books are divided. Also listed are chapter numbers and the sections and subsections, if any. Look at the sample table of contents below:

Table of Contents

Chapter One   Chapter Two   Chapter Three

Directions: Using the table of contents above, answer the following questions.

1. How many chapters are in this book? _____

2. What chapter contains information about things to plant? _____

3. On what page does information about fences begin? _____

4. What chapter tells you what you can use to help your garden grow better? _____

5. What page tells you how to use fertilizer? _____

6. What page tells you how far apart to plant pumpkin seeds? _____

7. What is on page 11? _____

8. What is on page 4? _____

GRADE
6

I. Reading
  A. Directions
  B. Sequencing
  C. Main Idea
II. Writing
  A. Capitalization
  B. Proofreading

Name _____

Indexes

An **index** is an alphabetical listing of names, topics, and important words and is found in the back of a book. An index lists every page on which these items appear. For example, in a book about music, dulcimer might be listed this way: Dulcimer 2, 13, 26, 38. Page numbers may also be listed like this: Guitars 18–21. That means that information about guitars begins on page 18 and continues through page 21. **Subject** is the name of the item in an index. **Sub-entry** is a smaller division of the subject. For example, "apples" would be listed under *fruit*.

Index

N
Neptune 27
NGC 5128 (galaxy) 39
Novas 32

O
Observatories. *See* El Caracol.
Orbits of planets 10
Orion rocket 43

P
Planetoids. *See* Asteroids.
Planet rings
   Jupiter 23
   Saturn 9, 25
   Uranus 26
Planets
   discovered by Greeks 7
   outside the solar system 40
   visible with the naked eye 9

   See also planet names.
Pleiades 32
Pluto 12, 27
Polaris 35, 36
Pole star. *See* Polaris.
Project Ozma 41

R
Rings. *See* Planet rings.

S
Sagittarius 37
Satellites
   Jupiter 24
   Neptune 27
   Pluto 27
   Saturn 25
   Uranus 26
   See also Galilean satellites.
Saturn 25

Directions: Answer the questions about the index from this book about the solar system.

1. On what pages is there information about Pluto?_____

2. On what pages is information about Saturn's first ring found?_____

3. What is on page 41?_____

4. Where is there information about the pole star?_____

5. What is on page 43?_____

6. On what page would you find information about planets that are visible to the eye?

_____

7. On what page would you find information about Jupiter's satellites?

_____

GRADE 6

I. Reading
   A. Directions
   B. Sequencing
   C. Main Idea
II. Writing
   A. Capitalization
   B. Proofreading

Name _____

Biographical Research

A **biography** is a written history of a person's life. Often, information for a biography can be obtained from an encyclopedia, especially if a person is famous. Of course, not everyone is listed in a main article in an encyclopedia. Use the encyclopedia's index, which is the last book in the set, to find which volume contains the information you need. Look at this listing taken from an encyclopedia index for Henry Moore, an English artist:

Moore, Henry English sculptor, 1898–1986

    main article Moore 12:106b, illus.
    references in Sculpture 15:290a, illus.

Notice that the listing includes Henry Moore's dates of birth and death and illustrations (illus.). It also includes a short description of his accomplishments: He was an English sculptor. Look below at part of the index from the *Children's Britannica* encyclopedias.

Lincoln, Abraham president of US, 1809–1865
    main article Lincoln 11:49a, illus.
    references in
        Assassination 2:64b
        Caricature, illus. 4:87
        Civil War, American 4:296a fol.
        Confederate States of America 5:113b fol.
        Democracy 6:17a
        Gettysburg, Battle of 8:144a
        Illinois 9:259b
        Thanksgiving Day 17:199a
        United States of America, history of 18:137a fol.
        Westward Movement 19:49a
Lincoln, Benjamin army officer, 1733–1810
    references in American Revolution 1:204b

Lind, Jenny Swedish singer, 1820–87 operatic soprano admired for vocal purity and control; made debut 1838 in Stockholm and sang in Paris and London, becoming known as the "Swedish Nightingale"; toured US with P.T. Barnum 1850; last concert 1883.
    references in Barnum 2:235a
Lindbergh, Anne US author and aviator, b. 1906
    references in Lindbergh 11:53a, illus.
Lindbergh, Charles Augustus US aviator, 1902–1974
    main article Lindbergh 11:53a, illus.
    references in
        Aviation, history of 2:140b, illus.
        Medals and decorations, 11:266b
        Saint Louis, 15:215b
Linde, Karl Von German engineer, 1842–1934
    references in Refrigeration 15:32b

Directions: Answer these questions from the index above.

1. Where is the main article for Abraham Lincoln? _____

2. In addition to the main article, how many other places are there references to Abraham Lincoln? _____

3. In which encyclopedia volume is there information about Anne Lindbergh?

_____

Test Practice Table of Contents

GRADE 6

I. Reading
A. Directions
B. Sequencing
C. Main Idea
II. Writing
A. Capitalization
B. Proofreading

About the Tests

What Are Standardized Achievement Tests?

Achievement tests measure what children know in particular subject areas such as reading, language arts, and mathematics. They do not measure your child's intelligence or ability to learn.

When tests are standardized, or *normed,* children's test results are compared with those of a specific group who have taken the test, usually at the same age or grade.

Standardized achievement tests measure what children around the country are learning. The test makers survey popular textbook series, as well as state curriculum frameworks and other professional sources, to determine what content is covered widely.

Because of variations in state frameworks and textbook series, as well as grade ranges on some test levels, the tests may cover some material that children have not yet learned. This is especially true if the test is offered early in the school year. However, test scores are compared to those of other children who take the test at the same time of year, so your child will not be at a disadvantage if his or her class has not covered specific material yet.

Different School Districts, Different Tests

There are many flexible options for districts when offering standardized tests. Many school districts choose not to give the full test battery, but select certain content and scoring options. For example, many schools may test only in the areas of reading and mathematics. Similarly, a state or district may use one test for certain grades and another test for other grades. These decisions are often based on

the amount of time and money a district wishes to spend on test administration. Some states choose to develop their own statewide assessment tests.

On pages 255–257 you will find information about these five widely used standardized achievement tests:

- California Achievement Tests (CAT)
- Terra Nova/CTBS
- Iowa Test of Basic Skills (ITBS)
- Stanford Achievement Test (SAT9)
- Metropolitan Achievement Test (MAT).

However, this book contains strategies and practice questions for use with a variety of tests. Even if your state does not give one of the five tests listed above, your child will benefit from doing the practice questions in this book. If you're unsure about which test your child takes, contact your local school district to find out which tests are given.

Types of Test Questions

Traditionally, standardized achievement tests have used only multiple choice questions. Today, many tests may include constructed response (short answer) and extended response (essay) questions as well.

In addition, many tests include questions that tap students' higher-order thinking skills. Instead of simple recall questions, such as identifying a date in history, questions may require students to make comparisons and contrasts or analyze results among other skills.

What the Tests Measure

These tests do not measure your child's level of intelligence, but they do show how well your child knows material that he or she has learned and that

is also covered on the tests. It's important to remember that some tests cover content that is not taught in your child's school or grade. In other instances, depending on when in the year the test is given, your child may not yet have covered the material.

If the test reports you receive show that your child needs improvement in one or more skill areas, you may want to seek help from your child's teacher and find out how you can work with your child to improve his or her skills.

California Achievement Test (CAT/5)

What Is the *California Achievement Test?*

The *California Achievement Test* is a standardized achievement test battery that is widely used with elementary through high school students.

Parts of the Test

The CAT includes tests in the following content areas:

Reading
- Word Analysis
- Vocabulary
- Comprehension

Spelling

Language Arts
- Language Mechanics
- Language Usage

Mathematics

Science

Social Studies

Your child may take some or all of these subtests if your district uses the *California Achievement Test.*

Terra Nova/CTBS (Comprehensive Tests of Basic Skills)

What Is the *Terra Nova/CTBS?*

The *Terra Nova/Comprehensive Tests of Basic Skills* is a standardized achievement test battery used in elementary through high school grades.

While many of the test questions on the *Terra Nova* are in the traditional multiple choice form, your child may take parts of the *Terra Nova* that include some open-ended questions (constructed-response items).

Parts of the Test

Your child may take some or all of the following subtests if your district uses the *Terra Nova/CTBS:*

Reading/Language Arts
Mathematics
Science
Social Studies

Supplementary tests include:
- Word Analysis
- Vocabulary
- Language Mechanics
- Spelling
- Mathematics Computation

Critical thinking skills may also be tested.

Iowa Test of Basic Skills (ITBS)

What Is the *ITBS?*

The *Iowa Test of Basic Skills* is a standardized achievement test battery used in elementary through high school grades.

Parts of the Test

Your child may take some or all of these subtests if your district uses the *ITBS*, also known as the *Iowa:*

Reading
- Vocabulary
- Reading Comprehension

Language Arts
- Spelling
- Capitalization
- Punctuation
- Usage and Expression

Math
- Concepts/Estimate
- Problems/Data Interpretation

Social Studies

Science

Sources of Information

Stanford Achievement Test (SAT9)

What Is the *Stanford Achievement Test?*

The *Stanford Achievement Test, Ninth Edition (SAT9)* is a standardized achievement test battery used in elementary through high school grades.

Note that the *Stanford Achievement Test (SAT9)* is a different test from the *SAT* used by high school students for college admissions.

While many of the test questions on the *SAT9* are in traditional multiple choice form, your child may take parts of the *SAT9* that include some open-ended questions (constructed-response items).

Parts of the Test

Your child may take some or all of these subtests if your district uses the *Stanford Achievement Test.*

Reading
- Vocabulary
- Reading Comprehension

Mathematics
- Problem Solving
- Procedures

Language Arts

Spelling

Study Skills

Listening

Critical thinking skills may also be tested.

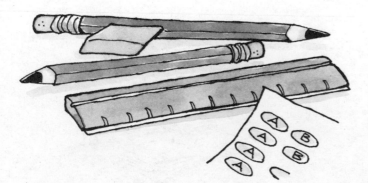

GRADE 6

I. Reading
  A. Directions
  B. Sequencing
  C. Main Idea
II. Writing
  A. Capitalization
  B. Proofreading

Metropolitan Achievement Test (MAT7 and MAT8)

What Is the *Metropolitan Achievement Test*?

The *Metropolitan Achievement Test* is a standardized achievement test battery used in elementary through high school grades.

Parts of the Test

Your child may take some or all of these subtests if your district uses the *Metropolitan Achievement Test*.

Reading
- Vocabulary
- Reading Comprehension

Math
- Concepts and Problem Solving
- Computation

Language Arts
- Pre-writing
- Composing
- Editing

Science

Social Studies

Research Skills

Thinking Skills

Spelling

Statewide Assessments

Today, the majority of states give statewide assessments. In some cases, these tests are known as *high-stakes assessments*. This means that students must score at a certain level in order to be promoted. Some states use minimum competency or proficiency tests. Often, these tests measure more basic skills than other types of statewide assessments.

Statewide assessments are generally linked to state curriculum frameworks. Frameworks provide a blueprint, or outline, to ensure that teachers are covering the same curriculum topics as other teachers in the same grade level in the state. In some states, standardized achievement tests (such as the five described in this book) are used in connection with statewide assessments.

When Statewide Assessments Are Given

Statewide assessments may not be given at every grade level. Generally, they are offered at one or more grades in elementary school, middle school, and high school. Many states test at grades 4, 8, and 10.

State-by-State Information

You can find information about statewide assessments and curriculum frameworks at your state Department of Education Web site. To find the address for your individual state go to www.ed.gov, click on Topics A–Z, and then click on State Departments of Education. You will find a list of all the state departments of education, mailing addresses, and Web sites.

How to Help Your Child
Prepare for Standardized Testing

Preparing All Year Round

Perhaps the most valuable way you can help your child prepare for standardized achievement tests is by providing enriching experiences. Keep in mind also, that test results for younger children are not as reliable as for older students. If a child is hungry, tired, or upset, this may result in a poor test score. Here are some tips on how you can help your child do his or her best on standardized tests.

Read aloud with your child. Reading aloud helps develop vocabulary and fosters a positive attitude toward reading. Reading together is one of the most effective ways you can help your child succeed in school.

Share experiences. Baking cookies together, planting a garden, or making a map of your neighborhood are examples of activities that help build skills that are measured on the tests such as sequencing and following directions.

Become informed about your state's testing procedures. Ask about or watch for announcements of meetings that explain about standardized tests and statewide assessments in your school district. Talk to your child's teacher about your child's individual performance on these state tests during a parent-teacher conference.

Help your child know what to expect. Read and discuss with your child the test-taking tips in this book. Your child can prepare by working through a couple of strategies a day so that no practice session takes too long.

Help your child with his or her regular school assignments. Set up a quiet study area for homework. Supply this area with pencils, paper, markers, a calculator, a ruler, a dictionary, scissors, glue, and so on. Check your child's homework and offer to help if he or she gets stuck. But remember, it's your child's homework, not yours. If you help too much, your child will not benefit from the activity.

Keep in regular contact with your child's teacher. Attend parent-teacher conferences, school functions, PTA or PTO meetings, and school board meetings. This will help you get to know the educators in your district and the families of your child's classmates.

Learn to use computers as an educational resource. If you do not have a computer and Internet access at home, try your local library.

Remember—simply getting your child comfortable with testing procedures and helping him or her know what to expect can improve test scores!

GRADE 6

I. Reading
   A. Directions
   B. Sequencing
   C. Main Idea
II. Writing
   A. Capitalization
   B. Proofreading

Getting Ready for the Big Day

There are lots of things you can do on or immediately before test day to improve your child's chances of testing success. What's more, these strategies will help your child prepare him- or herself for school tests, too, and promote general study skills that can last a lifetime.

Provide a good breakfast on test day.

Instead of sugar cereal, which provides immediate but not long-term energy, have your child eat a breakfast with protein or complex carbohydrates such as an egg, whole grain cereal or toast, or a banana-yogurt shake.

Promote a good night's sleep. A good night's sleep before the test is essential. Try not to overstress the importance of the test. This may cause your child to lose sleep because of anxiety. Doing some exercise after school and having a quiet evening routine will help your child sleep well the night before the test.

Assure your child that he or she is not expected to know all of the answers on the test. Explain that other children in higher grades may take the same test, and that the test may measure things your child has not yet learned in school. Help your child understand that you expect him or her to put forth a good effort—and that this is enough. Your child should not try to cram for these tests. Also avoid threats or bribes; these put undue pressure on children and may interfere with their best performance.

Keep the mood light and offer encouragement. To provide a break on test days, do something fun and special after school— take a walk around the neighborhood, play a game, read a favorite book, or prepare a special snack together. These activities keep your child's mood light—even if the testing sessions have been difficult—and show how much you appreciate your child's effort.

Taking Standardized Tests

No matter what grade you're in, this is information you can use to prepare for standardized tests. Here is what you'll find:

- Test-taking tips and strategies to use on test day and year-round.
- Important terms to know for Language Arts and Reading.
- General study/homework tips.

By opening this book, you've already taken your first step towards test success. The rest is easy—all you have to do is get started!

What You Need to Know

There are many things you can do to increase your test success. Here's a list of tips to keep in mind when you take standardized tests—and when you study for them, too.

Keep up with your school work. One way you can succeed in school and on tests is by studying and doing your homework regularly. Studies show that you remember only about one-fifth of what you memorize

the night before a test. That's one good reason not to try to learn it all at once! Keeping up with your work throughout the year will help you remember the material better. You also won't be as tired or nervous as if you try to learn everything at once.

Feel your best. One of the ways you can do your best on tests and in school is to make sure your body is ready. To do this, get a good night's sleep each night and eat a healthy breakfast (not sugary cereal that will leave you tired by the middle of the morning). An egg or a milkshake with yogurt and fresh fruit will give you lasting energy. Also, wear comfortable clothes, maybe your lucky shirt or your favorite color on test day. It can't hurt, and it may even help you relax.

Be prepared. Do practice questions and learn about how standardized tests are organized. Books like this one will help you know what to expect when you take a standardized test.

GRADE 6

I. Reading
   A. Directions
   B. Sequencing
   C. Main Idea
II. Writing
   A. Capitalization
   B. Proofreading

When you are taking the test, follow the directions. It is important to listen carefully to the directions your teacher gives and to read the written instructions carefully. Words like *not, none, rarely, never,* and *always* are very important in test directions and questions. You may want to circle words like these.

Look at each page carefully before you start answering. In school you usually read a passage and then answer questions about it. But when you take a test, it's helpful to follow a different order.

If you are taking a Reading test, first read the directions. Then read the *questions* before you read the passage. This way you will know exactly what kind of information to look for as you read. Next, read the passage carefully. Finally, answer the questions.

On math and science tests, look at the labels on graphs and charts. Think about what each graph or chart shows. Questions often will ask you to draw conclusions about the information.

Manage your time. *Time management* means using your time wisely on a test so that you can finish as much of it as possible and do your best. Look over the test or the parts that you are allowed to do at one time. Sometimes you may want to do the easier parts first. This way, if you run out of time before you finish, you will have completed a good chunk of the work.

For tests that have a time limit, notice what time it is when the test begins and figure out when you need to stop. Check a few times as you work through the test to be sure you are making good progress and not spending too much time on any particular section.

You don't have to keep up with everyone else. You may notice other students in the class finishing before you do. Don't worry about this. Everyone works at a different pace. Just keep going, trying not to spend too long on any one question.

GRADE 6

I. Reading
  A. Directions
  B. Sequencing
  C. Main Idea
II. Writing
  A. Capitalization
  B. Proofreading

Fill in answer circles properly. Even if you know every answer on a test, you won't do well unless you fill in the circle next to the correct answer.

Fill in the entire circle, but don't spend too much time making it perfect. Make your mark dark, but not so dark that it goes through the paper! And be sure you only choose one answer for each question, even if you are not sure. If you choose two answers, both will be marked as wrong.

It's usually not a good idea to change your answers. Usually your first choice is the right one. Unless you realize that you misread the question, the directions, or some facts in a passage, it's usually safer to stay with your first answer. If you are pretty sure it's wrong, of course, go ahead and change it. Make sure you completely erase the first choice and neatly fill in your new choice.

Use context clues to figure out tough questions. If you come across a word or idea you don't understand, use context clues—the words in the sentences nearby— to help you figure out its meaning.

Sometimes it's good to guess. Should you guess when you don't know an answer on a test? That depends. If your teacher has made the test, usually you will score better if you answer as many questions as possible, even if you don't really know the answers.

On standardized tests, here's what to do to score your best. For each question, most of these tests let you choose from four or five answer choices. If you decide that a couple of answers are clearly wrong but you're still not sure about the answer, go ahead and make your best guess. If you can't narrow down the choices at all, then you may be better off skipping the question. Tests like these take away extra points for wrong answers, so it's better to leave them blank. Be sure you skip over the answer space for these questions on the answer sheet, though, so you don't fill in the wrong spaces.

GRADE
6

I. Reading
  A. Directions
  B. Sequencing
  C. Main Idea
II. Writing
  A. Capitalization
  B. Proofreading

Sometimes you should skip a question and come back to it. On many tests, you will score better if you answer more questions. This means that you should not spend too much time on any single question. Sometimes it gets tricky, though, keeping track of questions you skipped on your answer sheet.

If you want to skip a question because you don't know the answer, put a very light pencil mark next to the question in the test booklet. Try to choose an answer, even if you're not sure of it. Fill in the answer lightly on the answer sheet.

Check your work. On a standardized test, you can't go ahead or skip back to another section of the test. But you may go back and review your answers on the section you just worked on if you have extra time.

First, scan your answer sheet. Make sure that you answered every question you could. Also, if you are using a bubble-type answer sheet, make sure that you filled in only one bubble for each question. Erase any extra marks on the page.

Finally—avoid test anxiety! If you get nervous about tests, don't worry. *Test anxiety* happens to lots of good students. Being a little nervous actually sharpens your mind. But if you get very nervous about tests, take a few minutes to relax the night before or the day of the test. One good way to relax is to get some exercise, even if you just have time to stretch, shake out your fingers, and wiggle your toes. If you can't move around, it helps just to take a few slow, deep breaths and picture yourself doing a great job!

GRADE 6

I. Reading
  A. Directions
  B. Sequencing
  C. Main Idea
II. Writing
  A. Capitalization
  B. Proofreading

Name _____

READING: VOCABULARY

● **Lesson 1: Synonyms**

Directions: Read each item. Choose the answer that means the same or about the same as the underlined word. Fill in the circle for the correct answer.

Examples

A. cheap gift
- (A) generous
- (B) stingy
- (C) expensive
- (D) charitable

B. A frank answer is —
- (F) short
- (G) honest
- (H) long
- (J) complicated

Clue Look carefully at all the answer choices.

● **Practice**

1. **tiresome job**
   - (A) hurried
   - (B) slow
   - (C) tedious
   - (D) dim

2. **arrogant man**
   - (F) heavy
   - (G) proud
   - (H) cunning
   - (J) humble

3. **surly individual**
   - (A) wild
   - (B) anxious
   - (C) gruff
   - (D) calm

4. **agile body**
   - (F) clumsy
   - (G) heavy
   - (H) nimble
   - (J) thin

5. **To be in the midst is to be in the —**
   - (A) center
   - (B) dark
   - (C) crowd
   - (D) outskirts

6. **A person in peril is in —**
   - (F) clothing
   - (G) safety
   - (H) luck
   - (J) danger

7. **To thrive is to —**
   - (A) withdraw
   - (B) wither
   - (C) prosper
   - (D) participate

8. **An ally is a —**
   - (F) metal
   - (G) friend
   - (H) neighbor
   - (J) enemy

STOP

Name _____

READING: VOCABULARY

● **Lesson 2: Vocabulary Skills**

Directions: Read each item. Choose the answer that means the same or about the same as the underlined word. Fill in the circle for the correct answer.

Examples

A. A <u>diminutive</u> woman
- (A) tiny
- (B) industrious
- (C) slow
- (D) energetic

B. It was an <u>ambush</u>. <u>Ambush</u> means —
- (F) a courageous fight
- (G) a surprise attack
- (H) a change in plans
- (J) a flowering plant

Clue If a question is too difficult, skip it and come back to it later.

● **Practice**

1. <u>Prolong</u> the agony
- (A) stretch
- (B) shorten
- (C) stop
- (D) postpone

2. <u>Scour</u> the tub
- (F) preserve
- (G) fill
- (H) scrub
- (J) lug

3. <u>Unruly</u> behavior
- (A) ridiculous
- (B) obedient
- (C) calm
- (D) willful

4. <u>Concealed</u> the evidence
- (F) avoided
- (G) revealed
- (H) hid
- (J) examined

5. Her <u>bias</u> was plain to see. <u>Bias</u> means —
- (A) point of view
- (B) loss
- (C) wisdom
- (D) slip

6. The boy had a <u>hunch</u>. A <u>hunch</u> is a —
- (F) feeling
- (G) bad attitude
- (H) hump
- (J) cramp

7. The professor <u>rambled</u>. <u>Rambled</u> means —
- (A) to get lost
- (B) babbled
- (C) argued
- (D) stopped

8. The twins <u>mustered</u> their courage. <u>Mustered</u> means —
- (F) lost
- (G) faked
- (H) proclaimed
- (J) gathered

STOP

Name _____

READING: VOCABULARY

● **Lesson 3: Antonyms**

Directions: Read each item. Choose the word that means the opposite of the underlined word. Fill in the circle for the correct answer.

Examples

A. willing to leave
- Ⓐ able
- Ⓑ eager
- Ⓒ reluctant
- Ⓓ allowed

B. simple room
- Ⓕ ornate
- Ⓖ empty
- Ⓗ full
- Ⓙ unusual

Clue If you are not sure which answer is correct, take your best guess. Eliminate answers that mean the same thing as the underlined word.

● **Practice**

1. **dissimilar answers**
- Ⓐ identical
- Ⓑ strange
- Ⓒ unusual
- Ⓓ unlike

2. **The play commenced.**
- Ⓕ concluded
- Ⓖ began
- Ⓗ continued
- Ⓙ failed

3. **benign host**
- Ⓐ kind
- Ⓑ spiteful
- Ⓒ young
- Ⓓ gracious

4. **opened gingerly**
- Ⓕ carefully
- Ⓖ carelessly
- Ⓗ swiftly
- Ⓙ gradually

5. **absurd situation**
- Ⓐ ridiculous
- Ⓑ horrible
- Ⓒ funny
- Ⓓ sensible

6. **hoist the sails**
- Ⓕ lift
- Ⓖ lower
- Ⓗ display
- Ⓙ mend

7. **vacant room**
- Ⓐ clean
- Ⓑ ancient
- Ⓒ empty
- Ⓓ inhabited

8. **motivated worker**
- Ⓕ energized
- Ⓖ uninspired
- Ⓗ roused
- Ⓙ new

STOP

GRADE 6

I. Reading
  A. Directions
  B. Sequencing
  C. Main Idea
II. Writing
  A. Capitalization
  B. Proofreading

Name _____

READING: VOCABULARY

● Lesson 4: Multi-Meaning Words

Directions: Read the directions carefully. For items A, 1, and 2, choose the correct answer. For items B, 3, and 4, choose the word that fits in both sentences.

Examples

A. Because of her fever, she felt faint. In which sentence does the word faint mean the same thing as in the sentence above?

- (A) Her dress was a faint pink.
- (B) When he saw the blood, he felt faint.
- (C) The writing on the yellowing paper was very faint.
- (D) Her voice was so faint I could barely hear it.

B. Did someone _____ the cookies?

Leather is the _____ of an animal.

- (F) eat
- (G) hide
- (H) skin
- (J) bake

Clue Use the meaning of the sentences to find the right answer. Check your answer again before you fill in the circle.

● Practice

1. Will you brush my hair? In which sentence does the word brush mean the same thing as in the sentence above?

- (A) She bought a new brush.
- (B) After the storm, the yard was littered with brush.
- (C) I need to brush the dog.
- (D) She felt the kitten brush against her leg.

2. He plans to store the corn in his barn. In which sentence does the word store mean the same thing as in the sentence above?

- (F) She went to the grocery store.
- (G) My dad will store the lawn mower in the shed.
- (H) The owner will store his shelves with merchandise.
- (J) My favorite store is in the mall.

3. The _____ piece goes here. The first _____ of the tournament is over.

- (A) square
- (B) part
- (C) round
- (D) circular

4. The second _____ of our encyclopedia set is missing. Please turn down the _____ on your stereo.

- (F) sound
- (G) volume
- (H) book
- (J) dial

STOP

GRADE 6

I. Reading
  A. Directions
  B. Sequencing
  C. Main Idea
II. Writing
  A. Capitalization
  B. Proofreading

Name _____

READING: VOCABULARY

● Lesson 5: Words in Context

Directions: Read the paragraph. Find the word that fits best in each numbered blank. Fill in the circle for the correct answer.

Examples

Ashley was _____ **(A)** when she won the honor of representing her school in the spelling bee. This annual event gave students the opportunity to represent their schools in a statewide competition. Ashley could hardly wait. The winner would be _____ **(B)** the state champion.

A.
- Ⓐ disappointed
- Ⓑ indifferent
- Ⓒ bothered
- Ⓓ delighted

B.
- Ⓕ declared
- Ⓖ invited
- Ⓗ justified
- Ⓙ deceived

Clue If you aren't sure which answer is correct, substitute each answer in the blank.

● Practice

People who travel or cross the Amazon and Orinoco Rivers of South America are careful never to _____ **(1)** a foot or hand from the side of their boat. For just below the surface of these mighty waters _____ **(2)** a small fish feared throughout the _____ **(3)**. That fish is the flesh-eating piranha. It has a nasty _____ **(4)** and an even nastier _____ **(5)**. Although smaller fish make up most of its diet, the piranha will _____ **(6)** both humans and other animals.

1.
- Ⓐ lift
- Ⓑ dangle
- Ⓒ withdraw
- Ⓓ brush

2.
- Ⓕ lurks
- Ⓖ nests
- Ⓗ plays
- Ⓙ boasts

3.
- Ⓐ universe
- Ⓑ town
- Ⓒ continent
- Ⓓ village

4.
- Ⓕ habit
- Ⓖ friend
- Ⓗ flavor
- Ⓙ disposition

5.
- Ⓐ smile
- Ⓑ brother
- Ⓒ appetite
- Ⓓ memory

6.
- Ⓕ befriend
- Ⓖ bully
- Ⓗ attack
- Ⓙ analyze

STOP

GRADE 6

I. Reading
   A. Directions
   B. Sequencing
   C. Main Idea
II. Writing
   A. Capitalization
   B. Proofreading

Name _____

READING: VOCABULARY

● Lesson 6: Word Study

Directions: Read each question. Fill in the circle for the correct answer.

Examples

A. Which of these words probably comes from the Spanish word *chaparro* meaning "evergreen oak"?

- (A) chapel
- (B) chaparral
- (C) chaplain
- (D) chapter

B. Golden retrievers _____ children well.

Which of these words would indicate that golden retrievers get along well with children?

- (F) reject
- (G) tolerate
- (H) display
- (J) manipulate

Clue Stay with your first answer. It is more often right than it is wrong.

● Practice

1. Eggs are to omelet as bread is to _____.
   - (A) lunch
   - (B) sandwich
   - (C) wheat
   - (D) cheese

2. Which of these words probably comes from the Greek *gumnastes* meaning "athletic trainer"?
   - (F) gumption
   - (G) gymnast
   - (H) gumshoe
   - (J) gusto

3. Carlos did not want to _____.
   Which word means "to interfere"?
   - (A) interval
   - (B) insult
   - (C) intrude
   - (D) surpass

4. The sailors _____ their water supplies.

   Which word means the sailors "refilled" their water supplies?
   - (F) detected
   - (G) allocated
   - (H) participated
   - (J) replenished

For numbers 5 and 6, choose the answer that best defines the underlined part.

5. **primer**   **primeval**
   - (A) elementary
   - (B) original
   - (C) first
   - (D) former

6. **courier**   **courser**
   - (F) running
   - (G) ruling
   - (H) coursing
   - (J) turning

STOP

I. Reading
   A. Directions
   B. Sequencing
   C. Main Idea
II. Writing
   A. Capitalization
   B. Proofreading

Name _____

READING: VOCABULARY
SAMPLE TEST

● **Directions:** For items E1 and 1–8, choose the word or words that mean the same or almost the same as the underlined word. For item E2, fill in the circle for the correct answer.

Examples

E1. <u>possessed</u> information

- (A) questioned
- (B) discovered
- (C) had
- (D) lost

E2. Which of these words probably comes from the Greek word *horama* meaning "sight."

- (F) orangutan
- (G) panorama
- (H) amazing
- (J) amass

---

1. important <u>data</u>
   - (A) computer
   - (B) meeting
   - (C) information
   - (D) announcement

2. <u>promptly</u> returned
   - (F) quickly
   - (G) quietly
   - (H) hesitantly
   - (J) gallantly

3. <u>emphatic</u> reply
   - (A) humorous
   - (B) forceful
   - (C) emotional
   - (D) weak

4. huge <u>commotion</u>
   - (F) noise
   - (G) concert
   - (H) disturbance
   - (J) crowd

5. To <u>urge</u> someone is to —
   - (A) encourage
   - (B) discourage
   - (C) invite
   - (D) conceal

6. To <u>crouch</u> is to —
   - (F) crawl
   - (G) jump up
   - (H) stoop
   - (J) shrink

7. <u>Gnarled</u> means —
   - (A) grumpy
   - (B) knotted
   - (C) lifelike
   - (D) smooth

8. If someone is <u>bewildered</u>, he is —
   - (F) enchanted
   - (G) enlightened
   - (H) confused
   - (J) correct

GO ON

Name _____

READING: VOCABULARY
SAMPLE TEST (cont.)

9. Her description was <u>precise</u>.

   To be <u>precise</u> is to be —

   (A) specific

   (B) inaccurate

   (C) imaginative

   (D) peculiar

10. Heather was <u>chagrined</u>.

    To be <u>chagrined</u> is to be —

    (F) happy

    (G) embarrassed

    (H) angry

    (J) enthusiastic

11. The brothers had to <u>fend</u> for themselves.

    To <u>fend</u> is to —

    (A) manage

    (B) discover

    (C) shop

    (D) reply

12. She had an airtight <u>alibi</u>.

    <u>Alibi</u> means —

    (F) raft

    (G) excuse

    (H) opinion

    (J) claim

13. It was a clever <u>device</u>.

    <u>Device</u> means —

    (A) gadget

    (B) announcement

    (C) trap

    (D) development

For numbers 14–19, choose the word that means the opposite of the underlined word.

14. a ship <u>adrift</u>

    (F) sinking

    (G) floating

    (H) anchored

    (J) lost

15. <u>rouse</u> someone

    (A) awaken

    (B) anger

    (C) soothe

    (D) enliven

16. good <u>chum</u>

    (F) quality

    (G) deed

    (H) friend

    (J) stranger

17. <u>acute</u> pain

    (A) intense

    (B) sharp

    (C) intermittent

    (D) dull

18. eat with <u>relish</u>

    (F) enjoyment

    (G) disgust

    (H) zest

    (J) pleasure

19. <u>outlandish</u> clothing

    (A) outrageous

    (B) peculiar

    (C) ordinary

    (D) ridiculous

GO ON

I. Reading
A. Directions
B. Sequencing
C. Main Idea
II. Writing
A. Capitalization
B. Proofreading

Name _____

READING: VOCABULARY
SAMPLE TEST (cont.)

For numbers 20–23, choose the word that correctly completes both sentences.

20. Please hand me a _____.
She needed a _____ transplant.

- (F) kidney
- (G) hand
- (H) tissue
- (J) hammer

21. That was _____.
There were an _____ number of players.

- (A) strange
- (B) odd
- (C) quick
- (D) outside

22. The stars _____ at night.
You _____ to be ill.

- (F) seem
- (G) pretend
- (H) appear
- (J) shine

23. What's all that _____?
He hit the ball with his _____.

- (A) noise
- (B) bat
- (C) commotion
- (D) racket

24. I don't recognize your accent.
In which sentence does the word accent mean the same thing as in the sentence above?

- (F) Place the accent above the second syllable.
- (G) You forgot to include the accent mark.
- (H) She has a southern accent.
- (J) There is an accent on reading programs.

25. The directions were very complex.
In which sentence does the word complex mean the same thing as in the sentence above?

- (A) Alicia had a spider complex.
- (B) This map is too complex for me.
- (C) What's a complex carbohydrate?
- (D) They lived in an apartment complex.

For numbers 26 and 27, choose the answer that best defines the underlined part.

26. manual   manuscript

- (F) hand
- (G) write
- (H) dictate
- (J) instead of

27. mistreat   mispronounce

- (A) almost
- (B) badly
- (C) not
- (D) opposite of

GO ON

Name _____

READING: VOCABULARY
SAMPLE TEST (cont.)

28. **Which of these words probably comes from the Old French word *aaisier* meaning "to put at ease"?**

    F. simple
    G. easy
    H. aisle
    J. alas

29. **Which of these words probably comes from the Latin word *ferox* meaning "fierce"?**

    A. ferret
    B. ferment
    C. ferocious
    D. fervor

30. **The design was very _____.**
    Which of these words means "elaborate"?

    F. intrepid
    G. serviceable
    H. intricate
    J. exclusive

31. **They gave _____ to the officer.**
    Which of these words means "to give honor to" the officer?

    A. homage
    B. flourish
    C. ballast
    D. image

Read the paragraph. Choose the word below the paragraph that fits best in each numbered blank.

Laughter is good medicine. Scientists believe that laughter _____ (32) the heart and lungs. Laughter burns calories and may help _____ (33) blood pressure. It also _____ (34) stress and tension. If you are _____ (35) about an upcoming test, laughter can help you relax.

32. F. heals
    G. stresses
    H. weakens
    J. strengthens

33. A. raise
    B. lower
    C. eliminate
    D. elongate

34. F. relieves
    G. increases
    H. revives
    J. releases

35. A. excited
    B. enthusiastic
    C. nervous
    D. knowledgeable

STOP

Name _____

READING: COMPREHENSION

● Lesson 7: Main Idea

Directions: Read the passage. Choose the best answer to each question. Fill in the circle for the answer of your choice.

Example

The experts are not always right. They advised the big mining companies to pass up the Cripple Creek region. They claimed that no gold could be found there. It was left up to local prospectors to uncover the incredible wealth of Cripple Creek. More than $400 million worth of ore was found in this area that experts ignored.

A. **What is the paragraph mainly about?**

Ⓐ what experts thought about Cripple Creek

Ⓑ when gold was found at Cripple Creek

Ⓒ how much the ore was worth

Ⓓ how big mining companies operate

Clue If a question sounds confusing, try to restate it in simpler terms. Be sure you understand the question before you choose an answer.

● Practice

The practice of wearing rings is a very ancient one. Throughout history, people in many lands have decorated their bodies by wearing rings on their fingers, ears, lips, necks, noses, ankles, and wrists. In some cultures, a married woman wore a ring on the big toe of her left foot; a man might have put rings on his second and third toes. Today, the practice of wearing rings in some cases includes multiple facial rings, as well as rings in many other areas of the body.

1. **What is the paragraph mainly about?**

Ⓐ why some people wore rings on their toes

Ⓑ what kinds of rings were the most popular

Ⓒ when the practice of wearing rings began

Ⓓ how people throughout history have worn rings

2. **Which title best summarizes this passage?**

Ⓕ Rings Worn Today

Ⓖ Rings Throughout the Ages

Ⓗ Rings in Unusual Places

Ⓙ Rings Are Fun

STOP

READING: COMPREHENSION
● **Lesson 8: Recalling Details**

Directions: Read the passage. Choose the best answer to each question. Fill in the circle for the answer of your choice.

Example

The frankfurter, named for the city of Frankfurt, Germany, is easily the most popular sausage in the world. Frankfurters, popularly known as "hot dogs," are sold almost everywhere in the United States. They are consumed in great quantities at sporting events and amusement parks. People from other countries often associate hot dogs with the American way of life.

A. **Where are huge numbers of hot dogs eaten?**

   Ⓐ in Frankfurt, Germany
   Ⓑ in other countries
   Ⓒ at sporting events
   Ⓓ in stores

Clue Look for key words in the question, and then find the same or similar words in the passage. This will help you locate the correct answer.

● **Practice**

Around the year 370 B.C., the Greek philosopher Plato wrote about a huge continent that once existed in the Atlantic Ocean. Plato called the continent Atlantis and stated that it was approximately the size of Europe. Atlantis was supposedly the home of a mighty nation with powerful armies that had subdued parts of Europe and North Africa.

Plato's account of Atlantis came from his research of the records of an earlier Athenian ruler named Solon. Solon was supposed to have visited Egypt several hundred years before, and it was there that he heard about Atlantis.

Atlantis was said to have beautiful cities with advanced technologies. The climate was so ideal that two growing seasons were possible. The land teemed with herbs, fruits, and other plants and was the habitat of many animals. Life was good until,

according to Plato, the citizens of Atlantis became greedy and incurred the wrath of the gods. Then, great earthquakes and floods that continued nonstop for a day and night caused the continent to sink into the ocean.

1. **Who was Plato?**

   Ⓐ a citizen of Atlantis
   Ⓑ a philosopher
   Ⓒ a ruler
   Ⓓ a warrior

2. **Where did Plato believe the continent of Atlantis was located?**

   Ⓕ near Egypt
   Ⓖ in the Pacific Ocean
   Ⓗ in the Atlantic Ocean
   Ⓙ in the North Sea

STOP

Name _____

READING: COMPREHENSION

● **Lesson 9: Drawing Conclusions**

Directions: Read the passage. Choose the best answer to each question. Fill in the circle for the answer of your choice.

Example

English women once thought they looked best with wigs that rose two or even three feet above their heads. It certainly made them look taller. Wool, cotton, and goats' hair were used to give the hairpieces the desired height. The finest high-piled wigs were often decorated with imitation fruit, model ships, horses, and figurines.

A. **From the story you cannot tell —**

- (A) the color of the wigs
- (B) the height of the wigs
- (C) what the wigs were made of
- (D) how wigs were decorated

Clue

Skim the passage so you have an understanding of what it is about. Then, skim the questions. Answer the easiest questions first, then look back at the passage to find the answers.

● Practice

I'll admit the list is long. I broke Mom's favorite blue vase playing baseball in the house. It was a home run, but that didn't count much with Mom. I broke the back window. I didn't think I could break a window by shoving my hip against a door. It must have been bad glass. I ruined the living room carpet by leaving a red spot the size of a basketball. I know the rule—no drinking in the living room—but I wasn't really drinking. I didn't even get a sip before I dropped the glass.

I guess "Trouble" is my middle name. At least that's what Mom says. So you won't be surprised when I tell you I'm in trouble once again.

1. What is the main problem in the story?

- (A) The narrator drinks red pop in the living room.
- (B) The narrator breaks and destroys things.
- (C) The narrator disobeys the rules.
- (D) The narrator is in trouble again.

2. What do you think happens next in the story?

- (F) The narrator gets a paper route to pay for all the damages.
- (G) The narrator apologizes for ruining the carpet.
- (H) The narrator tells about the latest trouble he caused.
- (J) The narrator asks for a new middle name.

GO ON

GRADE
6

I. Reading
  A. Directions
  B. Sequencing
  C. Main Idea
II. Writing
  A. Capitalization
  B. Proofreading

Name _____

READING: COMPREHENSION
● **Lesson 9: Drawing Conclusions (cont.)**

Directions: Read the passage. Choose the best answer to each question. Fill in the circle for the answer of your choice.

Example

By actually fishing for and catching other fish, the anglerfish grows to be almost four feet long. It lies quietly in mud at the bottom of the water. Three worm-like "fingers" on the top of its head attract other fish. When the fish come close, the anglerfish gets its meal. If fishing is slow, the anglerfish may rise to the surface and swallow ducks, loons, or even geese.

B. **From this passage, what can you conclude about anglerfish?**
  (F) Anglerfish prefer fish to other animals.
  (G) They have worms growing out of their heads.
  (H) Birds often eat anglerfish.
  (J) They always remain at the bottom of the water.

Skip crossed only one set of fingers when he made a wish. He avoided black cats and never stepped on cracks in the sidewalk. He thought he was a perfect candidate to win something, anything.

Skip knew that winning took more than avoiding cracks and black cats. That's why he tried out for the track team. Skip wanted to hear the words, "You are the winner!" He imagined hearing his name announced over the loud speaker. However, Skip didn't work very hard at practice and didn't make the team.

Skip spent his free time kicking stones down the street. He pretended he was an NFL kicker in a championship game. The score was always 0–0, and his kick would cinch the title. In his imagination, he always scored.

Skip believed he would be a football star when he grew up. He decided it didn't matter that he hadn't made the track team. He would play football when he got to high school. He was such a great kicker; he would easily make the team. He might even

play in college, he thought. He really wanted to be a winner.

3. **Which sentence best summarizes this story?**
  (A) Skip was very superstitious.
  (B) Skip really wanted to be a winner.
  (C) Skip had a vivid imagination.
  (D) Track was not the right sport for Skip.

4. **Which sentence best describes what Skip will need to do to be a winner?**
  (F) Skip will need to stop being so superstitious.
  (G) Skip will need to work hard to succeed.
  (H) Skip will need to find someone to coach him.
  (J) Skip will need to stop kicking stones.

Name _____

READING: COMPREHENSION

● **Lesson 10: Fact and Opinion/Cause and Effect**

Directions: Read the passage. Choose the best answer to each question. Fill in the circle for the answer of your choice.

Example

The shellfish shrimp is a popular food. Shrimp are found in both fresh and salt water. Most shrimp have five pairs of thin front legs and five pairs of back legs. The front legs are used for walking and the back legs for swimming. Unlike most animals, if a shrimp damages or loses a leg, it can grow a new one.

A. Which sentence below is an opinion, not a fact?

- Ⓐ Shrimp can grow new legs.
- Ⓑ Shrimp live in fresh and salt water.
- Ⓒ Shrimp prefer to walk, not swim.
- Ⓓ Shrimp have five pairs of front legs.

 **Clue** Skim the passage for facts. Remember: Facts can be proven.

● **Practice**

Jessica and Suzanne were friends and neighbors. They loved to solve mysteries so much that they began their own club, the Mystery Solvers Club.

One Saturday afternoon, the day of their weekly meeting, Suzanne went to her room at 2:00 to get her journal. It was missing! The journal contained all the information and all the notes from each of the club's meetings and cases. Suzanne ran to the meeting place in Jessica's backyard. Suzanne exclaimed, "My journal is missing! You must help me find it."

The club members were concerned. They needed the club notes to solve a mystery from the week before. Jessica said, "Tell us all you know."

Suzanne replied, "I keep the journal in the drawer of my bedside table. Last night I was writing in it while I ate a sandwich. I don't remember much else except that I was very tired. I didn't think about my journal again until just now. It wasn't in my drawer where I keep it."

1. Which sentence below is not a fact?

- Ⓐ The club met on Saturday.
- Ⓑ Jessica and Suzanne were friends.
- Ⓒ Suzanne went to her room at 2:00 to get the journal.
- Ⓓ Someone took Suzanne's journal.

2. Because Suzanne has lost her journal, what will the club members probably do next?

- Ⓕ The club will buy a new journal.
- Ⓖ They will search for the missing journal.
- Ⓗ They will move on to the next mystery.
- Ⓙ Suzanne and Jessica will no longer be friends.

I. Reading
  A. Directions
  B. Sequencing
  C. Main Idea
II. Writing
  A. Capitalization
  B. Proofreading

Name _____

READING: COMPREHENSION

● Lesson 11: Story Elements

Directions: Read the passage. Choose the best answer to each question. Fill in the circle for the answer of your choice.

Example

The space taxi's engine hummed. Nathan's teeth chattered. Little wells of moisture beaded up on his forehead and palms. *I can't fly*, he thought. *Mars is just around the corner, but it's still too far to be stuck in this taxi.* Nathan knew that his uncle was waiting for him, waiting for help with his hydroponic farm. At first, that didn't matter. In his mind, Nathan saw himself leaping out of his seat and bolting toward the door. But then he thought of his uncle. Nathan knew that if he did not help his uncle, the crops he had

worked so hard to nurture and grow would not be ready for the Mars 3 season. He took a deep breath and settled back for the remainder of the flight. He couldn't wait to see the look on his uncle's face when he stepped off the taxi.

A. **What is the setting of this story?**
- Ⓐ Earth
- Ⓑ a space farm
- Ⓒ a space taxi
- Ⓓ unknown

 Read the passage quickly for clues to the setting and problem.

● Practice

"What do you wanna play?" Will asked as he shoved a bite of pancake into his mouth.

"Scramble. We are Scramble maniacs at this house," said Scott.

Will poured more orange juice into his glass. "How about that game where you ask dumb questions about stuff everyone always forgets?"

"Trivial Questions," said Scott.

"Yeah, that's it."

"Can you name the seven dwarfs?" asked Eric.

"Snoopy, Sneezy, Dopey," said Scott.

"Nah, Snoopy's a dog," said Eric.

"Let's do something else," Will chimed in as he cut his pancake in half.

"Let's play Scramble," said Scott.

"That's too much like school. Let's play football," said Eric.

"It's too cold out," said Scott.

"Let's dig out your connector sets. I haven't

played with those for years," Eric said as he pushed his chair back and stood.

"Yeah," said Scott and Will as they jumped from their seats.

1. **What is the setting for this story?**
- Ⓐ Scott's bedroom
- Ⓑ Scott's living room
- Ⓒ Scott's kitchen
- Ⓓ Scott's basement

2. **What is the problem in this story?**
- Ⓕ The boys cannot remember the names of the seven dwarfs.
- Ⓖ The boys cannot decide what they want to do.
- Ⓗ The boys do not want to play Scramble.
- Ⓙ It's too cold to play football.

I. Reading
   A. Directions
   B. Sequencing
   C. Main Idea
II. Writing
   A. Capitalization
   B. Proofreading

Name _____

READING: COMPREHENSION

● Lesson 12: Fiction

Directions: Read the passage. Choose the best answer to each question. Fill in the circle for the answer of your choice.

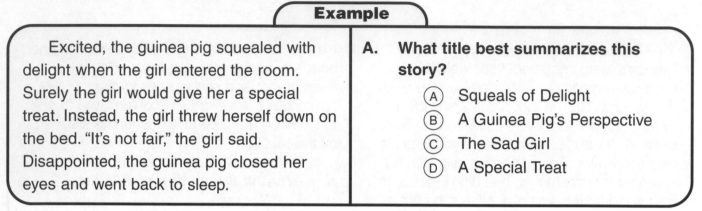

Example

Excited, the guinea pig squealed with delight when the girl entered the room. Surely the girl would give her a special treat. Instead, the girl threw herself down on the bed. "It's not fair," the girl said. Disappointed, the guinea pig closed her eyes and went back to sleep.

A. What title best summarizes this story?

- (A) Squeals of Delight
- (B) A Guinea Pig's Perspective
- (C) The Sad Girl
- (D) A Special Treat

Clue Skim the passage so you have an understanding of what it is about. Then, skim the questions. Answer the easiest questions first, and then look back to the passage to find the answers.

● Practice

"You said there was a river near here. Why don't we go swimming?" suggested Mara, wiping the sweat off her brow.

"Oh, you wouldn't want to swim in that river!" said Eva.

"Why not?" Mara asked. "I'm a strong swimmer. Even if the river's deep or the current's fast, it won't bother me."

"It's not that the river is deep or fast," said Eva. "If you like swimming with tires, broken bottles, and rusty cans, you can swim there."

"Well," said Mara, "I don't think I want to swim that badly. Unless—isn't there a public pool in town?"

1. Why did Mara probably want to go swimming?

- (A) It was a warm day.
- (B) Mara felt daring.
- (C) The girls were bored.
- (D) It was raining out.

2. What will the girls most likely do next?

- (F) visit a friend
- (G) go swimming in a pool
- (H) swim in the river
- (J) go back to Eva's house

STOP

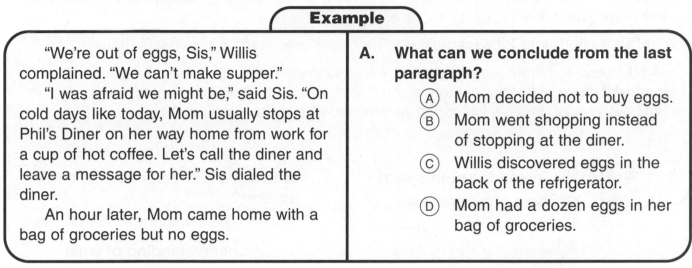

READING: COMPREHENSION

● **Lesson 13: Fiction**

Directions: Read the passage. Choose the best answer to each question. Fill in the circle for the answer of your choice.

Example

"We're out of eggs, Sis," Willis complained. "We can't make supper."

"I was afraid we might be," said Sis. "On cold days like today, Mom usually stops at Phil's Diner on her way home from work for a cup of hot coffee. Let's call the diner and leave a message for her." Sis dialed the diner.

An hour later, Mom came home with a bag of groceries but no eggs.

A. **What can we conclude from the last paragraph?**
- Ⓐ Mom decided not to buy eggs.
- Ⓑ Mom went shopping instead of stopping at the diner.
- Ⓒ Willis discovered eggs in the back of the refrigerator.
- Ⓓ Mom had a dozen eggs in her bag of groceries.

Skim the passage so you have an understanding of what it is about. Then, skim the questions. Answer the easiest questions first, and then look back to the passage to find the answers.

● **Practice**

The Special Gift

T.J. was poised to take a bite of his birthday cake when his mother said, "Not so fast, Mister. I think you have one more present coming."

"Really? What is it?" T.J. asked.

His father rose from his seat and walked around to T.J.'s chair. "Son, I have been waiting for this day to give you a very special gift. My father gave it to me when I was about your age, and it has been one of my most valued possessions. Now I want to give it to you." He then placed an old, dusty shoebox tied with string in front of T.J.

"This is my stamp collection, Son," his father began. "Your grandfather and I worked on it together. Now I want you to have it. I'll teach you about the different stamps and how to preserve them. We can go to the post office tomorrow after school, and you can pick out one of the new stamp sets to add to your collection."

T.J. tried to be excited about his gift, but he didn't understand what was so great about a box of old stamps. "Thanks, Dad," he said with a forced smile.

GO ON

READING: COMPREHENSION
● Lesson 13: Fiction (cont.)

Then, he noticed that Felicia had taken the box and was looking in each of the envelopes inside. "Look at this one!" she exclaimed. "It's from the year I was born. Hey, T.J., here's one from the year you were born, too!"

"That's right," said T.J.'s grandfather. "There are even stamps from my birthday!"

T.J. began to understand why the box was so important to his father and grandfather. He moved close to Felicia so that he could see the stamps better. Twenty minutes later, he didn't even notice that his ice cream was melted all over his cake.

1. **What is the main idea of this story?**
   - (A) Good manners are best.
   - (B) T.J. received a very special gift.
   - (C) Stamps are valuable.
   - (D) It's the thought that counts.

2. **When Felicia discovers the stamps from the years she and T.J. were born, what does T.J. begin to understand?**
   - (F) He and Felicia are about the same age.
   - (G) Some of the stamps are older than he is.
   - (H) The stamps are very meaningful.
   - (J) He was born after the collection was begun.

3. **Why didn't T.J. notice that his ice cream was melting?**
   - (A) He was no longer hungry.
   - (B) He was interested in the stamps.
   - (C) He did not like chocolate ice cream.
   - (D) He had already left the table.

4. **Which of these sentences is an opinion?**
   - (F) The stamp collection was very special to T.J.'s dad.
   - (G) At first, T.J. did not understand why the gift was so special.
   - (H) Collecting stamps is boring.
   - (J) Some of the stamps were very old.

5. **Who is the main character in this story?**
   - (A) Grandfather
   - (B) T.J.
   - (C) Father
   - (D) Felicia

6. **In the sentence, "I'll teach you about the different stamps and how to preserve them," the word *preserve* probably means —**
   - (F) to keep in good condition
   - (G) to store
   - (H) to sell to make money
   - (J) to keep from decay

I. Reading
A. Directions
B. Sequencing
C. Main Idea
II. Writing
A. Capitalization
B. Proofreading

Name _____

READING: COMPREHENSION

● **Lesson 14: Fiction**

Directions: Read the passage. Choose the best answer to each question. Fill in the circle for the answer of your choice.

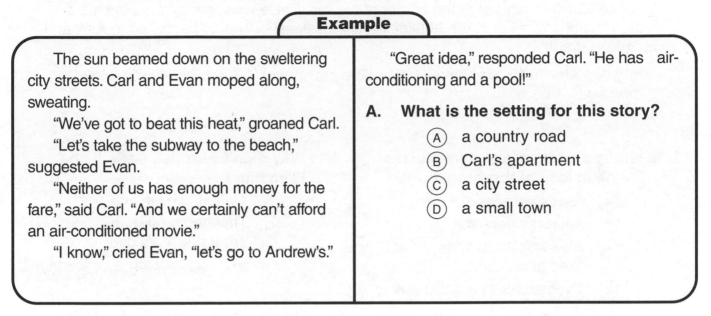

Example

The sun beamed down on the sweltering city streets. Carl and Evan moped along, sweating.

"We've got to beat this heat," groaned Carl.

"Let's take the subway to the beach," suggested Evan.

"Neither of us has enough money for the fare," said Carl. "And we certainly can't afford an air-conditioned movie."

"I know," cried Evan, "let's go to Andrew's."

"Great idea," responded Carl. "He has air-conditioning and a pool!"

A. **What is the setting for this story?**

- Ⓐ a country road
- Ⓑ Carl's apartment
- Ⓒ a city street
- Ⓓ a small town

Skim the passage so you have an understanding of what it is about. Then, skim the questions. Answer the easiest questions first, and then look back to the passage to find the answers.

● **Practice**

Cyber Love

Alex sat next to the girl of his dreams every day in science, math, and computer applications. Every day, CeCe smiled at Alex with her pretty, silver smile. Like Alex, she too wore braces. She wrote notes to him during class and laughed at all his jokes. Alex thought she liked him, but he was too shy to ask. He worried that the year would pass without ever learning for certain.

When Valentine's Day approached, Alex thought he had a chance. He would send her a special valentine. Unfortunately, he had no money. He was desperate, so desperate that he broke down and talked to his dad.

When Alex's dad said, "Try cyberspace," Alex was confused. He wondered how the Internet could help him. But when he visited the Free Virtual Valentine Web site, he knew his problem was solved. He chose a musical valentine and e-mailed it to CeCe at school.

GO ON

GRADE 6

I. Reading
  A. Directions
  B. Sequencing
  C. Main Idea
II. Writing
  A. Capitalization
  B. Proofreading

Name _____

READING: COMPREHENSION

● **Lesson 14: Fiction (cont.)**

On Valentine's Day, Alex waited patiently for CeCe to open her e-mail. He tried to look busy as he watched her out of the corner of his eye. CeCe whispered, "You sent me a message," as she clicked on the hot link to Alex's valentine. Then, she turned to Alex and said, "You're great."

I'm great, Alex thought to himself. *She likes me. If only I'd discovered cyberspace a long time ago.*

1. **Which sentence best summarizes the main idea of this story?**
   - (A) Alex liked school.
   - (B) Alex was very shy.
   - (C) Alex wanted to know if CeCe liked him.
   - (D) Cyberspace is a great way to show your love.

2. **Which detail from the story does not show that CeCe liked Alex?**
   - (F) She smiled at him.
   - (G) She laughed at his jokes.
   - (H) She sent him notes.
   - (J) She and Alex both wore braces.

3. **What can we conclude about CeCe from the first paragraph?**
   - (A) She had a good sense of humor.
   - (B) She was intelligent.
   - (C) She liked Alex.
   - (D) She liked Alex's braces.

4. **Why didn't Alex ask CeCe if she liked him?**
   - (F) He didn't think to ask.
   - (G) He was too shy.
   - (H) He didn't like girls.
   - (J) The year went by too quickly.

5. **What is the climax of this story?**
   - (A) Alex waits to see CeCe's response to his valentine.
   - (B) CeCe tells Alex that he is great.
   - (C) Alex talks to his dad.
   - (D) CeCe laughs at his jokes.

6. **What is the purpose of this story?**
   - (F) to illustrate how to combat shyness with girls
   - (G) to explain how Alex discovered that CeCe liked him
   - (H) to illustrate how to send a valentine through cyberspace
   - (J) to illustrate that it pays to ask parents for advice

GRADE
6
I. Reading
  A. Directions
  B. Sequencing
  C. Main Idea
II. Writing
  A. Capitalization
  B. Proofreading

Name _____

READING: COMPREHENSION

● **Lesson 15: Nonfiction**

Directions: Read the passage. Choose the best answer to each question. Fill in the circle for the answer of your choice.

Example

The Trans-Canadian Highway is the first ocean-to-ocean highway in Canada and the longest paved road in the world. After twelve years of work, the 4,859-mile highway was completed in September 1962. This highway made it possible for a person to drive from coast to coast and remain within Canada for the entire trip.

A. **This paragraph tells mainly —**

Ⓐ about highways in Canada

Ⓑ why the Trans-Canadian Highway is helpful

Ⓒ when the Trans-Canadian Highway was built

Ⓓ the location of the longest road

 **Clue** Skim the passage so you have an understanding of what it is about. Then, skim the questions. Answer the easiest questions first, and then look back to the passage to find the answer.

● **Practice**

Imagine this. You wake up to discover that a fresh layer of glistening snow covers the ground. After breakfast, you pull on your cold weather gear and hop on your bike. For some, this thought is unimaginable. For others, this activity, called *ice biking*, is an enjoyable form of recreation or even a way to commute to work. Ice bikers race and even go on camping trips.

If you think ice biking sounds fun, it is easy to get started. Ice bikers suggest that starting is just as easy as not putting your bike away when the weather grows cold. Just continue riding your bike. They suggest that you begin by riding your bike one day at a time. Plus, don't be foolhardy. Dress appropriately and watch the wind chill.

1. **What is the best way to begin ice biking?**

Ⓐ Go out and buy a new bike.

Ⓑ Don't put your bike away when it gets cold.

Ⓒ Ride just a few minutes each day.

Ⓓ Watch the wind chill.

2. **Which describes an activity enjoyed by ice bikers?**

Ⓕ commuting to work

Ⓖ camping

Ⓗ racing

Ⓙ All of the above

 STOP

I. Reading
  A. Directions
  B. Sequencing
  C. Main Idea
II. Writing
  A. Capitalization
  B. Proofreading

Name _____

READING: COMPREHENSION

● **Lesson 16: Nonfiction**

Directions: Read the passage. Choose the best answer to each question. Fill in the circle for the answer of your choice.

Example

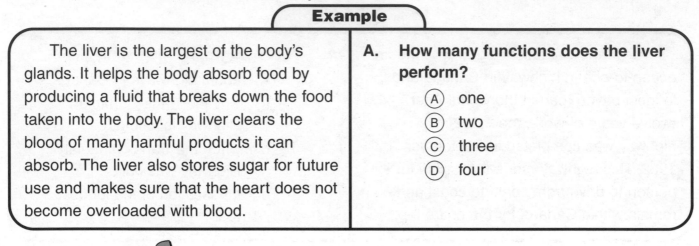

The liver is the largest of the body's glands. It helps the body absorb food by producing a fluid that breaks down the food taken into the body. The liver clears the blood of many harmful products it can absorb. The liver also stores sugar for future use and makes sure that the heart does not become overloaded with blood.

A. **How many functions does the liver perform?**

Ⓐ one
Ⓑ two
Ⓒ three
Ⓓ four

Clue Skim the passage and questions. Look back to the passage if you are unsure of the answers.

● **Practice**

The Ship of the Desert

Nomads who crisscross the Sahara Desert of North Africa rely on a most unique animal for transportation—the dromedary, or one-humped camel. Because it is indispensable to desert travel, the dromedary is sometimes called the "ship of the desert."

Several factors make the dromedary suitable for long desert trips. It can go for long periods without nourishment. The hump on a camel's back serves as its food reserve. When it has little to eat, it converts the fat from its hump into energy. The camel's hump can weigh up to 80 pounds or more. When the animal has to rely on its reservoir of fat, the hump becomes much smaller. Thus, it is easy to recognize a well-fed camel by the size of its hump.

Many people believe that camels store water in their humps. This is not true. Their ability to go for days without drinking is due to other factors. First, camels are able to drink large quantities of water at one time. Some have been known to gulp 53 gallons in one day. Second, the camel sweats very little and can tolerate greater body temperatures. Consequently, it retains most of the water it drinks and can travel several hundred miles before replenishing its supply.

Other physical characteristics enable the camel to endure harsh desert conditions. It can completely close its nostrils, thus protecting it from the stinging effects of sandstorms. Its eyes are shielded from sand and sun by overhanging lids and long lashes, and its broad, padded feet keep it from sinking into the soft sand. No other animal is better equipped for life in the desert than the camel.

GO ON

Name _____

READING: COMPREHENSION
● Lesson 16: Nonfiction (cont.)

1. What is the main idea expressed in this story?

- (A) The dromedary is the ideal animal for desert life.
- (B) The camel's hump serves as its food reservoir.
- (C) The dromedary is called the "ship of the desert."
- (D) Camels do not store water in their humps.

2. Which characteristic does not help the camel to survive in the desert?

- (F) A camel can drink up to 53 gallons of water in one day.
- (G) A camel can close its nostrils.
- (H) A camel sweats very little.
- (J) A camel is indispensable to desert travel.

3. What cannot be concluded from reading this passage?

- (A) A camel can survive a long time without eating.
- (B) A dromedary camel is easier to ride than a Bactrian camel.
- (C) Camels have many features that equip them for cold weather.
- (D) Both B and C

4. Which of these statements is a fact?

- (F) Nomads prefer camels to all other pack animals.
- (G) The Bactrian camel is the best camel for desert travel.
- (H) A camel's broad, padded feet protect it from sinking in soft sand.
- (J) Camels enjoy hot weather.

5. Which additional detail would support the title of this story?

- (A) Nomads use camel's hair to weave cloth to make tents.
- (B) Camels are strong animals capable of carrying loads up to a thousand pounds.
- (C) Camel's milk and meat are often part of the nomad's diet.
- (D) Camels can be stubborn.

6. What is the author's purpose for this passage?

- (F) to entertain
- (G) to inform
- (H) to persuade
- (J) to sell a product

GRADE

6

I. Reading
  A. Directions
  B. Sequencing
  C. Main Idea
II. Writing
  A. Capitalization
  B. Proofreading

Name _____

READING: COMPREHENSION

● **Lesson 17: Nonfiction**

Directions: Read the passage. Choose the best answer to each question. Fill in the circle for the answer of your choice.

Example

Though Americans take pride in the accomplishments of the pony express, few people know of an earlier and equally remarkable postal service. Eight hundred years before the pony express operated, messages traveled 150 miles a day without the aid of a horse. Incan runners were spaced about three miles apart over a stone road that stretched 5,000 miles. These relay runners were the "express mail" carriers of their time.

A. **The best nickname for these Incan messengers would be —**

  (A) the pony express

  (B) the Incan express

  (C) the horseless carriage

  (D) the horseless express

 **Clue**

Skim the passage and questions. Look back to the passage if you are unsure of the answers.

● **Practice**

The Man Behind the Faces

If you have never heard of Gutzon Borglum, you are not alone. Even though he was the sculptor responsible for the carvings on Mount Rushmore, many people do not know him by name.

Gutzon Borglum was born in Idaho in 1867 to Danish parents. He became interested in art early in life. He spent time studying in Paris then returned home to concentrate on sculpture. At the beginning of his career, Gutzon created many large sculptures, some which are quite famous. He also worked on the early stages of the carving of General Robert E. Lee at Stone Mountain, Virginia.

Gutzon was patriotic and outspoken. He lived during a time in American history called "the Colossal Age." This meant that big things were happening. For this reason, Gutzon Borglum became known as an artist who did things on a grand scale.

Borglum wanted to create a large monument to four American Presidents who brought our country into the modern age. He located Mount Rushmore, a 5,725-foot granite mountain in South Dakota and began his sculptures in 1927. Working on one at a time, Gutzon and his team carved the faces of George Washington, Thomas Jefferson, Abraham Lincoln, and Theodore Roosevelt into the mountainside.

 GO ON

GRADE
6

I. Reading
  A. Directions
  B. Sequencing
  C. Main Idea
II. Writing
  A. Capitalization
  B. Proofreading

READING: COMPREHENSION

● **Lesson 17: Nonfiction (cont.)**

Gutzon died in 1941, but his son, Lincoln, continued the work on Mount Rushmore. Today, Mount Rushmore is one of the most-visited national monuments.

1. **What is this article mainly about?**
   - (A) the beginning of "the Colossal Age"
   - (B) Gutzon Borglum's life
   - (C) Borglum's great work, Mount Rushmore
   - (D) art on a grand scale

2. **According to the passage, Gutzon Borglum did things on a grand scale. What does doing something "on a grand scale" probably mean?**
   - (F) creating things with intricate designs
   - (G) making things that are very large and impressive
   - (H) doing things well and with great care
   - (J) doing things that take artistic talent

3. **Based on your answer for number 2, which of the following would you consider to be done on a grand scale?**
   - (A) a painting as tall as a house
   - (B) a painting of a large, royal family
   - (C) a drawing of the tallest building in the world
   - (D) a life-size sculpture of a man

4. **Which of these statements about Mount Rushmore is true according to information in the article?**
   - (F) Mount Rushmore is located in North Dakota.
   - (G) It is located in South Dakota.
   - (H) It is more famous than Stone Mountain.
   - (J) It is the largest mountain in the country.

5. **What detail does not support the idea of Gutzon as an artist?**
   - (A) Gutzon went to Paris to study art.
   - (B) He became interested in art early in his life.
   - (C) Gutzon was patriotic and outspoken.
   - (D) He created many large sculptures.

STOP

I. Reading
A. Directions
B. Sequencing
C. Main Idea
II. Writing
A. Capitalization
B. Proofreading

READING: COMPREHENSION
SAMPLE TEST

● **Directions:** Read the passage. Choose the best answer to each question. Fill in the circle for the answer of your choice.

Example

Penny arrived early at the Johnson's because it was her first time to sit for their little girl, Lori. Lori looked at Penny. Lori was very petite. Her blond hair was pulled back into two ponytails, and her bright smile made even her freckles sparkle. Lori asked Penny to play dolls with her.

E1. **What can we know about Lori from reading the paragraph above?**

- (A) Lori is an intelligent little girl.
- (B) Lori is a pretty little girl.
- (C) Lori is a little girl with a bright smile.
- (D) Penny will have no problems babysitting Lori.

By Saturday Noon

Saturday noon is one of those special times in our house. When I say special, I don't mean good special. By Saturday noon, my sisters and I need to have our bedrooms pristine.

When Dad inspects our rooms, he is like an army sergeant doing the white-glove test. If anything is out of place, if any clothes are left on the floor, and if your dresser isn't cleaned off and shiny, you don't get to go anywhere that day.

That isn't hard for Margaret. She's a neat freak. But Chelsea and I are normal, which is the problem—two normal sisters sharing a bedroom. On Monday, we start our separate piles: dirty clothes, wrinkled clothes, clothes we decided not to wear but forgot to hang up. By Wednesday, it's hard to find the floor. By Friday, the tops of the dressers are loaded. Plus, Mom won't let us throw everything down the laundry chute. "Sort it," she says.

Usually, we have enough time to get our clothes all folded and hung by noon, but last Saturday, Chelsea got sick. She spent the morning in the bathroom. I was left to clean the room alone. I had plans to shop with Jen.

At 10:00, Jen decided she wanted to leave early. I was desperate, so I shoved everything under Chelsea's bed, dusted the dressers, plumped the pillows, and called Dad for a room check.

Dad started his checklist. Everything was okay until Dad got to my closet. He turned and asked, "Where are all your clothes, Sara?"

"Dirty," I confessed.

Dad looked around until he spied the clothes under Chelsea's bed.

"Dirty?" he asked.

GO ON

GRADE

6

I. Reading
  A. Directions
  B. Sequencing
  C. Main Idea
II. Writing
  A. Capitalization
  B. Proofreading

Name _____

READING: COMPREHENSION
SAMPLE TEST (cont.)

I winced. "I must have missed those."

"Call Jen. You're not going shopping today," he said.

By Saturday noon, I was sick right alongside Chelsea. Mom said, "It's a good thing you didn't go shopping." I figured it was just the opposite. If I had gone shopping, I would never have gotten sick.

1. **The words in the title "Saturday Noon" are used three times in the story. Why is that time important to Sara?**
   - (A) Chelsea wanted to go shopping.
   - (B) It was the deadline for having her room clean, which determined whether or not she could go out that day.
   - (C) It was the time Sara had to have the laundry done.
   - (D) It was when she got sick.

2. **How is Margaret different from Sara and Chelsea?**
   - (F) She is older.
   - (G) She is younger.
   - (H) She is very neat.
   - (J) She always goes out on Saturdays.

3. **What does the word *pristine* mean in this story?**
   - (A) very clean
   - (B) organized
   - (C) packed
   - (D) untidy

4. **Which of the following is not one of Sara's excuses for not getting her room clean?**
   - (F) Sara's mom will not let her throw clothes down the laundry chute.
   - (G) Chelsea got sick and couldn't help.
   - (H) Jen wanted to leave early.
   - (J) Her mom should clean her room.

5. **What is this story's plot?**
   - (A) Sara can't wait to go shopping.
   - (B) Sara knows she needs to have her room clean by Saturday noon, but blames everyone but herself for her room not being clean.
   - (C) Sara allows her laundry to build up.
   - (D) Sara's dad has unrealistic expectations for Sara.

6. **Which title below best fits this story?**
   - (F) The Blame Game
   - (G) Cleaning Is Not Normal
   - (H) Shopping With Jen
   - (J) Laundry Woes

GO ON

I. Reading
  A. Directions
  B. Sequencing
  C. Main Idea
II. Writing
  A. Capitalization
  B. Proofreading

Name _____

READING: COMPREHENSION
SAMPLE TEST (cont.)

Read the passage. Choose the best answer to each question. Fill in the circle for the answer of your choice.

Example

When a baby kangaroo is born, it is as big as your thumb. The baby, called a *joey*, cannot see, hear, walk, or jump. It crawls into the pouch on its mother's stomach and remains there about eight months. During that time, its body grows and develops more fully.

E2. **What is the main idea of this paragraph?**

  (F) Newborn joeys are small and defenseless.

  (G) Newborn joeys are as small as your thumb.

  (H) A mother kangaroo has it easy.

  (J) Joeys are baby kangaroos.

Maternal Fish Father

In the warm and temperate waters of the world live two unusual fish: the sea horse and its relative, the pipefish.

The sea horse, so-called because its head resembles a horse, is a small fish about two to eight inches long. It swims by moving the dorsal fin on its back. It is the only fish with a prehensile tail that it uses, like a monkey, to coil around and cling to seaweed.

The pipefish is named for its long snout, which looks like a thin pipe. When its body is straight, the pipefish resembles a slender snake. Its body forms an *S* shape and is propelled by its rear fins.

But it is not appearance that makes the sea horse and pipefish unique. It is their paternal roles. With both fish, the female's responsibility ends when she lays and deposits her eggs. From that point on, the male takes over and, in a manner of speaking, gives birth to the babies.

Both the male sea horse and pipefish have pouch-like organs on their undersides in which the female deposits her eggs. Here the young fish stay and are nourished for either a few days or for several weeks, depending on the species. When the baby sea horses are ready to be born, the father sea horse attaches itself to a plant and actually goes through the pangs of childbirth. As the sea horse bends back and forth, the wall of its brood pouch contracts. With each spasm, a baby fish is introduced into the world of the sea. The birth of the baby pipefish is less dramatic. The father's pouch simply opens, and the offspring swim off on their own.

GO ON

GRADE 6

I. Reading
  A. Directions
  B. Sequencing
  C. Main Idea
II. Writing
  A. Capitalization
  B. Proofreading

Name _____

READING: COMPREHENSION
SAMPLE TEST (cont.)

7. **What is the main idea of this passage?**

   (A) The pipefish and the sea horse fathers are unusual because of the way their offspring are born.

   (B) Sea horses resemble horses but have tales like monkeys.

   (C) Female pipefish and sea horses are lazy.

   (D) Sea horses make good pets.

8. **Which statement does not describe a sea horse?**

   (F) The sea horse's head resembles a horse.

   (G) The sea horse's body is propelled by a rear fin.

   (H) The sea horse uses its snout to cling to seaweed.

   (J) The sea horse has a prehensile tail.

9. **Which statement seems to say that the role of the pipefish is less difficult than that of the seahorse?**

   (A) The baby pipefish swim off.

   (B) The father's pouch simply opens.

   (C) The pipefish's body is shaped like an *S*.

   (D) The pipefish has a long, thin snout.

10. **Which statement is an opinion?**

    (F) Male sea horses and pipefish are very good fathers.

    (G) Sea horses are from two to eight inches long.

    (H) Sea horses move by the use of their dorsal fins.

    (J) The wall of the male sea horse's brood pouch contracts.

11. **What is the author's purpose?**

    (A) to compare and contrast two fish

    (B) to entertain

    (C) to persuade

    (D) to confuse

STOP

ANSWER SHEET

STUDENT'S NAME

LAST	FIRST	MI

SCHOOL

TEACHER

FEMALE ○   MALE ○

BIRTH DATE

MONTH	DAY	YEAR

JAN ○
FEB ○
MAR ○
APR ○
MAY ○
JUN ○
JUL ○
AUG ○
SEP ○
OCT ○
NOV ○
DEC ○

GRADE
⑤ ⑥ ⑦

Part 1: VOCABULARY

E1 Ⓐ Ⓑ Ⓒ Ⓓ	6 Ⓕ Ⓖ Ⓗ Ⓙ	13 Ⓐ Ⓑ Ⓒ Ⓓ	20 Ⓕ Ⓖ Ⓗ Ⓙ	27 Ⓐ Ⓑ Ⓒ Ⓓ	34 Ⓕ Ⓖ Ⓗ Ⓙ
E2 Ⓕ Ⓖ Ⓗ Ⓙ	7 Ⓐ Ⓑ Ⓒ Ⓓ	14 Ⓕ Ⓖ Ⓗ Ⓙ	21 Ⓐ Ⓑ Ⓒ Ⓓ	28 Ⓕ Ⓖ Ⓗ Ⓙ	35 Ⓐ Ⓑ Ⓒ Ⓓ
1 Ⓐ Ⓑ Ⓒ Ⓓ	8 Ⓕ Ⓖ Ⓗ Ⓙ	15 Ⓐ Ⓑ Ⓒ Ⓓ	22 Ⓕ Ⓖ Ⓗ Ⓙ	29 Ⓐ Ⓑ Ⓒ Ⓓ	
2 Ⓕ Ⓖ Ⓗ Ⓙ	9 Ⓐ Ⓑ Ⓒ Ⓓ	16 Ⓕ Ⓖ Ⓗ Ⓙ	23 Ⓐ Ⓑ Ⓒ Ⓓ	30 Ⓕ Ⓖ Ⓗ Ⓙ	
3 Ⓐ Ⓑ Ⓒ Ⓓ	10 Ⓕ Ⓖ Ⓗ Ⓙ	17 Ⓐ Ⓑ Ⓒ Ⓓ	24 Ⓕ Ⓖ Ⓗ Ⓙ	31 Ⓐ Ⓑ Ⓒ Ⓓ	
4 Ⓕ Ⓖ Ⓗ Ⓙ	11 Ⓐ Ⓑ Ⓒ Ⓓ	18 Ⓕ Ⓖ Ⓗ Ⓙ	25 Ⓐ Ⓑ Ⓒ Ⓓ	32 Ⓕ Ⓖ Ⓗ Ⓙ	
5 Ⓐ Ⓑ Ⓒ Ⓓ	12 Ⓕ Ⓖ Ⓗ Ⓙ	19 Ⓐ Ⓑ Ⓒ Ⓓ	26 Ⓕ Ⓖ Ⓗ Ⓙ	33 Ⓐ Ⓑ Ⓒ Ⓓ	

Part 2: READING COMPREHENSION

E1 Ⓐ Ⓑ Ⓒ Ⓓ	7 Ⓐ Ⓑ Ⓒ Ⓓ	14 Ⓕ Ⓖ Ⓗ Ⓙ	21 Ⓐ Ⓑ Ⓒ Ⓓ	28 Ⓕ Ⓖ Ⓗ Ⓙ
1 Ⓐ Ⓑ Ⓒ Ⓓ	8 Ⓕ Ⓖ Ⓗ Ⓙ	15 Ⓐ Ⓑ Ⓒ Ⓓ	22 Ⓕ Ⓖ Ⓗ Ⓙ	29 Ⓐ Ⓑ Ⓒ Ⓓ
2 Ⓕ Ⓖ Ⓗ Ⓙ	9 Ⓐ Ⓑ Ⓒ Ⓓ	16 Ⓕ Ⓖ Ⓗ Ⓙ	23 Ⓐ Ⓑ Ⓒ Ⓓ	
3 Ⓐ Ⓑ Ⓒ Ⓓ	10 Ⓕ Ⓖ Ⓗ Ⓙ	17 Ⓐ Ⓑ Ⓒ Ⓓ	24 Ⓕ Ⓖ Ⓗ Ⓙ	
4 Ⓕ Ⓖ Ⓗ Ⓙ	11 Ⓐ Ⓑ Ⓒ Ⓓ	18 Ⓕ Ⓖ Ⓗ Ⓙ	25 Ⓐ Ⓑ Ⓒ Ⓓ	
5 Ⓐ Ⓑ Ⓒ Ⓓ	12 Ⓕ Ⓖ Ⓗ Ⓙ	19 Ⓐ Ⓑ Ⓒ Ⓓ	26 Ⓕ Ⓖ Ⓗ Ⓙ	
6 Ⓕ Ⓖ Ⓗ Ⓙ	13 Ⓐ Ⓑ Ⓒ Ⓓ	20 Ⓕ Ⓖ Ⓗ Ⓙ	27 Ⓐ Ⓑ Ⓒ Ⓓ	

Name _____

READING PRACTICE TEST

● **Part 1: Vocabulary**

Directions: For item E1, find the word that means the same or almost the same as the underlined word. For item E2, fill in the circle for the answer you think is correct. Then, follow the directions for each part of this test.

Examples

E1. **artificial** diamond	E2. **Which of these words probably comes from the Latin word** *familiaris*, **which means "domestic"?**
Ⓐ fake	Ⓕ farmer
Ⓑ genuine	Ⓖ familiar
Ⓒ exquisite	Ⓗ famous
Ⓓ authentic	Ⓙ domicile

For numbers 1–13, find the word or words that mean the same or almost the same as the underlined word.

1. surprising **outcome**
   - Ⓐ relationship
   - Ⓑ appointment
   - Ⓒ result
   - Ⓓ announcement

2. **hideous** mask
   - Ⓕ lovely
   - Ⓖ funny
   - Ⓗ monstrous
   - Ⓙ false

3. **audible** sigh
   - Ⓐ heard
   - Ⓑ silent
   - Ⓒ austere
   - Ⓓ angry

4. **desolate** landscape
   - Ⓕ forested
   - Ⓖ barren
   - Ⓗ desirable
   - Ⓙ unnatural

5. To **subside** is to —
   - Ⓐ continue
   - Ⓑ grow louder
   - Ⓒ cease
   - Ⓓ be intermittent

6. A **cunning** plan is —
   - Ⓕ clever
   - Ⓖ unoriginal
   - Ⓗ original
   - Ⓙ detailed

7. A **monotone** speech is —
   - Ⓐ exciting
   - Ⓑ lively
   - Ⓒ dull
   - Ⓓ hesitant

8. To **assert** is to —
   - Ⓕ declare
   - Ⓖ argue
   - Ⓗ proceed
   - Ⓙ boast

GO ON

Name _____

READING PRACTICE TEST
Part 1: Vocabulary (cont.)

9. The old woman was very <u>frail</u>.
   Frail means —
   - (A) hardy
   - (B) determined
   - (C) delicate
   - (D) forgetful

10. Daphne's excuse was <u>legitimate</u>.
    Legitimate means the same as —
    - (F) false
    - (G) honest
    - (H) faulty
    - (J) incredible

11. Aaron Baron was very <u>illustrious</u>.
    Illustrious means —
    - (A) famous
    - (B) infamous
    - (C) intelligent
    - (D) sickly

12. Juanita's complexion was <u>wan</u>.
    Wan means —
    - (F) tan
    - (G) ashen
    - (H) bright
    - (J) swarthy

13. The crowd <u>jostled</u> Justin.
    Jostled means —
    - (A) ridiculed
    - (B) honored
    - (C) pushed
    - (D) ignored

For numbers 14–19, choose the word that means the opposite of the underlined word.

14. a <u>gleeful</u> response
    - (F) joyous
    - (G) gloomy
    - (H) cheerful
    - (J) reluctant

15. <u>absurd</u> situation
    - (A) ridiculous
    - (B) sensible
    - (C) unbelievable
    - (D) embarrassing

16. <u>arid</u> climate
    - (F) dry
    - (G) airy
    - (H) fertile
    - (J) barren

17. <u>animated</u> conversation
    - (A) lively
    - (B) dull
    - (C) energetic
    - (D) one-sided

18. <u>sodden</u> clothing
    - (F) soaked
    - (G) spongy
    - (H) dry
    - (J) filthy

19. <u>essential</u> ingredient
    - (A) necessary
    - (B) unnecessary
    - (C) important
    - (D) additional

GO ON

GRADE 6

I. Reading
A. Directions
B. Sequencing
C. Main Idea
II. Writing
A. Capitalization
B. Proofreading

Name _____

READING PRACTICE TEST
Part 1: Vocabulary (cont.)

For numbers 20–23, choose the word that correctly completes both sentences.

20. He discovered an underground _____.

Rachel read the _____ several times.

- (F) book
- (G) passage
- (H) civilization
- (J) letter

21. Michael's arm was in a _____.

Chondra was part of the _____.

- (A) sleeve
- (B) crew
- (C) cast
- (D) mold

22. Akiko had a _____ in her brow.

The farmer made a _____ with his plow.

- (F) furrow
- (G) wrinkle
- (H) trench
- (J) scar

23. Sara's hair was _____.

Matthew's friend _____ at him.

- (A) scowled
- (B) wild
- (C) tangled
- (D) snarled

24. Will the children <u>spruce</u> up their rooms?

In which sentence does the word <u>spruce</u> mean the same thing as in the sentence above?

- (F) They planted a <u>spruce</u>.
- (G) We used <u>spruce</u> to build our house.
- (H) The volunteers will <u>spruce</u> up the playground.
- (J) Maggie climbed up the <u>spruce</u>.

25. Andre <u>bounced</u> the ball.

In which sentence does the word <u>bounced</u> mean the same thing as in the sentence above?

- (A) Kate <u>bounced</u> back after her surgery.
- (B) Mrs. Smith's check <u>bounced</u>.
- (C) The Ping-Pong ball <u>bounced</u> off the table.
- (D) The kangaroo <u>bounced</u> across the field.

For numbers 26 and 27, choose the answer that best defines the underlined part.

26. <u>pre</u>pare <u>pre</u>occupy
- (F) after
- (G) before
- (H) because of
- (J) over

27. patience obedience
- (A) state or condition of being
- (B) full of
- (C) having, tending to
- (D) without

GO ON

GRADE
6

I. Reading
    A. Directions
    B. Sequencing
    C. Main Idea
II. Writing
    A. Capitalization
    B. Proofreading

Name _____

READING PRACTICE TEST

Part 1: Vocabulary (cont.)

28. Which of these words probably comes from the Latin word *gratia* meaning "grace"?

- (F) grade
- (G) grasp
- (H) gracious
- (J) regret

29. <u>Inhale</u> is to <u>exhale</u> as <u>tense</u> is to —

- (A) breathe
- (B) relax
- (C) nervous
- (D) gasp

30. Her favorite _____ was "Better safe than sorry."

Which of these words means "saying"?

- (F) craving
- (G) bias
- (H) maxim
- (J) gild

31. The man _____ an oak.

Which of these words means "to cut down with an ax"?

- (A) hewed
- (B) heaved
- (C) haunch
- (D) sliced

Read the paragraph. Choose the word below the paragraph that fits best in each numbered blank.

In October 1985, a whale caused quite a _____ **(32)** near the _____ **(33)** of California. The whale, a _____ **(34)** so large that its home is the Pacific Ocean, swam under the Golden Gate Bridge and up the Sacramento River. After more than three weeks, the whale finally reversed its _____ **(35)** and headed back toward the ocean.

32.
- (F) collision
- (G) stir
- (H) boycott
- (J) meddle

33.
- (A) city
- (B) island
- (C) coast
- (D) coax

34.
- (F) fish
- (G) amphibian
- (H) plebeian
- (J) creature

35.
- (A) bow
- (B) course
- (C) ballasts
- (D) opinion

STOP

GRADE 6

I. Reading
   A. Directions
   B. Sequencing
   C. Main Idea
II. Writing
   A. Capitalization
   B. Proofreading

Name _____

READING PRACTICE TEST

● Part 2: Reading Comprehension

Directions: Read the passage. Choose the best answer to each question. Fill in the circle for the answer of your choice.

Example

Jade begged her father to let her get a cat, but he worried that she wouldn't take care of it. So Jade worked hard to show how responsible she was. She even took out the trash every week and did all her homework every day after she got home from school.

When Jade's birthday came, she received a board game and some new clothes. Then, at the last minute, her father handed her a shoebox—something was squirming inside!

E1. What do you think will happen next?

- (A) Jade will open the box to find a puppy.
- (B) Jade will open the box to discover a kitten.
- (C) Jade will open the box to find her little brother.
- (D) Jade will not open the box.

Read this passage about a boy who discovers two coins. Then, answer the questions on the next page.

One Afternoon in March

One afternoon in March, I found two silver dollars shining in a half-melted snow bank. I instantly thought of buried treasure. So I dug through the snow searching for more. All I ended up with were two really cold hands. I slipped the two coins in my pocket and went home colder but richer.

The next morning, Megan and her little sister were searching the snow banks. *Finders keepers* was my first thought. I didn't need to get to the *losers weepers* part since Moira was already crying for real.

"I dropped them right here," she said between tears. Her hands were red from digging in the snow.

"Maybe they got shoved down the street by the snow plow. Let's try over there," Megan said optimistically.

They'll never know was my second thought, as I walked past them toward Tyler's house.

"Phil, have you seen two silver dollars?" Megan called. Moira looked up from the snow bank with hope bright in her eyes.

"Coins?" *Look innocent* was my third thought.

GO ON

READING PRACTICE TEST
Part 2: Reading Comprehension (cont.)

"Yes, Moira dropped two silver dollars somewhere around here yesterday."

"Yeah," said Moira, "they're big and heavy." She brushed her red hands off on her jacket and wiped the tears from her eyes. Her eyes were as red as her hands.

Lie, I thought, but said, "As a matter of fact," I hesitated, "I dug two coins out of that snow bank yesterday. I wondered who might have lost them."

Moira ran to me and gave me a bear hug. "Oh, thank you, thank you!"

I couldn't help but smile.

1. What is the main idea of this story?

(A) It is okay to lie if you think you will get away with it.

(B) It is always better to be honest than rich.

(C) "Finders keepers, losers weepers" is not a good saying to live by.

(D) Both B and C apply.

2. How did Phil probably feel at the end of the story? He felt —

(F) angry with himself for being honest.

(G) angry with Megan and Moira.

(H) hopeful that he would find another buried treasure.

(J) disappointed at having to give up the coins but glad that he had been honest.

3. What is the problem in this story?

(A) Moira has lost two silver dollars in the snow.

(B) Phil does not want to give up the coins he found.

(C) Phil does not want to help Moira find her coins.

(D) Megan does not want to help her sister.

4. Which statement below is a fact?

(F) Phil thinks only of his own wants.

(G) Moira cries a lot.

(H) Moira and Phil should be wearing mittens when out in the snow.

(J) Moira is crying because she has lost her silver dollars.

5. What is the setting of this story?

(A) outside on a March day

(B) outside on a warm, summer day

(C) a cold, winter day

(D) the view outside a window

6. What would be a good title for this story?

(F) Frostbitten Fingers

(G) Finders Keepers, Losers Weepers

(H) A Fistful of Dollars

(J) Honesty Is Best

GO ON

READING PRACTICE TEST
Part 2: Reading Comprehension (cont.)

Read this story about a Native American girl. Then, answer the questions on the next page.

A New Tipi

Fingers of frost tickled at Little Deer's feet. It was a chilly fall morning, but there was no time for Little Deer to snuggle beneath her buffalo skins. It was going to be a busy day, helping her mother to finish the cover for their family's new tipi.

Little Deer slid her tunic over her head and fastened her moccasins. Wrapping herself up in another skin, she walked outside to survey the work they had done so far. The tipi cover was beautiful and nearly complete. The vast semicircle was spread across the ground, a patchwork in various shades of brown. After her father and brothers had killed the buffalo, she and her mother had carefully cured and prepared the skins, stretching them and scraping them until they were buttery soft. Then with needles made from bone and thread made from animal sinew, they had carefully sewn the hides together until they formed a huge canvas nearly thirty feet across.

After they finished the cover today, it would be ready to mount on the lodge poles. Little Deer's father had traded with another tribe for fourteen tall, wooden poles. They would stack the poles together in a cone shape, lashing them together with more rope made from animal sinews.

Then, they would carefully stretch the cover over the poles, forming a snug, watertight home. Little Deer smiled in anticipation. She could just imagine the cozy glow of the fire through the tipi walls at night.

Name _____

READING PRACTICE TEST

Part 2: Reading Comprehension (cont.)

7. **What is this story mainly about?**
   - (A) hunting
   - (B) building a tipi
   - (C) the uses of buffalo
   - (D) the life of a Native American girl

8. **Which sentence below is not a step in the process of making a tipi?**
   - (F) Stretch the cover over the poles.
   - (G) Cure and prepare the skins.
   - (H) Sew the hides together.
   - (J) Make clothing from the remaining pieces of hide.

9. **How does Little Deer feel about finishing the tipi?**
   - (A) depressed
   - (B) angry
   - (C) excited
   - (D) cold

10. **Which of these statements shows personification?**
    - (F) Little Deer smiled in anticipation.
    - (G) Little Deer slid her tunic over her head and fastened her moccasins.
    - (H) The tipi cover was beautiful and nearly complete.
    - (J) Fingers of frost tickled at Little Deer's feet.

11. **Where would this passage most likely be found?**
    - (A) a historical novel
    - (B) an encyclopedia
    - (C) a science fiction story
    - (D) a diary

12. **Which characteristic most accurately describes Little Deer?**
    - (F) lazy
    - (G) hardworking
    - (H) clever
    - (J) intelligent

GO ON

GRADE
6

I. Reading
A. Directions
B. Sequencing
C. Main Idea
II. Writing
A. Capitalization
B. Proofreading

Name _____

READING PRACTICE TEST
Part 2: Reading Comprehension (cont.)

Read this story about a new girl at school. Then, answer the questions on the next page.

A Handful of Pretty Flowers

When Shanda first arrived at school, she discovered to her dismay that a freckle-faced boy in her sixth-grade class was smitten with her. Because Shanda's family was new to the city, Shanda had not yet made any friends. She didn't feel comfortable asking the other students the boy's name. And he didn't offer his name, just a handful of pretty flowers.

Shanda soon learned the redheaded boy's name, Tommy. Whenever the class lined up for assembly or gym, he always smiled a crooked smile in her direction. Shanda felt uncomfortable with the attention he gave her, small though it was. Why did he like her anyway? On several occasions, Shanda tried to start a conversation with Tommy. But he always blushed, put his hands in his pockets, and looked down in embarrassment.

Gradually, Shanda developed a circle of friends. She finally felt happy in her new school. The only thing that still made her uncomfortable was Tommy with his crooked, shy smiles.

One day, as Shanda was walking down the hallway, Tommy came up alongside her. "Do you like animals?" he asked. Shanda was shocked. He had actually spoken to her.

Shanda turned to him and replied, "Hi, Tommy. Yeah, I like animals. We have lots of pets at my house. How about you?"

Shanda noticed how nervous Tommy had become as she talked. He even appeared to stop breathing for a moment. He whispered something about a dog and then hurried away. Shanda wondered if she had hurt his feelings by calling him Tommy. Maybe he liked to be called Tom.

A week later, Tommy reverently handed Shanda a photo. It was a snapshot of a beautiful collie. She had intelligent eyes and almost seemed to be smiling. Her ears were alert, and her face tilted questioningly. Shanda knew this was an important moment for Tommy. "What's her name?" she asked softly.

"Sh-, sh-, she was Shanda . . . like you. We had her since I was in kindergarten. Sh-, she's gone now."

GO ON

GRADE

6

I. Reading
A. Directions
B. Sequencing
C. Main Idea
II. Writing
A. Capitalization
B. Proofreading

Name _____

READING PRACTICE TEST

Part 2: Reading Comprehension (cont.)

13. What is this story mainly about?

- (A) a girl has a hard time fitting in at a new school
- (B) a boy's love for his dog
- (C) a shy boy
- (D) a new girl at school and the shy boy who likes her

14. In this story, what does the word *smitten* mean?

- (F) struck by
- (G) attacked by
- (H) attracted to
- (J) bothered by

15. From reading this story, we can conclude that —

- (A) Tommy's dog has died, and he misses her.
- (B) Tommy's family now has a cat.
- (C) Tommy likes the name Shanda.
- (D) Tommy thinks Shanda is cute.

16. What probably caused Tommy to give Shanda flowers?

- (F) He felt sorry for her because she was a new girl.
- (G) She and his dog shared the name Shanda.
- (H) She had hair the same color as his collie.
- (J) She liked animals as much as he did.

17. From whose point of view is this story told?

- (A) Tommy's
- (B) Shanda's
- (C) the teacher's
- (D) Shanda's friend

18. Which statement best describes Shanda?

- (F) Shanda is popular.
- (G) Shanda likes Tommy.
- (H) Shanda shows kindness by asking about Tommy's dog.
- (J) Shanda is shy.

GO ON

GRADE 6

I. Reading
  A. Directions
  B. Sequencing
  C. Main Idea
II. Writing
  A. Capitalization
  B. Proofreading

Name _____

READING PRACTICE TEST
Part 2: Reading Comprehension (cont.)

Read this article about early radio. Then, answer the questions on the next page.

Hi-Yo, Silver!

What did people do for entertainment before television? Today, the average child spends more time watching television than reading. Television is so much a part of daily life that many people cannot imagine what life was like before it.

Before television, there was radio. Radio was invented around 1916 from the telegraph. At first, it was used to get information quickly from one part of the country to another. By 1926, radios were common in homes. People listened to music, news, and shows in the same way we watch TV today. Television was not invented until the 1940s, and it did not gain popularity in homes until 1955.

Families gathered around their radios to listen to shows broadcast all over the world. One of the most popular radio shows was *The Lone Ranger*. This show was about a Texas Ranger and a faithful Native American, named Tonto, who tirelessly worked to stop evil. The Lone Ranger rode a white horse named Silver and wore a black mask. The Lone Ranger hid his identity, because he had been left for dead by a gang that ambushed and killed five other Texas Rangers. He vowed to find these desperadoes. His white hat, white horse, black mask, and his famous call, "Hi-yo, Silver. Away!" became symbols of the American Wild West hero.

Other famous radio heroes were the Shadow and the Green Hornet. Eventually, radio shows became famous television shows as well. Comedians and vaudeville stars made the transition from the stage to radio to television. Comedians such as Jack Benny, Red Skelton, and George Burns had radio shows that became television favorites.

GO ON

GRADE
6

I. Reading
  A. Directions
  B. Sequencing
  C. Main Idea
II. Writing
  A. Capitalization
  B. Proofreading

Name _____

READING PRACTICE TEST
Part 2: Reading Comprehension (cont.)

19. What title best gives the main idea of this passage?

(A) The Lone Ranger Rides Again

(B) Before Television Came Radio

(C) Radio Stars Hit It Big on TV

(D) The History of Radio

20. What is not true of the passage?

(F) It gives a brief history of radio.

(G) It tells about the transition from radio to television.

(H) It focuses on *The Lone Ranger* show.

(J) It shows how radio was far more popular than television.

21. Which sentence below is an opinion?

(A) *The Lone Ranger* was the best radio show ever.

(B) The Lone Ranger wore a white hat and black mask.

(C) Tonto was the Lone Ranger's faithful companion.

(D) *The Lone Ranger* took place in the American West.

22. Which statement is true?

(F) Tonto rode a white horse named Silver.

(G) Radio was invented in 1926.

(H) Several radio shows later became popular TV shows.

(J) Radio stars could not make it as television stars.

23. Why do you suppose that *The Lone Ranger* was such a popular radio show?

(A) Families had nothing better to do with their free time.

(B) It had the classic good guy against bad guys theme.

(C) People liked the special effects.

(D) People liked to watch the Lone Ranger and Tonto catch the bad guys.

GO ON

GRADE

6

I. Reading
   A. Directions
   B. Sequencing
   C. Main Idea
II. Writing
   A. Capitalization
   B. Proofreading

Name _____

READING PRACTICE TEST
Part 2: Reading Comprehension (cont.)

Read this article about humankind's quest for flight. Then, answer the questions on the next page.

From Dreams to Reality

People have probably always dreamed of flight. As they watched birds fly, they wished that they could soar into the blue sky. As they watched the night sky, they wished they could explore the distant bright specks called stars. These dreams led inventors and scientists to risk their lives to achieve flight.

Orville and Wilbur Wright's first flight at Kitty Hawk in 1903 was only the beginning. Flight continued to improve and dreams soared further into space. The first manned space flight occurred in 1961 when Russian cosmonaut Yuri A. Gagarin orbited Earth a single time. In 1963, the first woman cosmonaut, Valentina Tereshkova, orbited Earth 48 times.

The Russians led the race for many years. In 1965, another cosmonaut, Alesksei A. Leonov, took the first space walk. In 1968, the Russians launched an unmanned spacecraft that orbited the moon. The pictures that returned to Earth encouraged man to take the next step to land on the moon.

The United States became the leader in the space race when *Apollo 11* landed on the moon in 1969. Neil Armstrong was the first man to step on the lunar surface. As he did so, he said these famous words, "That's one small step for a man, one giant leap for mankind." Later in 1969, Charles Conrad, Jr., and Alan L. Bean returned to the moon. In 1972, the United States completed its last mission to the moon, *Apollo 17*.

Today, people continue their quest for space, gathering data from the *Mir* Space Station, which was launched in 1986. In addition, unmanned probes have flown deep into space toward the planets, sending back pictures and scientific readings.

GO ON

Name _____

READING PRACTICE TEST

Part 2: Reading Comprehension (cont.)

24. What is this passage mainly about?

(F) famous cosmonauts

(G) a brief history of human flight

(H) the first flight

(J) the space race

25. What happened first?

(A) The *Mir* Space Station was launched.

(B) Yuri Gagarin orbited Earth a single time.

(C) Neil Armstrong walked on the moon.

(D) The first woman orbited Earth.

26. Why do you suppose the race to achieve firsts in space travel was so important?

(F) It prompted the United States to excel.

(G) It encouraged cooperation between the two countries.

(H) It discouraged people from being interested in space travel.

(J) It developed fierce rivalry that led to many mistakes.

27. Which of these is an opinion?

(A) The United States became the leader in the space race with the first landing on the moon.

(B) All people have dreamed about being able to fly.

(C) Today unmanned space probes explore space.

(D) The Russians led the space race for several years.

28. What is the purpose of this passage?

(F) to inform

(G) to advertise

(H) to entertain

(J) to promote an idea

29. Which statement is false?

(A) The first woman in space was Valentina Tereshkova.

(B) The first landing on the moon was in 1969.

(C) Russia achieved the first manned space flight.

(D) The last landing on the moon in 1972 ended the space race.

STOP

ANSWER KEY

READING: VOCABULARY
Lesson 1: Synonyms
• Page 264
- **A.** B
- **B.** G
- 1. C
- 2. G
- 3. C
- 4. H
- 5. A
- 6. J
- 7. C
- 8. G

READING: VOCABULARY
Lesson 2: Vocabulary Skills
• Page 265
- **A.** A
- **B.** G
- 1. A
- 2. H
- 3. D
- 4. H
- 5. A
- 6. F
- 7. B
- 8. J

READING: VOCABULARY
Lesson 3: Antonyms
• Page 266
- **A.** C
- **B.** F
- 1. A
- 2. F
- 3. B
- 4. G
- 5. D
- 6. G
- 7. D
- 8. G

READING: VOCABULARY
Lesson 4: Multi-Meaning Words
• Page 267
- **A.** B
- **B.** G
- 1. C
- 2. G
- 3. C
- 4. G

READING: VOCABULARY
Lesson 5: Words In Context
• Page 268
- **A.** D
- **B.** F

1. B
2. F
3. C
4. J
5. C
6. H

READING: VOCABULARY
Lesson 6: Word Study
• Page 269
- **A.** B
- **B.** G
- 1. B
- 2. G
- 3. C
- 4. J
- 5. C
- 6. F

READING: VOCABULARY
SAMPLE TEST
• Pages 270–273
- E1. C
- E2. G
- 1. C
- 2. F
- 3. B
- 4. H
- 5. A
- 6. H
- 7. B
- 8. H
- 9. A
- 10. G
- 11. A
- 12. G
- 13. A
- 14. H
- 15. C
- 16. J
- 17. D
- 18. G
- 19. C
- 20. H
- 21. B
- 22. H
- 23. D
- 24. H
- 25. B
- 26. F
- 27. B
- 28. G
- 29. C
- 30. H
- 31. A
- 32. J
- 33. B
- 34. F
- 35. C

READING: COMPREHENSION
Lesson 7: Main Idea
• Page 274
- **A.** A
- 1. D
- 2. G

READING: COMPREHENSION
Lesson 8: Recalling Details
• Page 275
- **A.** C
- 1. B
- 2. H

READING: COMPREHENSION
Lesson 9: Drawing Conclusions
• Pages 276–277
- **A.** A
- 1. B
- 2. H
- **B.** F
- 3. B
- 4. G

READING: COMPREHENSION
Lesson 10: Fact and Opinion/
Cause and Effect
• Page 278
- **A.** C
- 1. D
- 2. G

READING: COMPREHENSION
Lesson 11: Story Elements
• Page 279
- **A.** C
- 1. C
- 2. G

READING: COMPREHENSION
Lesson 12: Fiction
• Page 280
- **A.** B
- 1. A
- 2. G

I. Reading
  A. Directions
  B. Sequencing
  C. Main Idea
II. Writing
  A. Capitalization
  B. Proofreading

ANSWER KEY

READING: COMPREHENSION
Lesson 13: Fiction
• Pages 281–282
  A. B
  1. B
  2. H
  3. B
  4. H
  5. B
  6. F

READING: COMPREHENSION
Lesson 14: Fiction
• Pages 283–284
  A. C
  1. C
  2. J
  3. C
  4. G
  5. A
  6. G

READING: COMPREHENSION
Lesson 15: Nonfiction
• Page 285
  A. B
  1. B
  2. J

READING: COMPREHENSION
Lesson 16: Nonfiction
• Pages 286–287
  A. D
  1. A
  2. J
  3. D
  4. H
  5. B
  6. G

READING: COMPREHENSION
Lesson 17: Nonfiction
• Pages 288–289
  A. B
  1. B
  2. G
  3. A
  4. G
  5. C

READING: COMPREHENSION
SAMPLE TEST
• Pages 290–293
  E1. C
  1. B
  2. H
  3. A
  4. J
  5. B
  6. F
  E2. F
  7. A
  8. H
  9. B
  10. F
  11. A

READING PRACTICE TEST
Part 1: Vocabulary
• Pages 295–298
  E1. A
  E2. G
  1. C
  2. H
  3. A
  4. G
  5. C
  6. F
  7. C
  8. F
  9. C
  10. G
  11. A
  12. G
  13. C
  14. G
  15. B
  16. H
  17. B
  18. H
  19. B
  20. G
  21. C
  22. F
  23. D
  24. H
  25. C
  26. G
  27. A
  28. H
  29. B
  30. H
  31. A
  32. G
  33. C
  34. J
  35. B

READING PRACTICE TEST
Part 2: Reading Comprehension
• Pages 299–308
  E1. B
  1. D
  2. J
  3. B
  4. J
  5. A
  6. J
  7. B
  8. J
  9. C
  10. J
  11. A
  12. G
  13. D
  14. H
  15. A
  16. G
  17. B
  18. H
  19. B
  20. J
  21. A
  22. H
  23. B
  24. G
  25. B
  26. F
  27. B
  28. F
  29. D

GRADE
6

I. Reading
   A. Directions
   B. Sequencing
   C. Main Idea
II. Writing
   A. Capitalization
   B. Proofreading

Answer Key

Root and Base Words

Many words consist of one or more **Greek** or **Latin root**. For example, the Greek root **tele** means "far." When it is combined with **vis**, the Latin root for "see," we get **television**.

Directions: Fill in the blanks below to learn the meaning of more roots.

1. Telephones allow us to hear sounds from far away. **Tele** means ___**far**___ and **phone** comes from the Greek word meaning ___**ground**___.

2. **Ped** is a root word meaning "foot." Therefore, a **pedestrian** is a person who travels by ___**foot**___.

3. **Graph** comes from the Greek word meaning "to write," and **auto** is the root word for "self." Thus, an **autograph** is ___**your signature**___.

4. **Geo** is the Greek root for "Earth." **Geography**, then, is writing or drawing about the ___**Earth**___.

5. **Bio** is the root word meaning "life." When someone writes an **autobiography**, he or she writes about ___**their own life**___.

6. A **biographer** writes about ___**someone else's life**___.

7. The word **pedometer** combines the root **ped** with **meter**, a root meaning "measurement." A **pedometer** is an instrument for ___**measuring**___ the distance someone travels by ___**foot**___.

8. **Logy** is a Greek root for "study." When combined with the root **graph**, we get graphology or the study of ___**writing**___.

9. **Biology** is the study of ___**life**___.

10. **Geology** is the study of ___**Earth**___.

11. Writing that comes from far away is called a ___**telegraph**___.

12. Combine the root word for "sound" and the root word for "write." The machine we use to play records is a ___**phonograph**___.

5

More Root and Base Words

Add new words to your vocabulary by understanding these Greek or Latin roots.

1. **Magna** or **magni** is the Latin root for "great." **Magnificent** is an adjective that means "excellent" or "great."

2. **Aqua** is the Latin word meaning "water." An **aquarium** is a place for keeping water plants and aquatic animals.

3. **Flor** is the Latin root for "flower." A **florist** sells or grows flowers for a living.

4. **Dict** is the Latin root meaning "to speak." **Diction** means the manner in which words are spoken.

5. **Micro** comes from the Greek word mikros, meaning "tiny" or "small." A **microscope** is an instrument that allows us to see very small things.

Directions: Use a dictionary to find two words formed from each of the above roots. Write words and their definitions in the blanks below.

Root	Dictionary Word	Definition
1. magna or magni	(a) _____	(a) _____
	(b) _____	(b) _____
2. aqua	(a) _____	(a) _____
	(b) _____	(b) _____
3. flor	(a) _____	(a) _____
	(b) _____	(b) _____
4. dict	(a) _____	(a) _____
	(b) _____	(b) _____
5. micro	(a) _____	(a) _____
	(b) _____	(b) _____

Answers will vary.

6

Words With aqua and aque

aqua, aque	water
aqualung	breathing equipment for underwater swimming or diving
aquamarine	a bluish sea-green color
aquaplane	a wide board that is towed by a motorboat, like a single water ski
aquarium	an artificial pond or tank of water where live water animals and water plants are kept; a building where such collections are exhibited
aquatic	growing or living in water
aqueduct	a channel that carries large amounts of water

Directions: Divide the following words into parts so that **aqua (or aque)** is separate.

Example:	aqua	rium
1. aquamarine	**aqua**	**marine**
2. aqualung	**aqua**	**lung**
3. aquaplane	**aqua**	**plane**
4. aqueduct	**aque**	**duct**

Directions: Complete each sentence using a word from the word box.

1. To go scuba diving, you need to wear an ___**aqualung**___.

2. The children bought a variety of fish for the ___**aquarium**___.

3. Seaweed is an ___**aquatic**___ plant.

4. The Romans used an ___**aqueduct**___ to transport water from one place to another.

5. Susan liked to waterski, but her brother John preferred to use an ___**aquaplane**___.

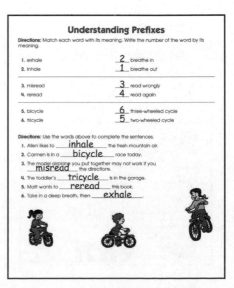

7

Words With dict

dict	to say
dictate	to say something aloud that will be written or recorded by another; to command or order
dictator	a ruler with unlimited power
diction	a style of speaking; the degree of preciseness or clarity in speech
predict	to foretell or say ahead of time that something will happen
verdict	a judgment or decision, especially that of a jury in a court case

Directions: Circle the root that means "to say" in the following words.

1. (dict)ion
2. pre(dict)
3. (dict)ator
4. ver(dict)

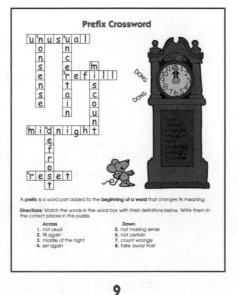

Directions: Complete each sentence using a word from the word box.

1. The foreman of the jury announced the ___**verdict**___: not guilty.

2. The actor was very careful of his ___**diction**___ during the audition.

3. The manager will ___**dictate**___ the new rules to the employees.

4. I ___**predict**___ that my little brother will have a dent in his new bike before the end of the week.

8

Prefix Crossword

A **prefix** is a word part added to the **beginning of a word** that changes its meaning.

Directions: Match the words in the word box with their definitions below. Write them in the correct places in the puzzle.

Across
1. not usual
2. fill again
3. middle of the night
4. set again

Down
5. not making sense
6. not certain
7. count wrongly
8. take away frost

9

Understanding Prefixes

Directions: Match each word with its meaning. Write the number of the word by its meaning.

1. exhale ___**2**___ breathe in
2. inhale ___**1**___ breathe out

3. misread ___**3**___ read wrongly
4. reread ___**4**___ read again

5. bicycle ___**6**___ three-wheeled cycle
6. tricycle ___**5**___ two-wheeled cycle

Directions: Use the words above to complete the sentences.

1. Allen likes to ___**inhale**___ the fresh mountain air.

2. Carmen is in a ___**bicycle**___ race today.

3. The model airplane you put together may not work if you ___**misread**___ the directions.

4. The toddler's ___**tricycle**___ is in the garage.

5. Matt wants to ___**reread**___ this book.

6. Take in a deep breath, then ___**exhale**___.

10

GRADE

6

I. Reading
A. Directions
B. Sequencing
C. Main Idea
II. Writing
A. Capitalization
B. Proofreading

Prefix Puzzle

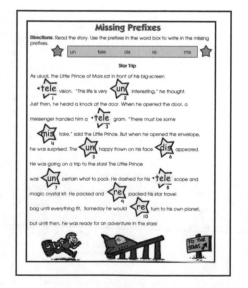

Directions: Match the words in the word box with their definitions below. Write them in the correct places in the puzzle.

Word box:
incorrect
ashore
unclear
renew
prepay
imperfect
dislike
mistreat

Puzzle answers:
ashore
prepay
renew
mistreat
imperfect
incorrect
dislike
unclear

Across
1. pay before
2. treat wrongly
3. not correct
4. not clear

Down
5. not like
6. not perfect
7. make new again
8. on shore

11

Prefix Meanings

Directions: Match each word with its meaning. Write the number of the word by its meaning.

1. increase   1 become larger
2. decrease   2 become smaller

3. indirect   4 direct again
4. redirect   3 not direct

5. inflate   6 to let out air
6. deflate   5 to blow air into

Directions: Use the words above to complete the sentences.
1. When I __deflate__ the tire, it will be flat.
2. To make more soup, __increase__ the amount of water.
3. Nick took an __indirect__ route to school.
4. If you are lost, a police officer can __redirect__ you.
5. Here are twenty balloons to __inflate__ for the party.
6. The price of shirts will __decrease__ during the big sale.

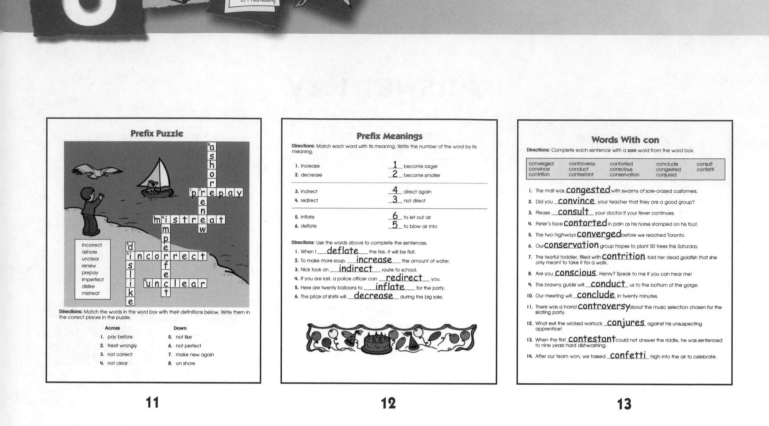

12

Words With con

Directions: Complete each sentence with a **con** word from the word box.

converged	controversy	contorted	conclude	consult
convince	conduct	conscious	congested	confetti
contrition	contestant	conservation	conjured	

1. The mall was __congested__ with swarms of sale-crazed customers.
2. Did you __convince__ your teacher that they are a good group?
3. Please __consult__ your doctor if your fever continues.
4. Peter's face __contorted__ in pain as his horse stomped on his foot.
5. The two highways __converged__ before we reached Toronto.
6. Our __conservation__ group hopes to plant 50 trees this Saturday.
7. The tearful toddler, filled with __contrition__ told her dead goldfish that she only meant to take it for a walk.
8. Are you __conscious__ Henry? Speak to me if you can hear me!
9. The brawny guide will __conduct__ us to the bottom of the gorge.
10. Our meeting will __conclude__ in twenty minutes.
11. There was a horrid __controversy__ about the music selection chosen for the skating party.
12. What evil the wicked warlock __conjures__ against his unsuspecting apprentice!
13. When the first __contestant__ could not answer the riddle, he was sentenced to nine years hard dishwashing.
14. After our team won, we tossed __confetti__ high into the air to celebrate.

13

Missing Prefixes

Directions: Read the story. Use the prefixes in the word box to write in the missing prefixes.

un   tele   dis   re   mis

Star Trip

As usual, the Little Prince of Mars sat in front of his big-screen __tele__ vision. "This life is very __un__ interesting," he thought.

Just then, he heard a knock at the door. When he opened the door, a messenger handed him a __tele__ gram. "There must be some __mis__ take," said the Little Prince. But when he opened the envelope, he was surprised. The __un__ happy frown on his face __dis__ appeared.

He was going on a trip to the stars! The Little Prince was __un__ certain what to pack. He dashed for his __tele__ scope and magic crystal kit. He packed and __re__ packed his star travel bag until everything fit. Someday he would __re__ turn to his own planet, but until then, he was ready for an adventure in the stars!

14

Suffixes

A **suffix** is a word part added to the **end of a word** that changes its meaning.

Directions: Use the suffix definitions in the box to write a definition of each word below.

ist means "one who practices"
ous means "full of"
ance means "the state of"

1. artist   one who makes art
2. courageous   full of courage
3. admittance   the state of admitting
4. appearance   the state of appearing
5. guitarist   one who practices guitar
6. humorous   full of humor
7. inheritance   the state of inheriting
8. mountainous   full of mountains
9. poisonous   full of poison
10. violinist   one who practices the violin

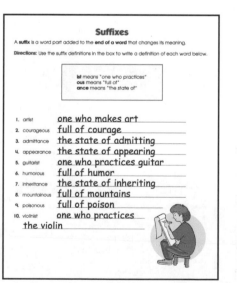

15

Suffixes ful and ly

Directions: Add the suffix **ful** or **ly** to the word from the box that makes sense in the sentence.

harm	easy
care	glad
use	brave
rest	sudden
hope	clear

1. Please be __careful__ when you use the iron.
2. __Suddenly__ a flock of geese swept across the sky.
3. Our vacation at the beach was so __restful__.
4. Sandy got an "A" on her speech because she spoke so __clearly__.
5. Our team is __hopeful__ that we will make the playoffs.
6. Some activities are __harmful__ to your health.
7. Manuel __bravely__ climbed the tree to get his sister's escaped parakeet.
8. I will __gladly__ deliver your papers for you while you are gone.
9. Your notes will be __useful__ as you prepare for the test.
10. The class aced the test __easily__.

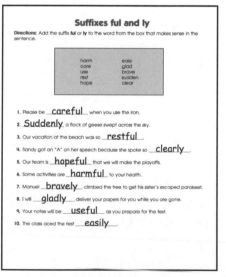

16

Suffixes less and ness

Directions: Add the suffix **less** or **ness** to complete each sentence.

1. We adopted a home **less** _____ dog from the pound.
2. My favorite thing about the dog is the soft **ness** _____ of its fur.
3. The thick **ness** _____ of its fur keeps the dog warm.
4. Dark **ness** _____ scared our dog at first, so it slept in my brother's room.
5. It was use **less** _____ to try to break the dog of that habit!
6. Our house was never spot **less** _____ before the dog arrived, but it is definitely messy now.
7. Feeling at home with our new pet was pain **less** _____.
8. We were not care **less** _____ when we named our dog.

17

Selecting Suffixes

Directions: Write the word with a suffix from the word box that fits the definition.

supportive	patience
absence	intelligence
truthful	forgetful
thoughtful	doubtful
cheerful	active

1. thinking carefully _____ **thoughtful**
2. has trouble remembering _____ **forgetful**
3. having a sunny attitude _____ **cheerful**
4. keeping busy _____ **active**
5. disbelieving or questioning _____ **doubtful**
6. always telling the truth _____ **truthful**
7. the state of not being present _____ **absence**
8. smartness _____ **intelligence**
9. showing great care or concern _____ **supportive**
10. ability to wait calmly _____ **patience**

18

Suffix Definitions

Directions: Write the definition of each word using the suffix definitions in the word box.

ness means "quality of being"
ble means "capable of being"

1. bleakness **quality of being bleak**
2. permissible **capable of being permitted**
3. breakable **capable of being broken**
4. blindness **quality of being blind**
5. steadiness **quality of being steady**
6. admissible **capable of being admitted**
7. furriness **quality of being furry**
8. believable **capable of being believed**

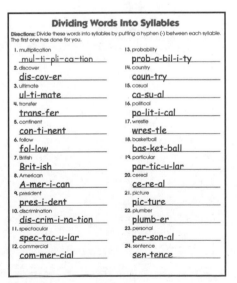

19

Selecting More Suffixes

Directions: Complete each sentence using a word with a suffix from the word box.

collection	invitation
capable	improvements
peaceful	addition
wonderful	marvelous

1. My birthday was **wonderful**.
2. This is my **collection** of stamps.
3. It is so **peaceful** up in the mountains.
4. In **addition** to dance lessons, I take piano and clarinet.
5. The **invitation** for the wedding came yesterday.
6. The movie was **marvelous**!
7. Dad is working on a few home **improvements**.
8. He is not **capable** of lifting all those heavy boxes himself.

20

Analyzing Words and Their Parts

A **syllable** is a word or part of a word with only one vowel sound.

Directions: Fill in the missing syllables. Use words from the box. Write the number of syllables after each word. The first one has been done for you.

expense	exist	aquarium	acquire	request
exact	expand	exit	quality	excellent
quiz	quantity	expression	exhibit	squirm

1. ex**cel**lent (3)
2. **—** squirm (1)
3. **ex**act (2)
4. **—** quiz (1)
5. aquar**i**um (4)
6. ac**quire** (2)
7. quali**ty** (3)
8. **ex**it (2)
9. ex**pres**sion (3)
10. **ex**ist (2)
11. **re**quest (2)
12. ex**hib**it (3)
13. **ex**pense (2)
14. **ex**pand (2)
15. quan**ti**ty (3)

Directions: Write words that rhyme. Use the words in the box.

1. fizz **quiz**
2. resist **exist**
3. fact **exact**
4. fence **expense**
5. sand **expand**
6. it's been sent **excellent**
7. this is it **exhibit**
8. made for me **quality**
9. reflection **expression**
10. worm **squirm**
11. fire **acquire**
12. best **request**
13. fit **exit**

A **root word** is a common stem which gives related words their basic meaning.

Directions: Write the root word for the bold word in each sentence.

1. I know **exactly** what I want. **exact**
2. Those shoes look **expensive**. **expense**
3. She didn't like my **expression** when I frowned. **express**
4. We went to the train **exhibition** at the park. **exhibit**

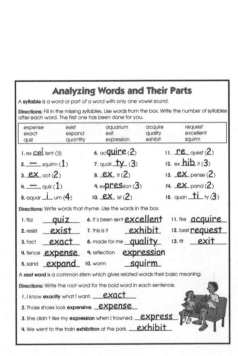

21

Dividing Words Into Syllables

Directions: Divide these words into syllables by putting a hyphen (-) between each syllable. The first one has been done for you.

1. multiplication **mul-ti-pli-ca-tion**
2. discover **dis-cov-er**
3. ultimate **ul-ti-mate**
4. transfer **trans-fer**
5. continent **con-ti-nent**
6. follow **fol-low**
7. British **Brit-ish**
8. American **A-mer-i-can**
9. president **pres-i-dent**
10. discrimination **dis-crim-i-na-tion**
11. spectacular **spec-tac-u-lar**
12. commercial **com-mer-cial**
13. probability **prob-a-bil-i-ty**
14. country **coun-try**
15. casual **ca-su-al**
16. political **po-lit-i-cal**
17. wrestle **wres-tle**
18. basketball **bas-ket-ball**
19. particular **par-tic-u-lar**
20. cereal **ce-re-al**
21. picture **pic-ture**
22. plumber **plumb-er**
23. personal **per-son-al**
24. sentence **sen-tence**

22

GRADE 6

I. Reading
  A. Directions
  B. Sequencing
  C. Main Idea
II. Writing
  A. Capitalization
  B. Proofreading

Tony's Tuxedo

banjo
buffalo
echo
halo
mosquito
patio
portfolio
ratio
rodeo
silo
soprano
stereo
studio
tobacco
tomato
tornado
tuxedo
zero

Directions: Write the words from the word box according to their number of syllables. The first one is done for you.

Two-Syllable Words

ban·jo
ec·ho
ha·lo
si·lo
ze·ro

Three-Syllable Words

to·bac·co
ra·ti·o
tom·a·to
mos·qui·to
so·pra·no
ster·e·o
tux·e·do
buf·fa·lo
tor·na·do
stu·di·o
ro·de·o
pat·i·o

Four-Syllable Word

port·fo·li·o

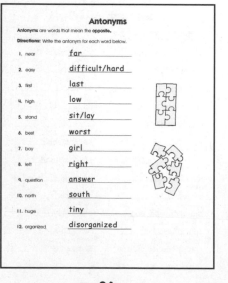

23

This Is So Fine

Directions: Rewrite each sentence below, replacing the word **fine** with one of the synonyms given. Since the synonyms have slight differences in meaning, be careful to choose the correct one.

Fine: clear, delicate, elegant, small, sharp, subtle

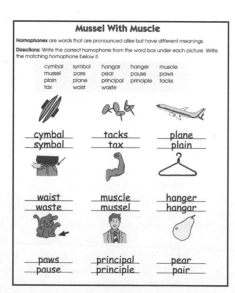

1. The queen wore a **fine** gown encrusted with jewels.

   The queen wore an elegant gown encrusted with jewels.

2. I wash this blouse by hand because of its **fine** lace collar.

   I wash this blouse by hand because of its delicate lace collar.

3. The sand in an hourglass must be very **fine** to trickle as it does.

   The sand in an hourglass must be very small to trickle as it does.

4. We need **fine** weather for sailing.

   We need clear weather for sailing.

5. Dad used a whetstone to put a **fine** edge on the knife.

   Dad used a whetstone to put a sharp edge on the knife.

6. Sometimes there is a **fine** line between innocence and guilt.

   Sometimes there is a subtle line between innocence and guilt.

24

Synonyms

Synonyms are words that mean nearly the **same**.

Directions: Write a word from the word box below its synonym.

refuse	occur	shake	choose
purchase	fright	rough	reply
copy	vacant	worth	pledge
genuine	depart	simple	tardy

| empty | shiver | real | late |
| vacant | shake | genuine | tardy |

| leave | used | decline | value |
| depart | choose | refuse | worth |

| happen | coarse | buy | answer |
| occur | rough | purchase | reply |

| promise | easy | tear | imitate |
| pledge | simple | fright | copy |

25

Antonyms

Antonyms are words that mean the **opposite**.

Directions: Write the antonym for each word below.

1. near — far
2. easy — difficult/hard
3. first — last
4. high — low
5. stand — sit/lay
6. best — worst
7. boy — girl
8. left — right
9. question — answer
10. north — south
11. huge — tiny
12. organized — disorganized

26

Antonyms

Snake Charmer

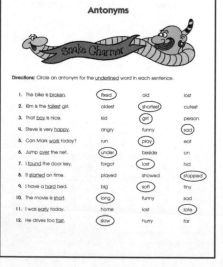

Directions: Circle an antonym for the underlined word in each sentence.

1. The bike is broken. — (fixed) / old / lost
2. Kim is the tallest girl. — oldest / (shortest) / cutest
3. That boy is nice. — kid / (girl) / person
4. Steve is very happy. — angry / funny / (sad)
5. Can Mark work today? — run / (play) / eat
6. Jump over the net. — (under) / beside / on
7. I found the door key. — forgot / (lost) / hid
8. It started on time. — played / showed / (stopped)
9. I have a hard bed. — big / (soft) / tiny
10. The movie is short. — (long) / funny / sad
11. I was early today. — home / lost / (late)
12. He drives too fast. — (slow) / hurry / far

27

Mussel With Muscle

Homophones are words that are pronounced alike but have different meanings.

Directions: Write the correct homophone from the word box under each picture. Write the matching homophone below it.

cymbal	symbol	hangar	hanger	muscle
mussel	pare	pear	pause	paws
plain	plane	principal	principle	tacks
tax	waist	waste		

cymbal / symbol

tacks / tax

plane / plain

waist / waste

muscle / mussel

hanger / hangar

paws / pause

principal / principle

pear / pair

28

GRADE 6

I. Reading
  A. Directions
  B. Sequencing
  C. Main Idea
II. Writing
  A. Capitalization
  B. Proofreading

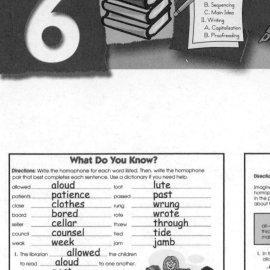

What Do You Know?

Directions: Write the homophone for each word listed. Then, write the homophone pair that best completes each sentence. Use a dictionary if you need help.

allowed	**aloud**	loot	**lute**
patients	**patience**	passed	**past**
close	**clothes**	rung	**wrung**
board	**bored**	rote	**wrote**
seller	**cellar**	threw	**through**
council	**counsel**	tied	**tide**
weak	**week**	jam	**jamb**

1. The librarian **allowed** the children to read **aloud** to one another.
2. This **past** year **passed** by so quickly.
3. The child **wrote** the entire passage by **rote**.
4. According to the agreement, the **seller** must repair the **cellar** windows before the sale is final.
5. A priceless **lute** was among the **loot** stolen from the museum last night.
6. We **tied** our boat to the dock and waited for low **tide**.
7. Caring for so many **patients** requires great **patience**.
8. Please **close** the door of my **clothes** closet.
9. The attorney will **counsel** his clients before the next **council** meeting.
10. We were so **bored** that we decided to leave the **board** meeting.

29

A Crown of Wild Olive Leaves

Directions: Read the selections and fill in each blank with the correct homophones.

Imagine yourself as a spectator at the ancient Greek games! Use the word bank of homophones to fill in each blank within the sentence. Then, use the other homophone in the pair to write your own sentence on the line provided. Try to write sentences about the Olympics.

Word Bank

all—awl	scent—sent	waits—weights	site—sight
throne—thrown	way—weigh	him—hymn	toes—tows
mail—male	scene—seen	war—wore	one—won

1. In the ancient games all athletes were **male**. Unmarried women were allowed to attend the spectacle, but married women were not.
   Answers will vary.
2. The **site** for the games was chosen carefully so that it was in full view of an important landmark.
   Answers will vary.
3. The temple of Zeus could be **seen** from the Games. The games were dedicated in honor of this god.
   Answers will vary.
4. One **way** that athletes relaxed was to swim in the pool at Olympia. But there were no swimming races in this one-and-only pool of ancient Greece.
   Answers will vary.
5. Every four years, three heralds would be **sent** from the town of nearby Elis to proclaim the games and announce the *Olympic Truce*.
   Answers will vary.
6. These heralds carried staffs and **wore** wreaths of olive leaves.
   Answers will vary.
7. The long-jump participants carried heavy lead **weights**. Yet distances of over 16 meters were recorded!
   Answers will vary.

30

8. The greatest honor was given to the winner of the stade. This was a run equal to about 192 meters. The winning sprinter had that year's Games named after **him**.
   Answers will vary.
9. Runners began from a standing start, feet together, **toes** gripping the grooves in the stone slabs which served as the starting line.
   Answers will vary.
10. Wrestlers **won** their events if their opponent had three falls. A fall was declared any time a wrestler's back or shoulder touched the ground.
    Answers will vary.
11. The Olympic Games were one of four all-Greek sports competitions. These games were open to **all** Greek men. At the all-Athens games, one event familiar to us today was a torch race.
    Answers will vary.
12. One chariot competitor, Emperor Nero, won his event even though he was **thrown** from his vehicle and failed to finish. Bribing the judges, Nero was named the champion with the excuse that he would have won if he had finished! After he died, the judges returned the bribe money.
    Answers will vary.

31

Present a Present

compact
conduct
conflict
content
contest
convict
impact
insult
object
permit
present
protest
rebel
record
refund
refuse
subject
suspect

Homographs are spelled alike but are different in meaning or pronunciation.

Directions: Fill in the blank with the correct homograph. Place an accent mark on the appropriate syllable of each homograph.

1. They had to **convíct** the **cónvict** for committing another terrible crime.
2. A young **rébel** will often **rebél** against parents or teachers.
3. I am **contént** with the **cóntent** of my research paper.
4. The nasty **ínsult** used to **insúlt** him made him feel bad.
5. I will **subjéct** myself to this **súbject**.
6. Someday, my parents will **permít** me to get my driver's **pérmit**.
7. The singer hopes to **recórd** a hit **récord**.
8. My mom will **objéct** if I throw this **óbject**.
9. We are expected to **condúct** ourselves with self-control and overall good **cónduct**.
10. I will **presént** her with a lovely **présent**.
11. I **refúse** to touch that stinky **réfuse**.
12. I **suspéct** he is the guilty **súspect**.

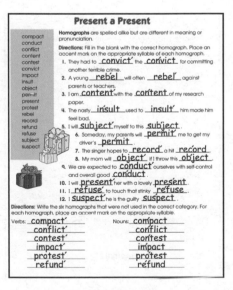

Directions: Write the six homographs that were not used in the correct category. For each homograph, place an accent mark on the appropriate syllable.

Verbs:	Nouns:
compáct	**cómpact**
conflíct	**cónflict**
contést	**cóntest**
impáct	**ímpact**
protést	**prótest**
refúnd	**réfund**

32

The Right Choice

Directions: Unscramble the scrambled word in each sentence. Write it on the line. Then, underline the correct meaning of the word.

1. The (anem) **mean** number between 2 and 8 is 5.
   intend   <u>average</u>   unkind
2. We heard the distant (yab) **bay** of a wolf last night.
   body of water   <u>howl</u>   reddish-brown
3. Help (olib) **bail** water from our boat before it sinks!
   <u>throw water out with a container</u>   pail handle   money for release
4. The race car driver has only one more (apl) **lap** to complete.
   <u>distance around a track</u>   drink up   body part formed when you sit
5. The man reads the (emtre) **meter** every month to see how much electricity we use.
   <u>device that measures flow</u>   rhythm of a poem   unit of length
6. Our pillows are filled with (nowd) **down**.
   grassy land   <u>soft feathers</u>   from higher to lower ground
7. The knight drew his (oilf) **foil** and charged at his enemy.
   keep from carrying out a plan   metal sheet   <u>long narrow sword</u>
8. We ate at the (unterco) **counter** because all the booths were occupied.
   <u>long table in a restaurant</u>   one who counts   opposite
9. You'd better (cudk) **duck**, or you'll bump your head on that branch.
   bird   <u>lower suddenly</u>   type of cloth
10. The (citk) **tick** is known to cause certain diseases in animals and people.
    pillow covering   sound of a clock   <u>a small insect</u>
11. We have to learn the steps of the (elre) **reel** for the school show.
    sway after being hit   spool for winding   <u>dance</u>
12. We left our waitress a twenty-percent (ipt) **tip**.
    slant   end point   <u>money for services</u>

33

Picture This!

A **compound word** is formed by two or more words.
Some compound words are written as one word. **Examples:** blueberry   motorcycle

Other compound words are joined by a hyphen. **Examples:** twenty-one   editor-in-chief

Directions: Write the compound word for each of the following cartoons.

___ + fish **shellfish**	steam + ___ **steamboat**
___ + story **three-story**	___ + frog **bullfrog**
___ + board **cupboard**	horse + ___ **horseshoe**
___ +flying **kite-flying**	lean + ___ **lean-to**
tea + ___ **teaspoon**	___ + round **year-round**
under + ___ **underfoot**	heart + ___ **heartbroken**

34

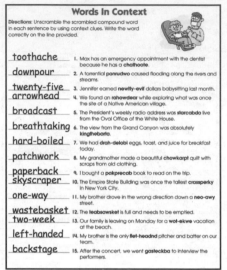

Compound Puzzles

Directions: Solve the word puzzles. Read the first part of the compound word vertically. Then, write the other part of the compound word horizontally. How many words can you make?

```
    FLY           ACHE
FIGHTER        LINE
  WORKS        BAND
  PLACE        STAND

    LORD    CRAFT    GLASSES
    MARK    LINE     BURN
   OWNER    PORT     DOWN
   SLIDE

    SHAKE       DAUGHTER
      BAG     MOTHER
  WRITING       FATHER
     MADE     SON
              CHILD

 GROUND    FIVE      COAT
  STAND    SIX         V
   SIDE    FOUR      COME
  WATER   EIGHT      BOARD
   WEAR      Y
```

35

Put-Them-Together Words

Directions: Choose a word from each box to make a compound word that correctly matches each definition.

folk	ginger	length
three-	trouble	land
court	live	vice-
seventy-	heart	head
chap	near-	sage

wise	broken	sighted
two	fourths	stock
brush	sticks	house
mark	president	quarters
tale	some	bread

Choose a word from each box.

1. not able to see far — **near-sighted**
2. annoying — **troublesome**
3. story handed down among people — **folktale**
4. farm animals — **livestock**
5. grayish-green bushy plant of the dry plains — **sagebrush**
6. a fraction of a whole — **three-fourths**
7. in the direction of the length — **lengthwise**
8. main office of operations — **headquarters**
9. building used for county government — **courthouse**
10. a two-digit number — **seventy-two**
11. kind of spicy cake — **gingerbread**
12. thin wooden sticks used in pairs for eating — **chopsticks**
13. something easily seen and used as a guide — **landmark**
14. officer next in rank to president — **vice-president**
15. crushed by sorrow — **heartbroken**

36

Words In Context

Directions: Unscramble the scrambled compound word in each sentence by using context clues. Write the word correctly on the line provided.

toothache 1. Max has an emergency appointment with the dentist because he has a **chathoote**.

downpour 2. A torrential **ponrudwo** caused flooding along the rivers and streams.

twenty-five 3. Jennifer earned **newtty-evif** dollars babysitting last month.

arrowhead 4. We found an **rahowdear** while exploring what was once the site of a Native American village.

broadcast 5. The President's weekly radio address was **starcabdo** live from the Oval Office of the White House.

breathtaking 6. The view from the Grand Canyon was absolutely **kingthebarta**.

hard-boiled 7. We had **drah-delobi** eggs, toast, and juice for breakfast today.

patchwork 8. My grandmother made a beautiful **chowkarpt** quilt with scraps from old clothing.

paperback 9. I bought a **pakprecab** book to read on the trip.

skyscraper 10. The Empire State Building was once the tallest **crassperky** in New York City.

one-way 11. My brother drove in the wrong direction down a **neo-awy** street.

wastebasket 12. The **leabsawsket** is full and needs to be emptied.

two-week 13. Our family is leaving on Monday for a **wot-ekwe** vacation at the beach.

left-handed 14. My brother is the only **flet-headnd** pitcher and batter on our team.

backstage 15. After the concert, we went **gasteckba** to interview the performers.

37

Messy Groups

Directions: Look at the groups in the chart [...] how all its members are alike. Then, add [...]

Answers will vary.

Group Name	Animals With Fur	Group Name	Countries
Members	bear	Members	United States
	dog		Mexico
	cat		China
	lion		Canada
	wolf		Ireland

Group Name	Bodies of Water	Group Name	Professions
Members	Caribbean	Members	lawyers
	Atlantic		scientists
	Mediterranean		writers
	Pacific Ocean		teachers
	Arctic Ocean		doctors

Group Name	Sounds	Group Name	Bodies in Space
Members	chirping	Members	asteroids
	growling		stars
	shouting		comets
	singing		planets
	talking		moon

38

What's in an Ad?

Directions: Read the advertisements. Classify information in each one as a fact or opinion. Statements of fact can be proven true. Statements of opinion cannot be proven because they present beliefs, judgments, or feelings.

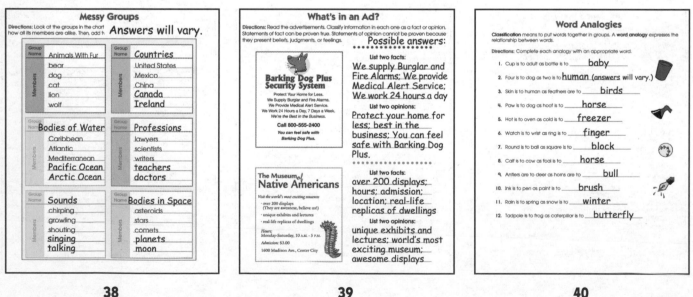

Possible answers:

Barking Dog Plus Security System
Protect Your Home for Less.
We Supply Burglar and Fire Alarms.
We Provide Medical Alert Service.
We Work 24 Hours a Day, 7 Days a Week.
We're the Best in the Business.
Call 800-555-2400
You can feel safe with Barking Dog Plus.

List two facts:
We supply Burglar and Fire Alarms; We provide Medical Alert Service; We work 24 hours a day

List two opinions:
Protect your home for less; best in the business; You can feel safe with Barking Dog Plus.

The Museum of Native Americans
Visit the world's most exciting museum!
- over 200 displays (They are awesome, believe us!)
- unique exhibits and lectures
- real-life replicas of dwellings

Hours: Monday-Saturday, 10 A.M. - 5 P.M.
Admission: $3.00
1600 Madison Ave., Center City

List two facts:
over 200 displays; hours; admission; location; real-life replicas of dwellings

List two opinions:
unique exhibits and lectures; world's most exciting museum; awesome displays

39

Word Analogies

Classification means to put words together in groups. A **word analogy** expresses the relationship between words.

Directions: Complete each analogy with an appropriate word.

1. Cup is to adult as bottle is to **baby**
2. Four is to dog as two is to **human (answers will vary.)**
3. Skin is to human as feathers are to **birds**
4. Paw is to dog as hoof is to **horse**
5. Hot is to oven as cold is to **freezer**
6. Watch is to wrist as ring is to **finger**
7. Round is to ball as square is to **block**
8. Calf is to cow as foal is to **horse**
9. Antlers are to deer as horns are to **bull**
10. Ink is to pen as paint is to **brush**
11. Rain is to spring as snow is to **winter**
12. Tadpole is to frog as caterpillar is to **butterfly**

40

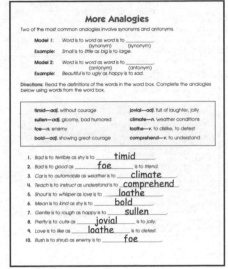

I. Reading
A. Directions
B. Sequencing
C. Main Idea
II. Writing
A. Capitalization
B. Proofreading

More Analogies

Two of the most common analogies involve synonyms and antonyms.

Model 1: Word is to word as word is to _____
(synonym)   (synonym)

Example: Small is to little as big is to large.

Model 2: Word is to word as word is to _____
(antonym)   (antonym)

Example: Beautiful is to ugly as happy is to sad.

Directions: Read the definitions of the words in the word box. Complete the analogies below using words from the word box.

timid—*adj.* without courage	**jovial**—*adj.* full of laughter, jolly
sullen—*adj.* gloomy, bad humored	**climate**—*n.* weather conditions
foe—*n.* enemy	**loathe**—*v.* to dislike, to detest
bold—*adj.* showing great courage	**comprehend**—*v.* to understand

1. Bad is to terrible as shy is to **timid**
2. Bad is to good as **foe** is to friend.
3. Car is to automobile as weather is to **climate**
4. Teach is to instruct as understand is to **comprehend**
5. Shout is to whisper as love is to **loathe**
6. Mean is to kind as shy is to **bold**
7. Gentle is to rough as happy is to **sullen**
8. Pretty is to cute as **jovial** is to jolly.
9. Love is to like as **loathe** is to detest.
10. Bush is to shrub as enemy is to **foe**

41

Word Work

Directions: Look up each of the following words in a dictionary and write the definitions on the line. Then, use these words to complete each analogy below.

1. punctual — on time, prompt
2. fragile — easily broken, delicate
3. discard — to throw out or sway, cast off
4. fraudulent — cheating, dishonest
5. peril — the condition of being in danger
6. prohibit — to not allow by law
7. monotonous — not interesting because of repetition
8. decade — a unit of time equaling 10 years
9. augment — to make greater in size or amount
10. soothe — to make less angry

11. Food is to eat as trash is to **discard**
12. Late is to early as tardy is to **punctual**
13. Metal is to sturdy as glass is to **fragile**
14. Accept is to reject as allow is to **prohibit**
15. Loud is to quiet as varied is to **monotonous**
16. Real is to genuine as fake is to **fraudulent**
17. One hundred is to century as ten is to **decade**
18. Hard is to soft as disturb is to **soothe**
19. Take is to give as subtract is to **augment**
20. Walk is to stroll as danger is to **peril**

42

Analogy Models

Directions: Read the analogy models. Then, circle the correct word to complete each analogy below. Use a dictionary if you need help.

Model 1: Tool is to its function as tool is to its _____
(function)

Example: Pen is to writing as shovel is to digging.

Model 2: Title is to specialty as title is to _____
(specialty)

Example: Dentist is to teeth as veterinarian is to animals.

Model 3: Cause is to effect as cause is to _____
(effect)

Example: Sadness is to tears as joy is to laughter.

Model 4: Worker is to product as worker is to _____
(product)

Example: Author is to book as artist is to painting.

1. Policeman is to crime as doctor is to _____
   (a. illness) b. nurse c. stethoscope d. patient
2. Carpenter is to hammer as doctor is to _____
   a. illness b. nurse (c. stethoscope) d. patient
3. Druggist is to pharmacy as teacher is to _____
   a. student (b. school) c. books d. teach
4. Baker is to bread as seamstress is to _____
   a. thread b. needle (c. dress) d. sewing
5. Scissors are to cut as ax is to _____
   (a. chop) b. burn c. tree d. sharpen
6. Sun is to sunburn as snow is to _____
   a. overcast (b. frostbite) c. umbrella d. climate
7. Fire is to burn as cold is to _____
   a. ice (b. freeze) c. snow d. wind
8. Hunger is to eat as thirst is to _____
   a. food b. cup c. milk (d. drink)

43

Fill Out the Form

Directions: Four people are going camping. Fill in the order form for their camping supplies. Remember to order enough supplies for four people. You can use your home address and phone number.

Item	Price	Order #	Item	Price	Order #
Super Sturdy Tent (4 person tent)	$200 each	97SJ800	First Aid Kit	$22 each	57CN249
Toasty Warm Sleeping Bag	$36 each	86GV394	Waterproof Camera	$25 each	16DK989
Tough Travel Backpack	$20 each	34TP283	Flashlight	$18 each	78PL234
PlastLight Water Bottle	$8 each	22SX436	Portable Stove	$40 each	9STO509

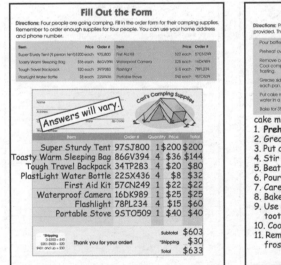

Answers will vary.

Carl's Camping Supplies

Name
Address
City State Zip Code

Item	Order #	Quantity	Price	Total
Super Sturdy Tent	97SJ800	1	$200	$200
Toasty Warm Sleeping Bag	86GV394	4	$36	$144
Tough Travel Backpack	34TP283	4	$20	$80
PlastLight Water Bottle	22SX436	4	$8	$32
First Aid Kit	57CN249	1	$22	$22
Waterproof Camera	16DK989	1	$25	$25
Flashlight	78PL234	4	$15	$60
Portable Stove	9STO509	1	$40	$40

*Shipping	Subtotal	$603
0-$200 = $10	*Shipping	$30
$201-$400 = $20		
$401 and up = $30 Thank you for your order!	Total	$633

44

Recipe Puzzle

Directions: Put the steps for this recipe in the correct order. Write them on the lines provided. Then, write a list of ingredients you will need.

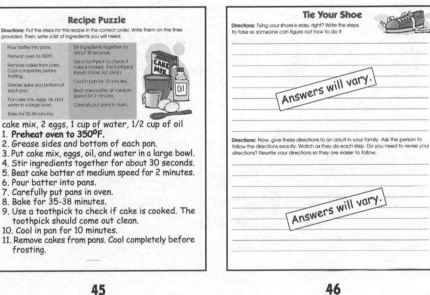

Pour batter into pans.

Preheat oven to 350°F.

Remove cakes from pans. Cool completely before frosting.

Grease sides and bottom of each pan.

Put cake mix, eggs, oil, and water in a large bowl.

Bake for 35-38 minutes.

Stir ingredients together for about 30 seconds.

Use a toothpick to check if cake is cooked. The toothpick should come out clean.

Cool in pan for 10 minutes.

Beat cake batter at medium speed for 2 minutes.

Carefully put pans in oven.

cake mix, 2 eggs, 1 cup of water, 1/2 cup of oil
1. **Preheat oven to 350°F.**
2. Grease sides and bottom of each pan.
3. Put cake mix, eggs, oil, and water in a large bowl.
4. Stir ingredients together for about 30 seconds.
5. Beat cake batter at medium speed for 2 minutes.
6. Pour batter into pans.
7. Carefully put pans in oven.
8. Bake for 35-38 minutes.
9. Use a toothpick to check if cake is cooked. The toothpick should come out clean.
10. Cool in pan for 10 minutes.
11. Remove cakes from pans. Cool completely before frosting.

45

Tie Your Shoe

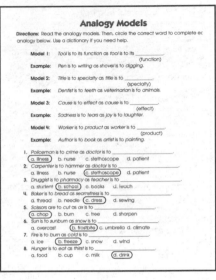

Directions: Tying your shoes is easy, right? Write the steps to take so someone can figure out how to do it.

Answers will vary.

Directions: Now, give these directions to an adult in your family. Ask the person to follow the directions exactly. Watch as they do each step. Do you need to revise your directions? Rewrite your directions so they are easier to follow.

Answers will vary.

46

GRADE 6

I. Reading
A. Directions
B. Sequencing
C. Main Idea
II. Writing
A. Capitalization
B. Proofreading

All in a Day

Directions: Read the activities. Then, write each next to a time that makes sense. Some lines will be blank.

Activities

Go to bed	Eat breakfast
Go to tennis practice	Play catch with a friend
Wake up	Eat dinner
Get out of school	Go to school
Do homework	Eat lunch

Hours in the Day   Answers will vary.

7 A.M. Wake up   Eat breakfast
8 A.M. Go to school
9 A.M.
10 A.M.
11 A.M.
12 P.M. Eat lunch
1 P.M.
2 P.M.
3 P.M. Get out of school   Go to tennis practice
4 P.M.
5 P.M. Do homework
6 P.M. Eat dinner
7 P.M. Play catch with friend
8 P.M.
9 P.M. Go to bed

47

Making a Mosaic

When you follow directions, be sure to read through them first, slowly. Look for special terms and time-order words, gather all materials, and follow the directions in the order they are written.

Directions: The pictures below show step-by-step directions for making a mosaic. Beside each picture, write the directions to explain each step. Be sure to use time-order words.

Step 1: First, cut construction paper to fit the box top.

Step 2: Then, glue construction paper to the box top.

Step 3: Next, draw a simple picture on the construction paper.

Step 4: Then, cut small pieces from magazines into shapes.

Step 5: Next, glue the pieces onto the drawing and over the entire box top to make the mosaic.

Step 6: Finally, paint the sides of the shoebox and the top.

48

Topic and Main Idea

Directions: Read each paragraph. Then, answer the questions.

You need a balanced diet to stay healthy. A balanced diet provides the amount of nutrients your body needs every day. By eating lots of different foods, you will get the nutrients you require to stay healthy.

1. What is the topic of this paragraph? Circle one.
   A. eating foods
   B. the importance of a balanced diet ◯
   C. planning your diet

2. Which sentence states the main idea about the topic?
   A. When you eat lots of different foods you get the nutrients you require.
   B. A balanced diet provides the amount of nutrients your body needs every day.
   C. You need a balanced diet to stay healthy. ◯

The food guide pyramid shows the five basic food groups. When choosing what to eat, you should think about these food groups. The food groups are Bread, Cereal, Rice, and Pasta; Vegetable; Fruit; Milk, Yogurt, and Cheese; and Meat, Poultry, Fish, Dry Beans, Eggs, and Nuts. The best way to plan a balanced diet is to choose a variety of foods from each of the five food groups.

3. What is the topic of this paragraph? Circle one.
   A. planning a balanced diet ◯
   B. vegetables
   C. the food guide pyramid

4. Which sentence states the main idea about the topic? Circle one.
   A. The food guide pyramid shows the five basic food groups.

B. When choosing what to eat, you should think about these food groups.
C. The best way to plan a balanced diet is to choose a variety of foods from each of the five food groups.

You should avoid eating cookies, candy, and sweetened soft drinks. These foods have a lot of sugar and very little nutritional value. They may also cause you to gain weight and your teeth to decay.

5. What is the topic of this paragraph? Circle one.
   A. foods to avoid eating ◯
   B. sugar
   C. how to avoid gaining weight

6. What is the unstated main idea? Circle one.
   A. Some foods have a lot of sugar and not much nutritional value.
   B. Cookies, candy, and sweetened soft drinks are not healthful foods. ◯
   C. Foods with a lot of sugar can cause you to gain weight.

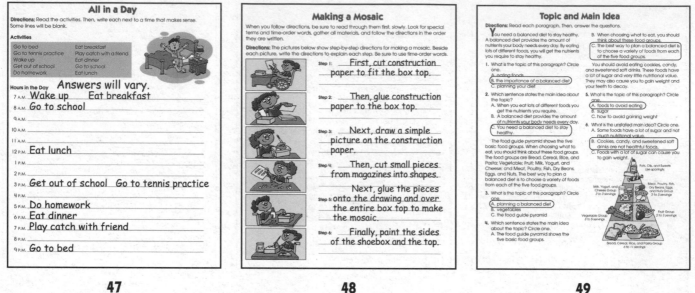

49

What's the Main Idea?

Often the main idea of a passage is **stated** in a sentence. Sometimes, however, you have to figure out the **unstated** main idea by looking at important details.

Directions: Read each paragraph. Then, write a sentence that states the main idea for each paragraph.

One of the most popular forms of entertainment today is playing computer games. Children are fascinated by these games. They are popular because they have exciting graphics, fun activities, and a wide variety of games.

Stated Main Idea: One of the most popular forms of entertainment today is playing computer games.

Some radio stations play jazz. Others play rock. Still others play country. Some stations just report the news and weather. What a lot of variety we get from radio!

Unstated Main Idea: Possible answer: There are a variety of listening options on the radio.

Do you have a hobby? One kind of hobby involves collecting things. Some people collect stamps. Others may collect dolls or stuffed animals. Many people collect and trade sports cards. Another kind of hobby involves building things. Some people build models of ships and airplanes from kits or build large structures from Legos. Other hobbies involve music, art, dance, and sports.

Unstated Main Idea: Possible answer: There are many kinds of hobbies.

50

What's the Idea?

Directions: Circle the sentence that best expresses the main idea of each paragraph.

1. Edmund began to question whether or not the lion in the Queen's courtyard was alive. The large creature looked as if it were about to pounce on a dwarf. But it did not move. Then Edmund noticed the snow on the lion's head and back. Only a statue would be covered like that!
   • The statue is snow-covered.
   • Edmund wonders if the lion is alive. ◯
   • The lion is ready to jump.

2. The resting party of children and beavers heard the sound of jingling bells. Mr. Beaver dashed out of his hiding place and soon called the others to join him. He could hardly contain himself with excitement. Father Christmas is here!
   • Mr. Beaver is a brave animal.
   • Father Christmas has come to Narnia. ◯
   • The group hears a jingling sound.

3. Poor Edmund! Because he came to the Queen, he expected her to reward him gratefully with Turkish delight. After all, he had traveled so far and had suffered miserably in the cold. When the Queen finally commanded that he receive food and drink, the cruel dwarf brought Edmund a bowl of water and a hunk of dry bread.
   • Edmund is not rewarded as he expects. ◯
   • The young boy suffered from the cold.
   • Edmund receives bread and water.

4. Peter knew he must rescue Susan from the wolf. When the wolf charged, Susan climbed up a nearby tree. The wolf's snapping and snarling mouth was inches away. When Peter looked more closely, he realized that his sister was about to faint. Rushing in with his sword, Peter slashed at the beast.
   • Peter kills the wolf.
   • Peter realizes he must save his sister. ◯
   • The wolf snarls at Susan.

51

Beth Is Sick

Poor Beth is sick, and she doesn't know why. She felt great yesterday, but this morning she woke up with a headache, a fever, and a horrible sore throat. Beth is disappointed because today is the day her class is going to the new science museum. Why did she have to be sick on a field trip day? How did she get ill so quickly?

Beth and Kim talk on the phone about Beth's situation for twenty minutes. Because they planned to be field trip partners, Kim is really sad Beth isn't going to school today. Kim tells Beth she probably got sick because she didn't wear a jacket to school yesterday, and it was a cold day. She tells Beth that if your body gets cold, you catch germs more easily. Beth tells Kim that is silly. She believes Kim has a virus.

Beth remembers learning about viruses in science class. Mr. Fridley told them that viruses are noncellular structures that can only be seen through an electron microscope, which magnifies them thousands of times. On its own, a virus is a lifeless particle that can't reproduce, but when a virus enters a living cell, it starts reproducing and can sometimes harm the host cell. Viruses that harm host cells cause disease like chicken pox, the flu, and colds. Mr. Fridley told them that shaking hands with or being sneezed or coughed on by an infected person may infect you with the virus. Beth believes that she became infected from someone since lots of people are sick at this time of year. Kim promises Beth a full report on the science museum.

Directions: Underline the main idea of the story.

Beth has a headache, fever, and a sore throat.
Beth and Kim try to discover why Beth is sick.
Viruses cause diseases.
Mr. Fridley taught them about viruses.

Directions: Check the correct answers.

Viruses...
☑ can't be seen through an ordinary light microscope.
☑ pass easily from one person to another.
☐ are thousands of times bigger than regular cells.
☑ enter living cells and start reproducing.

What are some ways to avoid viruses? Answers will vary.

52

GRADE 6

I. Reading
  A. Directions
  B. Sequencing
  C. Main Idea
II. Writing
  A. Capitalization
  B. Proofreading

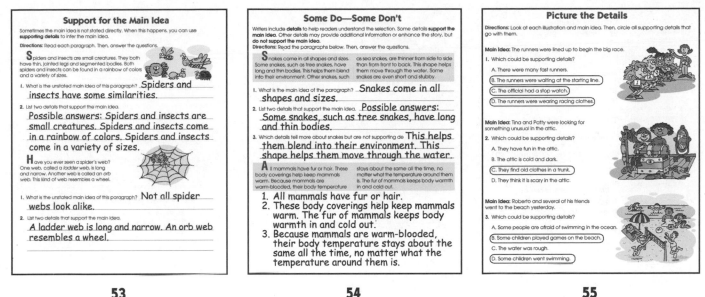

Support for the Main Idea

Sometimes the main idea is not stated directly. When this happens, you can use **supporting details** to infer the main idea.

Directions: Read each paragraph. Then, answer the questions.

Spiders and insects are small creatures. They both have thin, jointed legs and segmented bodies. Both spiders and insects can be found in a rainbow of colors and a variety of sizes.

1. What is the unstated main idea of this paragraph? Spiders and insects have some similarities.

2. List two details that support the main idea.
Possible answers: Spiders and insects are small creatures. Spiders and insects come in a rainbow of colors. Spiders and insects come in a variety of sizes.

Have you ever seen a spider's web? One web, called a ladder web, is long and narrow. Another web is called an orb web. This kind of web resembles a wheel.

1. What is the unstated main idea of this paragraph? Not all spider webs look alike.

2. List two details that support the main idea.
A ladder web is long and narrow. An orb web resembles a wheel.

53

Some Do—Some Don't

Writers include **details** to help readers understand the selection. Some details **support the main idea**. Other details may provide additional information or enhance the story, but do not support the main idea.

Directions: Read the paragraphs below. Then, answer the questions.

Snakes come in all shapes and sizes. Some snakes, such as tree snakes, have long and thin bodies. This helps them blend into their environment. Other snakes, such as sea snakes, are thinner from side to side than from front to back. This shape helps them move through the water. Some snakes are even short and stubby.

1. What is the main idea of the paragraph? Snakes come in all shapes and sizes.

2. List two details that support the main idea. Possible answers: Some snakes, such as tree snakes, have long and thin bodies.

3. Which details tell more about snakes but are not supporting de This helps them blend into their environment. This shape helps them move through the water.

All mammals have fur or hair. These body coverings help keep mammals warm. Because mammals are warm-blooded, their body temperature stays about the same all the time, no matter what the temperature around them is. The fur of mammals keeps body warmth in and cold out.

1. All mammals have fur or hair.
2. These body coverings help keep mammals warm. The fur of mammals keeps body warmth in and cold out.
3. Because mammals are warm-blooded, their body temperature stays about the same all the time, no matter what the temperature around them is.

54

Picture the Details

Directions: Look at each illustration and main idea. Then, circle all supporting details that go with them.

Main Idea: The runners were lined up to begin the big race.
1. Which could be supporting details?
A. There were many fast runners.
B. The runners were waiting at the starting line.
C. The official had a stop watch.
D. The runners were wearing racing clothes.

Main Idea: Tina and Patty were looking for something unusual in the attic.
2. Which could be supporting details?
A. They have fun in the attic.
B. The attic is cold and dark.
C. They find old clothes in a trunk.
D. They think it is scary in the attic.

Main Idea: Roberto and several of his friends went to the beach yesterday.
3. Which could be supporting details?
A. Some people are afraid of swimming in the ocean.
B. Some children played games on the beach.
C. The water was rough.
D. Some children went swimming.

55

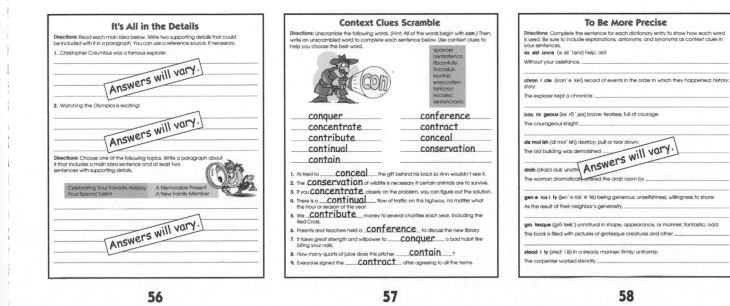

It's All in the Details

Directions: Read each main idea below. Write two supporting details that could be included with it in a paragraph. You can use a reference source, if necessary.

1. Christopher Columbus was a famous explorer.

Answers will vary.

2. Watching the Olympics is exciting!

Answers will vary.

Directions: Choose one of the following topics. Write a paragraph about it that includes a main idea sentence and at least two sentences with supporting details.

Celebrating Your Favorite Holiday | A Memorable Present
Your Special Talent | A New Family Member

Answers will vary.

56

Context Clues Scramble

Directions: Unscramble the following words. (Hint: All of the words begin with **con**.) Then, write an unscrambled word to complete each sentence. Use context clues to help you choose the best word.

quoncer
centratenco
ribcontute
tincoalun
inontac
enecacofem
tantcroc
nocalec
sentoncravia

conquer   conference
concentrate   contract
contribute   conceal
continual   conservation
contain

1. Al tried to **conceal** the gift behind his back so Ann wouldn't see it.
2. The **conservation** of wildlife is necessary if certain animals are to survive.
3. If you **concentrate** closely on the problem, you can figure out the solution.
4. There is a **continual** flow of traffic on this highway, no matter what the hour or season of the year.
5. We **contribute** money to several charities each year, including the Red Cross.
6. Parents and teachers held a **conference** to discuss the new library.
7. It takes great strength and willpower to **conquer** a bad habit like biting your nails.
8. How many quarts of juice does this pitcher **contain**?
9. Everyone signed the **contract** after agreeing to all the terms.

57

To Be More Precise

Directions: Complete the sentence for each dictionary entry to show how each word is used. Be sure to include explanations, antonyms, and synonyms as context clues in your sentences.

as sist ance (e sis´ tens) help; aid:
Without your assistance,

chron i cle (kron´ e kel) record of events in the order in which they happened; history; story:
The explorer kept a chronicle

cou ra geous (ke rā´ jes) brave; fearless; full of courage:
The courageous knight

de mol ish (di mol´ ish) destroy; pull or tear down:
The old building was demolished

drab (drab) dull, unatt
The woman dramatically altered the drab room by

Answers will vary.

gen e ros i ty (jen´ e ros´ e tē) being generous; unselfishness; willingness to share:
As the result of their neighbor's generosity,

gro tesque (grō tesk´) unnatural in shape, appearance, or manner; fantastic; odd:
The book is filled with pictures of grotesque creatures and other

stead i ly (sted´ l ē) in a steady manner; firmly; uniformly:
The carpenter worked steadily

58

GRADE
6

I. Reading
  A. Directions
  B. Sequencing
  C. Main Idea
II. Writing
  A. Capitalization
  B. Proofreading

Context Clues

A **context clue** is a clue or **hint from the sentence** that helps you to figure out words that you don't know.

Directions: Read each sentence carefully. Guess the definition of each underlined word based on the context clues in the sentence. Then, use a dictionary to see how good your guess was.

1. He didn't want to miss that game because the coach had said it was a crucial one in deciding the championship.
   Answers will vary. / very important
   your guess / dictionary definition

2. Although he tried to be punctual, he was always late.
   Answers will vary. / on time
   your guess / dictionary definition

3. The confusing instructions that come with some home computers perplex many people.
   Answers will vary. / puzzle, complicated
   your guess / dictionary definition

4. Light has a velocity of about 186,000 miles per second.
   Answers will vary. / speed
   your guess / dictionary definition

5. Our pet bird warbles happily in his cage all day long.
   Answers will vary. / to sing or whistle
   your guess / dictionary definition

59

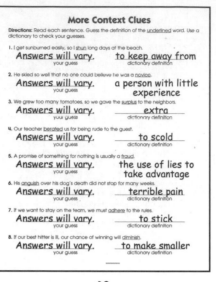

More Context Clues

Directions: Read each sentence. Guess the definition of the underlined word. Use a dictionary to check your guesses.

1. I get sunburned easily, so I shun long days at the beach.
   Answers will vary. / to keep away from
   your guess / dictionary definition

2. He skied so well that no one could believe he was a novice.
   Answers will vary. / a person with little experience
   your guess / dictionary definition

3. We grew too many tomatoes, so we gave the surplus to the neighbors.
   Answers will vary. / extra
   your guess / dictionary definition

4. Our teacher berated us for being rude to the guest.
   Answers will vary. / to scold
   your guess / dictionary definition

5. A promise of something for nothing is usually a fraud.
   Answers will vary. / the use of lies to take advantage
   your guess / dictionary definition

6. His anguish over his dog's death did not stop for many weeks.
   Answers will vary. / terrible pain
   your guess / dictionary definition

7. If we want to stay on the team, we must adhere to the rules.
   Answers will vary. / to stick
   your guess / dictionary definition

8. If our best hitter is ill, our chance of winning will diminish.
   Answers will vary. / to make smaller
   your guess / dictionary definition

60

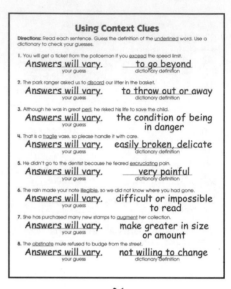

Using Context Clues

Directions: Read each sentence. Guess the definition of the underlined word. Use a dictionary to check your guesses.

1. You will get a ticket from the policeman if you exceed the speed limit.
   Answers will vary. / to go beyond
   your guess / dictionary definition

2. The park ranger asked us to discard our litter in the basket.
   Answers will vary. / to throw out or away
   your guess / dictionary definition

3. Although he was in great peril, he risked his life to save the child.
   Answers will vary. / the condition of being in danger
   your guess / dictionary definition

4. That is a fragile vase, so please handle it with care.
   Answers will vary. / easily broken, delicate
   your guess / dictionary definition

5. He didn't go to the dentist because he feared excruciating pain.
   Answers will vary. / very painful
   your guess / dictionary definition

6. The rain made your note illegible, so we did not know where you had gone.
   Answers will vary. / difficult or impossible to read
   your guess / dictionary definition

7. She has purchased many new stamps to augment her collection.
   Answers will vary. / make greater in size or amount
   your guess / dictionary definition

8. The obstinate mule refused to budge from the street.
   Answers will vary. / not willing to change
   your guess / dictionary definition

61

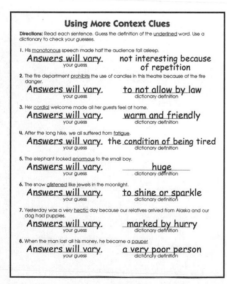

Using More Context Clues

Directions: Read each sentence. Guess the definition of the underlined word. Use a dictionary to check your guesses.

1. His monotonous speech made half the audience fall asleep.
   Answers will vary. / not interesting because of repetition
   your guess / dictionary definition

2. The fire department prohibits the use of candles in this theatre because of the fire danger.
   Answers will vary. / to not allow by law
   your guess / dictionary definition

3. Her cordial welcome made all her guests feel at home.
   Answers will vary. / warm and friendly
   your guess / dictionary definition

4. After the long hike, we all suffered from fatigue.
   Answers will vary. / the condition of being tired
   your guess / dictionary definition

5. The elephant looked enormous to the small boy.
   Answers will vary. / huge
   your guess / dictionary definition

6. The snow glistened like jewels in the moonlight.
   Answers will vary. / to shine or sparkle
   your guess / dictionary definition

7. Yesterday was a very hectic day because our relatives arrived from Alaska and our dog had puppies.
   Answers will vary. / marked by hurry
   your guess / dictionary definition

8. When the man lost all his money, he became a pauper.
   Answers will vary. / a very poor person
   your guess / dictionary definition

62

Understanding Context Clues

Directions: For each sentence, circle the pair of words that completes the meaning the sentence.

1. Their profits have been _____, and they wish to _____ their situation.
   a. decreasing—excuse
   b. declining—remedy
   c. comfortable—redress

2. Rats provide a _____ in reducing garbage, but this is outweighed by their _____ activities.
   a. help—useful
   b. trouble—dynamic
   c. service—harmful

3. Fact and Fancy were so _____ that no one could _____ them.
   a. connected—separate
   b. necessary—use
   c. respected—want

4. If one is to understand the _____, one must study the _____.
   a. facts—unnecessary
   b. unusual—sentences
   c. whole—parts

5. His father _____ him, for he realized the interest was more than a _____ fancy.
   a. encouraged—childish
   b. berated—sincere
   c. helped—mature

6. Safe driving prevents _____ and the awful _____ of knowing you have caused an accident.
   a. disease—remainder
   b. accidents—safe
   c. tragedy—remorse

63

Reviewing Context Clues

Directions: Circle the word which best fits each sentence.

Saving your (1) _____ to eat at a later date is not always (2) _____. It may not wait as long as you do!
1. land / greed / luck / **dessert**
2. golden / **wise** / fair / sure

Many (3) _____ may indeed make for light work, but only if they work (4) _____.
3. **shovels** / seas / hands / kitchens
4. **together** / alone / nearby / silently

"Put your money where your mouth is" may be a (5) _____ -inflicting proverb; but it sure (6) _____ people quiet!
5. plant / gold / wise / **germ**
6. invests / **keeps** / shuts / tempts

Go ahead and rollerblade along life's (7) _____, but keep those knee pads (8) _____ for the bumps along the way.
7. problems / **highways** / lamps / deeds
8. **ready** / quick / dangerous / softly

Music may indeed (9) _____ a savage beast, but only if the (10) _____ has an instrument nearby.
9. shoot / ride / **calm** / scale
10. lion / trumpet / radio / **musician**

The saying "A fool and his money are soon (11) _____" should not be discussed when (12) _____ allowance from our parents.
11. **parted** / happy / peaceful / shown
12. sewing / waving / giving / **asking**

As Uncle Gene (13) _____ on his inflatable raft on the (14) _____, we knew that some men are islands!
13. flew / **fetched** / floated / fared
14. dock / **lake** / sink / house

Hurtling downward into a deep, dark (15) _____, Bernard exclaimed, "Why sure! Gotta (16) _____ before ya' leap!"
15. mansion / Chevy / **chasm** / rim
16. **look** / shave / care / buy

64

GRADE 6

I. Reading
A. Directions
B. Sequencing
C. Main Idea
II. Writing
A. Capitalization
B. Proofreading

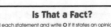

Just the Facts, Please

Directions: Read Ricky's paragraph. Underline each sentence that states an opinion rather than a fact. Then, list one valid and faulty opinion. Opinions are considered valid if they are supported by facts and faulty if they are not.

There are some really goofy laws still on the books in cities and towns throughout the United States. Many of these laws were passed a long time ago. Why they were passed is beyond me! People back then sure had some strange ideas about right and wrong.

In New Jersey, for example, it is against the law to slurp your soup in a public restaurant, and in the city of Newark, you must have a written note from your doctor if you want to buy ice cream after 6:00 P.M.!

If you happen to live within the city limits of Flowery Branch, Georgia, you had better not yell, "Snake!" Kids who live in Minneapolis, Minnesota, will like this next law, especially if they don't have a dishwasher. You see, it's against the law to wipe dishes dry. The lawmakers believed that dishes should drip dry. If you are a boy in Pulaski, Illinois, watch out where you throw snowballs! It's against the law for you to throw them at trees.

girls to throw snowballs, though, because they aren't mentioned in the law. That's really unfair.

Now here's another, you'll enjoy. I'm sure you'd agree that most little kids like lollipops. Well, guess what! If you live in Spokane, Washington, you are not allowed to buy a lollipop if you are a child. It's the law! If your family car drips oil or anything else for that matter, Green Bay, Wisconsin, is not the place to be. There is a one-dollar fine for every drop your car makes on the pavement. Speaking of cars, if you like comics, don't get caught reading them if you are riding in a car in Norman, Oklahoma. It's against the law.

Now here's the best one, in Winnetka, Illinois, it's against the law to take your shoes off in a theater if your feet smell.

Valid Opinion Possible answers: There are some really goofy laws still on the books; People back then had some strange ideas about right and wrong.

Faulty Opinion Possible answers: Why they were passed in the first place is beyond me; Now, here's another one you'll enjoy; I'm sure you'll agree that most kids like lollipops; Now here is the best one.

65

Is That a Fact?

Directions: Read each statement and write **O** if it states an opinion or **F** if it states a fact. Then, give a reason for each answer.

1. _O_ The most impressive view of China's Great Wall is from a space shuttle as it orbits Earth.

People will have different opinions about which view of the wall is most impressive.

2. _O_ Built between 400s B.C. and A.D. 1600s, the Great Wall was the greatest engineering feat of its time.

Other things constructed during that time period might be considered to be greater engineering feats.

3. _F_ The Great Wall is the longest human-made structure in existence, with the main part stretching over 2,100 miles.

The length of the Great Wall can be measured.

4. _F_ If you include the Great Wall's side sections and spurs, you can add another 1,800 miles or so to its total length, making it as long as the Nile River.

The sections and spurs can be measured, then compared to the actual length of the Nile River.

5. _O_ The Chinese should rebuild all the sections of the Great Wall that have crumbled over the centuries.

This is a matter for the people of China to decide.

6. _O_ Everyone says that the Great Wall is China's greatest national treasure.

There is no way to prove what everyone says about the wall, and China has other great treasures like the Imperial Palace.

66

Reading Skills: Fact or Opinion?

A **fact** is information that can be proved. An **opinion** is information that tells how someone feels or what he or she thinks about something.

Directions: For each sentence, write **F** for fact or **O** for opinion. The first one has been done for you.

_F_ 1. Each of the countries in South America has its own capital.

_O_ 2. All South Americans are good swimmers.

_O_ 3. People like the climate in Peru better than in Brazil.

_F_ 4. The continent of South America is almost completely surrounded by water.

_F_ 5. The only connection with another continent is a narrow strip of land, called the Isthmus of Panama, which links it to North America.

_F_ 6. The Andes Mountains run all the way down the western edge of the continent.

_F_ 7. The Andes are the longest continuous mountain barrier in the world.

_O_ 8. The Andes are the most beautiful mountain range.

_F_ 9. The Amazon River is the second longest river in the world—about 4,000 miles long.

_F_ 10. Half of the people in South America are Brazilians.

_O_ 11. Life in Brazil is better than life in other South American countries.

_O_ 12. Brazil is the best place for South Americans to live.

_F_ 13. Cape Horn is at the southern tip of South America.

_F_ 14. The largest land animal in South America is the tapir, which reaches a length of 6 to 8 feet.

67

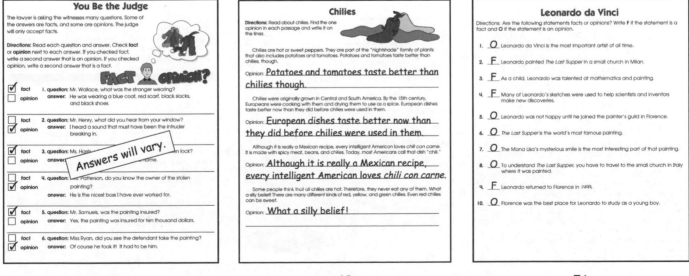

You Be the Judge

The lawyer is asking the witnesses many questions. Some of the answers are facts, and some are opinions. The judge will only accept facts.

Directions: Read each question and answer. Check **fact** or **opinion** next to each answer. If you checked fact, write a second answer that is an opinion. If you checked opinion, write a second answer that is a fact.

FACT **OPINION?**

☑ fact
☐ opinion **1. question:** Mr. Wallace, what was the stranger wearing?
answer: He was wearing a blue coat, red scarf, black slacks, and black shoes.

☐ fact
☑ opinion **2. question:** Mr. Henry, what did you hear from your window?
answer: I heard a sound that must have been the intruder breaking in.

☑ fact
☐ opinion **3. question:** Ms. Harris, ... lock?
answer: ... home.

☐ fact
☑ opinion **4. question:** ... Patterson, do you know the owner of the stolen painting?
answer: He is the nicest boss I have ever worked for.

☑ fact
☐ opinion **5. question:** Mr. Samuels, was the painting insured?
answer: Yes, the painting was insured for ten thousand dollars.

☐ fact
☑ opinion **6. question:** Miss Ryan, did you see the defendant take the painting?
answer: Of course he took it! It had to be him.

Answers will vary.

68

Chilies

Directions: Read about chilies. Find the one opinion in each passage and write it on the lines.

Chilies are hot or sweet peppers. They are part of the "nightshade" family of plants that also includes potatoes and tomatoes. Potatoes and tomatoes taste better than chilies, though.

Opinion: Potatoes and tomatoes taste better than chilies though.

Chilies were originally grown in Central and South America. By the 15th century, Europeans were cooking with them and drying them to use as a spice. European dishes taste better now than they did before chilies were used in them.

Opinion: European dishes taste better now than they did before chilies were used in them.

Although it is really a Mexican recipe, every intelligent American loves chili con carne. It is made with spicy meat, beans, and chilies. Today, most Americans call that dish "chili."

Opinion: Although it is really a Mexican recipe, every intelligent American loves chili con carne.

Some people think that all chilies are hot. Therefore, they never eat any of them. What a silly belief! There are many different kinds of red, yellow, and green chilies. Even red chilies can be sweet.

Opinion: What a silly belief!

69

Leonardo da Vinci

Directions: Are the following statements facts or opinions? Write **F** if the statement is a fact and **O** if the statement is an opinion.

1. _O_ Leonardo da Vinci is the most important artist of all time.

2. _F_ Leonardo painted The Last Supper in a small church in Milan.

3. _F_ As a child, Leonardo was talented at mathematics and painting.

4. _F_ Many of Leonardo's sketches were used to help scientists and inventors make new discoveries.

5. _O_ Leonardo was not happy until he joined the painter's guild in Florence.

6. _O_ The Last Supper is the world's most famous painting.

7. _O_ The Mona Lisa's mysterious smile is the most interesting part of that painting.

8. _O_ To understand The Last Supper, you have to travel to the small church in Italy where it was painted.

9. _F_ Leonardo returned to Florence in 1499.

10. _O_ Florence was the best place for Leonardo to study as a young boy.

71

GRADE
6

I. Reading
A. Directions
B. Sequencing
C. Main Idea
II. Writing
A. Capitalization
B. Proofreading

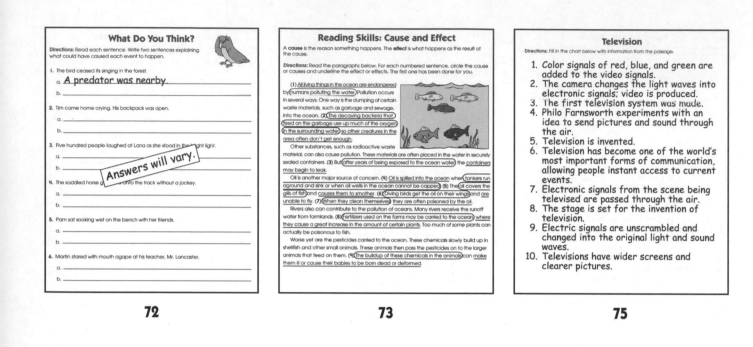

What Do You Think?

Directions: Read each sentence. Write two sentences explaining what could have caused each event to happen.

1. The bird ceased its singing in the forest.
   a. A predator was nearby.
   b. _____

2. Tim came home crying. His backpack was open.
   a. _____
   b. _____

3. Five hundred people laughed at Lana as she stood in the bright light.
   a. _____
   b. _____

Answers will vary.

4. The saddled horse g___ onto the track without a jockey.
   a. _____
   b. _____

5. Pam sat soaking wet on the bench with her friends.
   a. _____
   b. _____

6. Martin stared with mouth agape at his teacher, Mr. Lancaster.
   a. _____
   b. _____

72

Reading Skills: Cause and Effect

A **cause** is the reason something happens. The **effect** is what happens as the result of the cause.

Directions: Read the paragraphs below. For each numbered sentence, circle the cause or causes and underline the effect or effects. The first one has been done for you.

(1) All living things in the ocean are endangered by humans polluting the water. Pollution occurs in several ways. One way is the dumping of certain waste materials, such as garbage and sewage, into the ocean. (2) The decaying bacteria that feed on the garbage use up much of the oxygen in the surrounding water so other creatures in the area often don't get enough.

Other substances, such as radioactive waste material, can also cause pollution. These materials are often placed in the water in securely sealed containers. (3) But after years of being exposed to the ocean water, the containers may begin to leak.

Oil is another major source of concern. (4) Oil is spilled into the ocean when tankers run aground and sink or when oil wells in the ocean cannot be capped. (5) The oil covers the gills of fish and causes them to smother. (6) Diving birds get the oil on their wings and are unable to fly. (7) When they clean themselves, they are often poisoned by the oil.

Rivers also can contribute to the pollution of oceans. Many rivers receive the runoff water from farmlands. (8) Fertilizers used on the farms may be carried to the ocean where they cause a great increase in the amount of certain plants. Too much of some plants can actually be poisonous to fish.

Worse yet are the pesticides carried to the ocean. These chemicals slowly build up in shellfish and other small animals. These animals then pass the pesticides on to the larger animals that feed on them. (9) The buildup of these chemicals in the animals can make them ill or cause their babies to be born dead or deformed.

73

Television

Directions: Fill in the chart below with information from the passage.

1. Color signals of red, blue, and green are added to the video signals.
2. The camera changes the light waves into electronic signals; video is produced.
3. The first television system was made.
4. Philo Farnsworth experiments with an idea to send pictures and sound through the air.
5. Television is invented.
6. Television has become one of the world's most important forms of communication, allowing people instant access to current events.
7. Electronic signals from the scene being televised are passed through the air.
8. The stage is set for the invention of television.
9. Electric signals are unscrambled and changed into the original light and sound waves.
10. Televisions have wider screens and clearer pictures.

75

Put Them Together

Directions: Find the causes and effects that make sense together. Write the complete cause/effect sentences on the lines provided.

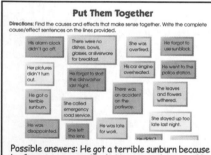

His alarm clock didn't go off. | There were no dishes, bowls, glasses, or silverware for breakfast. | She was overtired. | He forgot to use sunblock.

Her pictures didn't turn out. | He forgot to start the dishwasher last night. | His car engine overheated. | He went to the police station.

He got a terrible sunburn. | There was an accident on the parkway. | The leaves and flowers withered.

He was disappointed. | She called emergency road service. | He was late for work. | She stayed up too late last night.

She left the lens.

Possible answers: He got a terrible sunburn because he forgot to use sunblock; He got stuck in a traffic jam and his car engine overheated; There was an accident on the freeway so she called emergency road service; He went to the police station because his wallet was stolen; She stayed up too late last night so she was overtired; He didn't water the plants for two weeks so the leaves and flowers withered; He forgot to start the dishwasher last night so there were no dishes, bowls, glasses, or silverware for breakfast; Her pictures didn't turn out because she left the lens cap on her camera.

76

Shiloh

A **simile** is a comparison using the words *like* or *as*.

Example: The pile of laundry was *as high as a mountain* by the time our washer was fixed.

Directions: Underline the similes in these sentences. Write another simile with the same or nearly the same meaning.

1. My dream leaks out like water in a paper bag.
   Answers will vary.
2. I hold Shiloh as carefully as I carry Becky when she's asleep.
3. I'm as happy as a flea on a dog.
4. Keeping Shiloh a secret is like having a bomb waiting to go off.
5. I'm as tense as a cricket at night.
6. Ma hums to Shiloh like he's a baby in a cradle.

Directions: Complete these sentences with a simile of your own.

1. Shiloh looked at Dara Lynn like _____
2. Doc Murphy was as gentle as _____ *Answers will vary.*
3. Judd trying to be n_____
4. The Prestons were happy as _____ to have Shiloh.

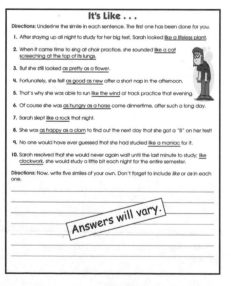

77

It's Like . . .

Directions: Underline the simile in each sentence. The first one has been done for you.

1. After staying up all night to study for her big test, Sarah looked like a lifeless plant.
2. When it came time to sing at choir practice, she sounded like a cat screeching at the top of its lungs.
3. But she still looked as pretty as a flower.
4. Fortunately, she felt as good as new after a short nap in the afternoon.
5. That's why she was able to run like the wind at track practice that evening.
6. Of course she was as hungry as a horse come dinnertime, after such a long day.
7. Sarah slept like a rock that night.
8. She was as happy as a clam to find out the next day that she got a "B" on her test!
9. No one would have ever guessed that she had studied like a maniac for it.
10. Sarah resolved that she would never again wait until the last minute to study; like clockwork, she would study a little bit each night for the entire semester.

Directions: Now, write five similes of your own. Don't forget to include *like* or *as* in each one.

_____
_____
Answers will vary.
_____

78

GRADE 6

I. Reading
  A. Directions
  B. Sequencing
  C. Main Idea
II. Writing
  A. Capitalization
  B. Proofreading

Compared to What?

A **simile** compares two different things and states the comparison directly by using the word *as* or *like*. A **metaphor** makes a comparison without stating it directly.

Example: The basketball player was a tower next to his other teammates.

Directions: Underline the metaphors in the following sentences. The first one has been done for you.

1. The airplane was a bullet in the sky.
2. From the plane, the river was a silver ribbon winding through the landscape.
3. The clouds were ghostly battleships sailing across the sky.
4. The snow-capped peaks were ice cream cones jutting into the sky.
5. The sunset was a bonfire in the sky.
6. The plane's shadow was a giant bird skimming effortlessly across the farm fields below.
7. Chicago was on fire with lights as we approached the airport at dusk.
8. The exciting city was a breath of fresh air to us folks from the country.

Directions: Now, write five metaphors of your own.

Answers will vary.

79

Which Is Which?

Directions: Label each sentence **simile** or **metaphor**.

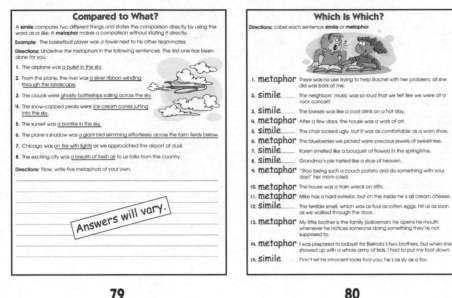

1. metaphor — There was no use trying to help Rachel with her problem; all she did was bark at me.
2. simile — The neighbors' music was so loud that we felt like we were at a rock concert.
3. simile — The breeze was like a cool drink on a hot day.
4. metaphor — After a few days, the house was a work of art.
5. simile — The chair looked ugly, but it was as comfortable as a worn shoe.
6. metaphor — The blueberries we picked were precious jewels of sweetness.
7. simile — Karen smelled like a bouquet of flowers in the springtime.
8. simile — Grandma's pie tasted like a slice of heaven.
9. metaphor — "Stop being such a couch potato and do something with your day!" her mom cried.
10. metaphor — The house was a train wreck on stilts.
11. metaphor — Mike has a hard exterior, but on the inside he's all cream cheese.
12. simile — The terrible smell, which was as foul as rotten eggs, hit us as soon as we walked through the door.
13. metaphor — My little brother is the family policeman; he opens his mouth whenever he notices someone doing something they're not supposed to.
14. metaphor — I was prepared to babysit for Belinda's two brothers, but when she showed up with a whole army of kids, I had to put my foot down.
15. simile — Don't let his innocent looks fool you; he's as sly as a fox.

80

Calling All Idioms

An **idiom** is a word or phrase that has taken on a different meaning than its actual one. Some idioms are so common that we don't even think about them. The expression "putting your foot in your mouth," for example, means saying something embarrassing or stupid.

Directions: Underline the idioms in the following sentences. The first one has been done for you.

1. You're lucky you keep winning, but don't push your luck.
2. My dad called me on the carpet after viewing my report card.
3. We're all in the same boat here!
4. Jared is putting me on.
5. By a vote of 8-3, the board turned down the proposal.
6. Since Mr. Smith was absent, they asked Ms. Nakano to fill in.
7. We ran into Nicki and Sammy at the fair.
8. The pizza at City Pies is out of this world.

Directions: Write a sentence using each of the idioms from the box:

break down	grow up	set up	run down
strike out	bottle up	shake down	check out

Answers will vary.

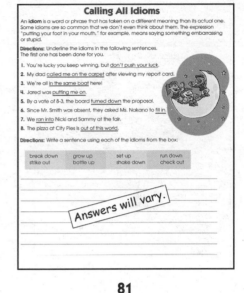

81

Extra! Extra!

Directions: The following are opening sentences for articles that appeared in the most recent edition of *Mercerville Monthly*. Read each one and predict the purpose of the article. Write **persuade**, **inform**, or **entertain** on the line.

There's no doubt in my mind that Michael Jordan is the best basketball player that has ever lived.

1. **persuade**

On Friday night, the Town Council voted unanimously to create a scholarship fund to send Mercerville's brightest students to college.

2. **inform**

Everyone has been wondering about our town's newest, most famous resident, comedian Slick Anderson. Well, Slick took me on a tour of his multi-million-dollar estate today, and what he showed me made me laugh so hard my stomach hurt. Wait until you hear about Slick's collection of humorous cartoon memorabilia!

3. **entertain**

Café de Cochon, located at 33 Main Street, serves light French food at reasonable prices.

4. **inform**

Some people say the solution to Mercerville's beetle problem is to spray a deadly insecticide. But why risk poisoning our pets, the environment, and even ourselves? I have a better plan for getting rid of the unwanted beetles, and not only is it safer for the environment but it won't cost the townspeople any money.

5. **persuade**

Six houses have been burglarized since the town's Neighborhood Watch program was dismantled, according to Police Chief Carmen DeSoto.

6. **inform**

As mayor of this town, Bob Thorpe has done nothing but deceive people. Mike Fernandez is an honest and hardworking alternative to Mr. Thorpe, and everyone should vote for him on Election Day.

7. **persuade**

How is it that this town can raise thousands of dollars for the Mercerville High boys' basketball team but the championship-winning girls' team can't even afford new uniforms? It's time for Mercerville to give female athletes the respect they deserve!

8. **persuade**

82

No Day at the Beach

Directions: Read each story fragment. Then, write a possible outcome. When you have finished, read your completed story!

All week, my family had been looking forward to spending Saturday at Brewster Beach. Then, on Friday night, my little sister got an earache, and my mom said we'd probably have to take her to the doctor the next day. Fortunately,

_____

Saturday started out as a beautiful day. We all woke up early and my dad made waffles. We put on our swimsuits and packed the car. But, when my mom tried to start the car, it

_____

Eventually, we were _____ again. But then, it began _____ minutes from the beach when sheets of water fell from the sky. We _____ rain would ruin our day for sure. So we pulled over, and

Answers will vary.

When we finally got to the beach, all the other families were already packing their things to go. My sister begged to stay for an hour or so, so we spread out our blanket even though the air was getting cool. I decided to feel the water. But I had no sooner dipped in my big toe when I was attacked by a swarm of mosquitoes! They were everywhere!

_____

We were all grumpy that night. What a disaster! I have a feeling it'll be a while before we plan another trip to Brewster Beach.

_____

83

What Will Happen?

Directions: Read each situation. Then, use what you know to make a prediction.

"Have a good day, and please don't forget to shut the windows before you leave for school!" said Mrs. Martin, rushing to catch her bus.

Max was eating breakfast and finishing the homework assignment he had forgotten to do last night. Twenty minutes later, he looked up at the clock. If he didn't hurry, he would miss his bus. Max shoved his homework and books into his backpack and ran out the door, making sure it was locked.

It was during math class that Max heard thunder and a howling wind and noticed the dark storm clouds.

"Oh, no," Max moaned to himself.

1. Predict what Max will find when he gets home. **Possible answers: Everything near the opened windows is wet; the newspapers and letters have been blown on the floor.**

Mary Beth had 10 more problems to finish before she could meet her friends. If she hadn't wasted so much time on the computer after dinner while she was supposed to be doing homework, she could have been outside having fun with them right now. Within a half-hour Mary Beth was out the door.

Only a few minutes later, she heard her mother calling her. "Mary Beth! It's time to come in!"

She barely had a chance to play. Reluctantly, Mary Beth left her friends and went inside. She was determined to do things differently tomorrow.

2. **Possible answers: Mary Beth will do her homework promptly and not waste time on the computer if she wants to meet her friends; she will start doing her homework as soon as she gets home from school.**

The Johnsons are away for the week. They have hired Dennis to get their mail and newspaper each afternoon while they are gone.

On Tuesday, he has soccer practice all afternoon and forgets. On Wednesday, he goes to a friend's house and stays overnight.

3. **Possible answers: The Johnsons will be upset to find their mailbox stuffed with letters and bills and newspapers piled up in their yard; the Johnsons will never hire Dennis to do anything for them again.**

84

GRADE
6

I. Reading
  A. Directions
  B. Sequencing
  C. Main Idea
II. Writing
  A. Capitalization
  B. Proofreading

What Happens Next?

Directions: Do you like to read comic strips? Have you ever tried to predict the outcome before reading the last frame? Well, here's your chance to show what you know about cats, predict what will happen, and be an artist, too! Read the frames below. Then, draw the ending.

Oh, look at that beautiful butterfly!

I'm going to catch you!

Oh, you're trying to get away from me!

Drawings/Dialogue will vary.

85

Athlete Mix-Up

Directions: Read each description of an athlete. Draw a conclusion about what type of athlete is described. Write your answers on the lines.

1. My sport can be played outside or inside. I don't usually play on a team, but, sometimes, I have a partner. I have to hit a ball over a net, but not with my hands. Once I pulled a muscle while practicing my killer serve.

I'm a **tennis player**

2. My sport is almost always played outside. I don't play on a team. I have to hit a ball over and over again, but not with my hands. My dream is to someday make a "hole in one." I can take a cart instead of walking to get from one part of the course to another.

I'm a **golfer**

3. My sport is always played inside. It involves trying to knock over things. I don't have to wear a uniform when I compete in my sport, but I do have to wear special shoes. I am happy when I make a "strike."

I'm a **bowler**

4. My sport is played outside by teams. There are lots of skills involved in my sport: kicking, throwing, catching, and running. Some of my teammates are pretty big, especially the linebacker. He looks even bigger when he's wearing his uniform and all his padding.

I'm a **football player**

5. When I was a little kid, I fantasized about swinging through the trees like a monkey. Now, I can swing, jump, dance, and do flips, too. My sport is usually played inside. I practice my routine and try to be graceful so I will impress the judges on competition day.

I'm a **gymnast**

6. My sport can be played outside or inside. However, it can't be played outside when the weather is cold. I go fast by kicking my legs as I pull with my arms. Sometimes, I race against other people, and, sometimes, I race against the clock. In long races, I have teammates who take over when I have finished my laps.

I'm a **swimmer**

7. Look, no hands needed in my sport! I am not allowed to touch the ball with my hands. Usually, I kick it, but I can bounce it off my head, too. I run from one end of the field to the other, trying to get the ball past the goalie and into the net.

I'm a **soccer player**

86

The Missing Painting

Directions: Read the following mystery and answer the questions.

Detective Doolittle couldn't sleep. He...

1. He knows that she is lying because she said she saw Fred at the Post Office the day after the robbery, which must have been a Sunday, but the Post Office isn't open on Sundays. Also, she said that the gardener had to take her daughter to school that day, but there is definitely no school on a Saturday in July.

2. Answers will vary, but may include: Miss Rappaport probably made up the whole story about the painting being stolen. There's no evidence and she's trying to blame it on everyone else.

...strange that day?" the detective asked.

1. Why does Detective Doolittle say that Miss Rappaport is lying?

2. What do you think happened to the painting? What makes you think so?

3. On another sheet of paper, write a conclusion to the story.

87

I Conclude . . .

Directions: When you read, you use information in the text as well as what you know to draw conclusions. Read the following facts and think about what you know. Make a check mark next to the correct conclusion. Then, write another conclusion for each of the facts.

1. Dolphins sleep just under the surface of the water but come up for air at three to four minute intervals.
   ✓ Dolphins are not fish but mammals.
   ___ Dolphins are light sleepers.
   Answers will vary.

2. Hydroponics, the cultivation of plants in water, was once used by the ancient Aztecs and Chinese, and is currently in use year-round in many greenhouses where the climate makes it impossible to grow plants outside.
   ___ Hydroponics is not a new method of growing plants.
   ___ Hydroponics is an efficient method of plant cultivation.
   Answers will vary.

3. Between 1950 and 1996, the population of New York City went from 7,891,957 to 7,380,906, while the population of Dallas went from 434,462 to 1,053,292.
   ___ New York City is one of the largest cities in the world.
   ✓ The population of a city can increase or decrease over time.
   Answers will vary.

4. An elephant eats about 1/20 of its own body weight daily, while a mouse eats as much as its weight.
   ___ An elephant eats an enormous amount of food each day.
   ✓ A smaller animal such as the mouse eats more in relation to its size.
   Answers will vary.

5. In less than a decade, the landfills in over half of the 50 states will be filled to capacity.
   ✓ We are running out of room for all the garbage we produce.
   ___ Landfills are not the best solution for disposing of garbage.
   Answers will vary.

88

Summarizing

A **summary** is a brief retelling of the main ideas of a reading selection. To summarize, write the author's most important points in your own words.

Directions: Write a two-sentence summary for each paragraph.

The boll weevil is a small beetle that is native to Mexico. It feeds inside the seed pods, or bolls, of cotton plants. The boll weevil crossed into Texas in the late 1800s. It has since spread into most of the cotton-growing areas of the United States. The boll weevil causes hundreds of millions of dollars worth of damage to cotton crops each year.

Summary:

Each spring, female boll weevils... plants with their snouts. They lay eggs... soon hatch into worm-like grubs. The... causing the buds to fall from the plant. They... one bud to another. Several generations of boll weevil... be produced in a single season.

Answers will vary.

Summary:

The coming of the boll weevil to the United States caused tremendous damage to cotton crops. Yet, there were some good results, too. Farmers were forced to plant other crops. In areas where a variety of crops were raised, the land is in better condition than it would have been if only cotton had been grown.

Summary:

89

At the Movies

Directions: What is your favorite movie of all time? Imagine that you are the arts and entertainment writer for a major newspaper. Write a summary of this movie including its topic, main idea, names of main characters, and the important events that took place. Then, write a paragraph at the end to tell why you think people should see it.

MOVIE TICKET

Answers will vary.

90

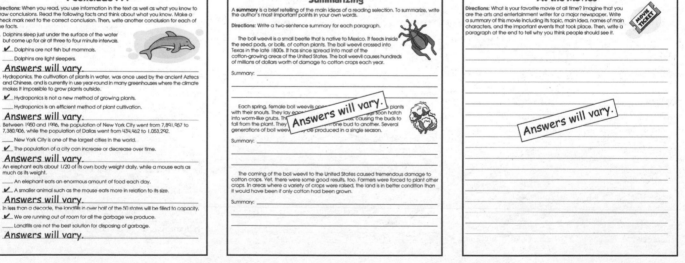

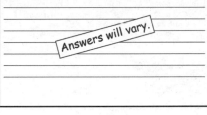

Neon Lights

Directions: A summary should include only the important details from a selection. Read the paragraph. Summarize it on the lines below. Then, go back and circle the sentences from the article that contained details that were not important for your summary.

When we think of neon lights, we think of the signs we see in store windows. That light is different from the light produced by an ordinary light bulb in a lamp. The light in neon lamps is produced by neon, a gas found in the air all around us. Neon gas, which is what is in neon lights, is colorless. When the sign is turned on, an electric current flows through the tube. The electrons in the neon gas get a burst of energy from the electric current. As each electron settles down, it releases a photon of light. The photons travel to our eyes and we see red light. Even though this light appears to glow continuously, the electrons are really like little lights blinking on and off. When the sign is turned off again, the neon gas becomes colorless.

Answers will vary.

91

Summarizing a Personal Narrative

Directions: Read the following narrative. Then, follow the directions.

My Greatest Fear

I am scared of spiders. I realize this is not a logical fear, but I cannot help myself. I have been frightened by spiders since I was very young.

The first reason that I am scared of spiders is their appearance. I do not like their eight wispy, creepy legs. Spiders are never easily seen, but rather dark and unattractive. They are often hairy, and the mere thought of multiple eyeballs gives me shivers.

Spiders are not well-behaved. They are sly and always ready to sneak up on innocent victims. Spiders have habits of scurrying across floors, dropping from ceilings, and dangling from cobwebs. One never knows what to expect from a spider.

Finally, I am scared of spiders due to a "spider experience" as a child. Having just climbed into bed, I noticed a particularly nasty-looking spider on the ceiling over my bed. My father came in to dispose of it, and it fell into bed with me. The thought of it crawling over me drove me from the bed shrieking. After that, I checked the ceiling nightly before getting into bed.

Many people love spiders. They are good for the environment and are certainly needed on our planet. However, because of my fear, irrational though it may be, I'd rather just avoid contact with arachnids.

Directions: Write a four-sentence summary of the narrative.

Answers will vary.

92

Facts to Back It Up

The statements you read in a newspaper article should be **objective**, or based on facts and not the writer's opinion. The writer should provide these facts to back up the story.

Directions: Read the following article carefully. Then, follow the instructions at the bottom of the page.

New Movie Theater Planned
By Marilyn Moore

Everyone who lives in the Oakdale section of town is excited about the movie theater planned for construction. The site where they want to build it is an empty lot. There is nothing there but trees and a bike path. Having a big movie theater is better than having only trees. The architect's plans for the building are perfect. And they will build a new sidewalk to let people who live south of Lawrence Street walk there. People will spend lots of time at the movie theater because everyone loves movies. The biggest benefit of having the theater is that when it opens, all the kids my age will get part-time jobs there.

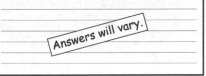

1. Circle all the facts that are given in the article.

2. Underline all the sentences from the article that reflect the author's opinion.

3. Tell why you do or do not think the article is objective. **This article is not objective, because many of the statements in it are based on the author's opinion.**

4. On the lines below, rewrite this article so that it is objective.

Answers will vary.

93

To Get the Vote

Directions: Read the following passage. Then, answer the questions.

Imagine how different life would be if women had never been given the right to vote! Before 1920, no woman in the United States could vote in an election. There were also laws that limited their right to own property, and many colleges and employers would not accept female applicants.

In the mid-1800s, women and men all over the country began speaking out in favor of giving women more rights. In 1848, a conference was held in Seneca Falls, New York, to bring famous people who believed in more rights for women. Many famous people attended the conference including Elizabeth Cady Stanton, Lucretia Mott, Frederick Douglass, and Sojourner Truth. They felt that, as long as women were unable to vote, other rights could be denied to them as well.

The struggle for women's right to vote continued for many years. Susan B. Anthony, another activist, actually cast a vote in the 1872 presidential election and was arrested as a result. During her trial, she told the judge that she had voted "to educate all women to do precisely as I have done, rebel against your man-made, unjust, unconstitutional forms of law."

Her plan may have worked, because the demand for the right to vote only increased in the late 19th and early 20th centuries. Finally, in 1920, Congress added the 19th Amendment to the Constitution: "The right of citizens of the United States to vote shall not be denied or abridged by the United States or by any State on account of sex."

1. What was the author's purpose for writing this passage— to inform, entertain, persuade, or express beliefs? **to inform**

2. **Possible answer: Women in the United States fought for the right to vote for a long time before they were granted it in 1920.**

3. **Answers will vary, but may include: Women could not own property, educate themselves, or get most jobs. Activists probably thought that if women could vote, they would change laws to give women other rights.**

94

Keep Behavin'

It was time for another of Mr. Fridley's science classes on behaviors. This time, the class was going to discuss learned behaviors. Mr. Fridley explained that learned behaviors are behaviors that change as a result of experience.

First, Mr. Fridley explained learning by association. This type of learning connects a stimulus with a particular response. He asked if anyone could give him an example. Lee suggested that when the bell rings at the end of class, the students put away their pens and pick up their books. Mr. Fridley congratulated Lee on his answer and said that the students learned to associate the stimulus of the bell with the response of leaving class.

There are several kinds of learning by association. One results in a conditioned response—a desired response to an unusual stimulus. Mr. Fridley reminded them of Ivan Pavlov's experiments with dogs. In the experiments, Pavlov found that dogs salivated when they smelled meat. Pavlov began ringing a bell every time he was about to give meat to a dog. In time, the dog salivated when the bell rang, whether or not there was any meat. Pavlov had trained the dogs to respond to the bell instead of the food.

Another kind of learning by association involves teaching animals to act in a certain way by rewarding them for their behavior. This is called positive reinforcement and may be as simple as a rat pressing a lever to get food. This type of learning, however, may also involve a complex series of tasks.

Match:

conditioned response ———— study hard—get a good grade

positive reinforcement ———— hear siren—panic

Underline:
Both types of learning by association involve . . .

<u>a stimulus.</u>   a learned association.

<u>a response.</u>   experiments.

Circle:
If a squirrel learns to climb into a bird feeder to obtain food, it has learned by . . .

conditioned response.   unconditioned response.

(positive reinforcement.)   negative reinforcement.

Write examples of something you have learned by a conditioned response and something you have learned by . . . *Answers will vary.*

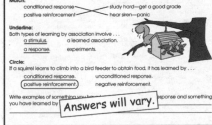

95

What's the Difference?

One day, David and Donald were discussing alligators. David insisted that alligators and crocodiles were the same animal but that people called them by different names. Donald insisted, however, that the two animals were entirely different reptiles. Kim walked up just in time to save the boys from further squabbling. Kim, who had lived in Florida for ten years, could settle this one.

She told David that alligators and crocodiles are separate reptiles. She told them that although they are similar-looking and are both called crocodilians, they are very different. Both have a long, low, cigar-shaped body, short legs, and a long, powerful tail to help them swim. But most crocodiles have a pointed snout instead of a round one like the alligator's. She also pointed out that while both have tough hides, long snouts, and sharp teeth to grasp their prey, the crocodile is only about two-thirds as heavy as an American alligator of the same length and can therefore move much more quickly. David and Donald were impressed with Kim's knowledge.

Kim also told the boys another way to tell the two reptiles apart. She said that both have an extra long lower fourth tooth. This tooth fits into a pit in the alligator's upper jaw, while in the crocodile, it fits into a groove in the side of the upper jaw and shows when the crocodile's mouth is closed. David and Donald thanked Kim for the information, looked at each other sheepishly, and walked away laughing.

Match:

crocodile — fourth tooth shows when mouth is shut
— round snout
— called *crocodilian*
alligator — fourth tooth is in a pocket in upper jaw
— pointed snout

Directions: Write three **Answers may include:** three ways they are different.

Alike	Different
tough hide	alligators have round snout, crocodiles have pointed
short legs	crocodiles are lighter
long, powerful tail	crocodiles are faster

Name two other animals that are sometimes thought to be the same.

Answers will vary.   toad   frog

96

GRADE 6

I. Reading
   A. Directions
   B. Sequencing
   C. Main Idea
II. Writing
   A. Capitalization
   B. Proofreading

Cats and Dogs

Directions: Magda is comparing and contrasting her cat Spike and her dog Fritz. Here's her chart.

	SPIKE	FRITZ
Tricks	does nothing on command	fetches, sits, shakes, begs
Destructiveness	claws furniture and drapes	chews shoes, slippers, and anything left around
Food	eats only one kind of cat food and only when he feels like it	eats anything and everything edible including stuff I don't like
Grooming	loves to be brushed	loves to be brushed
Breath	not too bad if you like fish, which I don't	bad enough to knock you out
Friendliness	cuddly only when he wants to be cuddled	always happy, wagging tail, licking my face, wanting to play
Vet Visits	could not care less	has to be dragged through the door

1. Both animals are destructive, like to be brushed, and have breath that is often bad.
2. Fritz does tricks, while Spike does not; Fritz is not a finicky eater like Spike; Fritz is friendly all the time, unlike Spike; Fritz does not like going to the vet, whereas Spike doesn't mind.
3. Answers will vary.

97

Pizza and Pie

Directions: You can use a **Venn diagram** to compare and contrast things, ideas, facts, and people. As you study the delicious-looking pizza and blueberry-peach pie, list their similarities and their distinguishing characteristics on the diagram below.

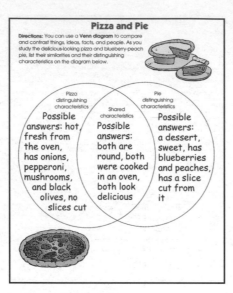

Pizza distinguishing characteristics

Possible answers: hot, fresh from the oven, has onions, pepperoni, mushrooms, and black olives, no slices cut

Shared characteristics

Possible answers: both are round, both were cooked in an oven, both look delicious

Pie distinguishing characteristics

Possible answers: a dessert, sweet, has blueberries and peaches, has a slice cut from it

98

Stranger Than Fiction

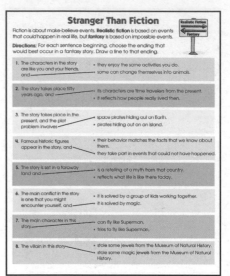

Fiction is about make-believe events. **Realistic fiction** is based on events that could happen in real life, but **fantasy** is based on impossible events.

Directions: For each sentence beginning, choose the ending that would best occur in a fantasy story. Draw a line to that ending.

1. The characters in the story are like you and your friends, and
   - they enjoy the same activities you do.
   - some can change themselves into animals.

2. The story takes place fifty years ago, and
   - its characters are time travelers from the present.
   - it reflects how people really lived then.

3. The story takes place in the present, and the plot problem involves
   - space pirates hiding out on Earth.
   - pirates hiding out on an island.

4. Famous historic figures appear in the story, and
   - their behavior matches the facts that we know about them.
   - they take part in events that could not have happened.

5. The story is set in a faraway land and
   - is a retelling of a myth from that country.
   - reflects what life is like there today.

6. The main conflict in the story is one that you might encounter yourself, and
   - it is solved by a group of kids working together.
   - it is solved by magic.

7. The main character in this story
   - can fly like Superman.
   - tries to fly like Superman.

8. The villain in this story
   - stole some jewels from the Museum of Natural History.
   - stole some magic jewels from the Museum of Natural History.

99

Make It Real

Directions: Liz wants to enter a story-writing contest. She wrote down all the ideas that came into her head. Then, she decided that she wants to make her story realistic. Circle the details that she might use in her story.

Possible settings:
a) the year 2525
b) (the present)
c) (five years ago)
d) (a small town)
e) (a softball field)
f) a spaceship going to Neptune
g) a castle where time is standing still
h) (a surprise party)
i) a mermaid's cave under the sea
j) a rocket going to the Moon

Possible plot problems:
s) A softball team has never won a game.
t) A magic pearl fell into the sea and must be found.
u) The main character wants to impress a new neighbor.
v) Space aliens are planning to steal Earth's water.
w) The character has to answer a riddle in order to free himself or herself from the prison of an evil princess.
x) The character gets upset when Grandfather moves in.
y) The character's two best friends have been quarreling.
z) The characters in a book come to life.

Possible characters:
k) the Boogie Monster
l) a talking frog
m) (a pet pig)
n) (a sixth-grade girl)
o) (someone's grandfather)
p) a girl who can fly
q) a mermaid
r) a boy who can do magic tricks

Get real!

100

It's Impossible!

Directions: Eli is visiting his cousin Jacob. He'd like to read a fantasy story at bedtime. He selects some books and reads a passage from each. Make a check mark in front of each passage that could have come from a fantasy book. Then, underline the words or sentences that make you feel sure of this.

☐ Suddenly the banging, clattering, and crashing stopped. The furious roar of the wind died down. The eerie silence was almost as scary as the raging of the storm. Ben started toward the cellar stairs, but his uncle pulled him back. "It's not safe yet," he said. "We're just in the eye of the tornado."

☑ Miranda closed her eyes and counted to ten, just as the old woman had told her to do. When she opened her eyes again, she was still sitting on the grass with Snowball, her cat, beside her. The difference, however, was that <u>she was now scarcely any taller than her cat.</u> Snowball narrowed his eyes and growled softly at her.

☑ Carlos waded to the shore, holding tight to the silver coin that Adrian had given him. What had Adrian said? "If you need help, <u>rub the coin and say my name and I will be there.</u> But I will come only once." Beyond the shimmering white beach stretched the dense, gloomy forest that he must pass through to reach Evershade.

☐ It seemed impossible that a castle should have so many halls and all of them so much alike. Gabrielle thought to herself as she darted around yet another corner. She was desperate to find a staircase. She dreaded being caught where she shouldn't have

been, yet she also hoped that someone would find her soon and lead her back to her tour group.

☑ The road beyond the wooden bridge forked in two directions. One followed the stream burbling and twinkling under the bridge. The other path, nearly overgrown with weeds, led up the hillside and toward the rocky cliffs. Emma hesitated, her map now useless. "<u>If I were you, I'd go to the left,</u>" remarked an ancient turtle that had been sunning itself on the bank. It then slid into the water with a soft plop.

☐ Jun watched his older brother with envy. This was going to be Ho's first year in the dragon, and he had taken what seemed like hours to dress. Now, he was carefully combing and recombing his hair in front of the mirror. "No one's going to see anything but your feet," Jun said crossly. "You'd think you were going to lead the whole parade."

101

Choices, Choices

Directions: Read each summary and write two more sentences that could be added to it. The first sentence should suggest a realistic plot. The second should turn the story into a fantasy. The first one has been done for you.

1. Brooke and Brendan's family has inherited Aunt May's old house in the country. They decide to spend the summer fixing it up. As they are cleaning out the basement, Brooke and Brendan make a surprising discovery.
   <u>They find a scrapbook with photos of a girl who looks like she could be Brooke's twin.</u>
   <u>They discover a tunnel that leads to a different world each time they follow it.</u>

2. Juan's older brother and his friends say Juan isn't good enough to play basketball with them. Feeling sad, Juan goes to practice by himself in the empty schoolyard.

3. Mrs. Maychek is a quiet, shy old woman who lives in the apartment next door to Malik's family. One day, Malik rescues Mrs. Maychek's cat from the fierce bulldog and carries the injured cat to its owner. Mrs. Maychek is grateful and gives him cake and cocoa. Then, Malik notices something strange around the living room.

4. Tony's friends have all gone away for the summer, and he is sure he'll have a rotten summer. However, Uncle Matthew stops by with an "unbirthday" gift that he says will solve Tony's problem. The gift is a box full of envelopes, and he is to open one each day. Eagerly, he tears open the first envelope.

Answers will vary.

102

GRADE
6

I. Reading
A. Directions
B. Sequencing
C. Main Idea
II. Writing
A. Capitalization
B. Proofreading

The Author's Purpose

Authors write to entertain, inform, or persuade. To **entertain** means to hold the attention of or to amuse someone. A fiction book about outer space entertains its reader, as does a joke book.

To **inform** means to give factual information. A cookbook informs the reader of new recipes. A newspaper tells what is happening in the world.

To **persuade** people means to convince them. Newspaper editorial writers try to persuade readers to accept their opinions. Doctors write health columns to persuade readers to eat nutritious foods.

Directions: Read each of the passages below. Tell whether they entertain, inform, or persuade. (They may do more than one.) Give the reasons why.

George Washington was born in a brick house near the Potomac River in Virginia on Feb. 11, 1732. When he was 11 [...] other, Lawrence, at Mount Vernon.

Author's Purpose: Inform

Reason: [Answers may include:] The passage contains only facts about George Washington.

When George Washington was a child, he always measured and counted things. Maybe that is why he became a surveyor when he grew up. Surveyors like to measure and count things, too.

Author's Purpose: Persuade and inform

Reason: The passage gives the author's opinion, as well as some facts.

George Washington was the best president America has ever had. He led a new nation to independence. He made all the states feel as if they were part of the United States. All presidents should be as involved with the country as George Washington was.

Author's Purpose: Persuade

Reason: Most of the information in this passage is opinion. The author tries to persuade the reader to agree with his point of view.

103

Llamas

Directions: Read each paragraph. Tell whether it informs, entertains, or persuades. One paragraph does more than one. Then, write your reasons on the lines below.

A llama (LAH'MAH) is a South American animal that is related to the camel. It is raised for its wool. Also, it can carry heavy loads. Some people who live near mountains in the United States train llamas to go on mou[...] they have two long [...]

[Answers may include:]

Author's Purpose: inform

Reason: All information is factual.

Llamas are the best animals to have if you're planning to backpack in the mountains. They can climb easily and carry your supplies. No one should ever go for a long hiking trip in the mountains without a llama.

Author's Purpose: persuade/inform

Reason: The paragraph contains some opinion and some fact. Sometimes, they suddenly stop walking for no reason. People have to push them to get them moving again. Stubborn llamas can be frustrating when hiking up a steep mountain.

Author's Purpose: inform

Reason: All information is factual.

Greg is an 11-year-old boy who raises llamas to climb mountains. One of his llamas is named Dallas. Although there are special saddles for llamas, Greg likes to ride bareback.

Author's Purpose: entertain

Reason: This information is presented to interest the reader. It tells a story.

Now use a separate sheet of paper to inform readers about llamas.

104

Roller Coasters

Directions: Read each paragraph and determine the author's purpose. Then, write down your reason on the line below.

Roller coaster rides are thrilling. The cars chug up the hills and then fly down them. People scre[...] metimes raise their arms above [...]

[Answers may include:]

Author's Purpose: inform/entertain

Reason: This is mostly fact but the author adds descriptive words. in Russia. That was more than 300 years ago! The slides were about 70 feet high, and people had to climb steep ladders to reach their tops. Riders got into carts and slid down very fast. Then, they climbed the ladders again. Early roller coasters were more work than fun.

Author's Purpose: inform

Reason: These are facts about the first roller coasters. America was built in 1884. It cost only a nickel to ride the "Switchback Gravity Pleasure Railway" at Coney Island in New York. Roller coasters did not become very popular until the late 1920s.

Author's Purpose: inform

Reason: These are facts about early roller coasters. giant roller coaster? Some of the most famous ones in the world include the "Mamba" at Worlds of Fun in Kansas City, Missouri; the "Ultra Twister" at Six Flags Astroworld in Houston, Texas; and the "Magnum" at Cedar Point in Sandusky, Ohio. Roller coasters are fun because they have thrilling twists and turns. Some go very high and some turn upside down. Everyone should go on a roller coaster at least once in his or her life.

Author's Purpose: entertain/inform/persuade

Reason: There are facts here but the author is trying to persuade the reader to join in his entertainment about roller coasters.

105

Review

Directions: Follow the instructions for each section.

1. Write a paragraph about a sport in which you are informing your audience.

2. Write a paragraph about the circus in whic[...] your audience.

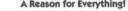
Answers will vary.

3. Write a paragraph about the desire for a later bedtime in which you are persuading your audience.

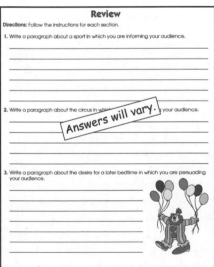

106

A Reason for Everything!

Directions: Below are the beginnings of some letters that David wrote. Tell why he wrote each one. Make sure to include the author's purpose for writing: to inform, to entertain, to persuade, or to express feelings, opinions, or beliefs.

Dear Aunt Grace,
Thanks so much for the kaleidoscope kit you sent for my birthday. I never would have guessed that making a kaleidoscope was so much fun. I have finished one, and I am about to try making some of the others shown in the book.

to express his thanks for a gift; to express the pleasure he got from it

Dear Miguel,
We arrived in Monterey yesterday. Monterey was California's capital city under the Mexican government, so it has many historic buildings. Today, we visited the old state custom house, a whaling station, and an old adobe house that is a museum. The adobe house had an old-fashioned garden and live farm animals you could pet.

to inform his friend about Monterey and what he has done there

Dear Jeff,
It's too bad you are away at camp. I have to tell you what you missed. While the Yees were away, they had a student house-sit and care for their hamster. He didn't know much about hamsters. Well, the hamster got out, and the house-sitter looked all over for it. He finally found it but had a terrible time catching it. When the Yees got back, they found a mouse in the hamster hut!

to entertain his friend with a funny story

Dear Editor,
Rocky Point Beach has become so littered that it is starting to look like a junkyard. You can see newspapers, cans, bottles, and food wrappers everywhere. I even saw parts of an old wet suit, a broken baby carrier, and a supermarket cart. The Recreation Department does not have the funds to clean it up, so it is up to the public. Two classes from my school will be there for a clean-up day on April 13. We'd like everyone who cares about the beach to come out and join us at 9:00 A.M.

to persuade people to join a beach clean-up party

107

Paws With a Cause

Directions: One way the author demonstrates a purpose for writing is in the information he or she chooses to include. Complete the story map with details from the passage.

I. PAWS provides three services:

A. rescues dogs from animal shelters   B. train dogs   C. educates the public on the need for these dogs

II. Dogs are trained to serve three types of clients:

A. hearing impaired   B. physically challenged   C. multiple handicapped

III. Training consists of:

A. basic obedience
  1. "sit" "come"
  2. "down"
B. sound-alert training
  1. respond to six sounds
C. training geared to needs   home placement training
  1. bonding with owner
  2. getting familiar with routines

IV. Write a sentence summarizing the author's purpose in giving these details in "Paws With a Cause."

Answers will vary.

109

GRADE 6

I. Reading
A. Directions
B. Sequencing
C. Main Idea
II. Writing
A. Capitalization
B. Proofreading

Comprehension: Fun With Photography

The word *photography* means "writing with light." *Photo* is from the Greek word *photos*, which means "light." *Graphy* is from the Greek word *graphic*, which means "writing." Cameras don't literally write pictures, of course. Instead, they imprint an image onto a piece of film.

Even the most sophisticated camera is basically a box with a piece of light-sensitive film inside. The box has a hole at the opposite end from the film. The light enters the box through the hole—the camera's lens—and shines on the surface of the film to create a picture. The picture that's created on the film is the image the camera's lens is pointed toward.

A lens is a circle of glass that is thinner at the edges and thicker in the center. The outer edges of the lens collect the light rays and draw them together at the center of the lens.

The shutter helps control the amount of light that enters the lens. Too much light will make the picture too light. Too little light will result in a dark picture. Electronic flash—either built into the camera or attached to the top of it—provides light when needed.

Cameras with automatic electronic flashes provide the additional light automatically. Electronic flashes—or simply "flashes," as they are often called—require batteries. If your flash quits working, a dead battery is probably the cause.

Directions: Answer these questions about photography.

1. From what language is the word *photography* derived? Greek
2. Where is the camera lens thickest? in the center
3. What do the outer edges of the lens do? collect the light rays and draw them together to the center of the lens
4. When is a flash needed? when there isn't enough light
5. What does the shutter do? It helps control the amount of light that enters the lens.

110

Comprehension: Photography Terms

Like other good professionals, photographers make their craft look easy. Their skill—like that of the graceful ice skater—comes from years of practice. Where skaters develop a sense of balance, photographers develop an "eye" for pictures. They can make important technical decisions about photographing, or "shooting," a particular scene in the twinkling of an eye.

It's interesting to know some of the technical language that professional photographers use. "Angle of view" refers to the angle from which a photograph is taken. "Depth of field" is the distance between the nearest point and the farthest point that is in focus in a photo.

"Filling the frame" refers to the amount of space the object being photographed takes up in the picture. A close-up picture of a dog, flower, or person would fill the frame. A far-away picture would not.

"ASA" refers to the speed of different types of films. "Speed" means the film's sensitivity to light. The letters *ASA* stand for the American Standards Association. Film manufacturers give their films ratings of 200ASA, 400ASA, and so on to indicate film speed. The higher the number on the film, the higher its sensitivity to light, and the faster its speed. The faster its speed, the better it will be at clearly capturing sports images and other action shots.

Directions: Answer these question about photography terms.

1. Name another term for photographing. "shooting"
2. This is the distance between the nearest point and the farthest point that is in focus in a photo.
   depth of field
3. This refers to the speed of different types of film. ASA
4. A close-up picture of someone's face would
   ☐ provide depth of field. ☐ create an ASA. ☒ fill the frame.
5. To photograph a swimming child, which film speed is better?
   ☐ 200ASA ☒ 400ASA

111

Comprehension: Photographing Animals

Animals are a favorite subject of many young photographers. Cats, dogs, hamsters, and other pets top the list, followed by zoo animals and the occasional lizard.

Because it's hard to get them to sit still and "perform on command," some professional photographers refuse to photograph pets. There are ways around the problem of short attention spans, however.

One way to get an appealing portrait of a cat or dog is to hold a biscuit or treat above the camera. The animal's longing look toward the food will be captured by the camera as a soulful gaze. Because it's above the camera—out of the camera's range—the treat won't appear in the picture. When you show the picture to your friends afterwards, they will be impressed by your pet's loving expression.

If you are using fast film, you can take some good, quick shots of a pet by simply snapping a picture right after calling its name. You'll get a different expression from your pet using this technique. Depending on your pet's disposition, the picture will capture an inquisitive expression or possibly a look of annoyance, especially if you've awakened Rover from a nap!

Taking pictures of zoo animals requires a little more patience. After all, you can't wake up a lion! You may have to wait for a while until the animal does something interesting or moves into a position for you to get a good shot. When photographing zoo animals, don't get too close to the cages, and never tap on the glass or throw things between the bars of a cage! Concentrate on shooting some good pictures, and always respect the animals you are photographing.

Directions: Answer these questions about photographing animals.

1. Why do some professionals dislike photographing animals? because it's difficult to get them to sit still
2. What speed of film should you use to photograph quick-moving pets? fast
3. To capture a pet's loving expression, hold this out of camera range. a treat
4. Compared to taking pictures of pets, what does photographing zoo animals require? more patience

112

Main Idea/Recalling Details: Kites

Kites are a familiar sight on breezy fall days. They come in a great variety of sizes, colors, and designs. It is not known who invented kites, but kites have been flown since the beginning of recorded history. While today children and adults use them for recreation, throughout history kites have had other uses.

In the United States, kites have been used in weather and other scientific research experiments. Before airplanes and weather balloons, the National Weather Service had kites carry weather instruments as high as 4 miles above the earth. In addition, the United States military used kites for observing the enemy and sending messages between troops.

In other countries, kites had cultural and religious importance. The ancient Chinese flew kites over their homes to drive out evil spirits. The Chinese still enjoy kites so much that one day each year they celebrate Kites' Day.

On some Pacific islands, kites were thought to have spiritual qualities. They were believed to symbolize both sides of nature—life and death. On some Polynesian islands, kites were used as protection against evil. These kites were often shaped like birds and used as soaring messengers to the heavens. In Hawaii, kites were also used to establish land ownership. A kite was released in the air, and a claim was given for the area where it came down.

Directions: Answer these questions about kites.

1. The main idea is:
   ☐ Kites come in a great variety of sizes, color, and designs.
   ☒ While today kites are used for recreation, throughout history they have had other uses.
2. Besides recreation, name two ways kites have been used in the United States.
   for weather and other scientific research
   The military used them for observation and to send messages.
3. holiday called Kites' Day? China
4. How did Hawaiians use kites to decide land ownership? A kite was released into the air, and a claim was given for the area where it came down.

113

Comprehension: Aerodynamics

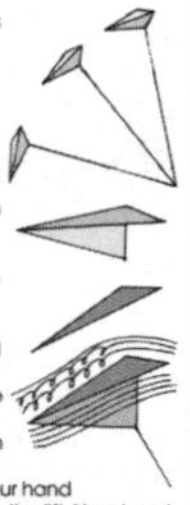

Kites are able to fly because of the principle of aerodynamics. This big word simply means the study of forces that are put into action by moving air. Three main forces work to keep a heavier-than-air kite flying—lift, gravity, and drag.

This is how it works: The flying lines, or strings, are attached to the kite to hold it at a slant. The wind pushes against the underside of the kite. At the same time, the wind rushes around the edges of the kite and "drags" some of the air from the upper side. This creates a partial vacuum there. The push of the air underneath is greater than the push of the air from the top, so the kite is held in the air. An airplane is held in the air in much the same way, except that it must keep moving rapidly to make the pressure above and below its wings different. The wind does this for the kite. In a steady airstream, a kite doesn't move backward or forward. It seems to be unaffected by gravity. This is possible because the lifting force of the wind overcomes the downward force of gravity.

If you have ever ridden a bicycle into a strong wind, you may have felt some of the forces of aerodynamics. If you held your hand out to your side, you could feel the air stream flowing around your hand. With your fingers pointed into the wind and your hand held level, there is little lift or drag. But if you raised your fingers slightly, the wind lifted your hand upwards. Raising your hand higher increases the drag and decreases the lift. Your hand is pushed downward. A kite flying in the sky is subject to these same forces.

Directions: Answer these questions about aerodynamics.

1. What is aerodynamics? the study of forces that are put into action by moving air
2. What three forces are at work to hold a kite in the air?
   lift gravity drag
3. An airplane is held in the air in much the same way, except that it must keep moving rapidly to keep the air above and below its wings different.
   (True) False

114

Comprehension: Getting Your Kite to Fly

There are some basic things to know about kite flying that can help you enjoy the sport more. Here are a few of the most important ones.

First, if you have ever seen someone flying a kite in a movie, you probably saw him or her get the kite off the ground by running into the wind. However, this is not the way to launch a kite. Most beginners will find a "high-start" launch to be the easiest. For a high-start launch, have a friend stand about 100 feet away, facing into the wind. Your friend should face you and hold the kite gently. Place some tension on the flying line by pulling gently on it. With a steady breeze behind you, tug gently on the line, and the kite will rise. If your kite begins to dive, don't panic or pull on the line. Dropping the reel will cause it to spin out of control and could cause someone to be hurt. Simply let the line go slack. This usually will right the kite in midair.

For a kite that is pulling hard away from you, have a friend stand behind you and take up the slack line as you bring it in. Hand over hand, pull down the kite. It is very important to have gloves on to do this, or you may burn or cut your hands. It is recommended that you always wear gloves while kite flying.

When two kite lines get crossed, pulling may cause enough friction to cut one or both of the lines. Instead of pulling, both fliers should walk toward one another until their lines uncross as they pass.

Directions: Circle **True** or **False** for these statements about kite flying.

1. To launch a kite, run into the wind holding the kite behind you. True (False)
2. In a high-start launch, a friend stands about 100 feet away from you, holding the kite. (True) False
3. If your kite begins to dive from the sky, immediately drop the reel. True (False)
4. It is recommended that you always wear gloves when kite flying. (True) False

115

GRADE
6
I. Reading
A. Directions
B. Sequencing
C. Main Idea
II. Writing
A. Capitalization
B. Proofreading

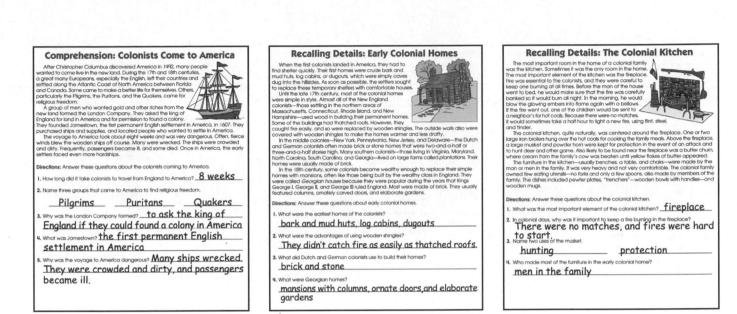

Comprehension: Colonists Come to America

After Christopher Columbus discovered America in 1492, many people wanted to come live in the new land. During the 17th and 18th centuries, a great many Europeans, especially the English, left their countries and settled along the Atlantic Coast of North America between Florida and Canada. Some came to make a better life for themselves. Others, particularly the Pilgrims, the Puritans, and the Quakers, came for religious freedom.

A group of men who wanted gold and other riches from the new land formed the London Company. They asked the king of England for land in America and for permission to found a colony. They founded Jamestown, the first permanent English settlement in America, in 1607. They purchased ships and supplies, and located people who wanted to settle in America.

The voyage to America took about eight weeks and was very dangerous. Often, fierce winds blew the wooden ships off course. Many were wrecked. The ships were crowded and dirty. Frequently, passengers became ill, and some died. Once in America, the early settlers faced even more hardships.

Directions: Answer these questions about the colonists coming to America.

1. How long did it take colonists to travel from England to America? 8 weeks
2. Name three groups that came to America to find religious freedom.
   Pilgrims Puritans Quakers
3. Why was the London Company formed? to ask the king of England if they could found a colony in America
4. What was Jamestown? the first permanent English settlement in America
5. Why was the voyage to America dangerous? Many ships wrecked. They were crowded and dirty, and passengers became ill.

116

Recalling Details: Early Colonial Homes

When the first colonists landed in America, they had to find shelter quickly. Their first homes were crude bark and mud huts, log cabins, or dugouts, which were simply caves dug into the hillsides. As soon as posssible, the settlers sought to replace these temporary shelters with comfortable houses.

Until the late 17th century, most of the colonial homes were simple in style. Almost all of the New England colonists—those settling in the northern areas of Massachusetts, Connecticut, Rhode Island, and New Hampshire—used wood in building their permanent homes. Some of the buildings had thatched roofs. However, they caught fire easily, and so were replaced by wooden shingles. The outside walls also were covered with wooden shingles to make the homes warmer and less drafty.

In the middle colonies—New York, Pennsylvania, New Jersey, and Delaware—the Dutch and German colonists often made brick or stone homes that were two-and-a-half or three-and-a-half stories high. Many southern colonists—those living in Virginia, Maryland, North Carolina, South Carolina, and Georgia—lived on large farms called *plantations*. Their homes were usually made of brick.

In the 18th century, some colonists became wealthy enough to replace their simple homes with mansions, often like those being built by the wealthy class in England. They were called *Georgian houses* because they were popular during the years that Kings George I, George II, and George III ruled England. Most were made of brick. They usually featured columns, ornately carved doors, and elaborate gardens.

Directions: Answer these questions about early colonial homes.

1. What were the earliest homes of the colonists?
   bark and mud huts, log cabins, dugouts
2. What were the advantages of using wooden shingles?
   They didn't catch fire as easily as thatched roofs.
3. What did Dutch and German colonists use to build their homes?
   brick and stone
4. What were Georgian homes?
   mansions with columns, ornate doors,and elaborate gardens

117

Recalling Details: The Colonial Kitchen

The most important room in the home of a colonial family was the kitchen. Sometimes it was the only room in the home. The most important element of the kitchen was the fireplace. Fire was essential to the colonists, and they were careful to keep one burning at all times. Before the man of the house went to bed, he would make sure that the fire was carefully banked so it would burn all night. In the morning, he would blow the glowing embers into flame again with a bellows. If the fire went out, one of the children would be sent to a neighbor's for hot coals. Because there were no matches, it would sometimes take a half hour to light a new fire, using flint, steel, and tinder.

The colonial kitchen, quite naturally, was centered around the fireplace. One or two large iron broilers hung over the hot coals for cooking the family meals. Above the fireplace, a large musket and powder horn were kept for protection in the event of an attack and to hunt deer and other game. Also likely to be found near the fireplace was a butter churn, where cream from the family's cow was beaten until yellow flakes of butter appeared.

The furniture in the kitchen—usually benches, a table, and chairs—were made by the man or men in the family. It was very heavy and not very comfortable. The colonial family owned few eating utensils—no forks and only a few spoons, also made by members of the family. The dishes included pewter plates, "trenchers"—wooden bowls with handles—and wooden mugs.

Directions: Answer these questions about the colonial kitchen.

1. What was the most important element of the colonial kitchen? fireplace
2. In colonial days, why was it important to keep a fire burning in the fireplace?
   There were no matches, and fires were hard to start.
3. Name two uses of the musket.
   hunting protection
4. Who made most of the furniture in the early colonial home?
   men in the family

118

Main Idea: The *Gettysburg Address*

On November 19, 1863, President Abraham Lincoln gave a short speech to dedicate a cemetery for Civil War soldiers in Gettysburg, Pennsylvania, where a famous battle was fought. He wrote five drafts of the *Gettysburg Address*, one of the most stirring speeches of all time. The war ended in 1865.

> Four score and seven years ago, our fathers brought forth on this continent a new nation, conceived in liberty, and dedicated to the proposition that all men are created equal.
>
> Now we are engaged in a great civil war, testing whether that nation, or any nation so conceived and so dedicated, can long endure. We are met on a great battlefield of that war. We have come to dedicate a portion of that field as a final resting place for those who here gave their lives that this nation might live. It is altogether fitting and proper that we should do this.
>
> But, in a larger sense, we cannot dedicate—we cannot consecrate—we cannot hallow—this ground. The brave men, living and dead, who struggled here have consecrated it far above our poor power to add or detract. The world will little note nor long remember what we say here, but it can never forget what they did here. It is for us the living, rather, to be dedicated to the unfinished work which they who fought here have thus far so nobly advanced. It is rather for us to be here dedicated to the great task remaining before us—that from these honored dead we take increased devotion to that cause for which they gave their last full measure of devotion—that we here highly resolve that these dead shall not have died in vain—that this nation, under God, shall have a new birth of freedom—and that government of the people, by the people, for the people shall not perish from this earth.

Directions: Answer the questions about the *Gettysburg Address*.

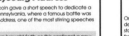

1. Circle the main idea:

   This speech will be long remembered as a tribute to the dead who died fighting in the Civil War.

   (This speech is to honor the dead soldiers who gave their lives so that the nation could have freedom for all citizens.)
2. What happened on the ground where the cemetery stood? A great battle was fought and many lives were lost.

119

Comprehension: The *Emancipation Proclamation*

On September 22, 1862, a year before delivering the *Gettysburg Address*, President Lincoln delivered the *Emancipation Proclamation*, which stated that all slaves in Confederate states should be set free. Since the Confederate states had already seceded (withdrawn) from the Union, they ignored the proclamation. However, the proclamation did strengthen the North's war effort. About 200,000 black men—mostly former slaves—enlisted in the Union Army. Two years later, the 13th Amendment to the Constitution ended slavery in all parts of the United States.

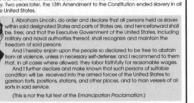

> I, Abraham Lincoln, do order and declare that all persons held as slaves within said designated States and parts of States are, and henceforward shall be, free; and that the Executive Government of the United States, including military and naval authorities thereof, shall recognize and maintain the freedom of said persons.
>
> And I hereby enjoin upon the people so declared to be free to abstain from all violence, unless in necessary self-defense; and I recommend to them that, in all cases where allowed, they labor faithfully for reasonable wages.
>
> And I further declare and make known that such persons of suitable condition will be received into the armed forces of the United States to garrison forts, positions, stations, and other places, and to man vessels of all sorts in said service.
>
> (This is not the full text of the *Emancipation Proclamation*.)

Directions: Answer the questions about the *Emancipation Proclamation*.

1. How did the *Emancipation Proclamation* strengthen the North's war effort?
   About 200,000 Black men enlisted in the Union army.
2. Which came first, the *Emancipation Proclamation* or the *Gettysburg Address*?
   The *Emancipation Proclamation*
3. Which amendment to the Constitution grew out of the *Emancipation Proclamation*?
   13th
4. *Secede* means to ☐ quit. ☐ fight. ☒ withdraw.

120

Comprehension: Lincoln and the South

Many people think that Abraham Lincoln publicly came out against slavery from the beginning of his term as president. This is not the case. Whatever his private feelings, he did not criticize slavery publicly. Fearful that the southern states would secede, or leave, the Union, he pledged to respect the southern states' rights to own slaves. He also pledged that the government would respect the southern states' runaway slave laws. These laws required all citizens to return runaway slaves to their masters.

Clearly, Lincoln did not want the country torn apart by a civil war. In the following statement, written in 1861 shortly after he became president, he made it clear that the federal government would do its best to avoid conflict with the southern states.

> I hold that, in contemplation of the universal law and the Constitution, the Union of these states is perpetual. . . . No state, upon its own mere motion, can lawfully get out of the Union. . . . I shall take care, as the Constitution itself expressly enjoins upon me, that the laws of the Union be faithfully executed in all the states. . . . The power confided to me will be used to hold, occupy, and possess the property and places belonging to the government, and to collect the duties and imposts. . . .
>
> In your hands, my dissatisfied fellow-countrymen, and not in mine, is the momentous issue of civil war. The government will not assail you. You can have no conflict without yourselves being the aggressors. You have no oath registered in heaven to destroy the government, while I shall have the most solemn one to "preserve, protect, and defend" it.

Directions: Use context clues for these definitions.

1. What is the correct definition of *assail*? to attack, to confront
2. What is the correct definition of *enjoin*? to impose a rule or law
3. What is the correct definition of *contemplation*? meditation, considering before making a decision

Directions: Answer these questions about Lincoln and the southern states.

1. Lincoln is telling the southern states that the government
   ☐ does want a war. ☒ doesn't want a war. ☐ will stop a war.
2. As president, Lincoln pledged to "preserve, protect, and defend"
   ☐ slavery. ☐ the northern states. ☒ the Union.

121

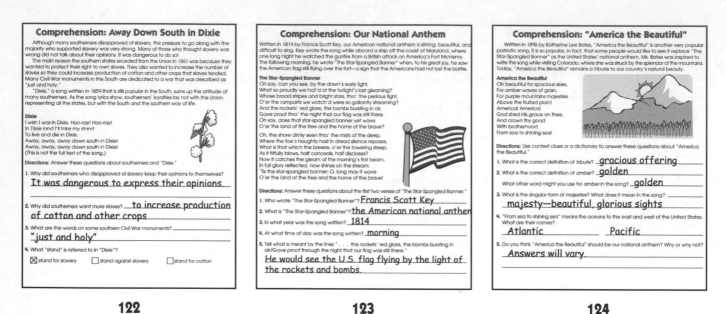

GRADE
6

I. Reading
  A. Directions
  B. Sequencing
  C. Main Idea
II. Writing
  A. Capitalization
  B. Proofreading

Comprehension: Away Down South in Dixie

Although many southerners disapproved of slavery, the pressure to go along with the majority who supported slavery was very strong. Many of those who thought slavery was wrong did not talk about their opinions. It was dangerous to do so!

The main reason the southern states seceded from the Union in 1861 was because they wanted to protect their right to own slaves. They also wanted to increase the number of slaves so they could increase production of cotton and other crops that slaves tended. Many Civil War monuments in the South are dedicated to a war that was described as "just and holy."

"Dixie," a song written in 1859 that is still popular in the South, sums up the attitude of many southerners. As the song lyrics show, southerners' loyalties lay not with the Union representing all the states, but with the South and the southern way of life.

Dixie
I wish I was in Dixie, Hoo-ray! Hoo-ray!
In Dixie land I'll take my stand!
To live and die in Dixie.
Away, away, away down south in Dixie!
Away, away, away down south in Dixie!
(This is not the full text of the song.)

Directions: Answer these questions about southerners and "Dixie."

1. Why did southerners who disapproved of slavery keep their opinions to themselves?
   It was dangerous to express their opinions.

2. Why did southerners want more slaves? to increase production of cotton and other crops

3. What are the words on some southern Civil War monuments? "just and holy"

4. What "stand" is referred to in "Dixie"?
   ☒ stand for slavery   ☐ stand against slavery   ☐ stand for cotton

122

Comprehension: Our National Anthem

Written in 1814 by Francis Scott Key, our American national anthem is stirring, beautiful, and difficult to sing. Key wrote the song while aboard a ship off the coast of Maryland, when one long night he watched the gunfire from a British attack on America's Fort McHenry. The following morning, he wrote "The Star-Spangled Banner" when, to his great joy, he saw the American flag still flying over the fort—a sign that the Americans had not lost the battle.

The Star-Spangled Banner
Oh say, can you see, by the dawn's early light,
What so proudly we hail'd at the twilight's last gleaming?
Whose broad stripes and bright stars, thro' the perilous fight,
O'er the ramparts we watch'd were so gallantly streaming?
And the rockets' red glare, the bombs bursting in air,
Gave proof thro' the night that our flag was still there.
Oh say, does that star-spangled banner yet wave
O'er the land of the free and the home of the brave?

Oh, the shore dimly seen thro' the mists of the deep,
Where the foe's haughty host in dread silence reposes,
What is that which the breeze, o'er the towering steep,
As it fitfully blows, half conceals, half discloses?
Now it catches the gleam of the morning's first beam,
In full glory reflected, now shines on the stream:
'Tis the star-spangled banner; O, long may it wave
O'er the land of the free and the home of the brave!

Directions: Answer these questions about the first two verses of "The Star-Spangled Banner."

1. Who wrote "The Star-Spangled Banner"? Francis Scott Key

2. What is "The Star-Spangled Banner"? the American national anthem

3. In what year was the song written? 1814

4. At what time of day was the song written? morning

5. Tell what is meant by the lines ". . . the rockets' red glare, the bombs bursting in air/Gave proof through the night that our flag was still there."
   He would see the U.S. flag flying by the light of the rockets and bombs.

123

Comprehension: "America the Beautiful"

Written in 1895 by Katherine Lee Bates, "America the Beautiful" is another very popular patriotic song. It is so popular, in fact, that some people would like to see it replace "The Star-Spangled Banner" as the United States' national anthem. Ms. Bates was inspired to write the song while visiting Colorado, where she was struck by the splendor of the mountains. Today, "America the Beautiful" remains a tribute to our country's natural beauty.

America the Beautiful
Oh beautiful for spacious skies,
For amber waves of grain,
For purple mountains majesties
Above the fruited plain!
America! America!
God shed His grace on thee,
And crown thy good
With brotherhood
From sea to shining sea!

Directions: Use context clues or a dictionary to answer these questions about "America the Beautiful."

1. What is the correct definition of tribute? gracious offering

2. What is the correct definition of amber? golden
   What other word might you use for amber in the song? golden

3. What is the singular form of majesties? What does it mean in the song?
   majesty—beautiful, glorious sights

4. "From sea to shining sea" means the oceans to the east and west of the United States. What are their names?
   Atlantic   Pacific

5. Do you think "America the Beautiful" should be our national anthem? Why or why not?
   Answers will vary.

124

Comprehension: Civil War Marching Song

When soldiers march, they sometimes sing a song to help them keep in step. One of the most famous marching songs of the Civil War was the "Battle Hymn of the Republic," written in 1861 by Julia Ward Howe. Mrs. Howe wrote the song after visiting a Union army camp in the North. The words are about how God is on the side of the soldiers.

Battle Hymn of the Republic
Mine eyes have seen the glory of the coming of the Lord.
He is trampling out the vintage where the grapes of wrath are stored.
He has loosed the fateful lightning of his terrible swift sword,
His truth is marching on.

Glory, glory hallelujah! Glory, glory hallelujah!
Glory, glory hallelujah! His truth is marching on.

I have seen him in the watchfires of a hundred circling camps,
I have builded him an altar in the evening dews and damps,
I can read his righteous sentence by the dim and flaring lamps,
His day is marching on.

Glory, glory hallelujah! Glory, glory hallelujah!
Glory, glory hallelujah! His truth is marching on.

Directions: Answer these questions about the "Battle Hymn of the Republic."

1. Who wrote the "Battle Hymn of the Republic"? Julia Ward Howe

2. When was the song written? 1861

3. What war was in progress at the time? Civil War

4. Why did soldiers sing while they marched? to help keep in step

5. What marches along with the soldiers? God

6. What did the soldiers sing about building in the evening?
   an altar

125

Recalling Details: The Island Continent, Australia

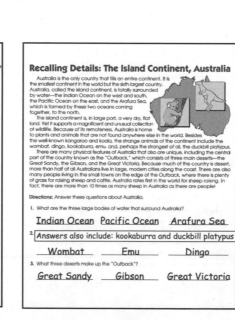

Australia is the only country that fills an entire continent. It is the smallest continent in the world but the sixth largest country. Australia, called the island continent, is totally surrounded by water—the Indian Ocean on the west and south, the Pacific Ocean on the east, and the Arafura Sea, which is formed by these two oceans coming together, to the north.

The island continent is, in large part, a very dry, flat land. Yet it supports a magnificent and unusual collection of wildlife. Because of its remoteness, Australia is home to plants and animals that are not found anywhere else in the world. Besides the well-known kangaroo and koala, the strange animals of the continent include the wombat, dingo, kookaburra, emu and, perhaps the strangest of all, the duckbill platypus.

There are many physical features of Australia that also are unique, including the central part of the country known as the "Outback," which consists of three main deserts—the Great Sandy, the Gibson, and the Great Victoria. Because much of the country is desert, more than half of all Australians live in large, modern cities along the coast. There are also many people living in the small towns on the edge of the Outback, where there is plenty of grass for raising sheep and cattle. Australia rates first in the world for sheep raising. In fact, there are more than 10 times as many sheep in Australia as there are people!

Directions: Answer these questions about Australia.

1. What are the three large bodies of water that surround Australia?
   Indian Ocean   Pacific Ocean   Arafura Sea

2. Answers also include: kookaburra and duckbill platypus
   Wombat   Emu   Dingo

3. What three deserts make up the "Outback"?
   Great Sandy   Gibson   Great Victoria

126

Comprehension: The Aborigines

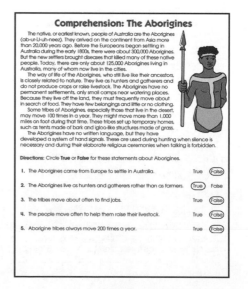

The native, or earliest known, people of Australia are the Aborigines (ab-ur-IJ-uh-neez). They arrived on the continent from Asia more than 20,000 years ago. Before the Europeans began settling in Australia during the early 1800s, there were about 300,000 Aborigines. But the new settlers brought diseases that killed many of these native people. Today, there are only about 125,000 Aborigines living in Australia, many of whom now live in the cities.

The way of life of the Aborigines, who still live like their ancestors, is closely related to nature. They live as hunters and gatherers and do not produce crops or raise livestock. The Aborigines have no permanent settlements, only small camps near watering places. Because they live off the land, they must frequently move about in search of food. They have few belongings and little or no clothing.

Some tribes of Aborigines, especially those that live in the desert, may move 100 times in a year. They might move more than 1,000 miles on foot during that time. These tribes set up temporary homes, such as tents made of bark and igloo-like structures made of grass.

The Aborigines have no written language, but they have developed a system of hand signals. These are used during hunting when silence is necessary and during their elaborate religious ceremonies when talking is forbidden.

Directions: Circle True or False for these statements about Aborigines.

1. The Aborigines came from Europe to settle in Australia.   True (False)

2. The Aborigines live as hunters and gatherers rather than as farmers.   (True) False

3. The tribes move about often to find jobs.   True (False)

4. The people move often to help them raise their livestock.   True (False)

5. Aborigine tribes always move 200 times a year.   True (False)

127

GRADE 6

I. Reading
  A. Directions
  B. Sequencing
  C. Main Idea
II. Writing
  A. Capitalization
  B. Proofreading

Main Idea/Comprehension: The Boomerang

The Aborigines have developed a few tools and weapons, including spears, flint knives, and the boomerang. The boomerang comes in different shapes and has many uses. This curved throwing stick is used for hunting, playing, digging, cutting, and even making music.

You may have seen a boomerang that, when thrown, returns to the thrower. This type of boomerang is sometimes used in duck hunting, but it is most often used as a toy and for sporting contests. It is lightweight—about three-fourths of a pound—and has a big curve in it. However, the boomerang used by the Aborigines for hunting is much heavier and is nearly straight. It does not return to its thrower.

Because of its sharp edges, the boomerang makes a good knife for skinning animals. The Aborigines also use boomerangs as digging sticks, to sharpen stone blades, to start fires, and as swords and clubs in fighting. Boomerangs sometimes are used to make music—two clapped together provide rhythmic background for dances. Some make musical sounds when they are pulled across one another.

To throw a boomerang, the thrower grasps it at one end and holds it behind his head. He throws it overhanded, adding a sharp flick of the wrist at the last moment. It is thrown into the wind to make it come back. A skillful thrower can do many tricks with his boomerang. He can make it spin in several circles or make a figure eight in the air. He can even make it bounce on the ground several times before it soars into the air and returns.

Directions: Answer these questions about boomerangs.

1. The main idea is:
   - ☐ The Aborigines have developed a few tools and weapons, including spears, flint knives, and the boomerang.
   - ☒ The boomerang comes in different shapes and has many uses.

2. To make it return, the thrower tosses the boomerang
   - ☒ into the wind.   ☐ against the wind.

3. List three uses for the boomerang.
   hunting | Sample answers: |
   playing
   digging

128

Comprehension: The Kangaroo

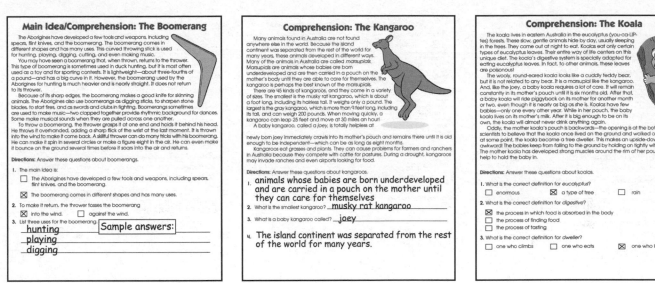

Many animals found in Australia are not found anywhere else in the world. Because the island continent was separated from the rest of the world for many years, these animals developed in different ways. Many of the animals in Australia are called *marsupials*. Marsupials are animals whose babies are born underdeveloped and are then carried in a pouch on the mother's body until they are able to care for themselves. The kangaroo is perhaps the best known of the marsupials.

There are 45 kinds of kangaroos, and they come in a variety of sizes. The smallest is the musky rat kangaroo, which is about a foot long, including its hairless tail. It weighs only a pound. The largest is the gray kangaroo, which is more than 9 feet tall, including its tail, and can weigh 200 pounds. When moving quickly, a kangaroo can leap 25 feet and move at 30 miles an hour! A baby kangaroo, called a *joey*, is totally helpless at newly born joey immediately crawls into its mother's pouch and remains there until it is old enough to be independent—which can be as long as eight months.

Kangaroos eat grasses and plants. They can cause problems for farmers and ranchers in Australia because they compete with cattle for pastures. During a drought, kangaroos may invade ranches and even airports looking for food.

Directions: Answer these questions about kangaroos.

1. animals whose babies are born underdeveloped and are carried in a pouch on the mother until they can care for themselves

2. What is the smallest kangaroo?   musky rat kangaroo

3. What is a baby kangaroo called?   joey

4. The island continent was separated from the rest of the world for many years.

129

Comprehension: The Koala

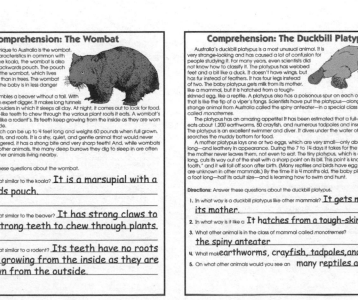

The koala lives in eastern Australia in the eucalyptus (you-ca-LIP-tes) forests. These slow, gentle animals hide by day, usually sleeping in the trees. They come out at night to eat. Koalas eat only certain types of eucalyptus leaves. Their entire way of life centers on this unique diet. The koala's digestive system is specially adapted for eating eucalyptus leaves. In fact, to other animals, these leaves are poisonous!

The wooly, round-eared koala looks like a cuddly teddy bear, but it is not related to any bear. It is a marsupial like the kangaroo. And, like the joey, a baby koala requires a lot of care. It will remain constantly in its mother's pouch until it is six months old. After that, a baby koala will ride piggyback on its mother for another month or two, even though it is nearly as big as she is. Koalas have few babies—only one every other year. While in her pouch, the baby koala lives on its mother's milk. After it is big enough to be on its own, the koala will almost never drink anything again.

Oddly, the mother koala's pouch is backwards—the opening is at the bottom. This leads scientists to believe that the koala once lived on the ground and walked on all fours. But at some point, the koala became a tree dweller. This makes an upside-down pouch very awkward! The babies keep from falling to the ground by holding on tightly with their mouths. The mother koala has developed strong muscles around the rim of her pouch that also help to hold the baby in.

Directions: Answer these questions about koalas.

1. What is the correct definition for *eucalyptus*?
   - ☐ enormous   ☒ a type of tree   ☐ rain

2. What is the correct definition for *digestive*?
   - ☒ the process in which food is absorbed in the body
   - ☐ the process of finding food
   - ☐ the process of tasting

3. What is the correct definition for *dweller*?
   - ☐ one who climbs   ☐ one who eats   ☒ one who lives in

130

Comprehension: The Wombat

Another animal unique to Australia is the wombat. The wombat has characteristics in common with other animals. Like the koala, the wombat is also a marsupial with a backwards pouch. The pouch is more practical for the wombat, which lives on the ground rather than in trees. The wombat walks on all fours so the baby is in less danger of falling out.

The wombat resembles a beaver without a tail. With its strong claws, it is an expert digger. It makes long tunnels beneath cliffs and boulders in which it sleeps all day. At night, it comes out to look for food. It has strong, beaver-like teeth to chew through the various plant roots it eats. A wombat's teeth have no roots, like a rodent's. Its teeth keep growing from the inside as they are worn down from the outside.

The wombat, which can be up to 4 feet long and weighs 60 pounds when full grown, eats only grass, plants, and roots. It is a shy, quiet, and gentle animal that would never attack. But when angered, it has a strong bite and very sharp teeth! And, while wombats don't eat or attack other animals, the many deep burrows they dig to sleep in are often dangerous to the other animals living nearby.

Directions: Answer these questions about the wombat.

1. How is the wombat similar to the koala? It is a marsupial with a backwards pouch.

2. How is the wombat similar to the beaver? It has strong claws to dig and strong teeth to chew through plants.

3. How is the wombat similar to a rodent? Its teeth have no roots but keep growing from the inside as they are worn down from the outside.

131

Comprehension: The Duckbill Platypus

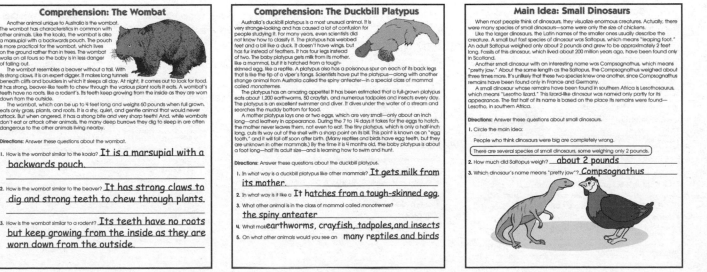

Australia's duckbill platypus is a most unusual animal. It is very strange-looking and has caused a lot of confusion for people studying it. For many years, even scientists did not know how to classify it. The platypus has webbed feet and a bill like a duck. It doesn't have wings, but has fur instead of feathers. It has four legs instead of two. The baby platypus gets milk from its mother, like a mammal, but it is hatched from a tough-skinned egg, like a reptile. A platypus also has a poisonous spur on each of its back legs that is like the tip of a viper's fangs. Scientists have put the platypus—along with another strange animal from Australia called the spiny anteater—in a special class of mammal called *monotremes*.

The platypus has an amazing appetite! It has been estimated that a full-grown platypus eats about 1,200 earthworms, 50 crayfish, and numerous tadpoles and insects every day. The platypus is an excellent swimmer and diver. It dives under the water of a stream and searches the muddy bottom for food.

A mother platypus lays one or two eggs, which are very small—only about an inch long—and leathery in appearance. During the 7 to 14 days it takes for the eggs to hatch, the mother never leaves them, not even to eat. The tiny platypus, which is only a half-inch long, cuts its way out of the shell with a sharp point on its bill. This point is known as an "egg tooth," and it will fall off soon after birth. (Many reptiles and birds have egg teeth, but they are unknown in other mammals.) By the time it is 4 months old, the baby platypus is about a foot long—half its adult size—and is learning how to swim and hunt.

Directions: Answer these questions about the duckbill platypus.

1. In what way is a duckbill platypus like other mammals? It gets milk from its mother.

2. In what way is it like a It hatches from a tough-skinned egg.

3. What other animal is in the class of mammal called *monotremes*? the spiny anteater

4. What make earthworms, crayfish, tadpoles, and insects

5. On what other animals would you see an many reptiles and birds

132

Main Idea: Small Dinosaurs

When most people think of dinosaurs, they visualize enormous creatures. Actually, there were many species of small dinosaurs—some were only the size of chickens.

Like the larger dinosaurs, the Latin names of the smaller ones usually describe the creature. A small but fast species of dinosaur was Saltopus, which means "leaping foot." An adult Saltopus weighed only about 2 pounds and grew to be approximately 2 feet long. Fossils of this dinosaur, which lived about 200 million years ago, have been found only in Scotland.

Another small dinosaur with an interesting name was Compsognathus, which means "pretty jaw." About the same length as the Saltopus, the Compsognathus weighed about three times more. It's unlikely that these two species knew one another, since Compsognathus remains have been found only in France and Germany.

A small dinosaur whose remains have been found in southern Africa is Lesothosaurus, which means "Lesotho lizard." This lizard-like dinosaur was named only partly for its appearance. The first half of its name is based on the place its remains were found—Lesotho, in southern Africa.

Directions: Answer these questions about small dinosaurs.

1. Circle the main idea:

   People who think dinosaurs were big are completely wrong.

   (There are several species of small dinosaurs, some weighing only 2 pounds.)

2. How much did Saltopus weigh?   about 2 pounds

3. Which dinosaur's name means "pretty jaw"?   Compsognathus

133

GRADE 6

I. Reading
  A. Directions
  B. Sequencing
  C. Main Idea
II. Writing
  A. Capitalization
  B. Proofreading

Comprehension: Dinosaur History

Dinosaurs are so popular today that it's hard to imagine this not always being the case. The fact is, no one had any idea that dinosaurs ever existed until about 150 years ago.

In 1841, a British scientist named Richard Owen coined the term *Dinosauria* to describe several sets of recently discovered large fossil bones. *Dinosauria* is Latin for "terrible lizards," and even though some dinosaurs were similar to lizards, modern science now also links dinosaurs to birds. Today's birds are thought to be the closest relatives to the dinosaurs.

Like birds, most dinosaurs had fairly long legs that extended straight down from beneath their bodies. Because of their long legs, many dinosaurs were able to move fast. They were also able to balance themselves well. Long-legged dinosaurs, such as the Iguanodon, needed balance to walk upright.

The Iguanodon walked on its long hind legs and used its stubby front legs as arms. On the end of its arms were five hoof-like fingers, one of which functioned as a thumb. Because it had no front teeth for tearing meat, scientists believe the Iguanodon was a plant eater. Its large, flat back teeth were useful for grinding tender plants before swallowing them.

Directions: Answer these questions about the history of dinosaurs.

1. How were dinosaurs like today's birds? **most had fairly long, straight legs that extended straight down beneath their bodies**

2. This man coined the term *Dinosauria*.
☐ Owen Richards   ☐ Richard Owens   ☒ Richard Owen

3. Which of these did the Iguanodon not have?
☐ short front legs   ☒ front teeth   ☐ back teeth

4. List other ways you can think of that dinosaurs and birds are alike. **Answers will vary.**

134

Comprehension: Tyrannosaurus Rex

The largest meat-eating animal ever to roam Earth was Tyrannosaurus Rex. *Rex* is Latin for "king," and because of its size, Tyrannosaurus certainly was at the top of the dinosaur heap. With a length of 46 feet and a weight of 7 tons, there's no doubt this dinosaur commanded respect!

Unlike smaller dinosaurs, Tyrannosaurus wasn't tremendously fast on its huge feet. It could stroll along at a walking speed of 2 to 3 miles an hour. Not bad, considering Tyrannosaurus was pulling along a body that weighed 14,000 pounds! Like other dinosaurs, Tyrannosaurus walked upright, probably balancing its 16-foot-long head by lifting its massive tail.

Compared to the rest of its body, Tyrannosaurus' front claws were tiny. Scientists aren't really sure what the claws were for, although it seems likely that they may have been used for holding food. In that case, Tyrannosaurus would have had to lower its massive head down to its short claws to take anything in its mouth. Maybe it just used the claws to scratch nearby itches!

Because of their low metabolism, dinosaurs did not require a lot of food for survival. Scientists speculate that Tyrannosaurus ate off the same huge piece of meat—usually the carcass of another dinosaur—for several weeks. What do you suppose Tyrannosaurus did the rest of the time?

Directions: Answer these questions about Tyrannosaurus Rex.

1. Why was this dinosaur called "Rex"? **It means king.**

2. For what might Tyrannosaurus Rex have used its claws? **to hold food**

3. How long was Tyrannosaurus Rex? **about 46 feet**

4. Tyrannosaurus weighed
☐ 10,000 lbs.   ☐ 12,000 lbs.   ☒ 14,000 lbs.

5. Tyrannosaurus ate
☐ plants.   ☒ other dinosaurs.   ☐ birds.

135

Comprehension: Dinosaur Fossils

Imagine putting together the world's largest jigsaw puzzle. That is what scientists who reassemble the fossil bones of dinosaurs must do to find out what the creatures looked like. Fossilized bones are imbedded, or stuck, in solid rock, so scientists must first get the bones out of the rocks without breaking or otherwise damaging them. This task requires enormous patience.

In addition to hammers, drills, and chisels, sound waves are used to break up the rock. The drills, which are similar to high-speed dentist drills, cut through the rock very quickly. As the bones are removed, scientists begin trying to figure out how they attach to one another. Sometimes the dinosaur's skeleton is preserved just as it was when it died. This, of course, shows scientists exactly how to reassemble it. Other times, parts of bone are missing. It then becomes a guessing game to decide what goes where.

When scientists discover dinosaur fossils, it is called a "find." A particularly exciting find in 1978 occurred in Montana when, for the first time, fossilized dinosaur eggs, babies, and several nests were found. The species of dinosaur in this exciting find was Maiasaura, which means "good mother lizard." From the size of the nest, which was 23 feet, scientists speculated that the adult female Maiasaura was about the same size.

Unlike birds' nests, dinosaur nests were not made of sticks and straw. Instead, since they were land animals, nests were made of dirt hollowed out into a bowl shape. The Maiasaura's nest was 3 feet deep and held about 20 eggs.

Directions: Answer these questions about dinosaur fossils.

1. Name four tools used to remove dinosaur bones from rock. **hammers, drills, chisels, sound waves**

2. What do scientists do with the bones they remove? **They try to reassemble them.**

3. The type of dinosaur fossils found in Montana in 1978 were
☐ Mayiasaura.   ☐ Masaura.   ☒ Malasaura.

4. When scientists discover dinosaur fossils, it is called a
☐ found.   ☒ find.   ☐ nest.

136

Comprehension: Dinosaur Tracks

Some scientists refer to dinosaurs' fossilized tracks as "footprints in time." The tracks that survived in Texas for 120 million years had been made in sand or mud. These large footprints were of the Apatosaurus. The footprints were more than 3 feet across!

Although Apatosaurus had a long, heavy tail, there is no sign that the tail hit the ground along with the feet. Scientists speculate that the place where the tracks were made was once a riverbed, and that Apatosaurus' tail floated in the water and thus left no tracks. Another theory is that the dinosaur always carried its tail out behind it. This second theory is not as popular, because scientists say it's unlikely the dinosaur would consistently carry its long, heavy tail off the ground. When Apatosaurus rested, for example, the tail would have left its mark.

Besides Texas, fossilized tracks have been found in England, Canada, Australia, and Brazil. Some tracks have also been found in New England. The tracks discovered in Canada were quite a find! They showed a pattern made by 10 species of dinosaurs. In all, about 1,700 fossilized footprints were discovered. Maybe the scientists uncovered what millions of years ago was a dinosaur playground.

Directions: Answer these questions about dinosaur tracks.

1. Circle the main idea:

  (Fossilized dinosaur tracks provide scientists with information from which to draw conclusions about dinosaur size and behavior.)

  Fossilized dinosaur tracks are not very useful because so few have been found in the United States.

2. Explain how a dinosaur might have crossed a river without its tail leaving a track. **It may have floated.**

3. Name five countries where dinosaur tracks have been found. **England, Canada, Australia, Brazil, and U.S.**

4. Circle the valid generalization about dinosaur tracks.

  The fact that 10 species of tracks were found together proves dinosaurs were friends with others outside their groups.

  (The fact that 10 species of tracks were found together means the dinosaurs probably gathered in that spot for water or food.)

137

Recalling Details: The Earth's Atmosphere

The most important reason that life can exist on Earth is its atmosphere—the air around us. Without it, plant and animal life could not have developed. There would be no clouds, weather, or even sounds, only a death-like stillness and an endlessly black sky. Without the protection of the atmosphere, the sun's rays would roast the Earth by day. At night, with no blanketing atmosphere, the stored heat would escape into space, dropping the temperature of the planet hundreds of degrees.

Held captive by Earth's gravity, the atmosphere surrounds the planet to a depth of hundreds of miles. However, all but 1 percent of the atmosphere is in a layer about 20 miles deep just above the surface of the Earth. It is made up of a mixture of gases and dusts. About 78 percent of it is a gas called nitrogen, which is very important as food for plants. Most of the remaining gas, 21 percent, is called oxygen, which all people and animals depend on for life. The remaining 1 percent is made up of a blend of other gases—including carbon dioxide, argon, ozone, and helium—and tiny dust particles. These particles come from ocean salt crystals, bits of rocks and sand, plant pollen, volcanic ash, and even meteor dust.

You may not think of air as matter, as something that can be weighed. In fact, the Earth's air weighs billions and billions of tons. Near the surface of the planet, this "air pressure" is greatest. Right now, about 10 tons of air is pressing in on you. Yet, like the fish living near the floor of the ocean, you don't notice this tremendous weight because your body is built to withstand it.

Directions: Answer these questions about the Earth's atmosphere.

1. What is the atmosphere? **the air around us**

2. Of what is the atmosphere? **a mixture of gases and dusts**

3. What is the most abundant gas in the atmosphere? **nitrogen**

4. Which of the atmosphere's gases is most important to humans and animals? **oxygen**

5. What is air pressure? **the weight of the air on Earth**

138

Comprehension: Causes and Effects of Weather

The behavior of the atmosphere, which we experience as weather and climate, affects our lives in many important ways. It is the reason no one lives on the South Pole. It controls when a farmer plants the food we will eat, which crops will be planted, and whether those crops will grow. The weather tells us what clothes to wear and how we will play after school. Weather is the sum of the conditions of the air that may affect the Earth's surface and its living things. These conditions include the temperature, air pressure, wind, and moisture. Climate refers to these conditions but generally applies to larger areas and longer periods of time, such as the annual climate of South America rather than today's weather in Oklahoma City.

Climate is influenced by many factors. It depends first and foremost on latitude. Areas nearest the equator are warm and wet, while the poles are cold and relatively dry. The poles also have extreme seasonal changes, while the areas at the middle latitudes have more moderate climates, neither as cold as the poles nor as hot as the equator. Other circumstances may alter this pattern, however. Land near the oceans, for instance, is generally warmer than inland areas.

Elevation also plays a role in climate. For example, despite the fact that Africa's highest mountain, Kilimanjaro, is just south of the equator, its summit is perpetually covered by snow. In general, high land is cooler and wetter than nearby low land.

Directions: Check the answers to these questions about the causes and effects of weather.

1. What is the correct definition for *atmosphere?*
☐ the clouds   ☐ the sky   ☒ where weather occurs

2. What is the correct definition for *foremost?*
☒ most important   ☐ highest number   ☐ in the front

3. What is the correct definition for *circumstances?*
☐ temperatures   ☐ seasons   ☒ conditions

4. What is the correct definition for *elevation?*
☒ height above Earth   ☐ nearness to equator   ☐ snow covering

5. What is the correct definition for *perpetually?*
☐ occasionally   ☐ rarely   ☒ always

139

GRADE
6

I. Reading
  A. Directions
  B. Sequencing
  C. Main Idea
II. Writing
  A. Capitalization
  B. Proofreading

Comprehension: Hurricanes

The characteristics of a hurricane are powerful winds, driving rain, and raging seas. Although a storm must have winds blowing at least 74 miles an hour to be classified as a hurricane, it is not unusual to have winds above 150 miles per hour. The entire storm system can be 500 miles in diameter, with lines of clouds that spiral toward a center called the "eye." Within the eye itself, which is about 15 miles across, the air is actually calm and cloudless. But this eye is enclosed by a towering wall of thick clouds where the storm's heaviest rains and highest winds are found.

All hurricanes begin in the warm seas and moist winds of the tropics. They form in either of two narrow bands to the north and south of the equator. For weeks, the blistering sun beats down on the ocean water. Slowly, the air above the sea becomes heated and begins to swirl. As the hot, moist air is pulled skyward. Gradually, this circle grows larger and spins faster. As the hot, moist air at the top is cooled, great rain clouds are formed. The storm's fury builds until it moves over land or a cold area of the ocean where its supply of heat and moisture is finally cut off.

Hurricanes that strike North America usually form over the Atlantic Ocean. West coast storms are less dangerous because they tend to head out over the Pacific Ocean rather than toward land. The greatest damage usually comes from the hurricanes that begin in the western Pacific, because they often batter heavily populated regions.

Directions: Answer these questions about hurricanes.

1. What is necessary for a storm to be classified as a hurricane? **winds blowing at least 74 miles an hour**

2. What is **lines of clouds that spiral toward the center**

3. Where do **warm seas and moist winds of the tropics**

4. **It moves over land or a cold area of the ocean where its supply of heat and moisture is cut off.**

5. Why do hurricanes formed in the western Pacific cause the most damage? **They often batter heavily populated areas.**

140

Comprehension: Thunderstorms

With warm weather comes the threat of thunderstorms. The rapid growth of the majestic thunderhead cloud and the damp, cool winds that warn of an approaching storm are familiar in most regions of the world. In fact, it has been estimated that at any given time, 1,800 such storms are in progress around the globe.

As with hurricanes and tornadoes, thunderstorms are formed when a warm, moist air mass meets with a cold air mass. Before long, bolts of lightning streak across the sky, and thunder booms. It is not entirely understood how lightning is formed. It is known that a positive electrical charge builds near the top of the cloud, and a negative charge forms at the bottom. When enough force builds up, a powerful current of electricity zigzags down an electrically charged pathway between the two, causing the flash of lightning.

The clap of thunder you hear after a lightning flash is created by rapidly heated air that expands as the lightning passes through it. The distant rumbling is caused by the thunder's sound waves bouncing back and forth within clouds or between mountains. When thunderstorms rumble through an area, many people begin to worry about tornadoes. But they need to be just as fearful of thunderstorms. In fact, lightning kills more people than any other severe weather condition. In 1988, lightning killed 68 people in the United States, while tornadoes killed 32.

Directions: Answer these questions about thunderstorms.

1. How many thunderstorms are estimated to be occurring at any given time around the world? **1,800**

2. When are thunderstorms formed? **when a warm, moist air mass meets a cold air mass**

3. What causes thunder? **rapidly heated air that expands as lightning passes through it**

4. On average, which causes more deaths, lightning or tornadoes? **lightning**

141

Nouns

A **noun** names a person, place, thing, or idea. There are several types of nouns.

Examples:
proper nouns: Joe, Jefferson Memorial
common nouns: dog, town
concrete nouns: book, stove
abstract nouns: fear, devotion
collective nouns: audience, flock

A word can be more than one type of noun.

Example: **Dog** is both a common and a concrete noun.

Directions: Write the type or types of each noun on the lines.

1. desk — **common, concrete**
2. ocean — **common, concrete**
3. love — **common, abstract**
4. cat — **common, concrete**
5. herd — **common, concrete, collective**
6. compassion — **common, abstract**
7. reputation — **common, abstract**
8. eyes — **common, concrete**
9. staff — **common, concrete, collective**
10. day — **common, concrete**
11. Roosevelt Building — **proper, concrete**
12. Mr. Timken — **proper, concrete**
13. life — **common, abstract**
14. porch — **common, concrete**
15. United States — **proper, concrete or abstract**

142

Possessive Nouns

A **possessive** noun owns something. To make a singular noun possessive, add an apostrophe and **s**. Example: mayor's campaign.

To make a plural noun possessive when it already ends with **s**, add only an apostrophe. Example: dogs' tails

To make a plural noun possessive when it doesn't end with **s**, add an apostrophe and **s**. Example: men's shirts

Directions: Write the correct form of the word for each sentence in the group. Words may be singular, plural, singular possessive, or plural possessive. The first one has been done for you.

teacher 1. How many **teachers** does your school have?
         2. Where is the **teacher's** coat?
         3. All the **teachers'** mailboxes are in the school office.

reporter 4. Two **reporters** were assigned to the story.
          5. One **reporter's** car broke down on the way to the scene.
          6. The other **reporter** was riding as a passenger.
          7. Both **reporters'** notes ended up missing.

child 8. The **children** are hungry.
       9. How much spaghetti can one **child** eat?
      10. Put this much on each **child's** plate.
      11. The **children's** spaghetti is ready for them.

mouse 12. Some **mice** made a nest under those boards.
       13. I can see the **mice's** hole from here.
       14. A baby **mouse** has wandered away from the nest.
       15. The **mouse's** mother is coming to get it.

143

Concrete or Abstract?

A **concrete noun** is something you can see, touch, taste, hear, or smell. An **abstract noun** is something you may not be able to see—an idea, a feeling, an emotion, or a quality.

Directions: Underline all the nouns and pronouns in the story. Then, write the concrete nouns on the left side of the chart and the abstract nouns on the right. If a noun is repeated, you don't have to rewrite it.

Michael told Stephie she was going to ride her bicycle today. She put her hands on the handlebars. He could see the fear on her face as she began to cry. He held the bike as she pushed on the pedals. Her balance was good and the bike started to move. Her ability to ride was better today than ever before. Her anger at him was going away.

Then, Michael let go without telling her. She rode the bicycle all by herself. She didn't pick up much speed, but she did ride around the whole block by herself.

When Stephie was finished, she realized that she had ridden the bike on her own. Michael saw the pride on her face, and they went inside to tell their dad about her accomplishment.

Concrete Nouns		Abstract Nouns
Michael	face	fear
Stephie	pedals	balance
she	balance	ability
bicycle	him	anger
hands	herself	speed
handlebars	block	pride
he	dad	accomplishment
bike	they	

144

Collective Crossword

A **collective noun** names a group of things.

Examples: a class of students   a troupe of mimes   a committee of citizens

Directions: Use the clues below to complete the crossword puzzle. If necessary, use a dictionary or encyclopedia to help you.

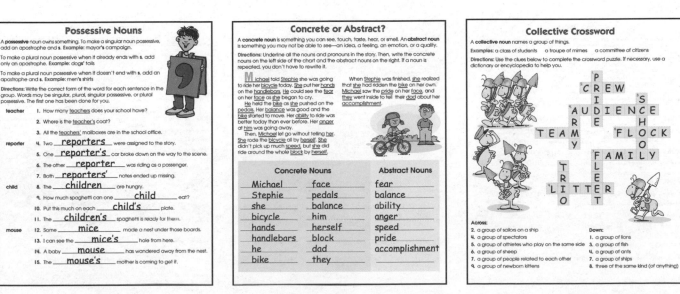

Across:
2. a group of sailors on a ship
4. a group of spectators
5. a group of athletes who play on the same side
6. a group of sheep
7. a group of people related to each other
8. a group of newborn kittens

Down:
1. a group of lions
3. a group of fish
4. a group of ants
7. a group of ships
8. three of the same kind (of anything)

145

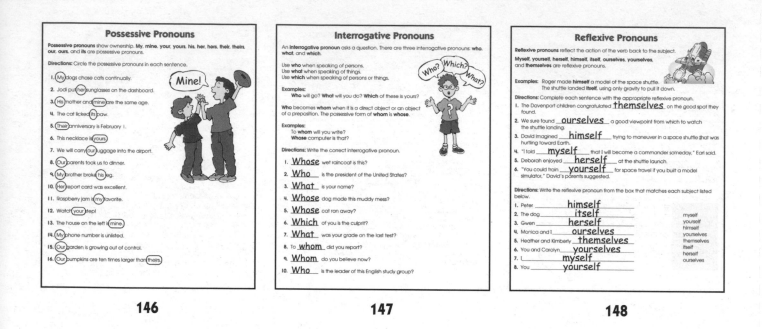

I. Reading
A. Directions
B. Sequencing
C. Main Idea
II. Writing
A. Capitalization
B. Proofreading

Possessive Pronouns

Possessive pronouns show ownership. **My, mine, your, yours, his, her, hers, their, theirs, our, ours,** and **its** are possessive pronouns.

Directions: Circle the possessive pronouns in each sentence.

1. (My) dogs chase cats continually.
2. Jodi put (her) sunglasses on the dashboard.
3. (His) mother and (mine) are the same age.
4. The cat licked (its) paw.
5. (Their) anniversary is February 1.
6. This necklace is (yours).
7. We will carry (our) luggage into the airport.
8. (Our) parents took us to dinner.
9. (My) brother broke (his) leg.
10. (Her) report card was excellent.
11. Raspberry jam is (my) favorite.
12. Watch (your) step!
13. The house on the left is (mine).
14. (My) phone number is unlisted.
15. (Our) garden is growing out of control.
16. (Our) pumpkins are ten times larger than (theirs).

Mine!

146

Interrogative Pronouns

An **interrogative pronoun** asks a question. There are three interrogative pronouns: **who, what,** and **which.**

Use **who** when speaking of persons.
Use **what** when speaking of things.
Use **which** when speaking of persons or things.

Examples:
Who will go? **What** will you do? **Which** of these is yours?

Who becomes **whom** when it is a direct object or an object of a preposition. The possessive form of **whom** is **whose.**

Examples:
To **whom** will you write?
Whose computer is that?

Who? Which? What?

Directions: Write the correct interrogative pronoun.

1. __Whose__ wet raincoat is this?
2. __Who__ is the president of the United States?
3. __What__ is your name?
4. __Whose__ dog made this muddy mess?
5. __Whose__ cat ran away?
6. __Which__ of you is the culprit?
7. __What__ was your grade on the last test?
8. To __whom__ did you report?
9. __Whom__ do you believe now?
10. __Who__ is the leader of this English study group?

147

Reflexive Pronouns

Reflexive pronouns reflect the action of the verb back to the subject.
Myself, yourself, herself, himself, itself, ourselves, yourselves, and **themselves** are reflexive pronouns.

Examples: Roger made **himself** a model of the space shuttle. The shuttle landed **itself,** using only gravity to pull it down.

Directions: Complete each sentence with the appropriate reflexive pronoun.

1. The Davenport children congratulated __themselves__ on the good spot they found.
2. We sure found __ourselves__ a good viewpoint from which to watch the shuttle landing.
3. David imagined __himself__ trying to maneuver in a space shuttle that was hurtling toward Earth.
4. "I told __myself__ that I will become a commander someday," Earl said.
5. Deborah enjoyed __herself__ at the shuttle launch.
6. "You could train __yourself__ for space travel if you built a model simulator," David's parents suggested.

Directions: Write the reflexive pronoun from the box that matches each subject listed below.

1. Peter __himself__
2. The dog __itself__
3. Gwen __herself__
4. Monica and I __ourselves__
5. Heather and Kimberly __themselves__
6. You and Carolyn __yourselves__
7. I __myself__
8. You __yourself__

myself
yourself
himself
yourselves
themselves
itself
herself
ourselves

148

Pursuing Pronouns

A **personal pronoun** takes the place of one or more nouns. An **interrogative pronoun** introduces a question. A **relative pronoun** introduces a group of words that acts as an adjective.

Examples: I am excited about the track meet today. (personal pronoun)
What event does Bill plan to enter? (interrogative pronoun)
The track meet, **which** we went to last week, was an exciting event. (relative pronoun)

Directions: Write **personal, interrogative,** or **relative** in the blank to identify each boldfaced pronoun.

1. **Which** sprinting race is your favorite? __interrogative__
2. **We** both like the same type of running shoes. __personal__
3. The high jump is a challenge **that** I would like to take on. __relative__
4. **Who** would like to warm up with me? __interrogative__
5. A boy **whom** I knew won the track meet. __relative__
6. **You** are a natural when it comes to long-distance running. __personal__
7. Is it true that **she** would like to join our running club? __personal__
8. **Whose** house should the team go to for the end-of-th __interrogative__

Directions: Complete each sentence with a pronoun.

1. I tried to find my shoes __that__ were lost. (relative)
2. __They__ told us it won't be a problem for them to run today. (personal)
3. The boy __who__ won the race is a great runner. (relative)
4. __Who__ would like to be our fourth runner in the relay race? (interrogative)

149

How Possessive!

Possessive pronouns take the place of possessive nouns. For example, instead of saying "That is Samantha's sandwich," you can say, "That is **her** sandwich."

Notice that the noun follows the pronoun and there is no apostrophe. A possessive pronoun can also be used without a noun following it. You can say, "That is **hers.**"

Directions: Use context clues to figure out the missing possessive pronouns. Write them on the lines.

"Hi, I'm Sam. What's __your__ name?" said Sam.

"Hi, __My__ name is Sidney," replied the boy.

"Nice to meet you, Sidney. Meet __my__ friend Simon and __his__ sister, Samantha. We're about to eat __our__ lunches. Did you bring __yours__?"

"No," answered Sidney. "I left __mine__ at home." Then, he placed __his__ backpack on the table.

"No problem," said Sam. "You can have some of __ours__. We have plenty. I have two tuna sandwiches. Simon and Samantha have subs. __Their__ mom makes the best sandwiches."

"Thanks," said Sidney, showing them __his__ big, toothy smile.

Challenge: Now, rewrite each of these sentences so it contains a possessive pronoun with no noun following it.

1. My favorite kind of sandwich is grilled cheese; what's yours?
2. I left my lunch at home, but Sara promised that I could have some of hers.
3. My sister is in the fifth grade, but yours is older.
4. I offered Tommy some of mine, but he said he wanted to eat his first.

150

Pronoun Play-Off

A **subject pronoun** is used as the subject of a sentence or after a linking verb. An **object pronoun** is used as a direct object, an indirect object, or an object of a preposition.

Directions: Here's a game for you to play. Patricia Proud is a pronoun pro. She has written five sentences with subject and object pronouns. Can you beat her score? Here's what to do:

1. Read Patricia Proud's sentences.
2. Write the correct label in the circle underneath each underlined word: label subject pronouns **S,** direct object pronouns **DO,** indirect object pronouns **IO,** and objects of a preposition **OP.**
3. Calculate Patricia's score as follows:
   subject pronoun = 1 point   object of a preposition = 3 points
   direct object = 2 points   indirect object = 4 points
4. Then, write five sentences of your own. Underline and label all the subject and object pronouns.
5. Figure out your score. Who won?

Patricia's Sentences   **Patricia's Score:** __34__

1. My friends said that <u>they</u> really amused <u>them</u> with their antics.
   (S)   (DO)
2. <u>You</u> and your friends pulled quite a joke on <u>us</u>.
   (S)   (OP)
3. My parents and I gave <u>her</u> a gift for her eleventh birthday.
   (S)   (IO)
4. <u>They</u> listened as <u>we</u> told <u>them</u> what happened to <u>you</u>.
   (S)   (S)   (IO)   (OP)
5. Jack's brother told <u>me</u> that <u>you</u> need help, so <u>we</u> will take care of <u>it</u> for <u>you</u> and <u>him</u>.
   (DO)   (S)   (S)   (OP) (OP) (OP)

Your Sentences   **Your Score:** _____

Answers will vary.

151

GRADE 6

I. Reading
  A. Directions
  B. Sequencing
  C. Main Idea
II. Writing
  A. Capitalization
  B. Proofreading

Spelling: Plurals

Is **heros** or **heroes** the correct spelling? Many people aren't sure. These rules have exceptions, but they will help you spell the plural forms of most words that end with **o**.
- If a word ends with a consonant and **o**, add **es**: heroes.
- If a word ends with a vowel and **o**, add **s**: radios.

Here are some other spelling rules for plurals:
- If a word ends with **s, ss, x, ch**, or **sh**, add **es**: buses, kisses, taxes, peaches, wishes.
- If a word ends with **f** or **fe**, drop the **f** or **fe** and add **ves**: leaf, leaves; wife, wives.
- Some plurals don't end with **s** or **es**: geese, deer, children.

Directions: Write the plural forms of the words.

1. Our area doesn't often have (tornado).   **tornadoes**
2. How many (radio) does this store sell every month?   **radios**
3. (Radish) are the same color as apples.   **radishes**
4. Does this submarine carry (torpedo)?   **torpedoes**
5. Hawaii has a number of active (volcano).   **volcanoes**
6. Did you pack (knife) in the picnic basket?   **knives**
7. We heard (echo) when we shouted in the canyon.   **echoes**
8. Where is the list of (address)?   **addresses**
9. What will you do when that plant (reach) the ceiling?   **reaches**
10. Sometimes my dad (fix) us milkshakes.   **fixes**
11. Every night, my sister (wish) on the first star she sees.   **wishes**
12. Who (furnish) the school with pencils and paper?   **furnishes**
13. The author (research) every detail in her books.   **researches**

heros or heroes?

152

Generating Gerunds

Gerunds are verbs that end in **ing** and are used as nouns.

Examples: **Laughing** is my sister's favorite pastime.
Jimmy's responsibility will be **sweeping** the porch.

Directions: Use gerunds to fill in the blanks below. Be sure your answers make sense with the meaning of the paragraph.

The Obstacle Course

_____ isn't everything when you compete in an obstacle course. First, you have to complete the course once to register a starting time. Then, your challenge is to do the course in a faster time. The competitors at today's obstacle course really gave it... ... the hardest part for Kurt... couldn't keep his two feet together. _____ was easier because he could jump and run at the same time. In the end, he improved his time by one whole minute. _____ was the hardest part for Trish. Her arms just didn't move as fast as she wanted them to. On the other hand, she thought that _____ over the pond was easy. She improved her time by more than a minute. Other

competitors said that _____ was the easiest part of the course. But everyone agreed that _____ down the water slide was the most fun. The _____ from the crowd... human-made mud pond. ...reamed with laughter when Maxwell slid into it.

In the end, Donna had the most improved time. She was given a ribbon and a free pass to a nearby water park. But all the kids that participated enjoyed themselves. Sometimes, just _____ your hardest is the best reward!

Answers will vary.

153

To Infinitives and Beyond!

An **infinitive** is a verb, usually preceded by **to**, that is used as a noun, adjective, or adverb.

Examples: Everyone wanted **to leave**.
To turn down Alice's offer would be rude.
My little brother tried **to solve** the problem.

Directions: Underline the infinitives in each sentence.

1. *When Aliens Attack Part 2* is the movie to watch this summer!
2. The tennis player was determined to win the game.
3. I invited Dr. Lewis to speak to my class on Career Day.
4. "Not to be a pain," she said, "but can you turn down the TV while I do my homework?"
5. Angie's mother insisted that we were to come to the park as soon as the movie was over.
6. Yvetta's ability to make friends turned her into one of the most well-liked kids in school.
7. I told my little sister not to answer the door to strangers while I was across the street.
8. Even though she found it to be difficult, Michelle learned to play the violin beautifully.
9. The girl longed to run, skip, and ride her bicycle for the whole month she had to use crutches.

Challenge: Now, use infinitives to write five sentences of your own.

Answers will vary.

154

Scrambled Verbs

Here's a game for two players that tests what you know about verb tenses.

You will need: a number cube, adhesive tape, a timer or stopwatch, two crayons or markers of different colors, scratch paper, a pencil

Directions:
1. First, cover a number cube with adhesive tape. Then, write present, past, and future on the faces of the cube. Write each verb tense on two faces.
2. Each player must select a crayon or marker.
3. The first player should set the timer for 1 minute.
4. Then, this player must choose a verb from the chart below and unscramble it. He or she should write it in the box.
5. Then, he or she rolls the cube to determine a verb tense.
6. This player must use the verb correctly in a sentence. If it is used correctly, the player can color in the square. If not, the other player gets a chance to use the verb in a sentence and color the square. Then, the second player can take a regular turn.
7. Continue taking turns in this fashion.
8. The first player to complete a row across, down, or diagonally wins the game. Remember, you have only 1 minute per turn!

mitda **admit**	shlaf **flash**	casee **cease**	dysut **study**	remgee **emerge**
parepa **appear**	chekts **sketch**	actprice **practice**	velpode **develop**	veres **serve**
rowk **work**	covedris **discover**	FREE	rashe **share**	cande **dance**
riccel **circle**	ageman **manage**	tollecc **collect**	shinif **finish**	macres **scream**
dritec **direct**	sitnel **listen**	blimc **climb**	vidpore **provide**	oncusef **confuse**

PAST PRESENT

155

Just Perfect

Here are three more verb tenses to remember:

present perfect   action started in the past and just completed or still going on.
   I **have started** my homework already.

past perfect   action completed before another action.
   I **had finished** my math homework long before his call.

future perfect   action that will be started and completed in the future.
   I **will have finished** all my homework long before I go to bed.

Now, this page is just perfect!

Directions: Arrange each group of words to make a complete sentence. Then, write the sentence, underline the verb, and write its tense. The first one has been done for you.

1. present perfect   so traveled My summer this has countries six family far so
   My family <u>has traveled</u> to six countries so far this summer.
2. future perfect
   We <u>will have visited</u> 12 countries by the end of our trip.
3. past perfect
   I <u>had</u> never <u>ridden</u> a camel until a week ago in Egypt.
4. present perfect
   I <u>have tasted</u> some of the most unusual foods on this trip.
5. future perfect
   By this time tomorrow we <u>will have sailed</u> to Greece.
6. present perfect
   I <u>have written</u> at least 50 postcards to my friends back home.
7. past perfect
   I <u>had</u> only <u>taken</u> a few shots of the pyramids when I realized the camera was out of film.

156

How Irregular!

Some verbs are **irregular**. That means you don't just add **d** or **ed** when you change the verb to the past participle.
Example: I **ate** pancakes yesterday.
   I **have eaten** breakfast already.

Directions: Find and circle the past tense and past participle for each of the following irregular verbs. Words may appear up, down, across, diagonally, and backwards. Then, use the circled words to complete the sentences below.

tear	strive	arise
lie	break	fall
write	ride	

F A L L E N X Y
Z B T O R E Z
N S T R O V E
E D L A Y D I A
D I R N I S A R O
D R T O R X R O S
I R A B R O K E N
X W R I T T E N

1. My sister and I **arose** at 7:00 A.M. Our parents had **arisen** an hour earlier to start the campfire.
2. I **fell** off my horse yesterday. I have never **fallen** off a horse before.
3. I had already **ridden** several miles along the rocky trail when the accident occurred, but I got back on and **rode** back to camp.
4. Last night, a raccoon **broke** into our cooler to look for food. That's better than the bear that had **broken** into Mr. Alexander's cabin last summer.
5. After a long hike, I **lay** down on a flat rock. I had only **lain** there about two minutes when I saw a bald eagle fly overhead.
6. My sister **strove** to reach the top of the mountain before everyone else, but then she has always **striven** to be the first at everything.
7. I slipped and **tore** a hole in my jeans. When I took off my jacket, I noticed that I had **torn** that, too.
8. I was flipping through the pages of my journal when I found an unopened note my friend had **written** me. I immediately read it and **wrote** her back.

157

GRADE 6

I. Reading
  A. Directions
  B. Sequencing
  C. Main Idea
II. Writing
  A. Capitalization
  B. Proofreading

More Irregularities

For some irregular verbs, the past tense and past participle are the same.

Example: The past tense and past participle of the verb **stand** is **stood**.
  We **stand** to salute the flag.
  The children **stood** in line for 15 minutes.
  Our house has **stood** for 150 years.

Directions: To complete each sentence, write the past tense or past participle of the verb that is bold. Then, write the boxed letters in order at the bottom of the page to answer the riddle.

1. shine It has been days since the sun has **s h o n e**.
2. deal The president's speech **d e a l t** with education.
3. slide The children **s l i d** down the hill.
4. flee The frightened child **f l e d** to safety.
5. hold The boy had **h e l d** on as long as he could.
6. spin The car had **s p u n** out of control.
7. leave Everyone **l e f t** about an hour ago.
8. sit He **s a t** at the bus stop for over an hour.
9. keep You have never **k e p t** a single promise!
10. hang The portrait had **h u n g** in the hall for generations.
11. lay They had no sooner **l a i n** down when the children ran through the room in their muddy shoes.
12. catch I had **c a u g h t** a glimpse of her just in time.
13. shrink Ann cried when she saw that her new sweater had **s h r u n k** so much.
14. sting The hornet **s t u n g** me on the leg.

How could the man go without sleep for seven days and not be tired?
He slept at night.

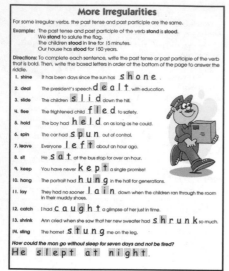

158

Choose, Chose, Chosen

Irregular verbs can be confusing because you don't just add **d** or **ed** to form the past tense or the past participle. You also don't need a helping verb such as **have**, **has**, or **had** to form the past tense, but you do need a helping verb with a past participle.

Examples: present: I **choose** to read.
  past: You **chose** wisely.
  past participle: He has **chosen** a blue shirt.

Directions: Underline the correct verb form from the choices in parentheses.

1. I (brung, <u>brought</u>) my wallet with me but I have (forgot, <u>forgotten</u>) my keys again!
2. I had (did, <u>done</u>) everything humanly possible to help so I (<u>went</u>, gone) home.
3. I accidentally (<u>threw</u>, thrown) away all the notes I had (took, <u>taken</u>) in science class last week.
4. My friends (<u>saw</u>, seen) me coming before I had (saw, <u>seen</u>) them.
5. Jack (<u>began</u>, begun) to realize that he had (chose, <u>chosen</u>) the wrong clothes to wear on such a cold day.
6. We had not (<u>knew</u>, known) until this morning that you (<u>were</u>, been) in town.
7. Mack's parents had (forbade, <u>forbidden</u>) him to swim in the river, but he (<u>swam</u>, swum) there anyway.
8. Have you always (got, <u>gotten</u>) up so early, or have you just (began, <u>begun</u>) to get up at daybreak?
9. My computer had just (froze, <u>frozen</u>) for the third time, so I (<u>gave</u>, given) up and (<u>wrote</u>, written) my report by hand.
10. No one (<u>knew</u>, known) that I had (wrote, <u>written</u>) the song myself until I (<u>sang</u>, sung) it for them.
11. Mindy and I have not (spoke, <u>spoken</u>) since the last time she (<u>was</u>, been) at her grandparents' house.
12. It had (grew, <u>grown</u>) too cold to stay outside any longer, so everyone (<u>came</u>, come) inside.

159

Putting It All Together

Directions: Underline the incorrect forms of irregular verbs in each sentence. Then, write the correct ones on the line.

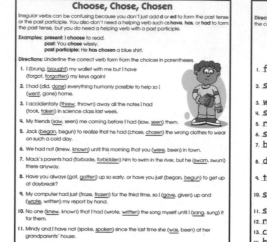

1. flung _____ My brother was so angry he <u>flinged</u> his backpack across the room.
2. seen _____ Until I had <u>saw</u> that documentary, I thought giant squids didn't really exist.
3. worn, shrank _____ The new sweatshirt I had <u>wore</u> only once <u>shrunk</u> two sizes.
4. spoken _____ Have you <u>spoke</u> to your parents yet about getting a puppy?
5. run, began _____ I had <u>ran</u> at least a mile before I <u>begun</u> to slow down.
6. swum _____ Have you ever <u>swam</u> across the lake?
7. begun, went _____ People had <u>began</u> smelling smoke just moments before the alarm <u>gone</u> off.
8. driven _____ Our family has <u>drove</u> to the shore countless times, but never has he had <u>drove</u> in the traffic been as bad as it was today.
9. taken _____ The plane had no sooner <u>took</u> off before the captain announced that we must return to the airport immediately.
10. sang, written _____ Our school chorus <u>sung</u> a song that a fifth-grade student had <u>wrote</u>.
11. stolen _____ The police caught the man who had <u>stole</u> our car.
12. rang _____ My alarm clock <u>rung</u> just as I awoke.
13. chosen _____ The outfit I had <u>chose</u> for the dance was really awesome.
14. hidden _____ She had <u>hid</u> the box so well that she herself couldn't find it.
15. swore _____ My brother <u>sweared</u> that he hadn't told anyone.

160

Who's Who?

Adjectives can be used to compare. Add **er** to most adjectives of one or two syllables to compare two people, places, or things. Add **est** to most adjectives of one or two syllables to compare three or more people, places, or things.

Directions: Write **er** or **est** to complete each adjective in the story. Then, write the name of each sibling above his or her picture and circle the item that each one purchases.

Maggie is the old**est** but not the tall**est** of five siblings. Although Max is the young**est** of all, he is tall**er** than both Maggie and Missy. Morris is young**er** than Maggie but not short**er** than Maggie or Missy. Melvin, three or four years old, is also the small**est**. Who's who?

Maggie, Morris, Max, Missy, and Melvin are shopping at the Coolkids' store at the mall. It has absolutely everything. As an avid stuffed animal collector, Maggie is buying the large**est** of two pandas. Max, who is always looking for a bargain, will get the

cheap**est** video he can find. Missy loves to read. She has just enough money to buy a book with the funni**est** jokes and riddles ever written. It is also the thick**est** and heavi**est** kids' book she's ever bought. Melvin really likes jigsaw puzzles. Today, he found four puzzles he'd like to have. He has decided on the puzzle with the few**est** number of pieces. Morris is trying to decide between two skateboards. After trying out both of them, he picks the long**er** and narrow**er** one. Which item did each sibling buy?

Maggie Melvin Max
Missy
Morris

161

This, That, These, Those

The adjectives **this** and **that** are singular. The adjectives **these** and **those** are plural. **This** and **these** refer to things that are nearby. **That** and **those** refer to things that are farther away.

Examples: **This** elevator we are riding is called a "lift" in England.
  Those apartments across the street are called "flats."

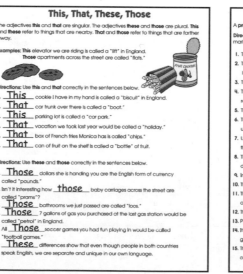

Directions: Use **this** and **that** correctly in the sentences below.

1. **This** _____ cookie I have in my hand is called a "biscuit" in England.
2. **That** _____ car trunk over there is called a "boot."
3. **This** _____ parking lot is called a "car park."
4. **That** _____ vacation we took last year would be called a "holiday."
5. **That** _____ box of French fries Monica has is called "chips."
6. **That** _____ can of fruit on the shelf is called a "bottle" of fruit.

Directions: Use **these** and **those** correctly in the sentences below.

1. **Those** _____ dollars she is handing you are the English form of currency called "pounds."
2. Isn't it interesting how **those** _____ baby carriages across the street are called "prams"?
3. **Those** _____ bathrooms we just passed are called "loos."
4. **Those** _____ 7 gallons of gas you purchased at the last gas station would be called "petrol" in England.
5. All **Those** _____ soccer games you had fun playing in would be called "football games."
6. **These** _____ differences show that even though people in both countries speak English, we are separate and unique in our own language.

162

Did You Know?

A **proper adjective** is formed from a proper noun. It always begins with a capital letter.

Directions: Identify the proper adjectives in the animal facts below and use proofreaders' marks to capitalize them.

Here's how to use proofreaders' marks to capitalize letters:
g̲erman i̲rish
s̲cottish

1. The k̲omodo dragon is actually a lizard, not a dragon.
2. The s̲outh a̲merican Goliath spider is four inches long, has a 10+ inch leg span, 1-inch fangs, and eats birds.
3. The animal we call the a̲merican buffalo is really a bison.
4. The c̲alifornia condor is a large bird that eats the remains of dead animals.
5. The a̲frican elephant is larger than the i̲ndian elephant.
6. The n̲ile crocodile will remain underwater more than an hour in order to surprise its unsuspecting prey.
7. Unable to do anything but fight, a̲mazon ants steal the larvae of other ants and keep them as slave ants to build their homes and feed them.
8. The a̲laskan brown bear is one of several mammals that is a scavenger, feeding on dead seals, walruses, and whales.
9. In e̲uropean folklore, the hoot of an owl is a warning of death.
10. The male d̲arwin frog has a pouch in his mouth in which he hatches eggs.
11. The adult s̲iberian tiger, the largest big cat, reaches a length of 10 feet and a weight of 585 pounds.
12. The kiwi, a n̲ew z̲ealand bird, is unable to fly.
13. Pandas eat c̲hinese bamboo shoots; koalas eat a̲ustralian eucalyptus leaves.
14. It is said that s̲iamese cats, a breed that likely originated in T̲hailand, were trained to guard the king's palace and attack intruders by jumping on their backs.
15. The chihuahua is the smallest breed of dog and was named after the m̲exican state of the same name.

163

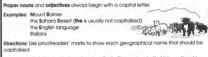

Proper Nouns and Adjectives

Proper nouns and **adjectives** always begin with a capital letter.

Examples: Mount Rainier
the Sahara Desert (**the** is usually not capitalized)
the English language
Italians

Directions: Use proofreaders' marks to show each geographical name that should be capitalized.

australia is the smallest continent on Earth. The western half of this continent is dominated by the great sandy desert, the gibson desert, and the great victoria desert. Two mountain ranges, the macdonnell range and the musgrave range, are located in this area. The great dividing range is a long mountain chain that runs along australia's eastern coastline. Surrounding this small continent are the indian ocean, the timor sea, the arafura sea, the coral sea, and the pacific ocean. You may have read about the great barrier reef, which lies between its northeast shoreline and the coral sea.
australia is divided into six main areas: western australia, south australia, the northern territory, queensland, new south wales, and victoria. The capital of australia is canberra, which is located in new south wales. Its highest point is mt. kosciusko, which is southwest of canberra. Two large lakes, lake eyre and lake torrens, lie in south australia. The darling, warrego, and murray rivers flow through the southeast corner. Much of australia's land is used for grazing sheep and cattle.

Directions: Use proofreaders' marks to show each word that should be capitalized.

1. americans and the english speak the english language.
2. english is a germanic language, as are german and dutch.
3. swedish, norwegian, and danish are also germanic languages.
4. italian and spanish are two romance languages.
5. The romance languages come from latin, the language of all romans.
6. The languages of the russians, poles, czechs, and slavs have a common origin.
7. Many africans speak hebrew and arabic.
8. The language of indians and pakistanis is hindustani.
9. Many american students study french and german.
10. spanish and latin are also often studied.

164

Comparing With Adjectives

The **comparative** form of an adjective is used to compare two nouns. It is formed in two ways: by adding the suffix **er** to the adjective or by using the words **more** or **less** with the adjective.

Examples:
David is a **faster** runner than Thomas.
David is **more** diligent at track practice than Thomas.

The **superlative** form of an adjective is used to compare three or more nouns. It is also formed in two ways: by adding the suffix **est** to the adjective or by using the words **most** or **least** with the adjective.

Examples:
David is the **fastest** runner on the track team.
David is the **most** diligent worker on the track team.

Directions: Circle the adjective of comparison in each of the following sentences. On the line, write if the adjective is written using the comparative form or the superlative form.

1. Central High has the (shortest) basketball team in the league. **superlative**

2. One of their (most skillful) plays is to pass the ball through their opponents' legs. **superlative**

3. Central wins a lot of games because the team's players are (more clever) dribblers than the opposing players. **comparative**

4. The opposing team is (dizzier) because Central dribbles circles around them. **comparative**

5. The (toughest) game of the year was against South High. **superlative**

6. Central's captain won the game with the (fanciest) shot of the game. **superlative**

165

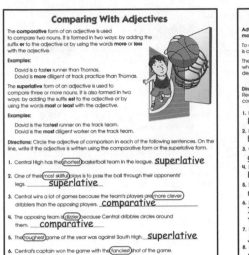

What Did You Say?

Adverbs can show comparison. To compare two actions, add the suffix **er** or use the words **more** or **less**. This is called using the **comparative degree**.

To compare more than two actions, add the suffix **est** or use the words **most** or **least**. This is called using the **superlative degree**.

The spellings of some adverbs change when you use comparative and superlative degrees. Here are some examples:

eagerly	more eagerly	most eagerly
carefully	less carefully	least carefully
well	better	best
low	lower	lowest

Directions: Benjamin Bing brags about everything, but he always uses adverbs incorrectly. Read what Benjamin has to say. Underline each mistake. Then, rewrite each sentence correctly.

1. Everyone knows I can do wheelies more better and more long than yo **Everyone knows I can do wheelies better and longer than you can!**

2. My older brother swims the most fast of all the kids at camp. **My older brother swims the fastest of all the kids at camp.**

3. Our dog Spike growls ferociouslier than the dog next door. **Our dog Spike growls more ferociously than the dog next door.**

4. I think the Rockets hockey team plays the most skillfullest of **I think the Rockets hockey team plays the most skillfully of all the teams.**

5. I finished my homework even more quickiler today than yesterday. **I finished my homework even more quickly today than yesterday.**

6. I'm a great tennis player because I serve the ball more hard than the other players. **I'm a great tennis player because I serve the ball harder than the other players.**

7. My mother jogs more farther in 15 minutes than your mother does. **My mother jogs farther in 15 minutes than your mother does.**

8. My sister writes more rapidlier and neatlier than Jenny does. **My sister writes more rapidly and neatly than Jenny does.**

166

Where and When

Some adverbs such as **here**, **there**, **outside**, and **nearby** tell where something is located. Other adverbs such as **always**, **never**, **today**, and **early** tell when something is taking place.

Directions: Write the adverb that correctly completes the sentence and fits in the puzzle. Each adverb must tell either **when** or **where**. The first one has been done for you.

Across:
1. We ____ go to the movies.
5. I take a vitamin ____.
7. Please play ____.
8. We saw him ____.
10. Do it right ____!
11. Please come ____!
14. The sky is ____.
16. Nothing lasts ____.
17. Not late but ____.
18. He lives ____.

Down:
2. Come here ____.
3. I haven't seen you ____.
4. We've looked ____.
6. We can't find it ____.
9. Please sit ____.
12. Don't ever say ____.
13. Do you come here ____?
15. She hid the cookies ____ the breadbox.

periodically

167

More About Adverbs

Adverbs that modify verbs function as adverbs of time, place, or manner. Adverbs that modify adjectives or other adverbs function as adverbs of degree, also called intensifiers.

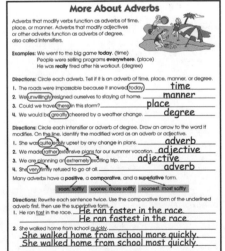

Examples: We went to the big game **today**. (time)
People were selling programs **everywhere**. (place)
He was **really** tired after his workout. (degree)

Directions: Circle each adverb. Tell if it is an adverb of time, place, manner, or degree.

1. The roads were impassable because it snowed (today). **time**
2. We (unwillingly) resigned ourselves to staying at home. **manner**
3. Could we travel (there) in this storm? **place**
4. We would be (greatly) cheered by a weather change. **degree**

Directions: Circle each intensifier or adverb of degree. Draw an arrow to the word it modifies. On the line, identify the modified word as an adverb or adjective.

1. She was (quite) easily upset by any change in plans. **adverb**
2. We made (rather) extensive plans for our summer vacation. **adjective**
3. We are planning an (extremely) exciting trip. **adjective**
4. She (very) firmly refused to go at all. **adverb**

Many adverbs have a **positive**, a **comparative**, and a **superlative** form.

soon, softly	sooner, more softly	soonest, most softly

Directions: Rewrite each sentence twice. Use the comparative form of the underlined adverb first, then use the superlative form.

1. He ran fast in the race. **He ran faster in the race.**
He ran fastest in the race.

2. She walked home from school quickly. **She walked home from school more quickly.**
She walked home from school most quickly.

168

Confusing Adjectives and Adverbs

Good, bad, sure, and **real** are adjectives. They modify nouns.
Examples: That was a **good** dinner. He made a **bad** choice.

Badly, surely, and **really** are adverbs. They modify verbs, adjectives, and other adverbs.
Examples: He ran **badly**. He **really** wanted to go.

Better, worse, best, and **worst** are adjectives if they modify nouns. They are adverbs if they modify verbs, adverbs, or adjectives.
Examples: That's my **best** work. (adjective)
He sang **best** last night. (adverb)

Well is an adjective if it refers to health.
Well is an adverb if it tells how something is done.
Examples: She feels **well** today. (adjective)
He rode the horse **well**. (adverb)

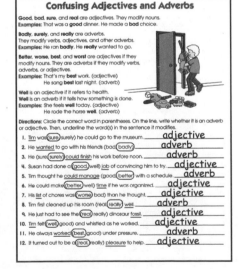

Directions: Circle the correct word in parentheses. On the line, write whether it is an adverb or adjective. Then, underline the word(s) in the sentence that it modifies.

1. Tim was (sure) surely) he could go to the museum. **adjective**
2. He wanted to go with his friends (bad (badly)). **adverb**
3. He (sure (surely)) could finish his work before noon. **adverb**
4. Susan had done a (good) well) job of convincing him to try. **adjective**
5. Tim thought he could manage (good (better)) with a schedule. **adverb**
6. He could make (better) well) time if he was organized. **adjective**
7. His list of chores was (worse) bad) than he thought. **adjective**
8. Tim first cleaned up his room (real (really)) well. **adverb**
9. He just had to see the (real) really) dinosaur fossil. **adjective**
10. Tim felt (well) good) and whistled as he worked. **adjective**
11. He always worked (best) good) under pressure. **adverb**
12. It turned out to be a (real) really) pleasure to help. **adjective**

169

Total Reading Grade 6

GRADE

6

I. Reading
  A. Directions
  B. Sequencing
  C. Main Idea
II. Writing
  A. Capitalization
  B. Proofreading

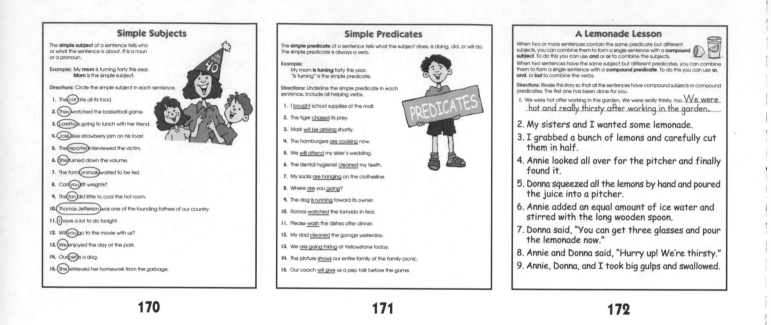

Simple Subjects

The **simple subject** of a sentence tells who or what the sentence is about. It is a noun or a pronoun.

Example: My **mom** is turning forty this year.
    Mom is the simple subject.

Directions: Circle the simple subject in each sentence.

1. The (cat) ate all its food.
2. (They) watched the basketball game.
3. (Loretta) is going to lunch with her friend.
4. (Jose) likes strawberry jam on his toast.
5. The (reporter) interviewed the victim.
6. (She) turned down the volume.
7. The farm (animals) waited to be fed.
8. Can (you) lift weights?
9. The (fan) did little to cool the hot room.
10. (Thomas Jefferson) was one of the founding fathers of our country.
11. (I) have a lot to do tonight.
12. Will (you) go to the movie with us?
13. (We) enjoyed the day at the park.
14. Our (pet) is a dog.
15. (She) retrieved her homework from the garbage.

170

Simple Predicates

The **simple predicate** of a sentence tells what the subject does, is doing, did, or will do. The simple predicate is always a verb.

Example:
My mom **is turning** forty this year.
"Is turning" is the simple predicate.

Directions: Underline the simple predicate in each sentence. Include all helping verbs.

1. I <u>bought</u> school supplies at the mall.
2. The tiger <u>chased</u> its prey.
3. Mark <u>will be arriving</u> shortly.
4. The hamburgers <u>are cooking</u> now.
5. We <u>will attend</u> my sister's wedding.
6. The dental hygienist <u>cleaned</u> my teeth.
7. My socks <u>are hanging</u> on the clothesline.
8. Where <u>are</u> you <u>going</u>?
9. The dog <u>is running</u> toward its owner.
10. Ramos <u>watched</u> the tornado in fear.
11. Please <u>wash</u> the dishes after dinner.
12. My dad <u>cleaned</u> the garage yesterday.
13. We <u>are going</u> hiking at Yellowstone today.
14. The picture <u>shows</u> our entire family at the family picnic.
15. Our coach <u>will give</u> us a pep talk before the game.

171

A Lemonade Lesson

When two or more sentences contain the same predicate but different subjects, you can combine them to form a single sentence with a **compound subject**. To do this you can use **and** or **or** to combine the subjects.

When two sentences have the same subject but different predicates, you can combine them to form a single sentence with a **compound predicate**. To do this you can use **or**, **and**, or **but** to combine the verbs.

Directions: Revise this story so that all the sentences have compound subjects or compound predicates. The first one has been done for you.

1. We were hot after working in the garden. We were really thirsty, too. <u>We were hot and really thirsty after working in the garden.</u>
2. My sisters and I wanted some lemonade.
3. I grabbed a bunch of lemons and carefully cut them in half.
4. Annie looked all over for the pitcher and finally found it.
5. Donna squeezed all the lemons by hand and poured the juice into a pitcher.
6. Annie added an equal amount of ice water and stirred with the long wooden spoon.
7. Donna said, "You can get three glasses and pour the lemonade now."
8. Annie and Donna said, "Hurry up! We're thirsty."
9. Annie, Donna, and I took big gulps and swallowed.

172

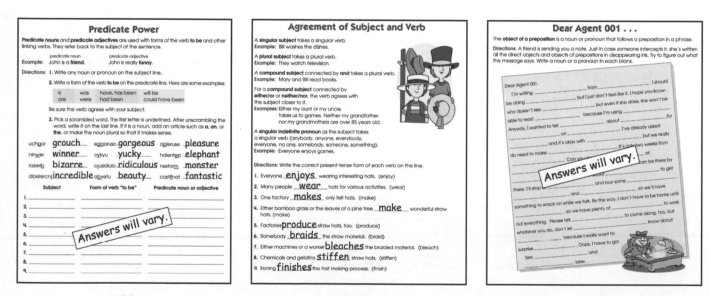

Predicate Power

Predicate nouns and **predicate adjectives** are used with forms of the verb **to be** and other linking verbs. They refer back to the subject of the sentence.

Example: John is a **friend**.   John is really **funny**.
    predicate noun   predicate adjective

Directions: 1. Write any noun or pronoun on the subject line.

2. Write a form of the verb **to be** on the predicate line. Here are some examples:

| is | was | have, has been | will be |
| are | were | had been | could have been |

Be sure the verb agrees with your subject.

3. Pick a scrambled word. The first letter is underlined. After unscrambling the word, write it on the last line. If it is a noun, add an article such as **a, an,** or **the**, or make the noun plural so that it makes sense.

uchgor **grouch**   eggoruso **gorgeous**   apleruse **pleasure**
ninwer **winner**   cykyu **yucky**   halentep **elephant**
razerib **bizarre**   crusidiulo **ridiculous**   nestorm **monster**
dibelercni **incredible**   abyetu **beauty**   casttfnat **fantastic**

Subject	Form of verb "to be"	Predicate noun or adjective
1.		
2.		
3.		
4.	*Answers will vary.*	
5.		
6.		
7.		
8.		
9.		

173

Agreement of Subject and Verb

A **singular subject** takes a singular verb.
Example: Bill washes the dishes.

A **plural subject** takes a plural verb.
Example: They watch television.

A **compound subject** connected by **and** takes a plural verb.
Example: Mary and Bill read books.

For a **compound subject** connected by **either/or** or **neither/nor**, the verb agrees with the subject closer to it.
Examples: Either my aunt or my uncle takes us to games. Neither my grandfather nor my grandmothers are over 85 years old.

A **singular indefinite pronoun** as the subject takes a singular verb (anybody, anyone, everybody, everyone, no one, somebody, someone, something).
Example: Everyone enjoys games.

Directions: Write the correct present-tense form of each verb on the line.

1. Everyone **enjoys** wearing interesting hats. (enjoy)
2. Many people **wear** hats for various activities. (wear)
3. One factory **makes** only felt hats. (make)
4. Either bamboo grass or the leaves of a pine tree **make** wonderful straw hats. (make)
5. Factories **produce** straw hats, too. (produce)
6. Somebody **braids** the straw material. (braid)
7. Either machines or a worker **bleaches** the braided material. (bleach)
8. Chemicals and gelatins **stiffen** straw hats. (stiffen)
9. Ironing **finishes** the hat making process. (finish)

174

Dear Agent 001 . . .

The **object of a preposition** is a noun or pronoun that follows a preposition in a phrase.

Directions: A friend is sending you a note. Just in case someone intercepts it, she's written all the direct objects and objects of prepositions in disappearing ink. Try to figure out what the message says. Write a noun or a pronoun in each blank.

Answers will vary.

175

Missing Objects

Directions: Each of the following sentences tells about a well-known character from a nursery rhyme or fairy tale. Each sentence is also missing either a direct object or an indirect object. Use the ^ symbol to show where the missing object should be. Then, insert it. The first one has been done for you.

1. After they were summoned by Old King Cole, the three fiddlers played ^ a merry tune. *him*

   a bowl of curds and whey
2. Mrs. Muffet fixed her lovely young daughter^ *Her dog*
3. Old Mother Hubbard threw^ a big bone after returning from the market.

   a brick house
4. The very practical third little pig built himself^ *his friends*
5. Each time Pinocchio tells another lie, his nose grows longer.

   the pail
6. Jill handed Jack^ and ran up the hill with him to get some water. *Simple simon*
7. The pie man didn't offer^ any of his wares for he had no money.

   her grandmother
8. Red Riding Hood brought^ a basket of goodies.
9. Hansel broke off a chunk of gingerbread from the witch's cottage and gave his sister^. Gretel *a taste*

   Jack
10. A trickster gave^ a handful of magical beans for the cow.

    water
11. Jack fetched^ on the hill.

    wool
12. Baa, baa, black sheep gave^ to his master.

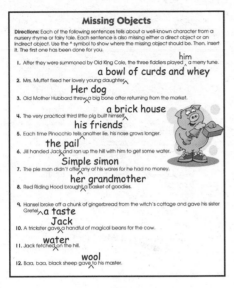

176

Be Brief

An **abbreviation** is the shortened form of a word. Many abbreviations begin with a capital letter and end with a period. **Initials** are a type of abbreviation you can use for certain names and expressions. They replace a word or a whole name.

Directions: Lisa Lewis is always making lists. To save time, she uses abbreviations and initials. Read Lisa's list and underline the abbreviations and initials she used. Then, list the abbreviations and initials and write out what each means. Don't forget to include capital letters and periods where they belong.

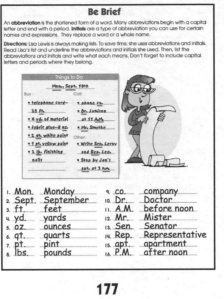

Things to Do
Mon., Sept. 10th

Buy:
- telephone cord— 25 ft.
- 4 yd. of material
- fabric glue—8 oz.
- 2 qt. white paint
- 1 pt. yellow paint
- 2 lb. finishing nails

Call:
- phone co.
- Dr. Jamison at 11 A.M.
- Mr. Smythe

Other:
- Write Sen. Leroy and Rep. Lee.
- Stop by Jen's apt. at 3 P.M.

1. Mon. — Monday
2. Sept. — September
3. ft. — feet
4. yd. — yards
5. oz. — ounces
6. qt. — quarts
7. pt. — pint
8. lbs. — pounds
9. co. — company
10. Dr. — Doctor
11. A.M. — before noon
12. Mr. — Mister
13. Sen. — Senator
14. Rep. — Representative
15. apt. — apartment
16. P.M. — after noon

177

State It

The United States Postal Service has a standard abbreviation for every state. For example, Alabama is abbreviated as AL, Kansas as KS, and Tennessee as TN. When you write an address in letters and on envelopes, you should use these abbreviations. Can you identify all fifty states and the postal abbreviation for each? Test yourself and see.

Directions: Write the abbreviation for each state on the map.

178

Abbreviation Station

Directions: How well do you know your abbreviations? Play this game to find out. Each player needs a coin and small button to use as a marker.

1. Flip the coin to determine how many spaces to move your marker. Move 2 spaces if it's heads up, and 1 space if it's tails up.
2. You will land on an abbreviation. Tell what it means and how to use it. For example, **Dr.** is the abbreviation for the title "Doctor." It is written before a person's name.
3. The first player who goes from START to FINISH along any of the paths wins. Then, write all the words on the lines.

START
cont. — continued
bldg. — building
°F — Fahrenheit
Inc. — Incorporated
m.p.h. — miles per hour
Gen. — General
Nov. — November
Jr. — Junior
mi. — mile
cm — centimeter
SW — Southwest
chap. — chapter
etc. — et cetera
Pres. — President
Rd. — Road
tsp. — teaspoon
°C — Celsius
Mt. — Mount or Mountain
oz. — ounce
pp. — pages
km — kilometer
AZ — Arizona
dept. — department
No. — number
FINISH
lb. — pound
Corp. — Corporation

179

A Recipe for a Sentence

And, but, yet, or, and **so** are **coordinating conjunctions**. Use them to join together words, phrases, and sentences. Be sure to add a comma before a conjunction when you use it to combine two sentences.

Directions: Read the sentences in the first column. Find related sentences in the second column. Look in the third column to find the best conjunction to combine the sentences. Write your new sentences on the lines below.

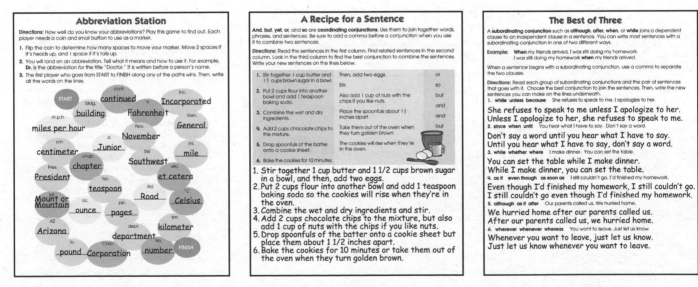

1. Stir together 1 cup butter and 1½ cups brown sugar in a bowl.	Then, add two eggs.	or
2. Put 2 cups flour into another bowl and add 1 teaspoon baking soda.	Stir.	so
	Also add 1 cup of nuts with the chips if you like nuts.	but
3. Combine the wet and dry ingredients.	Place the spoonfuls about 1½ inches apart.	and
4. Add 2 cups chocolate chips to the mixture.	Take them out of the oven when they turn golden brown.	and
5. Drop spoonfuls of the batter onto a cookie sheet.	The cookies will rise when they're in the oven.	but
6. Bake the cookies for 10 minutes.		

1. Stir together 1 cup butter and 1 1/2 cups brown sugar in a bowl, and then, add two eggs.
2. Put 2 cups flour into another bowl and add 1 teaspoon baking soda so the cookies will rise when they're in the oven.
3. Combine the wet and dry ingredients and stir.
4. Add 2 cups chocolate chips to the mixture, but also add 1 cup of nuts with the chips if you like nuts.
5. Drop spoonfuls of the batter onto a cookie sheet but place them about 1 1/2 inches apart.
6. Bake the cookies for 10 minutes or take them out of the oven when they turn golden brown.

180

The Best of Three

A **subordinating conjunction** such as **although, after, when,** or **while** joins a dependent clause to an independent clause in a sentence. You can write most sentences with a subordinating conjunction in one of two different ways.

Example: **When** my friends arrived, I was still doing my homework.
I was still doing my homework **when** my friends arrived.

When a sentence begins with a subordinating conjunction, use a comma to separate the two clauses.

Directions: Read each group of subordinating conjunctions and the pair of sentences that goes with it. Choose the best conjunction to join the sentences. Then, write the new sentences you can make on the lines underneath.
1. while unless because   She refuses to speak to me. I apologize to her.

She refuses to speak to me unless I apologize to her.
Unless I apologize to her, she refuses to speak to me.
2. since when until   You hear what I have to say. Don't say a word.

Don't say a word until you hear what I have to say.
Until you hear what I have to say, don't say a word.
3. while whether where   I make dinner. You can set the table.

You can set the table while I make dinner.
While I make dinner, you can set the table.
4. as if even though as soon as   I still couldn't go. I'd finished my homework.

Even though I'd finished my homework, I still couldn't go.
I still couldn't go even though I'd finished my homework.
5. although as if after   Our parents called us. We hurried home.

We hurried home after our parents called us.
After our parents called us, we hurried home.
6. wherever whenever whereas   You want to leave. Just let us know.

Whenever you want to leave, just let us know.
Just let us know whenever you want to leave.

181

GRADE
6

I. Reading
A. Directions
B. Sequencing
C. Main Idea
II. Writing
A. Capitalization
B. Proofreading

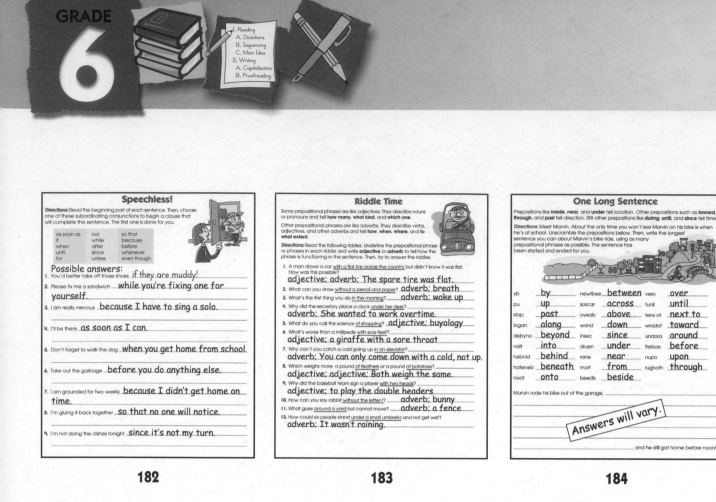

Speechless!

Directions: Read the beginning part of each sentence. Then, choose one of these subordinating conjunctions to begin a clause that will complete the sentence. The first one is done for you.

as soon as	nor	so that
if	while	because
when	after	before
until	since	whenever
for	unless	even though

Possible answers:

1. You'd better take off those shoes _if they are muddy!_
2. Please fix me a sandwich _while you're fixing one for yourself._
3. I am really nervous _because I have to sing a solo._
4. I'll be there _as soon as I can._
5. Don't forget to walk the dog _when you get home from school._
6. Take out the garbage _before you do anything else._
7. I am grounded for two weeks _because I didn't get home on time._
8. I'm gluing it back together _so that no one will notice._
9. I'm not doing the dishes tonight _since it's not my turn._

182

Riddle Time

Some prepositional phrases are like adjectives. They describe nouns or pronouns and tell **how many, what kind,** and **which one.**

Other prepositional phrases are like adverbs. They describe verbs, adjectives, and other adverbs and tell **how, when, where,** and **to what extent.**

Directions: Read the following riddles. Underline the prepositional phrase or phrases in each riddle and write **adjective or adverb** to tell how the phrase is functioning in the sentence. Then, try to answer the riddles.

1. A man drove a car with a flat tire across the country but didn't know it was flat. How was this possible?
   adjective; adverb; The spare tire was flat.
2. What can you draw without a pencil and paper? adverb; breath
3. What's the first thing you do in the morning? adverb; wake up
4. Why did the secretary place a clock under her desk?
   adverb; She wanted to work overtime.
5. What do you call the science of shopping? adjective; buyology
6. What's worse than a millipede with sore feet?
   adjective; a giraffe with a sore throat
7. Why can't you catch a cold going up in an elevator?
   adverb; You can only come down with a cold, not up.
8. Which weighs more, a pound of feathers or a pound of potatoes?
   adjective; adjective; Both weigh the same.
9. Why did the baseball team sign a player with two heads?
   adjective; to play the double headers
10. How can you say rabbit without the letter r? adverb; bunny
11. What goes around a yard but cannot move? adverb; a fence
12. How could six people stand under a small umbrella and not get wet?
    adverb; It wasn't raining.

183

One Long Sentence

Prepositions like **inside, near,** and **under** tell location. Other prepositions such as **toward, through,** and **past** tell direction. Still other prepositions like **during, until,** and **since** tell time.

Directions: Meet Marvin. About the only time you won't see Marvin on his bike is when he's at school. Unscramble the prepositions below. Then, write the longest sentence you can about Marvin's bike ride, using as many prepositional phrases as possible. The sentence has been started and ended for you.

yb	**by**	newtbee	**between**	vero	**over**
pu	**up**	soscar	**across**	tunli	**until**
stap	**past**	oveab	**above**	tenx ot	**next to**
logan	**along**	wond	**down**	wradot	**toward**
debyno	**beyond**	insec	**since**	undora	**around**
noit	**into**	druen	**under**	freboe	**before**
hebnid	**behind**	rane	**near**	nupo	**upon**
hateneb	**beneath**	morf	**from**	rughoth	**through**
noot	**onto**	beedls	**beside**		

Marvin rode his bike out of the garage, _____

Answers will vary.

_____ and he still got home before noon!

184

The Object Is . . .

A **prepositional phrase** begins with a preposition and ends with the object of the preposition. When you use a pronoun as the object of a preposition, be sure to use an object pronoun. The object pronouns are **me, you, him, her, it, us,** and **them.**

Directions: As you read the following story, you will notice that Greg did not complete the prepositional phrases. Help him out by adding the missing objects and any other words that describe the object.

Last night, my friend Steve and I decided to sleep outside in _____. According to _____ the weather forecast called for clear skies with _____. I found the sleeping bags underneath _____ in _____. I also packed some snacks for _____. We could hardly wait for it to get dark. We unrolled our sleeping bags and put them _____ just beyond _____. It finally got dark. Soon we'd hear the owls and some _____ critters that live in the woods around _____ _Answers will vary._ e games and talked about _____ nack and crawled into _____ ool asleep when we were startled by a rustling sound.

"It's probably just a raccoon," I said, as I nervously reached for _____. Steve didn't say anything, but I could tell he was scared. Well, it wasn't a critter. It was my little brother Tommy, dragging his blanket and pillow behind _____.

"What are you doing here?" I asked. "You know, Tommy, you almost scared the wits out of _____."

"Sorry, Greg," he said. "I wanted to sleep outside with _____."

"Well, okay," I sighed. "Just wrap the blanket around _____ and come lie down next to _____."

"Goodnight, Greg and Steve," said Tommy, "and thanks."

185

Prepositional Phrases

A **prepositional phrase** is a group of words that begins with a preposition and ends with a noun or pronoun. It can act as an adjective or adverb.

Examples: Pineapple is also grown outside of Hawaii. (adverb)
The sandwiches with the peanut butter were the best ones. (adjective)
We ate the peanut butter sandwiches at night. (adverb)

Directions: Underline the prepositional phrase in each sentence.

1. Peanuts are enjoyed around the world.
2. Peanuts are native to South America.
3. Peanut pods develop beneath the ground.
4. The pegs, which are the pod stems, push their way under the soil.
5. Peanuts are part of the legume family.
6. Most peanuts are grown in Africa and Asia.

Directions: Tell whether each prepositional phrase acts as an **adjective** or an **adverb.**

1. Wait until choir practice is over to eat peanut butter. adverb
2. Peanut butter on a spoon is a delicious and quick snack. adjective
3. Have you ever enjoyed celery with peanut butter and raisins? adjective
4. Try your peanut butter sandwich with cold milk. adverb
5. I love peanut butter on toast. adjective
6. I enjoy eating peanuts at a ball game. adverb

186

Preposition, Adverb, or Verb?

Don't confuse prepositions with adverbs or with phrases made of **to** plus a verb.

Examples: All the students went to the zoo. (preposition)
We really wanted to go. (verb part)
We started getting excited before the trip. (preposition)
Have you gone to the zoo before? (adverb)

Directions: Identify each **bold** word as a preposition, adverb, or verb part.

1. It was incredible how they had trained the animals to move like that! verb part
2. A monkey followed me to the concession stand. preposition
3. A beautiful dove flew around the audience. preposition
4. A seal tossed a ball around to show off. adverb
5. We took pictures of the walrus before the show. preposition
6. I had never seen a walrus up close before. adverb
7. The walrus waddled beyond the stage over to the audience. preposition
8. My friends were brave, and they decided to stay and pet him. verb part
9. David asked us, "Who wants to see the Dolphin Show at 2:00?" verb part
10. The whale catapulted to the top and grabbed the fish. preposition
11. The monkeys would have liked to swing through the trees. verb part
12. I looked up when I heard the parrot talk. adverb
13. I noticed a pigeon flying around. adverb
14. The elephants came near. adverb
15. The pigeon carried the message to its destination. preposition
16. The chimpanzees shouted across the water. preposition

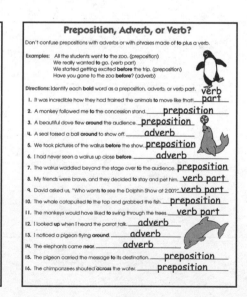

187

I. Reading
  A. Directions
  B. Sequencing
  C. Main Idea
II. Writing
  A. Capitalization
  B. Proofreading

Simple, Compound, and Complex Sentences

A simple sentence has a complete subject and predicate.
Example: The little brown rabbit hopped all around the yard.

A compound sentence has two or more simple sentences joined together.
Example: Patrick tried to pick the rabbit up, but it quickly hopped away.

A complex sentence contains one independent clause and one or more dependent clauses.
Example: After several tries, Patrick finally caught the frightened rabbit.

Directions: Label the sentences below as simple, compound, or complex.
1. Jack and Sam were planning their summer vacation. **simple**
2. Jack, who loved to hike and climb, wanted to go to the mountains. **complex**
3. Sam called the travel agency, but no one answered the phone. **compound**
4. They needed some advice about their travel plans. **simple**
5. Since they had been to the mountains last year, Sam thought going to a lake would be better this time. **complex**
6. They finally decided to fish the first week of their vacation and head for the mountains the second week. **complex**

Directions: Write the sentences below according to the directions.
1. Write a simple sentence with a compound subject.

2. Write a simple sentence with a compound verb.

3. Write a compound s...   **Answers will vary.**

4. Write a complex sent... ...ing the subordinating conjunction *after.*

188

Windy Weather

Remember: Follow punctuation rules whenever you write a sentence.
  Periods are used at the end of a sentence.
  Commas are used to separate items in a list or to separate parts of a sentence.
  Question marks are placed at the end of a question.
  Exclamation points end a command or sentence that expresses a strong emotion.

Directions: Read the following letter and insert the commas or end marks that are missing from each sentence.

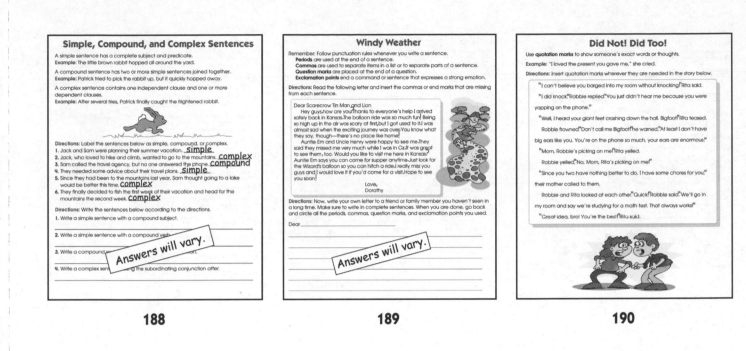

Dear Scarecrow, Tin Man, and Lion
  Hey guys, how are you? Thanks to everyone's help I arrived safely back in Kansas. The balloon ride was so much fun! Being so high up in the air was scary at first, but I got used to it. I was almost sad when the exciting journey was over. You know what they say, though—there's no place like home!
  Auntie Em and Uncle Henry were happy to see me. They said they missed me very much while I was in Oz. It was great to see them, too. Would you like to visit me here in Kansas? Auntie Em says you can come for supper anytime. Just look for the Wizard's balloon so you can hitch a ride. I really miss you guys and I would love it if you'd come for a visit. Hope to see you soon!
      Love,
      Dorothy

Directions: Now, write your own letter to a friend or family member you haven't seen in a long time. Make sure to write in complete sentences. When you are done, go back and circle all the periods, commas, question marks, and exclamation points you used.

Dear _____

Answers will vary.

189

Did Not! Did Too!

Use **quotation marks** to show someone's exact words or thoughts.

Example: "I loved the present you gave me," she cried.

Directions: Insert quotation marks wherever they are needed in the story below.

"I can't believe you barged into my room without knocking!" Rita said.

"I did knock," Robbie replied. "You just didn't hear me because you were yapping on the phone."

"Well, I heard your giant feet crashing down the hall. Bigfoot!" Rita teased.

Robbie frowned. "Don't call me Bigfoot," he warned. "At least I don't have big ears like you. You're on the phone so much, your ears are enormous."

"Mom, Robbie's picking on me!" Rita yelled.

Robbie yelled, "No, Mom, Rita's picking on me!"

"Since you two have nothing better to do, I have some chores for you," their mother called to them.

Robbie and Rita looked at each other. "Quick!" Robbie said. "We'll go in my room and say we're studying for a math test. That always works!"

"Great idea, bro! You're the best!" Rita said.

190

Fix the Ads

Use capital letters at the beginning of a sentence and at the beginning of proper nouns and adjectives.

Directions: Rewrite the following newspaper ads using capital letters in the correct places.

is time running out for You? do you have Some time on your hands? whatever your problem, connie's clock store Can Help! stop by our store on main street to see our huge selection! just remember to hurry, Because "time waits for No One!"

Is time running out for you? Do you have some time on your hands? Whatever your problem, Connie's Clock Store can help! Stop by our store on Main Street to see our huge selection! Just remember to hurry, because "Time waits for no one!"

got a strong longing for Chocolate? a burning yearning for candy hearts? at david's candy Depot, you'll find chocolates in all shapes and sizes, caramels and Nougats to satisfy your sweet tooth, and Delicious jellybeans in 100 gourmet flavors. so stop by our store in the greenleaf mall. tell the clerk, "david sent me," and you'll get a free sample of our famous chocolate cherries!

Got a strong longing for chocolate? A burning yearning for candy hearts? At David's Candy Depot, you'll find chocolates in all shapes and sizes, caramels and nougats to satisfy your sweet tooth, and delicious jellybeans in 100 gourmet flavors. So stop by our store in the Greenleaf Mall. Tell the clerk, "David sent me," and you'll get a free sample of our famous chocolate cherries!

191

One Noisy Storm

There can be more than one way to say something correctly, so try using different types of sentences when you write.

1. Possible answers include: Scooby had always been a silly cat. However, he was acting strangely that morning./Scooby had always been a silly cat. But that morning he was acting strangely.
2. Possible answers include: He was jumping and howling more than usual and even pounced on our other cat, Fluffernutter, while she was sleeping!/ He was jumping and howling more than usual, and he even pounced on our other cat, Fluffernutter, while she was sleeping!
3. Possible answers include: Fluffernutter woke up. She started acting crazy, too./Fluffernutter woke up and then she started acting crazy, too.
4. Possible answers include: Our dog, Lucy, came to see what was going on because the two of them were making so much noise./Our dog, Lucy, came to see what was going on when she heard the two of them making so much noise.
5. Possible answers include: Lucy started barking. Then, she ran into the bathroom and wouldn't come out./Lucy started barking and ran into the bathroom, but she wouldn't come out.

192

Commas

Use **commas** . . .
  . . . after introductory phrases
  . . . to set off nouns of direct address
  . . . to set off appositives from the words that go with them
  . . . to set off words that interrupt the flow of the sentence
  . . . to separate words or groups of words in a series

Examples:
  Introductory phrase: Of course, I'd be happy to attend.
  Noun of direct address: Ms. Williams, please sit here.
  To set off appositives: Lee, the club president, sat beside me.
  Words interrupting flow: My cousin, who's 13, will also be there.
  Words in a series: I ate popcorn, peanuts, oats, and barley.

Directions: Identify how the commas are used in each sentence.
  Write: **I** for introductory phrase
  N for noun of direct address
  A for appositive
  WF for words interrupting flow
  WS for words in a series

I 1. Yes, she is my sister.
A 2. My teacher, Mr. Hopkins, is very fair.
WS 3. Her favorite fruits are oranges, plums, and grapes.
A 4. The city mayor, Carla Ellison, is quite young.
WS 5. I will buy bread, milk, fruit, and ice cream.
WF 6. Her crying, which was quite loud, soon gave me a headache.
N 7. Stephanie, please answer the question.
I 8. So, do you know her?
I 9. Unfortunately, the item is not returnable.
WS 10. My sister, my cousin, and my friend will accompany me on vacation.
A 11. My grandparents, Rose and Bill, are both 57 years old.

193

GRADE 6

I. Reading
  A. Directions
  B. Sequencing
  C. Main Idea
II. Writing
  A. Capitalization
  B. Proofreading

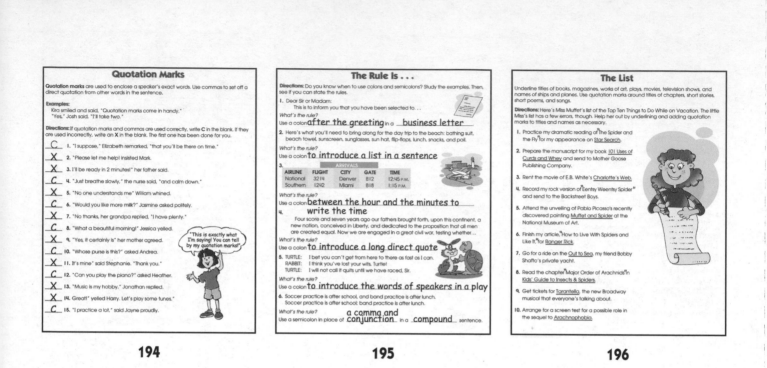

Quotation Marks

Quotation marks are used to enclose a speaker's exact words. Use commas to set off a direct quotation from other words in the sentence.

Examples:
Kira smiled and said, "Quotation marks come in handy."
"Yes," Josh said, "I'll take two."

Directions: If quotation marks and commas are used correctly, write **C** in the blank. If they are used incorrectly, write an **X** in the blank. The first one has been done for you.

C 1. "I suppose," Elizabeth remarked, "that you'll be there on time."
X 2. "Please let me help! Insisted Mark.
X 3. I'll be ready in 2 minutes!" her father said.
C 4. "Just breathe slowly," the nurse said, "and calm down."
X 5. "No one understands me" William whined.
C 6. "Would you like more milk?" Jasmine asked politely.
X 7. "No thanks, her grandpa replied, "I have plenty."
C 8. "What a beautiful morning!" Jessica yelled.
X 9. "Yes, it certainly is" her mother agreed.
C 10. "Whose purse is this?" asked Andrea.
X 11. It's mine" said Stephanie. "Thank you."
C 12. "Can you play the piano?" asked Heather.
X 13. "Music is my hobby," Jonathan replied.
X 14. Great!" yelled Harry. Let's play some tunes."
C 15. "I practice a lot," said Jayne proudly.

"This is exactly what I'm saying! You can tell by my quotation marks!"

194

The Rule Is . . .

Directions: Do you know when to use colons and semicolons? Study the examples. Then, see if you can state the rules.

1. Dear Sir or Madam:
   This is to inform you that you have been selected to. . .
What's the rule?
Use a colon **after the greeting** in a **business letter**

2. Here's what you'll need to bring along for the day trip to the beach: bathing suit, beach towel, sunscreen, sunglasses, sun hat, flip-flops, lunch, snacks, and pail.
What's the rule?
Use a colon **to introduce a list in a sentence**

3.

ARRIVALS				
AIRLINE	FLIGHT	CITY	GATE	TIME
National	3214	Denver	B12	12:45 P.M.
Southern	1242	Miami	B18	1:15 P.M.

Use a colon **between the hour and the minutes to write the time**

4. Four score and seven years ago our fathers brought forth, upon this continent, a new nation, conceived in Liberty, and dedicated to the proposition that all men are created equal. Now we are engaged in a great civil war, testing whether. . .
What's the rule?
Use a colon **to introduce a long direct quote**

5. TURTLE: I bet you can't get from here to there as fast as I can.
  RABBIT: I think you've lost your wits, Turtle!
  TURTLE: I will not call it quits until we have raced, Sir.
What's the rule?
Use a colon **to introduce the words of speakers in a play**

6. Soccer practice is after school, and band practice is after lunch.
  Soccer practice is after school; band practice is after lunch.
What's the rule?
Use a semicolon in place of **a comma and conjunction** in a **compound** sentence.

195

The List

Underline titles of books, magazines, works of art, plays, movies, television shows, and names of ships and planes. Use quotation marks around titles of chapters, short stories, short poems, and songs.

Directions: Here's Miss Muffet's list of the Top Ten Things to Do While on Vacation. The little Miss's list has a few errors, though. Help her out by underlining and adding quotation marks to titles and names as necessary.

1. Practice my dramatic reading of The Spider and the Fly "for my appearance on Star Search.

2. Prepare the manuscript for my book 101 Uses of Curds and Whey and send to Mother Goose Publishing Company.

3. Rent the movie of E.B. White's Charlotte's Web.

4. Record my rock version of "Eentsy Weentsy Spider" and send to the Backstreet Boys.

5. Attend the unveiling of Pablo Picasso's recently discovered painting Muffet and Spider at the National Museum of Art.

6. Finish my article, "How to Live With Spiders and Like It," for Ranger Rick.

7. Go for a ride on the Out to Sea, my friend Bobby Shafto's private yacht.

8. Read the chapter "Major Order of Arachnids" in Kids' Guide to Insects & Spiders.

9. Get tickets for Tarantella, the new Broadway musical that everyone's talking about.

10. Arrange for a screen test for a possible role in the sequel to Arachnophobia.

196

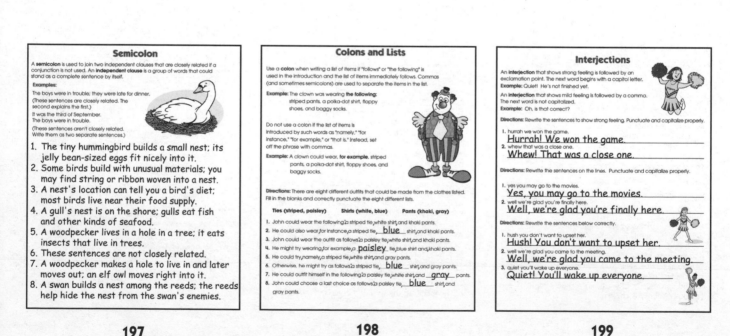

Semicolon

A **semicolon** is used to join two independent clauses that are closely related if a conjunction is not used. An **independent clause** is a group of words that could stand as a complete sentence by itself.

Examples:
The boys were in trouble; they were late for dinner.
(These sentences are closely related. The second explains the first.)
It was the first of September.
The boys were in trouble.
(These sentences aren't closely related. Write them as two separate sentences.)

1. The tiny hummingbird builds a small nest; its jelly bean-sized eggs fit nicely into it.
2. Some birds build with unusual materials; you may find string or ribbon woven into a nest.
3. A nest's location can tell you a bird's diet; most birds live near their food supply.
4. A gull's nest is on the shore; gulls eat fish and other kinds of seafood.
5. A woodpecker lives in a hole in a tree; it eats insects that live in trees.
6. These sentences are not closely related.
7. A woodpecker makes a hole to live in and later moves out; an elf owl moves right into it.
8. A swan builds a nest among the reeds; the reeds help hide the nest from the swan's enemies.

197

Colons and Lists

Use a **colon** when writing a list of items if "follows" or "the following" is used in the introduction and the list of items immediately follows. Commas (and sometimes semicolons) are used to separate the items in the list.

Example: The clown was wearing **the following:**
  striped pants, a polka-dot shirt, floppy shoes, and baggy socks.

Do not use a colon if the list of items is introduced by such words as "namely," "for instance," "for example," or "that is." Instead, set off the phrase with commas.

Example: A clown could wear, **for example,** striped pants, a polka-dot shirt, floppy shoes, and baggy socks.

Directions: There are eight different outfits that could be made from the clothes listed. Fill in the blanks and correctly punctuate the eight different lists.

Ties (striped, paisley)   Shirts (white, blue)   Pants (khaki, gray)

1. John could wear the following: a striped tie, white shirt, and khaki pants.
2. He could also wear, for instance, a striped tie, **blue** shirt, and khaki pants.
3. John could wear the outfit as follows: a paisley tie, white shirt, and khaki pants.
4. He might try wearing, for example, a **paisley** tie, blue shirt and khaki pants.
5. He could try, namely, a striped tie, white shirt, and gray pants.
6. Otherwise, he might try as follows: a striped tie, **blue** shirt, and gray pants.
7. He could outfit himself in the following: a paisley tie, white shirt, and **gray** pants.
8. John could choose a last choice as follows: a paisley tie, **blue** shirt, and gray pants.

198

Interjections

An **interjection** that shows strong feeling is followed by an exclamation point. The next word begins with a capital letter.
Example: Quiet! He's not finished yet.
An **interjection** that shows mild feeling is followed by a comma. The next word is not capitalized.
Example: Oh, is that correct?

Directions: Rewrite the sentences to show strong feeling. Punctuate and capitalize properly.

1. hurrah we won the game.
Hurrah! We won the game.
2. whew that was a close one.
Whew! That was a close one.

Directions: Rewrite the sentences on the lines. Punctuate and capitalize properly.

1. yes you may go to the movies.
Yes, you may go to the movies.
2. well we're glad you're finally here.
Well, we're glad you're finally here.

Directions: Rewrite the sentences below correctly.

1. hush you don't want to upset her.
Hush! You don't want to upset her.
2. well we're glad you came to the meeting.
Well, we're glad you came to the meeting.
3. quiet you'll wake up everyone.
Quiet! You'll wake up everyone.

199

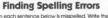

GRADE 6

I. Reading
A. Directions
B. Sequencing
C. Main Idea
II. Writing
A. Capitalization
B. Proofreading

Finding Spelling Errors

Directions: One word in each sentence below is misspelled. Write the word correctly on the line.

1. Jeff felt discoraged at the comparison between him and his older brother. **discouraged**
2. I got inpatient as my curiosity grew. **impatient**
3. She confided that she had not finished the asignment. **assignment**
4. They made the selection after a brief conference. **conference**
5. Obviusly, it's impolite to sneeze on someone. **Obviously**
6. This skin cream is practicaly invisible. **practically**
7. What would prevent you from taking on additonal work? **additional**
8. I can resite the words to that hymn. **recite**
9. In a previous columm, the newspaper explained the situation. **column**
10. He decieved me so many times that now I distrust him. **deceived**
11. Please have the curtesy to observe the "No Eating" signs. **courtesy**
12. The advertisement is so small that it's nearly invisible. **invisible**
13. The best way to communicate is in a face-to-face conservation. **conversation**
14. In a cost comparison, salmon is more expensive than tuna. **comparison**
15. Popularity among friends shouldn't depend on your accomplishments. **Popularity**
16. Her campaign was quite an achievment. **achievement**
17. He condemed it as a poor imitation. **condemned**

200

Finding Spelling Errors

Directions: Circle all misspelled words. Write the words correctly on the lines at the end of each paragraph. If you need help, consult a dictionary.

Sabrina wanted to aquire a saltwater acquarium. She was worried about the expence, though, so first she did some research. She wanted to learn the exact care saltwater fish need, not just to exist but to flourish. One sorce said she needed to put water in the aquarium and wait 6 weeks before she added the fish. "Good greif," Sabrina thought. She got a kitten from her neighbor instead.

acquire, aquarium, expense, research,
exact, exist, flourish, source, grief,
neighbor

One stormy day, Marcel was babysitting his neice. He happened to observe that the sky looked darker than norm. At first he ignored it, but then he noticed a black cloud expand and grow in hieght. Then a tail dropped from the twisting cloud and seized a tree. "It's a tornado!" Marcel shouted. "Maybe two tornados. This is an emergensy!" For a breef moment Marcel wished he hadn't shouted, because his niece looked at him with a very frightened expresion. Just then, the cieling began to sag as if it had a heavy wieght on it. "This is an excelent time to visit the basement," he told the little girl as calmly as possible.

niece, observe, normal, ignored, expand,
height, seized, tornadoes, emergency,
brief, expression, ceiling, weight, excellent

Just before Mother's Day, Bethany went to a flourist to buy some flowers for her mother. "Well, what is your reqest?" the clerk asked. "I don't have much money," Bethany told him. "So make up your mind," he said impatiently. "Do you want quallity or quanity?" Bethany wondered if he was giving her a quizz. She tried not to squirm as he stared down at her. "I want cortesy," she said, as she headed for the exit.

florist, request, quality, quantity, quiz,
squirm, courtesy, exit

201

Correcting Errors

Directions: Find six errors in each paragraph. Write the words correctly on the lines after each paragraph. Use a dictionary if you need help.

My brother Jim took a math course at the high school that was too hard for hymn. My father didn't want him to take it, but Jim said, "Oh, you're just too critical, Dad. Obviously you don't think I can do it." Jim ignored Dad. That's norm at our house.

course, him, critical, obviously, ignored, normal

Well, the first day Jim went to the course, he came home with a solem expreion on his face, like a condemed man. "That teacher assined us five pages of homework!" he said. "And two additonal problems that we have to reserch!"

solemn, expression, condemned, assigned,
additional, research

"He sounds like an excelent profesional teacher," my dad said. "We need more teachers of that qwality in our schools." Jim squirmed in his seat. Then he gradualy started to smile. "Dad, I need some help with a person problem," he said. "Five pages of problems, right?" Dad asked. Jim smiled and handed Dad his math book. That's typial at our house, too.

excellent, professional, quality, gradually,
personal, typical

One day, we had a medical emergeny at home. My sisters hand got stuck in a basket with a narrow opening, and she couldn't pull it out. I thought she would have to wear the basket on her hand permanentally. First, I tried to stretch and expand the baskets opening, but that didn't work.

medical, emergency, sister's, permanently,
expand, basket's

Then I smeared a quanity of butter on my sisters hand, and she pulled it right out. I thought she would have the curtesy to thank me, but she just stomped away, still mad. How childish! Sometimes she seems to think theres just to serve her. There are more importaner things in the world than her happiness!

quantity, sister's, courtesy, childish, exist,
important

202

Complete Sentences

A **complete sentence** has both a simple subject and a simple predicate. It is a complete thought. Sentences which are not complete are called **fragments**.

Example:
Complete sentence: The wolf howled at the moon.
Sentence fragment: Howled at the moon.

Directions: Write C on the line if the sentence is complete. Write F if it is a fragment.

1. **C** The machine is running.
2. **C** What will we do today?
3. **F** Knowing what I do.
4. **C** That statement is true.
5. **C** My parents drove to town.
6. **F** Watching television all afternoon.
7. **C** The storm devastated the town.
8. **C** Our friends can go with us.
9. **C** The palm trees bent in the wind.
10. **F** Spraying the fire all night.

Directions: Rewrite the sentence fragments from above to make them complete sentences.

Answers will vary.

203

Run-On Sentences

A **run-on sentence** occurs when two or more sentences are joined together without punctuation or a joining word. Run-on sentences should be divided into two or more separate sentences.

Example:
Run-on sentence: My parents, sister, brother, and I went to the park we saw many animals we had fun.
Correct: My parents, sister, brother, and I went to the park. We saw many animals and had fun.

Directions: Rewrite the run-on sentences correctly. *Sample answers:*

1. The dog energetically chased the ball I kept throwing him the ball for a half hour.
   The dog energetically chased the ball. I kept throwing him the ball for a half hour.

2. The restaurant served scrambled eggs and bacon for breakfast I had some and they were delicious.
   The restaurant served bacon and scrambled eggs for breakfast. I had some, and they were delicious.

3. The lightning struck close to our house it scared my little brother and my grandmother called to see if we were safe.
   The lightning struck close to our house. It scared my little brother. My grandmother called to see if we were safe.

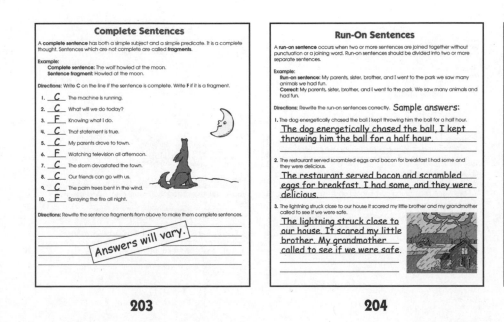

204

Run-On Wreck!

There is usually more than one way to fix a run-on sentence. You can rewrite it as two or more separate sentences. You can insert a comma or semicolon. You might also insert a conjunction such as **and**, **but**, or **with**.

Directions: Rew... **Possible answers include:**

in two different...

1. Sunday's Street Fair was very crowded, there were more than ten thousand people there.
   Sunday's Street Fair was very crowded. There were more than ten thousand people there./ Sunday's Street Fair was very crowded; there were more than ten thousand people there.

2. There were lots of booths set up. They were on First Avenue and Second Avenue, too./ There were lots of booths set up on First Avenue and Second Avenue, too.

3. You could buy lots of things at the fair. There were clothes, videos, pet supplies, food, and more./ You could buy lots of things at the fair; there were clothes, videos, pet supplies, food, and more.

4. My best friend found a cute T-shirt. It had a funny saying on it./ My best friend found a cute T-shirt with a funny saying on it.

5. We had so much fun at the fair. Now I can't wait until next year's!/ We had so much fun at the fair; I can't wait until next year's!

205

GRADE
6

I. Reading
  A. Directions
  B. Sequencing
  C. Main Idea
II. Writing
  A. Capitalization
  B. Proofreading

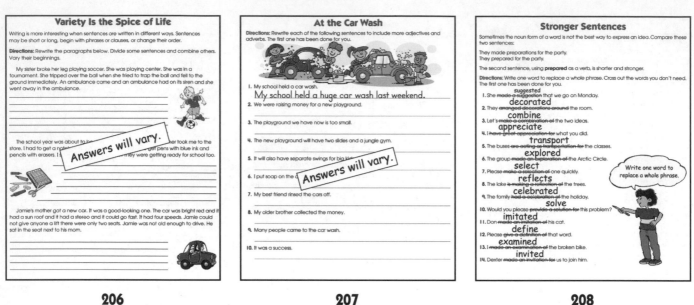

Variety Is the Spice of Life

Writing is more interesting when sentences are written in different ways. Sentences may be short or long, begin with phrases or clauses, or change their order.

Directions: Rewrite the paragraphs below. Divide some sentences and combine others. Vary their beginnings.

My sister broke her leg playing soccer. She was playing center. She was in a tournament. She tripped over the ball when she tried to trap the ball and fell to the ground immediately. An ambulance came and an ambulance had on its siren and she went away in the ambulance.

The school year was about to ... her took me to the store. I had to get a note... get pens with blue ink and pencils with erasers. I... they were getting ready for school too.

Answers will vary.

Jamie's mother got a new car. It was a good-looking one. The car was bright red and it had a sun roof and it had a stereo and it could go fast. It had four speeds. Jamie could not give anyone a lift there were only two seats. Jamie was not old enough to drive. He sat in the seat next to his mom.

206

At the Car Wash

Directions: Rewrite each of the following sentences to include more adjectives and adverbs. The first one has been done for you.

1. My school held a car wash.
   My school held a huge car wash last weekend.

2. We were raising money for a new playground.

3. The playground we have now is too small.

4. The new playground will have two slides and a jungle gym.

5. It will also have separate swings for big kids.

6. I put soap on the c...

7. My best friend rinsed the cars off.

8. My older brother collected the money.

9. Many people came to the car wash.

10. It was a success.

Answers will vary.

207

Stronger Sentences

Sometimes the noun form of a word is not the best way to express an idea. Compare these two sentences:

They made preparations for the party.
They prepared for the party.

The second sentence, using **prepared** as a verb, is shorter and stronger.

Directions: Write one word to replace a whole phrase. Cross out the words you don't need. The first one has been done for you.

1. She ~~made a suggestion~~ that we go on Monday. **suggested**
2. They ~~arranged decorations around~~ the room. **decorated**
3. Let's ~~make a combination of~~ the two ideas. **combine**
4. I have ~~great appreciation for~~ what you did. **appreciate**
5. The buses ~~are acting as transportation for~~ the classes. **transport**
6. The group ~~made an exploration of~~ the Arctic Circle. **explored**
7. Please ~~make a selection of~~ one quickly. **select**
8. The lake is ~~making a reflection of~~ the trees. **reflects**
9. The family ~~had a celebration of~~ the holiday. **celebrated**
10. Would you please ~~provide a solution to~~ this problem? **solve**
11. Don ~~made an imitation of~~ his cat. **imitated**
12. Please ~~give a definition of~~ that word. **define**
13. I ~~made an examination of~~ the broken bike. **examined**
14. Dexter ~~made an invitation for~~ us to join him. **invited**

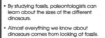 Write one word to replace a whole phrase.

208

Great Combinations

You can combine sentences by eliminating words that are repeated. When you eliminate words to put two or more subjects together into one sentence, you are making a **compound subject**. Make sure your subject agrees with your verb.

Example: **Lisa** went to soccer practice after school. **Tori** went to soccer practice.
Lisa and Tori went to soccer practice.

When you eliminate words to put two or more verbs together into one sentence, you are making a **compound predicate**.

Example: I **built** the birdhouse myself. I **painted** the birdhouse myself.
I **built and painted** the birdhouse myself.

Directions: Combine the following sets of sentences. Then, label each new sentence correctly with the words **compound subject** or **compound predicate** to tell which it contains.

1. My town just started a new recycling program. My town is asking everyone to participate.
   My town just started a new recycling program and is asking everyone to participate. compound predicate

2. We have to separate plastic, glass, aluminum, and paper. We have to put them all in different containers.
   We have to separate plastic, glass, aluminum, and paper and put them all in different containers. compound predicate

3. My sister has the job of taking the containers out to the curb so the truck can pick them up. I have the job of taking the containers out to the curb so the truck can pick them up.
   My sister and I have the job of taking the containers out to the curb so the truck can pick them up. compound subject

4. The truck picks up the containers. Then, the truck takes the containers to a recycling plant in the next town.
   The truck picks up the containers and takes them to a recycling plant in the next town. compound predicate

209

All About Teddy

Conjunctions are words that join words or groups of words. Using conjunctions is a good way to combine sentences.

Example: My teacher will be there. My best friend will not be there.
My teacher will be there, **but** my best friend will not be.

Directions: Combine each pair of sentences below by using one of the conjunctions from the box. There may be more than one way to combine the sentences, and some conjunctions may be used more than once.

but and Possible answers include:

1. Theodore Roosevelt was born on October 27, 1858, and died on January 16, 1919.

2. Roosevelt became vice president of the United States under William McKinley; when McKinley was assassinated, Roosevelt became president.

3. As president, Roosevelt arranged for the Panama Canal to be built and resolved disagreements between big mining companies and their workers.

4. He set aside over 200 million acres of land for parks and nature reserves because he wanted to preserve America's natural resources for future generations.

5. Roosevelt ran for president again in 1912 but was defeated by Woodrow Wilson.

210

Report-a-Sauras, Part 1

Directions: You are writing a report about dinosaurs. In each paragraph, you want to answer a certain research question. The following is a list of notes you took at the library. Write each piece of information under the paragraph it goes with.

- Dinosaurs roamed the earth for more than 180 million years, but they became extinct over 65 million years ago.
- By studying fossils, paleontologists can learn about the sizes of the different dinosaurs.
- Almost everything we know about dinosaurs comes from looking at fossils.
- Scientists who study dinosaur fossils are called paleontologists.
- Before paleontologists can study fossils, they must dig them from the ground and clean them very carefully.
- Then, the fossils can be taken to a university or museum and studied.
- By studying fossils, paleontologists can learn what the different types of dinosaurs ate.
- Fossils were formed from dinosaurs when their remains hardened into stone or were surrounded by mud or sand that hardened into stone.
- Fossils are formed over long periods of time from the bones, eggs, and other remains of dinosaurs.
- By studying fossils, paleontologists can learn how the different types of dinosaurs cared for their young.

First paragraph: When did the dinosaurs live?
- Dinosaurs roamed the earth for more than 180 million years, but they became extinct over 65 million years ago.

Second paragraph: What are fossils, and why are they important?
- Almost everything we know about dinosaurs comes from looking at fossils.
- Fossils were formed from dinosaurs when these remains hardened into stone or were surrounded by mud or sand that hardened into stone.
- Fossils are formed over long periods of time from the bones, eggs, and other remains of dinosaurs.

211

GRADE
6

I. Reading
A. Directions
B. Sequencing
C. Main Idea
II. Writing
A. Capitalization
B. Proofreading

Report-a-Sauras, Part 2

Directions: Continue to write each piece of information from page 211 under the paragraph it goes in.

Third paragraph: What are paleontologists, and what do they do?

· Scientists who study dinosaur fossils are called paleontologists.

· Before paleontologists can study fossils, they must dig them from the ground and clean them very carefully.

· Then the fossils can be taken to a university or museum and studied.

Fourth paragraph: What can paleontologists learn from looking at fossils?

· By studying fossils, paleontologists can learn about the sizes of the different dinosaurs.

· By studying fossils, paleontologists can learn what the different types of dinosaurs ate.

· By studying fossils, paleontologists can learn how the different types of dinosaurs cared for their young.

212

Give Me One Reason

Directions: Place each line of information below in the correct spot on the outline. A few are already done for you. Check off the information as you use it.

I would be supervising other children

I would be working as a member of a team

To keep busy after school

To help other children

Program offers activities for younger kids

Program runs until 5:00

Program offers tutoring for younger kids

Reading

Math

Science

You wouldn't have to worry about me while you're at work

Arts and crafts

Playground games

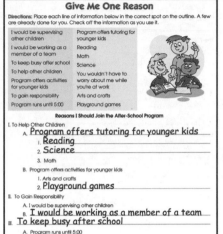

Reasons I Should Join the After-School Program

I. To Help Other Children
  A. Program offers tutoring for younger kids
    1. Reading
    2. Science
    3. Math
  B. Program offers activities for younger kids
    1. Arts and crafts
    2. Playground games
II. To Gain Responsibility
  A. I would be supervising other children
  B. I would be working as a member of a team
III. To keep busy after school
  A. Program runs until 5:00
  B. You wouldn't have to worry about me while you're at work.

213

The Three-Alarm Outline

Directions: Read the following article. Then, fill in the outline below with points from the story. Remember: Each subsection you fill in must answer the main question posed for that section.

On June 11, a terrible fire ripped through the old hat factory on Martin Street. For a short period of time the fire threatened a store nearby, but it was contained thanks to the local fire department.

It is believed that the fire started in a pile of rags that was too close to an old electrical outlet.

The fire started at around 9:30 in the morning and by 10:00 the whole building was in flames. It

took nearly three hours for firefighters to extinguish the blaze.

Ms. Liza Smith, of 32 Martin Street, reported the fire at 9:45 when she smelled smoke. "I thought for a while that the smell was coming from my house, and I was very scared," she said. "But when I went

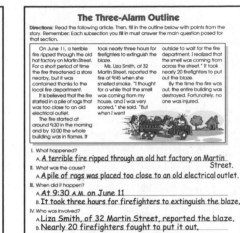

outside to wait for the fire department, I realized that the smell was coming from across the street." It took nearly 20 firefighters to put out the blaze.

By the time the fire was out, the entire building was destroyed. Fortunately, no one was injured.

I. What happened?
  A. A terrible fire ripped through an old hat factory on Martin Street.
II. What was the cause?
  A. A pile of rags was placed too close to an old electrical outlet.
III. When did it happen?
  A. At 9:30 A.M. on June 11
  B. It took three hours for firefighters to extinguish the blaze.
IV. Who was involved?
  A. Liza Smith, of 32 Martin Street, reported the blaze.
  B. Nearly 20 firefighters fought to put it out.
V. What was the result?
  A. The entire building was destroyed.
  B. No one was injured.

214

Writing: Outlining

An **outline** is a skeletal description of the main ideas and important details of a reading selection. Making an outline is a good study aid. It is particularly useful when you must write a paper.

Directions: Read the paragraphs, and then complete the outline below.

Weather has a lot to do with where animals live. Cold-blooded animals have body temperatures that change with the temperature of the environment. Cold-blooded animals include snakes, frogs, and lizards. They cannot live anywhere the temperatures stay below freezing for long periods of time. The body temperatures of warm-blooded animals do not depend on the environment. Any animal with hair or fur—including dogs, elephants, and whales—is warm-blooded. Warm-blooded animals can live anywhere in the world where there is enough food to sustain them.

Some warm-blooded animals live where snow covers the ground all winter. These animals have different ways to survive the cold weather. Certain animals store up food to last throughout the snowy season. For example, the tree squirrel may gather nuts to hide in his home. Other animals hibernate in the winter. The ___ in its burrow all winter long, living off the fat reserves ___

Sample answers:

Title: Animal Habitats

Main Topic: I. Weather has a lot to do with where animals live

  Subtopic: A. Cold-blooded animals' temperatures change with environment.
    Detail: 1. They cannot live anywhere it stays below freezing very long.
  Subtopic: B. Warm-blooded animals' temperatures do not depend on the environment.
    Detail: 1. They can live anywhere there is food.

Main Topic: II. Some warm-blooded animals can live in the snow all winter.

  Subtopic: A. Animals have different ways to survive the cold.
    Details: 1. Some animals store food for the winter.
      2. Some animals hibernate in the winter.

215

Organizing Paragraphs

A **topic sentence** states the main idea of a paragraph and is usually the first sentence. **Support sentences** follow, providing details about the topic. All sentences in a paragraph should relate to the topic sentence. A paragraph ends with a **conclusion sentence**.

Directions: Rearrange each group of sentences into a paragraph, beginning with the topic sentence. Cross out the sentence in each group that is not related to the topic sentence. Write the new paragraph.

Now, chalk drawings are considered art by themselves. The earliest chalk drawings were found on the walls of caves. Chalk is also used in cement, fertilizer, toothpaste, and makeup. Chalk once was used just to make quick sketches. Chalk has been used for drawing for thousands of years. Then, the artist would paint pictures from the sketches.

Chalk has been used for drawing for thousands of years. The earliest chalk drawings were found on the walls of caves. Chalk once was used just to make quick sketches. Then, the artist would paint pictures from the sketches. Now, chalk drawings are considered art by themselves.

Dams also keep young salmon from swimming downriver to the ocean. Most salmon live in the ocean but return to fresh water to lay their eggs and breed. Dams prevent salmon from swimming upriver to their spawning grounds. Pacific salmon die after they spawn the first time. One kind of fish pass is a series of pools of water that lead the salmon over the dams. Dams are threatening salmon by interfering with their spawning. To help with this problem, some dams have special "fish passes" to allow salmon to swim over the dam.

Dams are threatening salmon by interfering with their spawning. Most salmon live in the ocean but return to fresh water to lay their eggs and breed. Dams prevent salmon from swimming upriver to their spawning grounds. Dams also keep young salmon from swimming downriver to the ocean. To help with this problem, some dams have special "fish passes" to allow salmon to swim over the dam. One kind of fish pass is a series of pools of water that lead the salmon over the dams.

216

It Doesn't Belong

Directions: In each paragraph, there is one sentence that doesn't belong. Circle the topic sentence, and underline the unnecessary sentence.

1. (March is my favorite month of the year.) I like March because you never know what to expect. Sometimes it snows. It usually rains a lot in April. Sometimes it can be very hot in March. March is the kind of month when anything can happen!

2. (Yesterday, my mom and I planted flowers in our garden.) My sister was at work yesterday afternoon. We planted daffodils, irises, and petunias. It was a lot of hard work, but I bet our garden will look great when all those flowers are in bloom!

3. (We had an incredible thunderstorm last night!) It rained so hard, it sounded like someone was playing drums on our roof. And the thunder was so loud, all the windows rattled. There was a lot of lightning too. During the storm, we heard a huge crash. I looked outside and saw a big branch had fallen next to the house. We were lucky it didn't hit anybody! It's not raining today.

4. (Tomorrow, I will go to work with my dad for "Take Your Daughters to Work Day.") My dad is the manager of a sporting goods store. My mom works in an office. I like going to work with Dad because it's never boring at the store. There is lots of sports equipment to play with and one of Dad's co-workers, Theresa, always plays catch with me on her break.

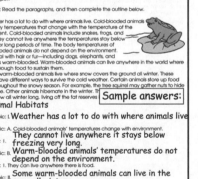

217

GRADE 6

I. Reading
   A. Directions
   B. Sequencing
   C. Main Idea
II. Writing
   A. Capitalization
   B. Proofreading

Hollywood Hound

Start a new paragraph every time you begin writing about a new idea or a new person begins speaking.

Directions: Lola Labrador is covering a movie premiere for *Hollywood Hound*. Help Lola organize her article into paragraphs by marking a paragraph indent symbol ¶ wherever Lola should start a new paragraph.

¶The air was full of wagging tails and excited barks when I arrived at the Canine Cinema. Tonight was the premiere of Hollywood's most eagerly awaited film, "Mission Impawsible." ¶The crowd surged forward with an excited woof as the first long black limousine arrived. Out stepped Thandie Newfoundland, the beautiful female star of the film. Thandie looked stunning in a sparkly diamond collar with matching diamond bracelets on her paws, and diamond earrings glistening in the fur of each ear. "How do you feel about being in this movie?" I asked the pretty pooch. ¶"Lola, it's a dream come true," she responded. "My tail's been wagging ever since my big chase scene with the exploding Frisbee." ¶Suddenly, excited howls filled the air. Who should step out of a limo but the star of "Mission Impawsible" himself, Tom Chow! ¶What a handsome dog he was, with his black leather jacket and muscular paws. ¶"Got to run," Tom called as he hurried inside with a wave to his fans. "I need to get a big bucket of doggie treats before the movie starts!"

218

Lost in the Zoo

One good way to start a paragraph is with an attention-grabbing introduction. If you can, finish your paragraph with a conclusion that sums up the paragraph's main point.

Directions: Write an I next to each statement that could make a good introduction to a paragraph. Write a C next to each sentence that could make a good conclusion.

1. **I** What's big, scaly, and has a really bad temper? The Komodo dragon!
2. **C** As you can see, you don't have to be big to be dangerous!
3. **I** Would you know what to do if you came face to face with a wild animal? Read on for some helpful tips for your next wildlife adventure.
4. **C** So the next time you hear someone say dragons aren't real, tell them about the Komodo dragon—a living, breathing monster!
5. **C** Even though wild animals can be deadly, if you follow the steps I just mentioned, you can keep yourself safe in the wild.
6. **I** When you think of deadly animals, you probably think of sharks, lions, or grizzly bears; but the animal that has killed more people in history isn't one of these creatures! It's the lowly mosquito.

Directions: Now, write a paragraph about your favorite animal. Include an attention-grabbing introduction and a concluding sentence that sums up your main point.

Answers will vary.

219

The School Newspaper

There are many different kinds of paragraphs. **Persuasive** paragraphs try to convince the reader; **expository** paragraphs give information about a topic and contains facts, opinions, or both; **descriptive** paragraphs describe things or events in detail.

Directions: Read each paragraph. On the lines below each one, tell what kind of paragraph it is (**persuasive**, **expository**, or **descriptive**) and its main message. The first one has been done for you.

1. Yesterday after school, the principal met with the new advisory board. This advisory board is made up of three teachers chosen by the principal, and three students chosen by the student body. The board hopes to address problems within the school and find ways for students and teachers to work together to solve them.

   Descriptive; the principal met with the advisory board to find ways for teachers and students to work together to solve problems.

2. Is it just me, or is the cafeteria food getting worse? Yesterday's special looked and tasted like cardboard. We used to have pizza all the time, but now we hardly ever have it. I think it would be great if we could have pizza more often instead of that gross cardboard stuff.

   Expository; the author thinks that the cafeteria food is getting worse.

3. I plan to vote for Chris McGuinness for class president. Why? Because he's honest and hard-working. Remember how great the Fall Fiesta Dance was last week? Chris did all of the organizing. If he can do such a great job planning a dance, just think of how good he'll be as our president!

   Persuasive; the author wants the reader to vote for Chris McGuinness for class president.

4. Chase Dribble scored the winning basket for our team with an amazing three-pointer.

   Descriptive; because of Chase Dribble's winning basket, the basketball team will be going to the state championships.

220

The Art of Persuasion

A good **persuasive paragraph** contains several elements. It contains a **topic sentence** that tells the author's opinion. It contains **support sentences** that give the author's reasons for feeling this way; these sentences may include **examples** to support or prove the author's argument. Finally, it includes a strong **concluding sentence** that sums up the author's opinion.

Directions: Complete each sentence below to express your own opinion. Then, turn each one into the topic sentence for a persuasive paragraph.

1. The best thing to do when you're feeling down is _____

Answers will vary.

2. The most fun day of _____ always _____

221

In a Blink

A **descriptive paragraph** contains a topic sentence telling who or what will be described. It also contains support sentences that introduce or give details about the topic, using specific examples.

Directions: Read this descriptive paragraph. Circle the topic sentence and underline the supporting sentences. If you see a sentence that does not relate to the main topic, cross it out.

Have you ever seen a firefly? (The firefly is a type of beetle that is known for producing a yellowish or greenish light.) ~~All beetles have wings.~~ The firefly produces light from a small organ on its abdomen called a lantern. The lantern contains special chemicals to make light. In most fireflies, the light blinks on and off; they actually use this to communicate with one another. When a male firefly blinks his light on and off, he is showing females that he is ready to mate. Female fireflies may blink their lights to show interest in mating, but sometimes they do it to trick male fireflies. A female firefly will blink her light at a male as if she wants to mate, but the joke's on him—she eats him instead! ~~Female black widow spiders are known for killing their male counterparts.~~

Directions: Now, write a descriptive paragraph of your own. Describe anything you want—your favorite food, a friend, a game you like to play. Remember to include a topic sentence and supporting sentences.

Answers will vary.

222

Keeping It Casual

You don't need to have a topic sentence or supporting sentences in every paragraph you write. When you write a letter or a diary entry, for example, you don't need to make a point and back it up in every paragraph. However, it's a good idea to start a new paragraph whenever you start talking about something new. This warns your reader that you will be changing the subject.

Directions: Write a diary entry to tell what you did yesterday. Include any important activities you did, thoughts or feelings you had, or plans you made. Make sure to begin a new paragraph whenever you introduce something new.

Date: _____

Dear Diary,

Answers will vary.

223

GRADE 6

I. Reading
  A. Directions
  B. Sequencing
  C. Main Idea
II. Writing
  A. Capitalization
  B. Proofreading

Prompt Paragraphs

Writing prompts are comments or questions that get your imagination working. In school and on standardized tests, you will be asked to write paragraphs or short essays in response to writing prompts.

Directions: Respond to the writing prompts below by writing one paragraph to go with each. Make sure to include a topic sentence and supporting sentences in each paragraph.

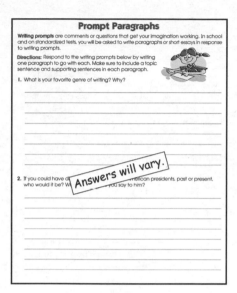

1. What is your favorite genre of writing? Why?

Answers will vary.

2. If you could have dinner with any American presidents, past or present, who would it be? What would you say to him?

224

Building Paragraphs

Directions: Read each group of questions and the topic sentence. On another sheet of paper, write support sentences that answer each question. Number your support sentences in order. Make any necessary changes so the sentences fit together in one paragraph. Then, write your paragraph after the topic sentence.

Questions: Why did Jimmy feel sad?
What happened to change how he felt?
How does he feel when he comes to school now?

Jimmy used to look so solemn when he came to school. _____

Questions: Why did Jennifer want to go to...
Why couldn't she and...
Does she he...

Jennifer always wanted... country. _____

Answers will vary.

Questions: What was Paulo's "new way to fix spaghetti"?
Did anyone else like it?
Did Paulo like it himself?

Paulo thought of a new way to fix spaghetti. _____

225

Prewriting Predicament

Prewriting is the process you go through before actually sitting down to write a story or report. There are several steps in the prewriting process.

Directions: Solve the crossword puzzle.

Across
3. First, _____ for ideas.
5. If necessary, _____ for more information.
6. Take _____ on the information you need or details you will include.

Down
1. Make an _____.
2. _____ your notes into groups that make sense.
4. Now, you're ready to write a _____ draft of your report or story!

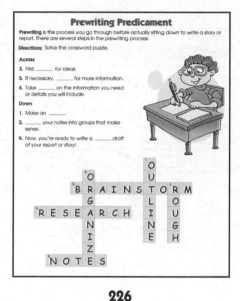

Crossword answers: OUTLINE, BRAINSTORM, ORGANIZE, RESEARCH, ROUGH, NOTES

226

Proofreading Puzzler

Directions: Proofread the following article for capitalization, punctuation, grammar, and spelling mistakes. Use the proofreading symbols below to mark any mistakes you find.

⌇ delete	# space	∕ lowercase
∧ insert	≡ capitalize	¶ new paragraph
⎘ transpose		

What do a Saint Bernard, a Chihuahua, and a german Shepherd have in common? That's easy—they are all dogs! But why don't all dogs look alike. Most terriers are small and low to the ground. Long ago, terriers were used to hunt rats and badgers. The dogs would follow the rats and badgers into their underground homes. Terriers are good diggers, their small size helps them get into tight places.

Greyhounds are racing dogs. They run very fast, a greyhound's long legs help it run. Another part of this dog's body that helps it run is its lungs. Just look at the greyhound's large chest! This dog's lungs are large and can hold a lot of air.

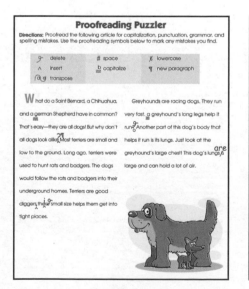

227

It's in the Revision

Revising is the process of reviewing your work and making changes to improve your writing. Once you've finished the prewriting stage and written a rough draft, you should—

• reread your work and look for problems.
• correct spelling and grammar errors.
• watch out for wordy phrases.
• get rid of text that does not relate to your topic.
• make sure your writing is clear and interesting.
• ask someone else to read your first draft.
• write your final draft.

Directions: Revise the following story according to the steps shown above.

This year I had the best summer vacaton ever. My whole family went to Masachusets, where grandparents live. They live near the ocean on cape cod. While we were there we did a lot of fun stuff. My grand father day camp so I didn't have to watch her all day like I usually do in the summer. I took sailing lessons. My boat tipped over many times but I learned how to take the water out of the boat and get back on it. I hope

This year I had the best summer vacation ever. My whole family went to Massachusetts, where my grandparents live. They live near the ocean on Cape Cod.

I had a lot of fun while I was at my grandparents' house. My little sister had day camp so I didn't have to watch her all day like I usually do in the summer. My grandfather taught me to play chess and I found out that I'm really good at it!

I also took sailing lessons while I was on Cape Cod. My boat tipped over many times, but I learned how to take the water out of the boat and get back on it. I hope I can go back to Cape Cod next summer!

228

A Message to You

Directions: Imagine that you are entering a writing contest. You will be writing a report about the Civil Rights movement and telling why it was important. Write the steps you will take to write your report, from the very first step to writing your final draft.

1. Brainstorm for ideas.
2. Do research on the Civil Rights movement.
3. Take notes.
4. Organize my notes into subjects.
5. Make an outline.
6. Write a rough draft.
7. Proofread my rough draft for errors.
8. Have someone else read my report and tell me what they think.
9. Fix any mistakes and/or add details or variety where necessary to make the report more interesting.
10. Write a final draft.

229

GRADE

6

I. Reading
  A. Directions
  B. Sequencing
  C. Main Idea
II. Writing
  A. Capitalization
  B. Proofreading

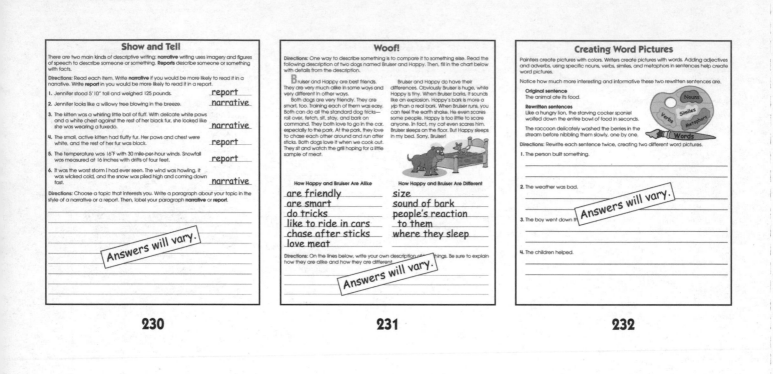

Show and Tell

There are two main kinds of descriptive writing: **narrative** writing uses imagery and figures of speech to describe someone or something. **Reports** describe someone or something with facts.

Directions: Read each item. Write **narrative** if you would be more likely to read it in a narrative. Write **report** in you would be more likely to read it in a report.

1. Jennifer stood 5'10" tall and weighed 125 pounds. — **report**
2. Jennifer looks like a willowy tree blowing in the breeze. — **narrative**
3. The kitten was a whirling little ball of fluff. With delicate white paws and a white chest against the rest of her black fur, she looked like she was wearing a tuxedo. — **narrative**
4. The small, active kitten had fluffy fur. Her paws and chest were white, and the rest of her fur was black. — **report**
5. The temperature was 16°F with 30 mile-per-hour winds. Snowfall was measured at 16 inches with drifts of four feet. — **report**
6. It was the worst storm I had ever seen. The wind was howling, it was wicked cold, and the snow was piled high and coming down fast. — **narrative**

Directions: Choose a topic that interests you. Write a paragraph about your topic in the style of a narrative or a report. Then, label your paragraph **narrative** or **report**.

Answers will vary.

230

Woof!

Directions: One way to describe something is to compare it to something else. Read the following description of two dogs named Bruiser and Happy. Then, fill in the chart below with details from the description.

Bruiser and Happy are best friends. They are very much alike in some ways and very different in other ways.

Both dogs are very friendly. They are smart, too. Training each of them was easy. Both can do all the standard dog tricks—roll over, fetch, sit, stay, and bark on command. They both love to go in the car, especially to the park. At the park, they love to chase each other around and run after sticks. Both dogs love it when we cook out. They sit and watch the grill hoping for a little sample of meat.

Bruiser and Happy do have their differences. Obviously Bruiser is huge, while Happy is tiny. When Bruiser barks, it sounds like an explosion. Happy's bark is more a yip than a real bark. When Bruiser runs, you can feel the earth shake. He even scares some people. Happy is too little to scare anyone. In fact, my cat even scares him. Bruiser sleeps on the floor. But Happy sleeps in my bed. Sorry, Bruiser!

How Happy and Bruiser Are Alike	How Happy and Bruiser Are Different
are friendly	size
are smart	sound of bark
do tricks	people's reaction to them
like to ride in cars	where they sleep
chase after sticks	
love meat	

Directions: On the lines below, write your own description of two things. Be sure to explain how they are alike and how they are different.

Answers will vary.

231

Creating Word Pictures

Painters create pictures with colors. Writers create pictures with words. Adding adjectives and adverbs, using specific nouns, verbs, similes, and metaphors in sentences help create word pictures.

Notice how much more interesting and informative these two rewritten sentences are.

Original sentence
The animal ate its food.

Rewritten sentences
Like a hungry lion, the starving cocker spaniel wolfed down the entire bowl of food in seconds.

The raccoon delicately washed the berries in the stream before nibbling them slowly, one by one.

(palette: Nouns, Similes, Verbs, Metaphors, Words)

Directions: Rewrite each sentence twice, creating two different word pictures.

1. The person built something.
2. The weather was bad.
3. The boy went down the...
4. The children helped.

Answers will vary.

232

Describe It!

Directions: You have just been the first person on Earth to see a space alien— shown at the right. It's very important that you give the most accurate description you can to the government investigators and reporters waiting to hear every detail. Take a good look. Then, write the most accurate description you can.

Answers will vary.

233

Persuasive Writing

To **persuade** means to convince someone that your opinion is correct. "Because I said so," isn't a very convincing reason. Instead, you need to offer reasons, facts, and examples to support your opinion.

Directions: Write two reasons or facts and two examples to persuade someone.

1. Riding a bicycle "no-handed" on a busy street is a bad idea.

Reasons/Facts: _____

Examples: _____

2. Taking medicine prescribed... ...se is dangerous.

Reasons/Facts: _____

Examples: _____

3. Learning to read well will help you in every other subject in school.

Reasons/Facts: _____

Examples: _____

Answers will vary.

234

Hire Me!

Persuasive writing tries to convince the reader of something. When you write a persuasive essay, you must back up your opinions with facts.

Directions: A landscape company has advertised for a young helper to do yard work. Imagine that you are applying for the job. Read each pair of sentences, and circle the letter of the sentence that is more persuasive. Remember that in persuasive writing, you want to back up opinions with facts.

(H) I am writing to apply for the job of yard work assistant because I am well qualified for it.
N. I want that job that you had in the paper.

O. I don't mind working if it's not too hot or raining.
(L) I can provide references from two neighbors as to my skills and reliability.

W. I want to use those cool riding mowers.
(R) I have used all kinds of lawn equipment and am eager to learn more.

(E) I have been doing yard work since I was six years old.
A. I haven't done much yard work, but it doesn't look that hard.

Y. I can work mornings only, except for Tuesdays and Fridays and only if you let me know at least a week in advance.
(D) I am ready to start and would be able to work any time you needed me.

Write the letters you circled to complete the following sentence.
If you wrote these sentences in a letter you would get **hired**.
Write the letters you didn't circle to complete the following sentence.
If you included these sentences in a letter, there is **no way** you would get the job.

Directions: Look through the want ads in your local newspaper. Imagine you are an adult, and pick a job you would like to have. Jot down a few notes on the lines below. Then, on another sheet of paper, write a letter applying for th... ...lude the education and experience that you might need to get the jo...

Answers will vary.

235

GRADE
6

I. Reading
  A. Directions
  B. Sequencing
  C. Main Idea
II. Writing
  A. Capitalization
  B. Proofreading

Back It Up!

Directions: Find a fact from **Column B** to back up each opinion in **Column A**. Write the letter that goes with each choice on the line.

Column A

1. **B** Many kids think the cafeteria food stinks.
2. **A** The cafeteria is crowded.
3. **E** The cafeteria serves unhealthy food.
4. **C** Safety is not a problem.
5. **D** Sixth graders are responsible about litter.

Column B

A. The seating capacity of the cafeteria is 150 kids per lunch period, yet it is now used by 200 kids each lunch period.

B. In a poll, 82 percent of sixth graders said they hate the cafeteria food.

C. Since this school is located in the middle of town, kids can go to stores to get lunch items without having to cross busy streets.

D. In the last three months, sixth graders have participated in three large recycling and community clean-up projects.

E. In the last month, 80 percent of hot lunch items were fried and greasy.

Directions: On the lines below, write a persuasive essay about something you would like to change about your school. Be sure to back up each opinion with a fact.

Answers will vary.

236

Let's Talk Business

Directions: Read the letter below. Then, write a reply as if you were Mr. Mechanic. Be sure to include all six parts of a business letter in your response: **heading, inside address, salutation, body, closing,** and **signature.**

999 Speedy Lane
Hot Dog, California 90102
February 29, 2000

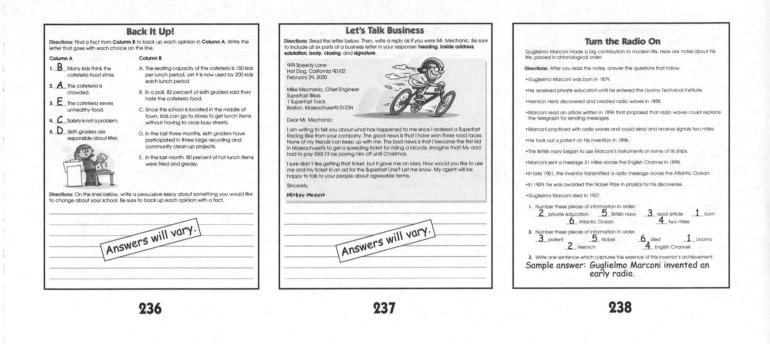

Mike Mechanic, Chief Engineer
Superfast Bikes
1 Superfast Track
Boston, Massachusetts 01234

Dear Mr. Mechanic:

I am writing to tell you about what happened to me since I ordered a Superfast Racing Bike from your company. The good news is that I have won three road races. None of my friends can keep up with me. The bad news is that I became the first kid in Massachusetts to get a speeding ticket for riding a bicycle. Imagine that! My dad had to pay $50! I'll be paying him off until Christmas.

I sure didn't like getting that ticket, but it gave me an idea. How would you like to use me and my ticket in an ad for the Superfast Line? Let me know. My agent will be happy to talk to your people about agreeable terms.

Sincerely,

Mickey Modest

Answers will vary.

237

Turn the Radio On

Guglielmo Marconi made a big contribution to modern life. Here are notes about his life, placed in chronological order.

Directions: After you read the notes, answer the questions that follow.

- Guglielmo Marconi was born in 1874.
- He received private education until he entered the Livorno Technical Institute.
- Heinrich Hertz discovered and created radio waves in 1888.
- Marconi read an article written in 1894 that proposed that radio waves could replace the telegraph for sending messages.
- Marconi practiced with radio waves and could send and receive signals two miles.
- He took out a patent on his invention in 1896.
- The British navy began to use Marconi's instruments on some of its ships.
- Marconi sent a message 31 miles across the English Channel in 1899.
- In late 1901, the inventor transmitted a radio message across the Atlantic Ocean.
- In 1909, he was awarded the Nobel Prize in physics for his discoveries.
- Guglielmo Marconi died in 1937.

1. Number these pieces of information in order.
   2 private education **5** British navy **3** read article **1** born
   6 Atlantic Ocean **4** two miles

2. Number these pieces of information in order.
   3 patent **5** Nobel **6** died **1** Livorno
   2 Heinrich **4** English Channel

3. Write one sentence which captures the essence of this inventor's achievement.

Sample answer: Guglielmo Marconi invented an early radio.

238

Franklin Facts

Directions: Here are paragraphs about the life of patriot Benjamin Franklin. Underline the effect in each cause-and-effect paragraph below. Then, choose a title from the box below and write it in the blank to match the paragraph.

1. **A Loving Father**
   Josiah Franklin was not a father blinded by his pride. When he saw that his son Ben was unhappy with the family candle-making trade, he sent him to work for an older son.

2. **A Lost Husband**
   Deborah Read was unable to marry Ben Franklin. This was due to the lack of proof that her long-missing first husband was really dead.

3. **Fighting the Fires Together**
   Observing Boston's volunteer fire company and noting his own city's problem with fires, Franklin instituted a number of firefighting companies for Philadelphia.

4. **Improving the Mail**
   Franklin traveled far along the eastern coast of the American colonies to inspect and improve the post offices during his tenure as the colonial Postmaster General.

5. **A Parent Grieves**
   Because Franky, Franklin's second son, died of smallpox at the age of four, Franklin regretted that he had not had the boy inoculated.

6. **An Electric Shock**
   While experimenting with electrical shock on a turkey, Franklin accidentally shocked himself, knocking himself unconscious for several minutes.

7. **Uncovering Murder**
   Angered by the murder of twenty Indians in 1763, Franklin wrote an attack on the white frontiersman who had killed these helpless victims.

8. **Banding Together**
   Franklin knew that the American colonies, in their quarrels with England, were weak individually. As a result he wrote, "Gentlemen, we must now all hang together, or we shall most assuredly hang separately."

9. **Finding Financial Aid**
   Franklin sailed to France because the Americans desperately needed loans for their war with Great Britain.

10. **Liberty for All**
    Franklin was puzzled that our young nation, which called for liberty and equality, practiced what he considered the abominable practice of slavery.

Titles

A Loving Father	A Parent Grieves
Uncovering Murder	Finding Financial Aid
Improving the Mail	An Electric Shock
Fighting the Fires Together	Banding Together
A Lost Husband	Liberty for All

239

Victorious

Directions: Read the time line to complete the story web below.

1940—Wilma Rudolph is born in Clarksville, Tennessee. She weighs four pounds. She has nineteen older brothers and sisters.

1945—At the age of five, Wilma contracts scarlet fever and polio. This leaves her with a left leg that is twisted inward. News spreads that she will never walk again.

Childhood: Although unable to walk, Wilma exercises. The nearest hospital willing to treat black people is 50 miles away. The local school will not accept her because of her disability.

Childhood: She is able to obtain a steel leg brace from the hospital. She can now go to school. Still she is unable to play with others. She exercises on her own.

Childhood: One Sunday as Wilma and her family come to church, Wilma removes her leg brace and walks without help.

1952—Wilma is able to take off her brace for the last time. Wilma and her mother mail the brace back to the hospital.

Teens: Wilma begins to play basketball. She had studied and memorized the moves of this game while watching classmates earlier.

Teens: In high school Wilma leads her team to the state championships. They lose in the finals. A college coach scouts the state final, and Wilma is given an athletic scholarship to attend the university and participate in track and field.

1960—Wilma represents the United States in the Olympic Games. She wins the gold medal in both the 100-meter and 200-meter events, despite a twisted ankle. Her 400-meter relay team also wins a gold medal.

1962—Wilma Rudolph becomes a second-grade teacher and a high school coach.

1994—Wilma Rudolph dies.

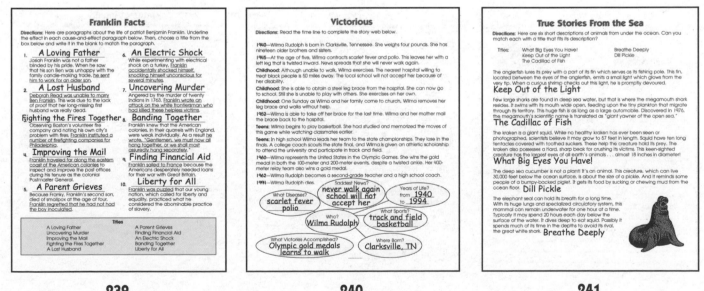

What Diseases? **scarlet fever polio**

Saddest News? **never walk again school will not accept her**

Years of Life? from **1940** to **1994**

Who? **Wilma Rudolph**

What Sports? **track and field basketball**

What Victories Accomplished? **Olympic gold medals learns to walk**

Where Born? **Clarksville, TN**

240

True Stories From the Sea

Directions: Here are six short descriptions of animals from under the ocean. Can you match each with a title that fits its description?

Titles: What Big Eyes You Have!   Breathe Deeply
     Keep Out of the Light   Dill Pickle
     The Cadillac of Fish

The anglerfish lures its prey with a part of its fin which serves as its fishing pole. This fin, located between the eyes of the anglerfish, emits a small light which glows from the very tip. When a curious shrimp checks out this light, he is promptly devoured.
Keep Out of the Light

Few large sharks are found in deep sea water, but that is where the megamouth shark resides. It swims with its mouth wide open, feeding upon the tiny plankton that migrate through its territory. This huge fish is as long as a large automobile. Discovered in 1976, the megamouth's scientific name is translated as "giant yawner of the open sea."
The Cadillac of Fish

The kraken is a giant squid. While no healthy kraken has ever been seen or photographed, scientists believe it may grow to 57 feet in length. Squid have ten long tentacles covered with toothed suckers. These help the creature hold its prey. The kraken also possesses a hard, sharp beak for crushing its victims. This keen-sighted creature has the largest eyes of all earth's animals...almost 18 inches in diameter!
What Big Eyes You Have!

The deep sea cucumber is not a plant! It's an animal. This creature, which can live 30,000 feet below the ocean surface, is about the size of a pickle. And it reminds some people of a bumpy-backed piglet. It gets its food by sucking or chewing mud from the ocean floor.
Dill Pickle

The elephant seal can hold its breath for a long time. With its huge lungs and specialized circulatory system, this mammal can remain underwater for one hour at a time. Typically it may spend 20 hours each day below the surface of the water. It dives deep to eat squid. Possibly it spends much of its time in the depths to avoid its rival, the great white shark. **Breathe Deeply**

241

I. Reading
  A. Directions
  B. Sequencing
  C. Main Idea
II. Writing
  A. Capitalization
  B. Proofreading

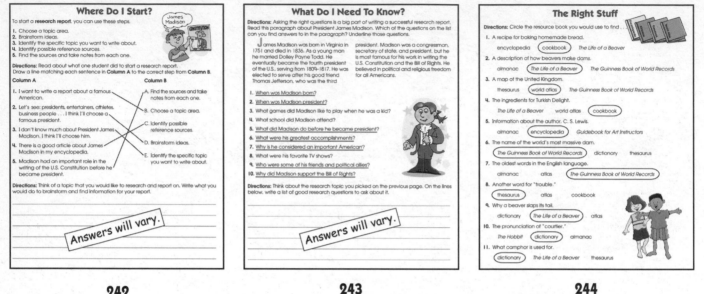

Where Do I Start?

To start a **research report**, you can use these steps.

1. Choose a topic area.
2. Brainstorm ideas.
3. Identify the specific topic you want to write about.
4. Identify possible reference sources.
5. Find the sources and take notes from each one.

Directions: Read about what one student did to start a research report. Draw a line matching each sentence in **Column A** to the correct step from **Column B.**

Column A

1. I want to write a report about a famous American.
2. Let's see: presidents, entertainers, athletes, business people . . . I think I'll choose a famous president.
3. I don't know much about President James Madison. I think I'll choose him.
4. There is a good article about James Madison in my encyclopedia.
5. Madison had an important role in the writing of the U.S. Constitution before he became president.

Column B

A. Find the sources and take notes from each one.
B. Choose a topic area.
C. Identify possible reference sources.
D. Brainstorm ideas.
E. Identify the specific topic you want to write about.

Directions: Think of a topic that you would like to research and report on. Write what you would do to brainstorm and find information for your report.

Answers will vary.

242

What Do I Need To Know?

Directions: Asking the right questions is a big part of writing a successful research report. Read this paragraph about President James Madison. Which of the questions on the list can you find answers to in the paragraph? Underline those questions.

James Madison was born in Virginia in 1751 and died in 1836. As a young man he married Dolley Payne Todd. He eventually became the fourth president of the U.S., serving from 1809-1817. He was elected to serve after his good friend Thomas Jefferson, who was the third president. Madison was a congressman, secretary of state, and president, but he is most famous for his work in writing the U.S. Constitution and the Bill of Rights. He believed in political and religious freedom for all Americans.

1. When was Madison born?
2. When was Madison president?
3. What games did Madison like to play when he was a kid?
4. What school did Madison attend?
5. What did Madison do before he became president?
6. What were his greatest accomplishments?
7. Why is he considered an important American?
8. What were his favorite TV shows?
9. Who were some of his friends and political allies?
10. Why did Madison support the Bill of Rights?

Directions: Think about the research topic you picked on the previous page. On the lines below, write a list of good research questions to ask about it.

Answers will vary.

243

The Right Stuff

Directions: Circle the resource book you would use to find . . .

1. A recipe for baking homemade bread.
  encyclopedia **(cookbook)** The Life of a Beaver

2. A description of how beavers make dams.
  almanac **(The Life of a Beaver)** The Guinness Book of World Records

3. A map of the United Kingdom.
  thesaurus **(world atlas)** The Guinness Book of World Records

4. The ingredients for Turkish Delight.
  The Life of a Beaver world atlas **(cookbook)**

5. Information about the author, C. S. Lewis.
  almanac **(encyclopedia)** Guidebook for Art Instructors

6. The name of the world's most massive dam.
  (The Guinness Book of World Records) dictionary thesaurus

7. The oldest words in the English language.
  almanac atlas **(The Guinness Book of World Records)**

8. Another word for "trouble."
  (thesaurus) atlas cookbook

9. Why a beaver slaps its tail.
  dictionary **(The Life of a Beaver)** atlas

10. The pronunciation of "courtier."
  The Hobbit **(dictionary)** almanac

11. What camphor is used for.
  (dictionary) The Life of a Beaver thesaurus

244

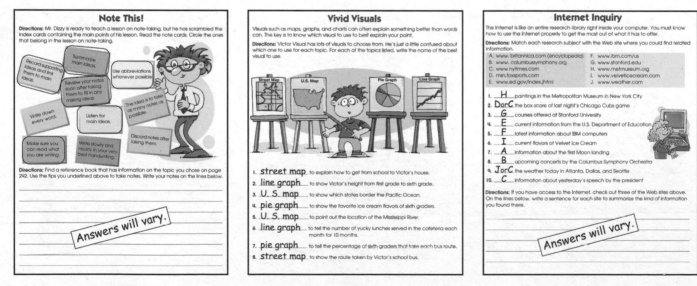

Note This!

Directions: Mr. Dizzy is ready to teach a lesson on note-taking, but he has scrambled the index cards containing the main points of his lesson. Read the note cards. Circle the ones that belong in the lesson on note-taking.

Record supporting ideas and link them to main ideas.
Summarize main ideas.
Use abbreviations whenever possible.
Review your notes soon after taking them to fill in any missing ideas.
The idea is to take as many notes as possible.
Write down every word.
Listen for main ideas.
Make sure you can read what you are writing.
Write slowly and neatly in your very best handwriting.
Discard notes after taking them.

Directions: Find a reference book that has information on the topic you chose on page 242. Use the tips you underlined above to take notes. Write your notes on the lines below.

Answers will vary.

245

Vivid Visuals

Visuals such as maps, graphs, and charts can often explain something better than words can. The key is to know which visual to use to best explain your point.

Directions: Victor Visual has lots of visuals to choose from. He's just a little confused about which one to use for each topic. For each of the topics listed, write the name of the best visual to use.

Street Map U.S. Map Pie Graph Line Graph

1. **street map** to explain how to get from school to Victor's house.
2. **line graph** to show Victor's height from first grade to sixth grade.
3. **U. S. map** to show which states border the Pacific Ocean.
4. **pie graph** to show the favorite ice cream flavors of sixth graders.
5. **U. S. map** to point out the location of the Mississippi River.
6. **line graph** to tell the number of yucky lunches served in the cafeteria each month for 10 months.
7. **pie graph** to tell the percentage of sixth graders that take each bus route.
8. **street map** to show the route taken by Victor's school bus.

246

Internet Inquiry

The Internet is like an entire research library right inside your computer. You must know how to use the Internet properly to get the most out of what it has to offer.

Directions: Match each research subject with the Web site where you could find related information.

A. www.britannica.com (encyclopedia)
B. www.columbussymphony.org
C. www.nytimes.com
D. msn.foxsports.com
E. www.ed.gov/index.jhtml
F. www.ibm.com/us
G. www.stanford.edu
H. www.metrnuseum.org
I. www.velveticecream.com
J. www.weather.com

1. **H** paintings in the Metropolitan Museum in New York City
2. **D or C** the box score of last night's Chicago Cubs game
3. **G** courses offered at Stanford University
4. **E** current information from the U.S. Department of Education
5. **F** latest information about IBM computers
6. **I** current flavors of Velvet Ice Cream
7. **A** information about the first Moon landing
8. **B** upcoming concerts by the Columbus Symphony Orchestra
9. **J or C** the weather today in Atlanta, Dallas, and Seattle
10. **C** information about yesterday's speech by the president

Directions: If you have access to the Internet, check out three of the Web sites above. On the lines below, write a sentence for each site to summarize the kind of information you found there.

Answers will vary.

247

GRADE 6

I. Reading
   A. Directions
   B. Sequencing
   C. Main Idea
II. Writing
   A. Capitalization
   B. Proofreading

Look It Up!

A **dictionary** gives word definitions and pronunciations.
A **thesaurus** provides synonyms and antonyms for words.
An **encyclopedia** has information on most subject matter.
An **almanac** contains information about recent events.
An **atlas** has maps and population information.

Directions: To complete the crossword puzzle, figure out which reference source you would use to find the information described in each clue.

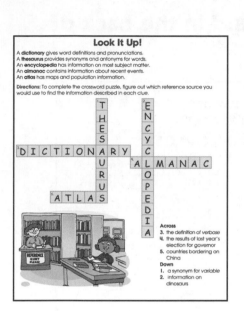

```
      T         E
      H         N
  D I C T I O N A R Y
      S         C
      A       A L M A N A C
      U         L
      R         O
  A T L A S     P
                E
                D
                I
                A
```

Across
3. the definition of *verbose*
4. the results of last year's election for governor
5. countries bordering on China

Down
1. a synonym for *variable*
2. information on dinosaurs

248

Chorus Program

Directions: Mr. Musichead is tired of his kids complaining about the chorus music. This year, he decided to let the kids vote on what kind of music they should perform. Look at the results of the election and enter the votes on the chart.

Of 100 fifth graders:
   45 chose pop tunes
   35 chose show tunes
   18 chose classical pieces
   2 chose hymns

Of 95 sixth graders:
   40 chose pop tunes
   40 chose show tunes
   10 chose classical pieces
   5 chose hymns

Of 105 seventh graders:
   55 chose show tunes
   30 chose pop tunes
   20 chose classical pieces

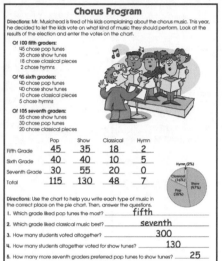

	Pop	Show	Classical	Hymn
Fifth Grade	45	35	18	2
Sixth Grade	40	40	10	5
Seventh Grade	30	55	20	0
Total	115	130	48	7

Pie chart: Hymn (2%), Classical (16%), Show (47%), Pop (35%)

Directions: Use the chart to help you write each type of music in the correct place on the pie chart. Then, answer the questions.
1. Which grade liked pop tunes the most? **fifth**
2. Which grade liked classical music best? **seventh**
3. How many students voted altogether? **300**
4. How many students altogether voted for show tunes? **130**
5. How many more seventh graders preferred pop tunes to show tunes? **25**

249

Table of Contents

The **table of contents**, located in the front of books or magazines, tells a lot about what is inside.

A table of contents in a book lists the headings and page numbers for each chapter. **Chapters** are the parts into which books are divided. Also listed are chapter numbers and the sections and subsections, if any. Look at the sample table of contents below:

Contents

Chapter 1: Planting a Garden	2
Location	4
Fences	5
Chapter 2: Seeds	8
Vegetables	
Potatoes	9
Beans	10
Tomatoes	11
Fruits	
Melons	13
Pumpkins	14
Chapter 3: Caring for a Garden	15
Weeding	16
Fertilizing	19

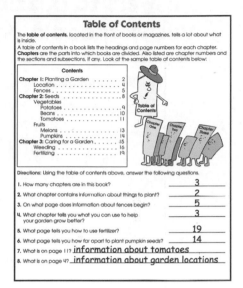

Directions: Using the table of contents above, answer the following questions.
1. How many chapters are in this book? **3**
2. What chapter contains information about things to plant? **2**
3. On what page does information about fences begin? **5**
4. What chapter tells you what you can use to help your garden grow better? **3**
5. What page tells you how to use fertilizer? **19**
6. What page tells you how far apart to plant pumpkin seeds? **14**
7. What is on page 11? **information about tomatoes**
8. What is on page 4? **information about garden locations**

250

Indexes

An **index** is an alphabetical listing of names, topics, and important words and is found in the back of a book. An index lists every page on which these items appear. For example, in a book about music, dulcimer might be listed this way: Dulcimer 2, 13, 26, 38. Page numbers may also be listed like this: Guitars 18–21. That means that information about guitars begins on page 18 and continues through page 21. **Subject** is the name of the item in an index. **Sub-entry** is a smaller division of the subject. For example, "apples" would be listed under *fruit*.

Index

See also planet names.

N
Neptune ... 27
NGC 5128 (galaxy) ... 39
Nova ... 32

O
Observatories. *See El Caracol.*
Orbits of planets ... 10
Orion rocket ... 43

P
Planetoids. *See Asteroids.*
Planet rings
   Jupiter ... 23
   Saturn ... 9, 26
   Uranus ... 26
Planets
   discovered by Greeks ... 7
   outside the solar system ... 40
   visible with the naked eye ... 25

Pleiades ... 32
Pluto ... 12, 27
Polaris ... 35, 36
Pole star. *See Polaris.*
Project Ozma ... 41

R
Rings. *See Planet rings.*

S
Sagittarius ... 37
Satellites
   Jupiter ... 24
   Neptune ... 27
   Pluto ... 25
   Saturn ... 25
   Uranus ... 26
   See also Galilean satellites.
   Saturn ... 25

Directions: Answer the questions about the index from this book about the solar system.
1. On what pages is there information about Pluto? **pages 12 and 27**
2. On what pages is information about Saturn's first ring found? **page 9 or 25**
3. What is on page 41? **information about Project Ozma**
4. Where is there information about the pole star? **pages 35 and 36**
5. What is on page 43? **information about the *Orion* rocket**
6. On what page would you find information about planets that are visible to the eye? **page 9**
7. On what page would you find information about Jupiter's satellites? **page 24**

251

Biographical Research

A **biography** is a written history of a person's life. Often, information for a biography can be obtained from an encyclopedia, especially if a person is famous. Of course, not everyone is listed in a main article in an encyclopedia. Use the encyclopedia's index, which is the last book in the set, to find which volume contains the information you need. Look at this listing taken from an encyclopedia index for Henry Moore, an English artist.

Moore, Henry English sculptor.
1898–1986
   main article Moore 12:106b, illus.
   references in Sculpture 15:290a, illus.

Notice that the listing includes Henry Moore's dates of birth and death and illustrations (illus.). It also includes a short description of his accomplishments: He was an English sculptor. Look below at part of the index from the *Children's Britannica* encyclopedias.

Lincoln, Abraham president of US.
1809–1865
   main article Lincoln 11:49a, illus.
   references in
      Assassination 2:69b
      Caricature, illus. 4:87
      Civil War, American 4:296a fol.
      Confederate States of America 5:113b fol.
      Democracy 6:17a
      Gettysburg, Battle of 8:199a
      Illinois 9:259b
      Thanksgiving Day 17:199a
      United States of America, history of 18:137a fol.
      Westward Movement 19:49a
Lincoln, Benjamin army officer.
1733–1810
   references in American Revolution 1:209b

Lind, Jenny Swedish singer. 1820–87
   operatic soprano admired for vocal purity
   and control; made debut 1838 in Stockholm
   and sang in Paris and London, becoming known
   as the "Swedish Nightingale"; toured US with P.T.
   Barnum 1850; last concert 1883.
   references in Barnum 2:235a
Lindbergh, Anne US author and aviator, b. 1906
   references in Lindbergh 11:53a, illus.
Lindbergh, Charles Augustus US aviator.
1902–1974
   main article Lindbergh 11:53a, illus.
   references in
      Aviation, history of 2:190b, illus.
      Medals and decorations, 11:266b
      Saint Louis, 15:215b
Linde, Karl Von German engineer.
1842–1934
   references in Refrigeration 15:32b

Directions: Answer these questions from the index above.
1. Where is the main article for Abraham Lincoln? **volume 11, page 44**
2. In addition to the main article, how many other places are there references to Abraham Lincoln? **10**
3. In which encyclopedia volume is there information about Anne Lindbergh? **volume 11**

252

Answers to puzzles printed on cardboard in the back of this workbook:

Brand Spankin' New | Winter

February 11 has been named Inventors' Day in honor of Thomas Edison's birthday. For each inventor you'll find letters encircling the name. Use these letters to discover what the person invented.

O A T S T
Robert Fulton
STEAMBOAT
B M A E

U A L U
Jacques Cousteau
AQUA LUNG
Q A G N

O I N T P E
Ladislao Biro
BALLPOINT PEN
P L L A B N

K E T S P
Sergei Korolev
SPACE ROCKET
C O R E C A

F E T Y P
Johan Vaaler
SAFETY PIN
A S N I

N G I N E 4 C Y L I N
Nikolaus Otto
4-CYLINDER GAS ENGINE
E S A G R E D

L E T F L
John Harington
FLUSH TOILET
I O T H S U

F I C L I G H
Garrett Morgan
TRAFFIC LIGHT
F A R T T

O P I E R
Chester Carlson
PHOTOCOPIER
C O T O H P

H O N O G
Thomas Edison
PHONOGRAPH
P H P A R

R B A R O
Evangelista Torricelli
BAROMETER
E T E M

R A M H
Dennis Gabor
HOLOGRAM
G O L O

A R M U
Chester Greenwood
EARMUFFS
E S F F

E G R A P
Samuel Morse
TELEGRAPH
L E T H

P E G Y R
J.B.L. Foucault
GYROSCOPE
O C S O

Rite of Spring or Stravinsky's Revenge | Spring

All the words in this cryptic puzzle follow the same code. A set of letters has been substituted for the correct letters of each word. These words relate to the topic *spring*. Can you figure them out?

1. PCWX — BUDS
2. VYTOJK — WARMTH
3. RGXUIJX — INSECTS
4. XKQVUTX — SHOWERS
5. OQVRGS — MOWING
6. AEQVUTX — FLOWERS
7. PRTWXQGS — BIRDSONG
8. HEYGJRGS — PLANTING
9. USSX — EGGS
10. STUUG — GREEN
11. PEQXXQOX — BLOSSOMS
12. PRTJK — BIRTH
13. TQPRGX — ROBINS
14. XUUWX — SEEDS
15. XCGXKRGU — SUNSHINE

CLUES:
1. The letter X represents S.
2. The letter Q represents O.
3. The letter S represents G.
4. The letter G represents N.

Lunar Madness | Summer

On July 20, 1969, American astronauts first landed on the moon. In honor of that event, try this puzzle about the moon and space. Each word or phrase below can be changed to a word or phrase relating to the space program. Use the definition clues whenever you become stuck. Good luck!

Words	Space Phrase	Definition Clue
1. TRACER (1 word)	CRATER	a pit in the moon's surface
2. CAPES (1 word)	SPACE	"the final frontier"
3. HEALTH DIES (2 words)	HEAT SHIELD	a protection against overheating upon re-entry
4. "LA LOOP" (1 word)	APOLLO	the craft type used in 1969
5. NASA TROUT (1 word)	ASTRONAUT	American space traveler
6. REMOTE (1 word)	METEOR	a shooting star
7. ARMS (1 word)	MARS	4th planet from the sun
8. DIET SOAR (1 word)	ASTEROID	"star shaped"
9. NEAR RIM (1 word)	MARINER	an early space satellite
10. THUS LET (1 word)	SHUTTLE	space taxi service
11. MINOR BOOST (2 words)	MOON'S ORBIT	lunar circle around us
12. GLANDULAR INN (2 words)	LUNAR LANDING	arrival on moon's surface
13. CLEFT NURSES (2 words)	REFLECTS SUN	how moon shines in night
14. ASK BITTY LOANS (2 words)	SKYLAB STATION	Earth's space platform
15. THE RAG VARSITY (2 words)	EARTH'S GRAVITY	what keeps us on Earth
16. MOTH MOAN NINE (4 words)	MAN-IN-THE-MOON	what some claim they see when they view our satellite

See You Real Soon | Fall

November 18th is the birthday of the most famous animated character of all time. Find 33 words related to Disney in the word search including Mickey's names in French (Michel), Japanese (Miki), Spanish (Miguel), and Danish (Mikkel).

Word Box

BAMBI	DONALD	LAND	MORTIMER	SOURIS
CABLE	DUCK	LIFE	MOUSE	STEAMBOAT
CAROL	DUMBO	LOUIE	MUS	THUMPER
CHRISTMAS	FANTASIA	MICHEL	PLAY	WALT
CRICKET	GOOFY	MICKEY	PLUTO	WILLIE
DAISY	HUEY	MIGUEL	RATONOCITO	WORLD
DEWEY	JIMINY	MIKI	SCROOGE	
DISNEY	KUCHI	MIKKEL		

What do the eleven remaining letters spell? **HERE'S MINNIE**

Brand Spankin' New

February 11 has been named Inventors' Day in honor of Thomas Edison's birthday. For each inventor you'll find letters encircling the name. Use these letters to discover what the person invented.

O A T S T
Robert Fulton
_____
B M A E

U A L U
Jacques Cousteau
_____
Q A G N

O I N T P E
Ladislao Biro
_____
P L L A B N

K E T S P
Sergei Korolev
_____
C O R E C A

F E T Y P
Johan Vaaler
_____
A S N I

N G I N E 4 C Y L I N
Nikolaus Otto
_____
E S A G R E D

L E T F L
John Harington
_____
I O T H S U

F I C L I G H
Garrett Morgan
_____
F A R T T

O P I E R
Chester Carlson
_____
C O T O H P

H O N O G
Thomas Edison
_____
P H P A R

R B A R O
Evangelista Torricelli
_____
E T E M

R A M H
Dennis Gabor
_____
G O L O

A R M U
Chester Greenwood
_____
E S F F

E G R A P
Samuel Morse
_____
L E T H

P E G Y R
J.B.L. Foucault
_____
O C S O

Rite of Spring or Stravinsky's Revenge

All the words in this cryptic puzzle follow the same code. A set of letters has been substituted for the correct letters of each word. These words relate to the topic *spring*. Can you figure them out?

1.   P C W X   _____
2.   V Y T O J K   _____
3.   R G X U I J X   _____
4.   X K Q V U T X   _____
5.   O Q V R G S   _____
6.   A E Q V U T X   _____
7.   P R T W X Q G S   _____
8.   H E Y G J R G S   _____
9.   U S S X   _____
10.   S T U U G   _____
11.   P E Q X X Q O X   _____
12.   P R T J K   _____
13.   T Q P R G X   _____
14.   X U U W X   _____
15.   X C G X K R G U   _____

CLUES: 1. The letter X represents S.
2. The letter Q represents O.
3. The letter S represents G.
4. The letter G represents N.

Lunar Madness

On July 20, 1969, American astronauts first landed on the moon. In honor of that event, try this puzzle about the moon and space. Each word or phrase below can be changed to a word or phrase relating to the space program. Use the definition clues whenever you become stuck.
Good luck!

Words	**Space Phrase**	**Definition Clue**
1. TRACER (1 word)	_____	a pit in the moon's surface
2. CAPES (1 word)	_____	"the final frontier"
3. HEALTH DIES (2 words)	_____	a protection against overheating upon re-entry
4. "LA LOOP" (1 word)	_____	the craft type used in 1969
5. NASA TROUT (1 word)	_____	American space traveler
6. REMOTE (1 word)	_____	a shooting star
7. ARMS (1 word)	_____	4th planet from the sun
8. DIET SOAR (1 word)	_____	"star shaped"
9. NEAR RIM (1 word)	_____	an early space satellite
10. THUS LET (1 word)	_____	space taxi service
11. MINOR BOOST (2 words)	_____	lunar circle around us
12. GLANDULAR INN (2 words)	_____	arrival on moon's surface
13. CLEFT NURSES (2 words)	_____	how moon shines in night
14. ASK BITTY LOANS (2 words)	_____	Earth's space platform
15. THE RAG VARSITY (2 words)	_____	what keeps us on Earth
16. MOTH MOAN NINE (4 words)	_____	what some claim they see when they view our satellite

See You Real Soon

November 18th is the birthday of the most famous animated character of all time. Find 33 words related to Disney in the word search including Mickey's names in French (Michel), Japanese (Miki), Spanish (Miguel), and Danish (Mikkel).

```
D H E Y E N S I D E W E Y E R
U O P F A N T A S I A H U E Y
M M N L I C E B E G O O R C S
B I E A A L A A L S M Y A H O
O K H B L Y M M E M O N T R U
G K L C S D B B H I U I O I R
O E C I U M O I C G S M N S I
O L A I N K A N I U E I O T S
F D R M O R T I M E R J C M I
Y W O R L D W I L L I E I A K
I A L A N D R E P M U H T S I
E L T E K C I R C E I U O L M
O T U L P M I C K E Y K C U D
```

Word Box

BAMBI	DONALD	LAND	MORTIMER	STEAMBOAT
CABLE	DUCK	LIFE	MOUSE	THUMPER
CAROL	DUMBO	LOUIE	MUS	WALT
CHRISTMAS	FANTASIA	MICHEL	PLAY	WILLIE
CRICKET	GOOFY	MICKEY	PLUTO	WORLD
DAISY	HUEY	MIGUEL	RATONOCITO	
DEWEY	JIMINY	MIKI	SCROOGE	
DISNEY	KUCHI	MIKKEL	SOURIS	

What do the eleven remaining letters spell?_____

Proofreading
Make It Correct
- Be sure all sentences are complete.
- Correct spelling, capitalization, and punctuation.
- Change words that are not used correctly.
- Have someone check your work.
- Recopy it correctly and neatly.

DICTIONARY

- Think about what others said about it.
- Rearrange words or sentences.
- Take out or add parts.
- Replace overused or unclear words.
- Read your writing aloud to be sure it flows smoothly.

Publishing
Share the Finished Product
- Read your writing aloud to a group.
- Create a book of your work.
- Send a copy to a friend or relative.
- Put your writing on display.
- Illustrate, perform, or set your creation to music.
- Congratulate yourself on a job well done!

The Writing Process

1 Prewriting
Think

- Decide on a topic to write about.
- Consider who will read or listen to your written work.
- Brainstorm ideas about the subject.
- List places where you can research information.
- Do your research.

2 Drafting
Write

- Put the information you researched into your own words.
- Write sentences and paragraphs even if they are not perfect.
- Read what you have written and judge if it says what you mean.
- Show it to others and ask for suggestions.

3 Revising
Make It Better

- Read what you have written again.